Fundamentals of OOP and Data Structures in Java

Fundamentals of OOP and Data Structures in Java is a text for an introductory course on classical data structures. Part One of the book presents the basic principles of Object-Oriented Programming (OOP) and Graphical User Interface (GUI) programming with Java. Part Two introduces each of the major data structures with supporting GUI-based laboratory programs designed to reinforce the basic concepts and principles of the text. These laboratories allow the reader to explore and experiment with the properties of each data structure. All source code for the laboratories is available on the Web.

By integrating the principles of OOP and GUI programming, this book takes the unique path of presenting the fundamental issues of data structures within the context of paradigms that are essential to today's professional software developer. From the very beginning, undergraduate students will be learning practical concepts that every professional must master during his or her career. In fact, professionals will find this book to be an excellent resource for upgrading their knowledge of OOP, GUI programming and classical data structures. The authors assume the reader has only an elementary understanding of Java and no experience with OOP.

Richard Wiener is Associate Professor of Computer Science at the University of Colorado at Colorado Springs and Editor-in-Chief of *The Journal of Object-Oriented Programming*. He is the author or co-author of twenty-one textbooks and professional books. In 1983 Richard Wiener received the Outstanding Teacher of the Year Award from the University of Colorado at Colorado Springs. His areas of research include object-oriented software development, simulated annealing and genetic algorithms, time series, and applied statistics.

Lewis J. Pinson is President of CIC and Associate Professor of Computer Science at the University of Colorado at Colorado Springs. His areas of expertise include computer software development, object-oriented problem solving, genetic algorithms, and complexity studies. He develops and presents training courses and intensive short courses and workshops on object-oriented problem solving and object-oriented languages. Dr. Pinson has authored or co-authored eight books.

4/2007

Fundamentals of OOP and Data Structures in Java

RICHARD WIENER
University of Colorado, Colorado Springs

LEWIS J. PINSON
University of Colorado, Colorado Springs

CAMBRIDGE
UNIVERSITY PRESS

PUBLISHED BY THE PRESS SYNDICATE OF THE UNIVERSITY OF CAMBRIDGE
The Pitt Building, Trumpington Street, Cambridge, United Kingdom

CAMBRIDGE UNIVERSITY PRESS
The Edinburgh Building, Cambridge CB2 2RU, UK   http://www.cup.cam.ac.uk
40 West 20th Street, New York, NY 10011-4211, USA http://www.cup.org
10 Stamford Road, Oakleigh, Melbourne 3166, Australia
Ruiz de Alarcón 13, 28014 Madrid, Spain

First published 2000

Printed in the United States of America

Typeface Century Schoolbook 10/12.5 pt. and ITC Franklin Gothic   *System* LATEX 2_ε [TB]

A catalog record for this book is available from the British Library.

Library of Congress Cataloging in Publication Data
Wiener, Richard, 1941–
    Fundamentals of OOP and data structures in Java / Richard Wiener, Lewis Pinson.
      p.   cm.
    ISBN 0-521-66220-6 (hb)
    1. Java (Computer program language)   2. Object-oriented programming (Computer
science)   3. Data structures (Computer science)   I. Pinson, Lewis J.   II. Title.
    QA76.73.J38 W53   2000
    005.1′17 – dc21
                                                                99-087328

ISBN 0 521 66220 6 hardback

To my children Henrik and Anna and my wife Hanne
who provide joy and love in my life.

r.w.

For Aspen. From the first moment she opened her
eyes, she captured my heart and added new meaning
to my life.

l.j.p.

Contents

Preface

This is a CS 2 book that presents classical data structures in an object-oriented programming (OOP) context using Java. This book also focuses on the basic principles of OOP and graphical user interface (GUI)-based programming – two paradigms essential for modern programming and problem solving. Our book is aimed principally at CS 2 students but may also be valuable to software development professionals who wish to upgrade their skills in the areas of OOP, GUI programming, and classical data structures.

The software development principles associated with OOP provide a strong framework for presenting and implementing classical data structures. We adhere to and emphasize these principles throughout this book.

Universities have been slow to introduce courses related to OOP into their curricula. Curriculum change has always occurred slowly at universities, but the past dozen years have been particularly disappointing in the area of OOP education. Often a department assumes that because it has switched language from Pascal or C to C++ or Java in CS 1 or CS 2 that it has made a commitment to object-oriented software education. This is simply not true. Object orientation embodies a set of principles often obscured by the intensive preoccupation with language details often evident in early university courses and the books that cater to these courses. The spate of CS 1 and CS 2 books featuring C++ or Java are often nothing more than warmed-over reruns of structured programming texts written originally for Pascal or C.

The principles of OOP and classical data structures are language independent. Our experience has shown that these principles need to be brought to life using well-crafted examples supported by a rich object-oriented programming language. In our view, Java fits this bill. It provides constructs and predefined standard libraries that directly support and connect to the rich body of underlying OOP and data structure principles. We have chosen Java because its usage is rising rapidly, it provides relative safety in programming, it is readily and inexpensively available (free in many cases), and it offers the user a clean and powerful object model. But make no mistake – this is not yet another book on Java programming. So what do we wish to achieve?

Part One of this book presents the basic principles of OOP and GUI programming. These principles are brought to life using examples crafted in Java. The principles and techniques presented in Part One of the book are carefully chosen to support Part Two of the book.

Part Two, the main part of the book, presents classical data structures. As the chapters of this part unfold, a Java-based package (package *foundations*) of data structure components evolves. Most of the source code for this package is available to the reader except in areas where, through exercises, the reader is expected to complete or enhance some data structure classes.

In Part Two, each of the major data structure presentations are supported by laboratories designed to support and reinforce the basic concepts and principles. Some of the laboratory programs allow the reader to extend his or her knowledge by adding additional features to a data structure class. The full Java source code for all laboratory programs is provided in a zip file, available for download at http://www.cup.org/Titles/66/0521662206.htm. These files also include the source code for all major programs presented in the book.

Some specific goals of this book are to:

- Present foundation concepts and principles of object-oriented programming: abstraction, encapsulation, object, class, instance, message, method, inheritance, polymorphism, abstract class, interface, and delegation.
- Present and illustrate subtleties of using objects: reference semantics, object creation, assignment, and cloning.
- Show how fundamental data elements including strings, arrays, vectors, and numbers are represented as objects. Explain details and subtleties of their representations and manipulation in Java.
- Present the conceptual framework underlying the construction of GUI-based programming: widgets, delegation/event handling, and model-view-controller design.
- Present and illustrate GUI software development with Java: use of AWT, Swing classes, event handling, and model-view-controller.
- Present a series of GUI-based interactive laboratories throughout Part Two of the book. These allow the reader to experiment with, visualize, and reinforce the basic concepts. These shall be provided with full Java source code online.
- Present the principles of class construction and documentation: external features (creation methods, class methods, commands, queries, and pre- and postconditions) and internal features (data and methods).
- Discuss the issues associated with error handling in Java.
- Present the important concept of collections. A hierarchy of collection interfaces is developed as a framework to support the concrete data structure classes in Part Two.
- Present the classical data structures in the context of OOP as concrete collection classes. This is the main focus and aim of the book.

We assume that the reader:

1. wishes to learn the fundamental principles of object-oriented software construction using Java

2. has prior experience with the elementary and basic aspects of the Java programming language or will learn these from basic programming books or language tutorials

3. has little or no experience with object-oriented programming

4. has not purchased this book as yet another book on Java programming

5. wishes to extend and reinforce Java programming skills with particular emphasis on GUI software development

6. wishes to see a GUI-based presentation of major programming examples and applications

7. desires a practical OOP-based presentation of data structures and their applications.

This book has evolved from a set of notes that has undergone several iterations based on class testing over a one-year period. We are grateful to our students for their thoughtful corrective feedback. We assume full responsibility for any errors or inaccuracies that remain. We thank our colleague Ben Nystuen for stimulating discussion and general support throughout the development of the notes that provide the basis for this book. We welcome feedback and corrections from you, the reader. You may provide these by sending e-mail to *rswiener@acm.org* or *ljp@acm.org*. We thank you in advance for your constructive comments.

Richard Wiener and Lewis J. Pinson
Colorado Springs, Colorado

PART ONE

Foundations

1

Cornerstones of OOP

The principles and practices of object-oriented software construction have evolved since the 1960s. Object-oriented programming (OOP) is preoccupied with the manipulation of software objects. OOP is a way of thinking about problem solving and a method of software organization and construction.

The concepts and ideas associated with object-oriented programming originated in Norway in the 1960s. A programming language called Simula developed by Christian Nygaard and his associates at the University of Oslo is considered the first object-oriented language. This language inspired significant thinking and development work at Xerox PARC (Palo Alto Research Center) in the 1970s that eventually led to the simple, rich, and powerful Smalltalk-80 programming language and environment (released in 1980). Smalltalk, perhaps more than any programming language before or after it, laid the foundation for object-oriented thinking and software construction. Smalltalk is considered a "pure" object-oriented language. Actions can be invoked only through objects or classes (a class can be considered an object in Smalltalk). The simple idea of sending messages to objects and using this as the basis for software organization is directly attributable to Smalltalk.

Seminal work on object-oriented programming was done in the mid-1980s in connection with the Eiffel language. Bertrand Meyer in his classic book *Object-Oriented Software Construction* (Prentice-Hall, 1988; Second Edition, 1997) set forth subtle principles associated with OOP that are still viable and alive today. The Eiffel programming language embodies many of these important principles and, like Smalltalk, is considered a pure object-oriented language. Eiffel, with its strong type checking (every object must have a type), is closer in structure to the languages that we use today than to Smalltalk.

OOP was popularized by a hybrid language developed at AT&T Bell Labs in the early 1980s, namely C++. This language evolved from the popular C language. C++ evolved rapidly during the late 1980s. Because of this rapid evolution and the need to retain a C-like syntax and backward compatibility with C, the syntax of C++ has become arcane and complex. The language continued to grow in complexity during the early 1990s before finally becoming standardized and is today considered one of the most complex programming languages ever devised. It is a hybrid language because one can invoke functions without classes or objects. In fact most C programs (C is not an object-oriented language) will compile and run as is using a C++ compiler. The hybrid nature of C++ makes it even more challenging to use since it allows a mixture of styles of software thinking and organization. In order to use C++ effectively as an object-oriented language, the programmer must impose rigorous constraints and style guidelines. Even with such discipline, the C-like nature of C++ allows programmers to work around basic OOP rules and principles such as encapsulation by using casts and pointers. The preoccupation with pointers in C++ makes the language potentially dangerous for large software projects because of the ever present specter of memory leakage (failure to de-allocate storage for objects that are no longer needed).

The Java programming language invented in the mid 1990s at Sun Microsystems and popularized in the late 1990s may be considered to be a third almost pure object-oriented language. Like Smalltalk and Eiffel, actions may be invoked only on objects and classes (except for a limited number of predefined operators used with primitive types). Also like Smalltalk and Eiffel and unlike C++, Java objects that are no longer needed are disposed of automatically using "garbage collection." The programmer is unburdened from having to devote time and effort to this important concern. It might be argued that the presence of primitive types in Java makes the language impure from an OOP perspective. Although this is strictly true, the basic nature and character of Java is that of a pure object-oriented language and we consider it such.

OOP got its popular start in Portland, Oregon in 1986 at the first Association for Computing Machinery (ACM)-sponsored OOPSLA (object-oriented programming, systems, languages, and applications) conference. At that time the first versions of C++ and Eiffel had recently been released. The three most highly developed languages that were showcased at this first OOPSLA conference were Object Pascal, Objective-C, and Smalltalk. The first release of the Java programming language was ten years away.

During the early days of object-oriented programming, attention was focused on the construction and development of OOP languages. Associated with these newly emerging languages were problem-solving methodologies and notations to support the software analysis and design processes. It was not until the late 1990s that standardization of the object-oriented analysis and design notation occurred with the Unified Modeling Language (UML).

The early application areas of OOP were the construction of libraries to support graphical user interfaces (GUIs), databases, and simulation. These application areas continue to provide fertile soil to support OOP development.

As we enter the twenty-first century, OOP has become widely accepted as a mainstream paradigm for problem solving and software construction. Its use may be found in a large number of application areas including compiler construction, operating system development, numerical software, data structures, communication and network software, as well as many other application areas.

In the following sections we introduce some fundamental concepts of OOP. Many of these concepts are elaborated on in later chapters of Part One.

1.1   Data Abstraction

The oldest cornerstone of OOP is the concept of data abstraction. This concept pre-dates OOP.

Data abstraction associates an underlying data type with a set of operations that may be performed on the data type. It is not necessary for a user of the data type to know how the type is represented (i.e., how the information in the type is stored) but only how the information can be manipulated. As an example, consider the notion of integer in a programming language. An integer is defined by the operations that may be performed on it. These include the binary operations of addition, subtraction, multiplication, and division as well as other well-known operations. A programmer can use an integer type without any knowledge of how it is internally stored or represented inside of the computer system. The internal representation is not accessible to the user.

Data abstraction derives its strength from the separation between the operations that may be performed on the underlying data and the internal representation of these data. If the internal representation of the data should be changed, as long as the operations on these data remain invariant, the software that uses the data remains unaffected.

1.2 Encapsulation

The fusion of underlying data with a set of operations that define the data type is called encapsulation. The internal representation of the data is encapsulated (hidden) but can be manipulated by the specified operations.

1.3 Object

OOP is based on the notion of object. A software object represents an abstraction of some reality. This reality may be a physical object but is more often an idea or concept that may be represented by an internal state. As an example consider a bouncing ball. If we were simulating the motion of the bouncing ball with software we would model the ball as an object and its dynamic state as its height above the surface on which it was bouncing. Here the software object represents a physical object. As a more abstract example consider a cashier line at a supermarket. If we were to represent the line as a software object, its internal state might be the number of customers waiting to check out. Associated with the line would be a set of behavioral rules. For example, the first customer to arrive would be the first customer to be served. The last customer to arrive would be the last to be served.

OOP is also based on the notion of sending messages to objects. Messages can **modify** or **return** information about the internal state of an object. We can send a line object the message *addCustomer*. This causes the internal state of the line to change. We can send a ball object the message *currentHeight*. This returns the ball's height above the surface.

The behavior of an object is codified in a class description. The object is said to be an instance of the **class** that describes its behavior. The class description specifies the internal state of the object and defines the types of messages that may be sent to all its instances. A class *Queue* might be defined to describe the behavior of line objects.

In a program an object is a program variable associated with a class type. The object encapsulates data. An object's "value" or information content is given by its internal state. This internal state is defined in terms of one or more fields. Each field holds a portion of the information content of the object. As indicated above, an object can receive messages that either change the internal state (i.e., change the value of one or more fields) or return information about the internal state of the object. These messages represent the operations that may be performed on the object.

1.4   Message

Messages are sent to or invoked on objects. In most object-oriented languages the syntax used to accomplish this is given as follows:

```
someObject.someMessage
```

The object precedes the message since it is the recipient of the message. A "dot" operator separates the object from the message. Reading from left to right places the emphasis on the first entity, the object. A message may sometimes have one or more parameters. For example,

```
line.addCustomer(joe)
```

Here the object *line*, an instance of class *Queue*, receives the message *addCustomer* with *joe* as a parameter. The object *joe* is presumed to be an instance of class *Customer*. Since a *Queue* object needs to hold other objects, in this case *Customer* objects, the method *addCustomer* must take a *Customer* object as a parameter.

Messages can be cascaded. Suppose we wish to determine the last name of the first customer in a line. The following expression might be appropriate:

```
line.first.lastName
```

Here *line* is assumed to be an instance of class *Queue*. The message *first* returns a *Customer* object (the lead customer in the *Queue*). The message *lastName* returns the last-name field of this lead customer. We are assuming that class *Queue* has a method *first* that returns the lead customer. We are assuming that class *Customer* has a method *lastName* that returns the last-name field.

1.5   Method

A method is a function or procedure that defines the action associated with a message. It is given as part of a class description. When a message is invoked on an object the details of the operation performed on the object are specified by the corresponding method.

1.6 Class

A class describes the behavior of objects, its instances. The external or "public" view of a class describes the messages that may be sent to instances. Each possible message is defined by a method. These include messages that affect the internal state of the object and messages that return information about this internal state. The internal or "private" view of a class describes the fields that hold the information content of instances. In addition to fields, the private view of a class may define private methods that are used to support public methods but cannot be invoked outside of the class.

The user of a class is concerned only with the public or external view of the class. The producer of a class is concerned with the public and private view. Chapter 3 describes the construction of Java classes in detail.

Let us consider a simple example to illustrate some of the ideas presented above. Consider class *Point*. The "actions" that one may take on a point object include:

1. setX(xValue)
2. setY(yValue)
3. x( )
4. y( )
5. distanceFromOrigin( )

Note: We prefer to use a noun phrase rather than a verb phrase for a message that returns internal information about an object. This is justified in Chapter 3.

The five external actions that have been defined for class *Point* are called accessor methods. They allow us to set and get the values of the x and y coordinates of a point object and get the distance of the point to the origin. The first two accessors, *setX* and *setY*, require a parameter.

Listing 1.1 presents a full Java class definition for *Point*.

Listing 1.1 Class *Point*

```
/** Details of class Point
*/
public class Point {

  // Fields
  private double x;          // x coordinate
  private double y;          // y coordinate
  private double distance;   // length of point

  // Methods
  public void setX (double x) {
    this.x = x;
    updateDistance();
  }
```

```
public void setY (double y) {
  this.y = y;
  updateDistance();
}

public double x () {
  return x;
}

public double y () {
  return y;
}

public double distanceFromOrigin () {
  return distance;
}

// Internal methods
private void updateDistance () {
  distance = Math.sqrt(x*x + y*y);
}
}
```

As will be our practice throughout this book, class names and public features shall be presented in boldface type. This highlights the external view of the class.

The three fields are designated with the *private* access specifier. This encapsulates the information content. This content can be modified using only the methods *setX* and *setY*. When either of these methods are invoked, the *distance* field is automatically updated and is available to the user with the method *distanceFromOrigin*.

If the fields information were not encapsulated, a user of class *Point* could directly modify the x coordinate or y coordinate and forget to update the *distance* field. Of course this quantity could be computed each time it is needed instead of updated each time the x or y coordinate of the point object is modified. In general, information about an object can be obtained either through storage (as in Listing 1.1) or through computation.

1.7 Inheritance

Another cornerstone of OOP is inheritance. Inspired from biological modeling, inheritance allows new classes to be constructed that inherit characteristics (fields and methods) from ancestor classes while typically introducing more specialized characteristics, new fields, or methods. A subclass is logically considered to be a specialized version or extension of its parent and by inference its ancestor classes.

In Java, every object before its creation must be declared to be of a given type, typically the class that the object is an instance of. This sometimes changes in the presence of inheritance because of an important principal, the principal of **polymorphic substitution**. This principal states that wherever an object of a given type is needed in an expression, it may be substituted for by an object that is a descendent of the given type. Although it may be difficult upon first contemplation to fully appreciate the power and implications of this principal, it is one of the most important and fundamental concepts in object-oriented software construction.

Since polymorphic substitution states that a descendent class object may be used in place of its ancestor object, the descendent class object must be considered to be of the ancestor type. This makes sense. Consider a high-level class *Vehicle* that encapsulates the properties of all vehicle objects. Now consider a more specific class *Bicycle* with its unique behavior that represents a specialization of class *Vehicle*. At the least, the methods of class *Vehicle* can be interpreted by class *Bicycle*. Thus it makes sense that a *Bicycle* object can be used in place of a *Vehicle* object (it will know how to respond to *Vehicle* messages). Clearly the opposite is not true. A *Vehicle* object cannot be used in place of a *Bicycle* object since it will not necessarily be able to respond to the specialized methods of class *Bicycle*. A bicycle is a vehicle.

In general a subclass should logically satisfy the constraint that it can also be considered to be of the parent class type. This is most fundamental. Regardless of what other purpose one may wish to achieve in using inheritance, this logical constraint should be satisfied. A *TeddyBear* class should not be construed to be a subclass of *Refrigerator*. This constraint is often referred to as the "is a" or "is kind of" relationship between subclass and parent. The subclass should satisfy the logical condition that it "is kind of" an instance of its parent. This logical constraint is sometimes referred to as **behavioral inheritance**. The subclass enjoys the same behavioral characteristics as its parent in addition to the more specialized behavior that distinguishes the subclass from the parent.

Another use of inheritance (some might argue "misuse") is **implementation inheritance**. Here the only purpose of creating a parent class is to factor code that is needed by other subclasses. Since ancestor methods are generally inherited by descendent classes (unless they are redefined in one or more descendent classes), the descendent class can consider the ancestor method to be one of its own. Although implementation inheritance makes it possible to reuse code, if the logical constraints of behavioral inheritance (the "is kind of" relationship) are not satisfied, the software architecture may become muddled and difficult to maintain. Often implementation inheritance flows as a natural and useful byproduct from behavioral inheritance.

It is not the goal of this introductory section on inheritance to present all the details of inheritance in Java. This is the goal of Chapter 4.

To clarify the above ideas, an example that illustrates the use of inheritance is presented in this section without extensive detail. Consider a *SpecializedPoint* class that extends the *Point* class presented in Listing 1.1.

SpecializedPoint Class

Suppose we wish to create a point class in which the x and y coordinates are constrained to be positive. That is, we wish our *SpecializedPoint* objects to be located in the first quadrant of the complex plane.

First we need to make small modifications to class *Point*, given in Listing 1.1. The Modified Point class is given in Listing 1.2.

Listing 1.2   Modified *Point* Class

```java
/** Modified Point class
*/
public class Point {

  // Fields
  protected double x;
  protected double y;
  protected double distance;

  // Constructor
  Point () {
    setX(0);
    setY(0);
  }

  Point (double x, double y) {
    setX(x);
    setY(y);
  }

  // Methods
  public void setX (double x) {
    this.x = x;
    updateDistance();
  }

  public void setY (double y) {
    this.y = y;
    updateDistance();
  }

  public double x () {
    return x;
  }

  public double y () {
    return y;
  }

  public double distanceFromOrigin () {
    return distance;
  }

  public String toString() {
    return "<" + x + "," + y + ">" ;
  }

  // Internal methods
  protected void updateDistance () {
    distance = Math.sqrt(x*x + y*y);
  }
}
```

Brief Explanation of Listing 1.2

The access modifiers for the three fields are changed from *private* to *protected*. This allows all subclasses to inherit these fields without changing the accessibility of the fields in outside classes – encapsulation of internal information is preserved while providing access to all descendent classes. If the fields were kept as *private* as in Listing 1.1, the subclass *SpecializedPoint* would effectively have no fields directly accessible. This violates the concept of behavioral inheritance in which a subclass is a kind of its parent. In order for a *SpecializedPoint* object to be of type *Point*, it must retain the three internal fields (i.e., have an x value, a y value, and a *distance* value).

Two constructors are added to the class definition. As shall be explained further in Chapter 3, a constructor is a function that always bears the name of its class and is used to produce new instances of the given class. In Listing 1.1 no constructor was provided. In this case Java provides a default constructor that initializes all fields to zero (if they are scalar fields as in Listing 1.1) and null if the fields are objects (reference types). This shall be explained in Chapter 2. Notice that the field *distance* is automatically updated based on the values used in the two constructors for fields x and y by invoking the *setX* and *setY* commands. This is an example of a good object-oriented design principle in action. A consistent set of steps is followed for setting the value of *distance*.

The method *toString()* is useful because it is automatically invoked whenever a string representation of a *Point* is desired. This is useful when doing input/output (I/O) as in the expression *System.out.println("pt = " + pt)*, where *pt* is a *Point* object. Here the "+" or concatenation operator causes the *toString()* method to be automatically invoked, converting the *pt* object to a string object. Class *String* and its important properties are discussed in Chapter 2.

Listing 1.3   Class *SpecializedPoint*

```
/** Details of a specialized Point class that extends class Point
*/
public class SpecializedPoint extends Point {

  // Constructor
  SpecializedPoint () {
    super(); // Invokes the parent class constructor
  }

  SpecializedPoint (double x, double y) {
    super(x, y);
  }

  // Methods
  public void setX (double x) { // Redefined method
    if (x < 0)
      throw new UnsupportedOperationException(
        "x must be greater than 0" );
```

```
    else {
      this.x = x;
      updateDistance();
    }
  }


  public void setY (double y) { // Redefined method
    if (y < 0)
      throw new UnsupportedOperationException(
        "y must be greater than 0" );
    else {
      this.y = y;
      updateDistance();
    }
  }
}
```

Brief Explanation of Listing 1.3

The key word **extends** establishes that class *SpecializedPoint* is a subclass of class *Point*. The methods *setX* and *setY* are redefined. Code is written to ensure that the values of the parameters *x* and *y* are non-negative. If this is violated an *UnsupportedOperationException* is generated. It is the responsibility of the caller (the block of code that invokes the constructor or *setX* or *setY*) to ensure that *x* and *y* are non-negative. This shall be explained in more detail in Chapter 4. All other methods from class *Point* are inherited in class *SpecializedPoint* and may be used as is.

Listing 1.4 presents a small test class that exercises some of the methods of classes *Point* and *SpecializedPoint*.

Listing 1.4 Class *PointTest*

```
/** A test program that exercises classes Point and SpecializedPoint
*/
public class PointTest {

  public static void main(String[] args) {
    Point p = new Point (-3, -4);
    SpecializedPoint sp1 = new SpecializedPoint ();
    SpecializedPoint sp2 = new SpecializedPoint ();

    sp1.setX(3);
    sp1.setY(4);
    System.out.println("sp1 = " + sp1);
```

```
    sp2.setX(-3); // Should cause an exception to be generated
    sp2.setY(4);
    System.out.println("sp1 = " + sp1);
  }
}
```

Brief Explanation of Listing 1.4

The code works fine and predictably until the method *setX* with parameter
−3 is invoked on the *SpecializedPoint* object *sp2*. This causes the *Unsupported-
OperationException* to be generated. Exceptions are discussed in Chapter 7. The
program output is:

```
sp1 = <3.0,4.0>
Exception in thread "main" java.lang.
  UnsupportedOperationException: x
and y must be greater than 0
at SpecializedPoint.setX(SpecializedPoint.java:24)
at PointTest.main(PointTest.java:15)
```

1.8 Late Binding Polymorphism

Late binding is closely related to inheritance. Since methods may be redefined in
descendent classes (like methods *setX* and *setY* in Listing 1.3), it is common for
several specialized versions of a given method to exist in a class hierarchy, each
with the same method signature (same function name, same return type, and
same set of parameters). The runtime system is able to bind the correct version of
a method to an object based on the specific type of the object. This late binding is
an important characteristic of object-oriented systems. The word *polymorphism*
derives from "many forms." In the case of OOP, many forms refer to the different
versions of a specific method defined in different subclasses. An example that
illustrates late binding is presented in the next section.

1.9 Abstract Classes

A class in which one or more methods are not implemented is defined as an **abstract class**. A class in which all methods are implemented is a **concrete class**.
Abstract classes are often defined near the top of a hierarchical structure of classes.
Undefined or abstract methods are used in an abstract class to establish required
behavior in any descendent concrete class. **An instance of an abstract class
cannot be created**.

Since some methods in an abstract class may be fully implemented, the benefit
of implementation inheritance can be realized along with behavior inheritance.

We illustrate the concepts of abstract class and late binding by considering
skeletal portions of a small hierarchy of *Vehicle* classes. We employ UML notation
(see Appendix A) to represent the *Vehicle* hierarchy, shown in Figure 1.1.

Class *Vehicle* is shown as the root class in the hierarchy. Class *Vehicle* is abstract. This implies that no instances of *Vehicle* can be constructed. The fields

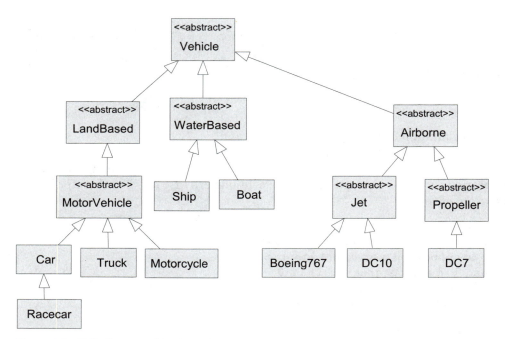

Figure 1.1. UML diagram of *Vehicle* class hierarchy.

of *Vehicle*, if any, and all its methods, are inherited by every class in Figure
1.1. The fields and methods of *Vehicle* describe behavior and state common to
all subclasses of *Vehicle* (all vehicle types). The three immediate subclasses of
Vehicle – LandBased, WaterBased, and *Airborne* – are also abstract classes (no instances can be constructed). More specialized characteristics (fields and methods)
for each of these vehicle types are defined. Under *LandBased* is the abstract class
MotorVehicle. There are three concrete subclasses of *MotorVehicle*: *Car, Truck*, and
Motorcycle. Each of these inherits the fields and methods defined in the abstract
classes *MotorVehicle, Landbased*, and *Vehicle* as well as introducing more specialized behavior. Class *Racecar* is shown as a subclass of *Car*. It inherits the fields
and methods of *Car* as well as introducing its own specialized behavior (additional
fields or methods).

What is the type associated with an instance of class *Racecar*? The answer:
Racecar, Car, MotorVehicle, LandBased, Vehicle, and *Object* (all classes inherit
from *Object*). Yes, a *Racecar* instance is of six distinct types. What does this mean
in practice?

Consider the following variable declaration:

```
Vehicle rc = new Racecar();
```

Here an object *rc* of formal type *Vehicle* is constructed of actual type *Racecar*.
The principle of polymorphic substitution discussed in Section 1.7 is utilized.
This allows an object of some descendent type to be substituted for the ances-
tor type.

Let us consider the construction of abstract class *Vehicle*. Listing 1.5 presents the code for this abstract class.

The method *accelerate( )* is designated as abstract. No details are shown. Every concrete descendent class must have an implementation of this method either through inheritance or redefinition.

Listing 1.5   Abstract Class *Vehicle*

```java
import java.awt.*;

public abstract class Vehicle {

  // Fields
  protected int weight;
  protected Color color;

  // Methods
  public abstract void accelerate();

  int weight() {
    return weight;
  }

  int color() {
    return color;
  }

  // Other methods not shown
}
```

Listing 1.6 shows class *Car*.

Listing 1.6   Class *Car*

```java
public class Car extends MotorVehicle {
  // Methods
  public void accelerate() { /* Details related to car. */ }
  // Other methods not shown
}
```

Listing 1.7 shows class *Racecar* with *accelerate( )* redefined.

Listing 1.7   Class *Racecar*

```java
public class Racecar extends Car {
  // Methods
  public void accelerate() { /* Details related to race car. */ }
  // Other methods not shown
}
```

To further illustrate the concept of late binding and type, consider a collection of vehicles defined in class *VehicleApp* in Listing 1.8. Arrays are discussed in Chapter 2 but shall be utilized here.

The line of code

```
Vehicle [] vehicles = new Vehicle[7];
```

constructs an array that may hold seven vehicles. Here *Vehicle* is a placeholder for some concrete descendent type. The next seven lines of code construct and assign specific vehicle objects to the *vehicles* array.

The code shown in boldface shows late binding polymorphism in action.

```
// Accelerate each vehicle
for (int index = 0; index < 7; index++)
  vehicles[index].accelerate();
```

Each vehicle object is sent the command *accelerate()*. There are seven distinct implementations of this method. The appropriate method is bound to the command at runtime based on whether the object at *vehicles[index]* is a *Car, Racecar, Truck, Motorcycle, Boeing767, DC10,* or *DC7* vehicle.

If later a new concrete vehicle subclass were added to the *Vehicle* hierarchy, with a unique *accelerate()* method, the code shown in boldface would not have to be changed.

Listing 1.8 Class *VehicleApp*

```
public class VehicleApp {

  static public void main(String[] args) {
    Vehicle [] vehicles = new Vehicle[7];
    // Construct 7 vehicles
    vehicles [0] = new Car();
    vehicles [1] = new Racecar();
    vehicles [2] = new Truck();
    vehicles [3] = new Motorcycle();
    vehicles [4] = new Boeing767();
    vehicles [5] = new DC10();
    vehicles [6] = new DC7();

    // Accelerate each vehicle
    for (int index = 0; index < 7; index++)
      vehicles[index].accelerate();
  }
}
```

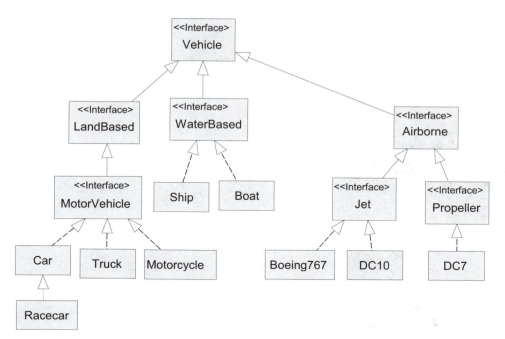

Figure 1.2. *Vehicle* classes using interfaces.

1.10 Interface

Java supports only single inheritance. That is, each class may have at most one parent. Suppose we wish to add a *Seaplane* class to the *Vehicle* hierarchy. Clearly a seaplane is a mixture of *Boat* and *Propeller*. How can we handle this with single inheritance?

A special type of abstract class, an **interface**, is available in Java. **No fields (except static constants) are allowed in an interface and all methods must be abstract**.

Suppose that each of the abstract classes presented in Figure 1.1 were interfaces. The new hierarchy would be as shown in Figure 1.2.

The interface *Vehicle* is given in Listing 1.9. The interface *LandBased* is given in Listing 1.10. The interface *MotorVehicle* is given in Listing 1.11. The revised class *Car* is given in Listing 1.12. An interface and all methods in an interface are abstract by default; the use of keyword *abstract* is optional.

Listing 1.9 Interface *Vehicle*

```
public interface Vehicle {
  // Methods
  public void accelerate();
  // Other methods not shown; all must be abstract
}
```

Listing 1.10 Interface *LandBased*

```
public interface LandBased extends Vehicle {
  // Methods not shown
}
```

Listing 1.11 Interface *MotorVehicle*

```
public interface MotorVehicle extends LandBased {
  // Methods not shown
}
```

Listing 1.12 Class *Car*

```
public class Car implements MotorVehicle {
  // Methods
  public void accelerate() { /* Details for class Car. */ }
  // Other methods not shown
}
```

It is noted that class *Car* implements *MotorVehicle* rather than extends *Motor-Vehicle*. An interface can only be extended by another interface (e.g., interface *MotorVehicle* extends interface *LandBased*). A concrete class such as *Car* can only "implement" an interface.

A concrete class can implement multiple interfaces. This is what distinguishes an interface from an ordinary class. Through multiple implementation, a concrete class can acquire the type and behavior of several interface classes.

Let us return to class *Seaplane*. This class can implement the interfaces *Water-Based* and *Propeller* as shown in Listing 1.13. When a class promises to implement an interface, it must implement every abstract method defined in that interface plus those inherited through extension of the interface.

Listing 1.13 Class *Seaplane*

```
public class Seaplane implements WaterBased, Propeller {
  // Methods
  public void accelerate() { /* Details related to this class. */ };
  // Other methods not shown
}
```

A Seaplane object is of the following six types: *Seaplane, WaterBased, Propeller, Airborne, Vehicle,* and *Object*. A *Seaplane* object may be used in place of any of these six types and can be said to be a kind of *WaterBased* or *Propeller* or *Airborne* or *Vehicle* or *Object* class.

Figure 1.3. Delegation.

Since an interface class is a special case of an abstract class, it is also used to establish behavioral properties that must be realized by any concrete class that implements the interface.

1.11 Delegation

Delegation is a mechanism of problem solving in which one class designates another to take responsibility for a set of actions. Typically an object of the class that carries out the set of actions (the delegate) is held as a field in the class that delegates the responsibility. This is shown in the UML diagram of Figure 1.3. The arrow connecting the classes indicates that the *Delegate* class is held as a field in the *DelegatesResponsibility* class.

Listing 1.14 shows the high-level structure of the relationship depicted in Figure 1.3.

Listing 1.14   **Java Code That Shows Delegation**

```
class DelegatesResponsibility {

  // Fields
  private Delegate delegate; // Carries out responsibilities

  // Methods
  public void takeAction() {
    delegate.takeAction();
  }
  // Other methods not shown
}
```

The method *takeAction* in class *DelegatesResponsibility* accomplishes its task by using the *delegate* object to perform this task.

1.12 Generic Classes and Interfaces

A generic class is one whose behavior is not dependent on some specific underlying type. As an example, let us consider a class that performs sorting on some underlying collection of objects. If one carefully examines the process of sorting (ordering information from smallest to largest or largest to smallest), it becomes evident that the only requirement that the underlying objects must satisfy is that they can be compared. That is, it can be determined whether one object is bigger or smaller than another object.

An important interface that is provided in the *java.util* package (starting with Version 1.2) is *Comparable*. Listing 1.15 shows this interface.

Listing 1.15 Interface *Comparable*

```
interface Comparable { // Given in package java.util

  int compareTo (Object o);
}
```

The function *compareTo* returns a value of −1 if the receiver is smaller than the object *o*, 0 if the receiver equals the object *o*, and 1 if the receiver is larger than object *o*.

Any class of objects that might serve as the basis for sorting must implement *Comparable*. Method *sort* has the signature given below:

```
public void sort (Comparable [] data, int size) { // Details not shown}
```

1.13 Summary

This chapter has introduced some of the basic foundation concepts underlying object-oriented programming. Further details regarding these concepts shall be presented in the next several chapters. Among the basic concepts introduced in this chapter are:

- ❏ Data abstraction – Associates an underlying data type with a set of operations that may be performed on the data type.
- ❏ Encapsulation – The fusion of underlying data with a set of operations. The internal representation of the data is encapsulated (hidden) but can be manipulated by the specified operations.
- ❏ Object – An abstraction of some reality. This reality may be a physical object but is more often an idea or concept that may be represented by an internal state and a set of actions that can modify or access this internal state.
- ❏ Message – Messages are sent to or invoked on objects.
- ❏ Method – A function or procedure that defines the action associated with a message.
- ❏ Class – Describes the behavior of objects, its instances. The external or public view describes the messages that may be sent to instances. Each possible message is defined by a method. These include messages that affect the internal state of the object and messages that return information about this internal state. The internal or private view describes the fields that hold the information content of instances. In addition to fields, the private view of a class may define private methods that are used to support public methods but cannot be invoked outside of the class.

❏ Inheritance – Inspired from biological modeling, inheritance allows new classes to be constructed that inherit characteristics (fields and methods) from ancestor classes while typically introducing more specialized characteristics, new fields, or methods. A subclass is logically considered to be a specialized version or extension of its parent and by inference its ancestor classes.

❏ Late binding – Late binding is closely related to inheritance. Since methods may be redefined in descendent classes it is common for several specialized versions of a given method to exist in a class hierarchy, each with the same method signature (same function name, same return type, and same set of parameters). The runtime system is able to bind the correct version of a method to an object based on the specific type of the object.

❏ Abstract class – A class in which one or more methods are not implemented. No instances may be created of an abstract class.

❏ Concrete class – A class in which all methods are implemented directly or through inheritance from another class.

❏ Interface – A special type of abstract class in which no fields (except for static constants) are allowed and all methods must be abstract.

❏ Generic class – The behavior is not dependent on a specific data type.

1.14 Exercises

1   List five data abstractions. For each, describe the operations that may be performed on the underlying data.

2   Describe several examples of inheritance. Explain the methods and fields of the parent class and its descendent classes.

3   Construct an example that illustrates late binding polymorphism. You need to identify a small hierarchy of classes and one or more methods that are redefined and behave polymorphically.

4   Construct an example where delegation might be useful.

5   Construct several generic classes. Describe their properties and why they are generic.

2

Objects

Objects, objects everywhere! OOP is about sending messages to objects. It is about the construction, manipulation, and destruction of objects.

This chapter looks at objects in more detail. In particular we focus on the creation, assignment, cloning, and equality testing of objects. We examine scalar types and contrast them with reference types. We discuss in some detail three basic collection types: array, string, and vector.

2.1 Reference Semantics and Creating Objects

In Java, an object is associated with a reference type – a class. An object is more specifically an instance of a class. Memory for the object and its contents (field values) is allocated dynamically using the object creation operator *new*. Before an object can be created it must be declared to be of a reference type.

Consider an object, *myStack*, that is declared to be of type *Stack*.

```
Stack myStack;
```

The initial value of *myStack* is *null*. An object with value *null* is really only a potential object. With value *null*, the object holds no information and no messages may be sent to the object. The object is said to be uninitialized.

To bring the object *myStack* to life, the object creation operator *new* must be used to activate a constructor in the class *Stack*. This might be accomplished as follows:

```
myStack = new Stack(); // Creating an instance of Stack
```

It is assumed that class *Stack* has a constructor with no parameters that creates and initializes an empty stack or if no explicit constructor is provided, a default constructor is activated that creates a *Stack* object and initializes all its fields of reference type to *null*. Fields of primitive type also have default initializations.

The object *myStack* could be declared and initialized at once as follows:

```
Stack myStack = new Stack();
```

Once initialized, the variable name *myStack* becomes a reference to the memory storage that holds the contents of this particular *Stack* object. Messages may be sent to this object using the usual dot operator that connects an object to its message. An example might be:

```
myStack.push(str1); // Sending message push to object myStack
```

Here the message *push* is sent to the object *myStack* with an object *str1* (a string object) as its parameter. This message changes the internal state of the object *myStack*.

If one attempts to send a message to an uninitialized object (one whose value is *null*), a runtime *NullPointerException* is generated by the system. This is a serious defect and can cause a program crash.

2.2 Assigning, Aliasing, and Cloning Objects

Several simple classes are constructed to assist in explaining the subtleties of assigning, copying, and cloning objects. As a convenience, Listing 2.1 repeats the implementation of class *Point* presented in Chapter 1.

Listing 2.1 Class *Point*

```
/** Details of class Point
*/
public class Point {

  // Fields
  protected double x;
  protected double y;
  protected double distance;

  // Constructor
  Point () {
    setX(0);
    setY(0);
  }

  Point (double x, double y) {
    setX(x);
    setY(y);
  }

  // Methods
  public void setX (double x) {
    this.x = x;
    updateDistance();
  }
```

```
public void setY (double y) {
  this.y = y;
  updateDistance();
}

public double x () {
  return x;
}

public double y () {
  return y;
}

public double distanceFromOrigin () {
  return distance;
}

public String toString() {
  return "<" + x + "," + y + ">";
}

// Internal methods
protected void updateDistance () {
  distance = Math.sqrt(x*x + y*y);
}
}
```

Listing 2.2 presents the details of a class *Line*.

Listing 2.2   Class *Line*

```
/** Encapsulates line
*/
public class Line {

  // Fields
  private Point pt1, pt2; // End points of line

  // Constructors
  public Line (Point pt1, Point pt2) {
    this.pt1 = pt1;
    this.pt2 = pt2;
  }

  // Methods
  public double length() {
```

```
      return Math.sqrt((pt2.y() - pt1.y()) * (pt2.y() - pt1.y()) +
                       (pt2.x() - pt1.x()) * (pt2.x() - pt1.x()));
    }

  public String toString() {
    return "point1: " + pt1 + " point2: " + pt2;
  }
}
```

Two end points, *pt1* and *pt2* give the internal fields that define the information content of a *Line*. The constructor takes these two end points as input and defines *pt1* and *pt2* using direct assignment of objects. We will examine the effect that such assignment has after considering a test program in Listing 2.3.

Listing 2.3 Effects of Object Assignment

```
public class CopyTest {

  public static void main(String[] args) {
    Point pt1 = new Point(1, 1);
    Point pt2 = new Point(2, 2);
    Line line1 = new Line(pt1, pt2);
    System.out.println ("line1 = " + line1);
    // Change starting point
    pt1.setX(0);
    pt1.setY(0);
    System.out.println(
          "After pt1.setX(0) and pt1.setY(0) \n line1 = " + line1);
  }
}
```

The output of Listing 2.3 is:

```
line1 = point1: <1.0,1.0> point2: <2.0,2.0>
After pt1.setX(0) and pt1.setY(0)
  line1 = point1: <0.0,0.0> point2: <2.0,2.0>
```

The value of *line1* has been affected by changing the values of *pt1* and *pt2*.

Let us analyze the code in Listings 2.2 and 2.3. Figure 2.1 shows the effect of the direct assignments in the constructor of class *Line* (see Listing 2.2). Figure 2.2 shows the objects *line1*, *pt1*, and *pt2* after changing the values in *pt1*.

The effect of the assignment statements in the constructor of class *Line* is to provide two

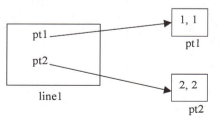

Figure 2.1. The objects *line1* and *pt1* and *pt2* before changing *pt1*.

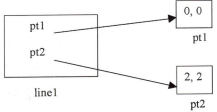

Figure 2.2. The objects *line1* and *pt1* and *pt2* after changing *pt1*.

sets of references to the point objects *pt1* and *pt2*. The values of these two points are stored in only one location in memory but are referenced in the fields of *line1* and the objects *pt1* and *pt2* (references to this storage). Therefore, any change that occurs in the point objects *pt1* or *pt2* as the program evolves directly affects the fields of the *line1* object. This is called an **aliasing** effect and is generally undesirable. When an object is constructed, such as *line1*, its internal state (end points *pt1* and *pt2*) should not be affected by external influences as occurred here.

We can correct the aliasing problem by modifying the constructor in class *Line*. The new constructor is given as follows:

```
public Line (Point pt1, Point pt2) {
  this.pt1 = new Point(pt1.x(), pt1.y());
  this.pt2 = new Point(pt2.x(), pt2.y());
}
```

Instead of performing a direct assignment, which caused the aliasing problem, we associate the fields *pt1* and *pt2* with entirely new *Point* objects constructed as shown above. The aliasing problem is solved.

Figure 2.3 shows the relationship among the various objects after the *pt1* object has been modified and using the alias-free version of *Line*.

Consider now a new class *LineHolder* given in Listing 2.4.

Listing 2.4   Class *LineHolder*

```
/** Holds two lines
*/
public class LineHolder {

  // Fields
  private Line line1, line2;

  // Constructor
  public LineHolder (Line line1, Line line2) {
    this.line1 = line1;
    this.line2 = line2;
  }

  // Methods
  public void setLine1 (Line line1) {
    this.line1 = line1;
  }
```

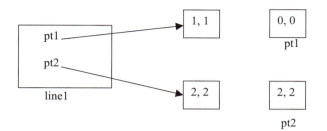

Figure 2.3. The object *line1* with its own independent field objects.

```
public void setLine2 (Line line2) {
  this.line2 = line2;
}

public String toString () {
  return "line1: " + line1 + " line2: " + line2;
}
}
```

Now consider a modified *CopyTest* program given in Listing 2.5.

Listing 2.5 Modified *CopyTest*

```
public class CopyTest {

  public static void main(String[] args) {
    Point pt1 = new Point(1, 1);
    Point pt2 = new Point(2, 2);
    Point pt3 = new Point(3, 3);
    Point pt4 = new Point(4, 4);
    Point pt5 = new Point(5, 5);
    Point pt6 = new Point(6, 6);
    Line line1 = new Line(pt1, pt2);
    Line line2 = new Line(pt3, pt4);
    Line line3 = new Line(pt5, pt6);

    LineHolder lineHolder1 = new LineHolder(line1, line2);
    LineHolder lineHolder2;
    lineHolder2 = lineHolder1;

    System.out.println("lineHolder2 = " + lineHolder2);

    lineHolder1.setLine2(line3);
    System.out.println("After line1 is changed, lineHolder2 = " +
                        lineHolder2);
  }
}
```

The constructor in class *LineHolder* produces the same aliasing effect because of the assignment statements. How can we fix this problem?

If we attempt the same solution as before we need to construct new *line1* and *line2* objects as we did when we corrected the aliasing problem in class *Line*. But we have a problem. We cannot construct these line objects since the constructor for class *Line* requires creating a line in terms of its two end points and we cannot access the end points for the two input lines in class *LineHolder* since they are private fields.

One approach to fixing the problem is to provide accessor methods in class *Line* that return its two end points. Then two new line objects could be created in the constructor for class *LineHolder* using end points of the input *line1* and *line2* objects in creating two new lines. We shall employ another approach.

An empty interface *Cloneable* is provided in package *java.lang*. A class that implements the *Cloneable* interface enables cloning for its instances. The class may redefine the *clone* method inherited from class *Object*. We define meaningful clone methods for classes *Line* and *LineHolder*. The modified class definitions are given in Listings 2.6 and 2.7.

Listing 2.6   Final Modification to Class *Line*

```
public class Line implements Cloneable {

  // Fields
  private Point pt1, pt2; // End points of line

  // Constructors
  public Line (Point pt1, Point pt2) {
    this.pt1 = new Point(pt1.x(), pt1.y());
    this.pt2 = new Point(pt2.x(), pt2.y());
  }

  // Methods
  public double length() {
    return Math.sqrt((pt2.y() - pt1.y()) * (pt2.y() - pt1.y()) +
                     (pt2.x() - pt1.x()) * (pt2.x() - pt1.x()));
  }

  public String toString () {
    return "point1: " + pt1 + " point2: " + pt2;
  }

  public Object clone () {
    return new Line(pt1, pt2);
  }
}
```

Listing 2.7 Final Modification to Class *LineHolder*

```
public class LineHolder implements Cloneable {

  // Fields
  private Line line1, line2;

  // Constructor
  public LineHolder (Line line1, Line line2) {
    this.line1 = (Line) line1.clone();
    this.line2 = (Line) line2.clone();
  }

  // Methods
  public void setLine1 (Line line1) {
    this.line1 = line1;
  }

  public void setLine2 (Line line2) {
    this.line2 = line2;
  }

  public String toString () {
    return "line1: " + line1 + " line2: " + line2;
  }

  public Object clone () {
    return new LineHolder((Line) line1.clone(),
            (Line) line2.clone());
  }
}
```

The clone method in class *Line* returns a new *Line* object containing the same fields. The clone method in class *LineHolder* returns a new *LineHolder* object using clones of its two fields. It is necessary to use the *(Line)* downcast operator since the clone function returns a formal type *Object* and a type *Line* is needed in the constructor for *LineHolder*. Listing 2.8 shows the final modification of the test class *CopyTest*.

Listing 2.8 Final Modification of Class *CopyTest*

```
public class CopyTest {

  public static void main(String[] args) {
    Point pt1 = new Point(1, 1);
    Point pt2 = new Point(2, 2);
    Point pt3 = new Point(3, 3);
```

```
    Point pt4 = new Point(4, 4);
    Point pt5 = new Point(5, 5);
    Point pt6 = new Point(6, 6);
    Line line1 = new Line(pt1, pt2);
    Line line2 = new Line(pt3, pt4);
    Line line3 = new Line(pt5, pt6);

    LineHolder lineHolder1 = new LineHolder(line1, line2);
    LineHolder lineHolder2;
    lineHolder2 = (LineHolder) lineHolder1.clone();

    System.out.println("lineHolder2 = " + lineHolder2);

    lineHolder1.setLine2(line3);
    System.out.println("After line1 is changed, lineHolder2 = " +
                    lineHolder2);
  }
}
```

The only line of code that has changed is shown in boldface. The downcast operator *(LineHolder)* must be used since *lineHolder1.clone()* returns a formal type *Object* and a *LineHolder* type is needed.

The aliasing problems that occurred in class *Line* and *LineHolder* were solved by creating fields that were totally new and independent objects that were decoupled from the objects sent in as parameters (*Point* objects for class *Line* and *Line* objects for class *LineHolder*).

2.3 Equality Testing

What does it mean to compare two objects using the predefined equality operator, "=="? The predefined equality operator returns *true* if the object references are identical. This is true only if there exist two separate references to the same underlying storage as when aliasing occurs. Consider the following code segment:

```
Point pt1 = new Point(1, 1);
Point pt2 = new Point(1, 1);
System.out.println("pt1 == pt2: " + (pt1 == pt2));
```

Although we know that *pt1* has the same internal content as *pt2* (they are equal in the usual sense) the output is *false* indicating that *pt1* and *pt2* are not equal.

The root class *Object* in the Java class library hierarchy has an *equals* method with the following signature:

```
public boolean equals(Object obj)
```

This default function works just as the predefined equality operator "==". It is fairly useless as is and should be redefined in classes that need it.

For class *Point* we need to add the following equals method:

```
public boolean equals (Object obj) {
   return ((Point) obj).x() == x && ((Point) obj).y() == y;
}
```

This method returns *true* if the x and y values of the point objects being compared are identical. The *(Point)* downcast operators are needed since the formal type of the parameter is *Object* whereas the actual type is *Point*.

2.4 Scalar versus Reference Types

Reference types include programmer-defined classes such as *Point*, *Line*, and *LineHolder* from Section 2.2 as well as the vast set of classes provided in the standard Java libraries. A reference type is associated with a class. In order to be usable, a variable declared to be of a reference type must be created using the object creation operator *new* before it can receive messages. When an object is created, storage for its contents is allocated.

Java provides several scalar types. These include primitive numeric types, plus *boolean* and *char*. The primitive types are not associated with a class and do not need to be created. They may be initialized at their point of declaration. The following segment of code contrasts the initialization of reference types and scalar types.

```
Point point1 = new Point(2, 2);
Point point2 = new Point(3, 3);
Line myLine = new Line(point1, point2);
int height = 72;
double weight = 175.4;
```

The three variables declared to be of reference types (*point1*, *point2*, and *myLine*) are each created and transformed into objects using the operator *new*. As each of these objects is created it is initialized.

The two variables declared to be of scalar type (*height* and *weight*) are declared and initialized in a single declaration/initialization expression. Storage for these variables does not have to be allocated by the programmer using *new*.

2.5 Scalar Types and Their Wrappers

Every scalar (primitive) type has an associated wrapper class or reference type. Table 2.1 lists the scalar types and their associated wrappers.

As we shall see in the next section, wrapper classes are essential when one wishes to store a collection of primitive values in many collection classes. In this

Table 2.1   Primitive Types and Their Associated Wrapper Classes

Primitive Type	Wrapper Class
int	Integer
long	Long
short	Short
float	Float
double	Double
boolean	Boolean
char	Character
byte	Byte
void	Void

case one needs to "wrap" the primitive type into a wrapper object and store the wrapper object in the collection class. When retrieving information from the collection class, one needs to "unwrap" the primitive from its wrapper.

Figure 2.4 is a UML diagram that shows the hierarchical relationship among wrapper classes.

2.6   Wrapping and Unwrapping – Conversion from Object to Scalar and Scalar to Object

Suppose one wishes to wrap an *int* to its wrapper *Integer*. The following line of code illustrates this process.

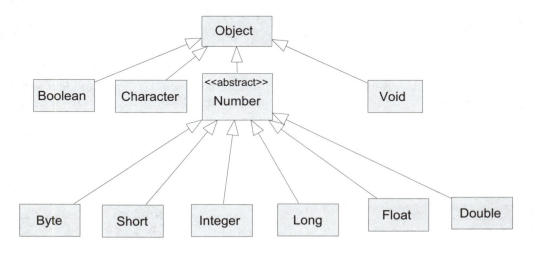

Figure 2.4. Hierarchy of wrapper classes.

```
int intValue = 25;
Integer integerValue = new Integer(intValue);
```

Suppose one wishes to retrieve the *int* value from its wrapper. This may be done as follows:

```
int intValue = integerValue.intValue();
```

The method *intValue()* is defined in class *Integer*.

The same process may be used to convert any of the numeric types, *char* or *boolean* to a wrapper and back again. For example,

```
double doubValue = 1.234;
Double doubleValue = new Double(doubValue);
double backAgain = doubleValue.doubleValue();
```

Often numeric information is input as a *String*. Class *String*, to be described in more detail in the next section, holds a sequence of *char* values. How can we convert a *String* to its scalar equivalent? We first illustrate this with a *String* representation of an *int*.

```
String str = "3456";
int intValue = Integer.valueOf(str).intValue();
```

The static method *valueOf*, in class *Integer*, converts the *String* to an *Integer* wrapper. The *intValue* function then converts the *Integer* to an *int*. An alternative method of doing the same thing is the following:

```
String str = "3456";
int intValue = (new Integer(str)).intValue();
```

This second approach is more general because it can be used in converting a *String* to any numeric type. For example, to convert the string "1.314" to a double one would do the following:

```
String str = "1.314";
double doubleValue = (new Double(str)).doubleValue();
```

In both cases, temporary wrapper objects (*Integer* in the first case and *Double* in the second case) are created as a means toward converting each to a scalar value.

2.7 Strings

One of the most widely used Java classes is class *String*. This reference type is used to represent sequences of characters.

A sequence of characters delimited by ordinary quotation marks forms a *String*. One can create a *String* in the usual way using the object creation operator *new* followed by a constructor. To create a string with the value "Hello" one could write the following code:

```
String str = new String("Hello" );
```

An alternative approach is possible with class *String*. This commonly used approach represents an exception to the requirement that the operator *new* must be used to create an object. One could write:

```
String str = "Hello";
```

Here the sequence of characters that defines the value of the *String* is used directly as if the variable *str* were a scalar type. In our view it is regrettable that this exception to object creation exists. Our experience suggests that inconsistencies should be avoided in a programming language if at all possible. Inconsistency leads to complexity that may lead to confusion and errors. The C++ language is a living example of an overly complex language that is riddled with inconsistencies.

Two basic features of class *String* are the methods *length* and *charAt*. The method *length* returns the number of characters in the string. The method *charAt* returns the character at a specified index (index 0 holding the first character of the string).

In any *String* method, an index position less than zero or greater than *length()* – *1* causes a *StringIndexOutOfBoundsException* to be thrown.

A *String* object is immutable. That is, once its value is set (through object creation), it cannot be changed. A *String* object may be thought of as "read only".

The "+" operator is used to create a new string by concatenation of existing strings. The string, str = "String 1" + "String 2", is a new string with the value "String1 String2". When a primitive type such as *int* or *boolean* is concatenated to a string using the "+" operator, the primitive type is automatically converted to a string prior to concatenation. So for example in the expression,

```
System.out.println ("The answer is " + myValue);
```

the variable *myValue*, assumed to be of type *double*, is automatically converted to a *String* object before the concatenation is performed.

String Methods

Table 2.2 lists several important *String* methods.

Table 2.2 Several Important *String* Methods		
Method	**Returns**	**Arguments**
toUpperCase()	Reference to a String object	None
toLowerCase()	Reference to a String object	None
length()	An integer	None
trim()	Reference to a String object	None
substring	Reference to a String object	Two integers

We illustrate the use of each of these in the following segment of code:

```
String str1 = "        ABcdEFghIJ";
System.out.println ("The length of str1 = " + str1.length());
System.out.println ("The uppercase value of str1 = " +
                  str1.toUpperCase());
System.out.println ("The lowercase value of str1 = " +
                  str1.toLowerCase());
System.out.println ("The trim value of str1 = " + str1.trim());
System.out.println ( "The last three characters of str1 = " +
                  str1.substring (str1.length() - 3,
                  str1.length()) );
```

The output of this program segment is:

```
The length of str1 = 15
The uppercase value of str1 =        ABCDEFGHIJ
The lowercase value of str1 =        abcdefghij
The trim value of str1 = ABcdEFghIJ
The last three characters of str1 = hIJ
```

The queries *toUpperCase()*, *toLowerCase()*, *trim()*, and *substring()* return a new string object. The original string object is unaffected by these operations.

String Comparisons

The method *compareTo* may be used to determine the lexicographic ordering of two strings. This ordering is based on Unicode character ordering.

Consider the expression

```
str1.compareTo(str2);
```

If the result returned is −1, *str1* is "smaller" than *str2* (would occur first if one were alphabetizing the two strings). If the result returned is 0, the two strings are equal (same length and contents). If the result returned is 1, *str1* is "larger" than *str2* (would occur second if one were alphabetizing the two strings).

One should always compare strings for equality using the *compareTo* method and not the double equals, "==" operator. The latter, as indicated earlier, compares only the object references that will be different when comparing two identical but independent strings.

2.8   Class *StringBuffer*

A *StringBuffer* object is not immutable, unlike a *String* object. A string buffer implements a mutable (changeable) sequence of characters.

In creating a *StringBuffer* object, one must specify its capacity (the maximum number of characters that can be held). If the capacity is exceeded, the capacity will be automatically increased. In the interest of efficiency, one should attempt to specify an initial capacity that is sufficient to hold all the characters that will be necessary.

A *StringBuffer* object can be converted to a *String* object by invoking the *toString()* method on the *StringBuffer* object. The principal operations for a *String-Buffer* object are *append* and *insert*. The following segment of code illustrates these and other basic operations in class *StringBuffer*.

```
StringBuffer strBuf = new StringBuffer(10);
strBuf.insert(0, 1234);
strBuf.append(567);
System.out.println(strBuf); // Output: 1234567
strBuf.setCharAt(3, '3');
System.out.println(strBuf); // Output: 1233567
strBuf.insert(2, "ABC");
System.out.println(strBuf); // Output: 12ABC33567
strBuf.replace(2, 5, "DEF");
System.out.println(strBuf); // Output: 12DEF33567
strBuf.reverse();
System.out.println(strBuf); // Output: 76533FED21
strBuf.insert(6, 7.777);
System.out.println(strBuf); // Output: 76533F7.777ED21
```

In applications in which a great deal of text manipulation is needed, a *String-Buffer* object can be created, the text manipulation can be performed on the *String-Buffer* object, and later, if desired, a *String* object can be produced that holds the result.

2.9   Arrays

Arrays have been a staple part of programming languages since Fortran. In many programming languages arrays are built-in types that are statically dimensioned and allow access to a collection of data through direct indexing. Static dimensioning means that once the size of an array is set it cannot be changed. Direct indexing means that data may be assigned or accessed at an index specified by an integer value within the range given by the size of the array.

In Java, an array is an object and is represented by a reference type. Like all reference types an array must be created before it can be used. Unlike other reference types a constructor is not explicitly invoked but the object creation operator *new* must be used in a different way. The *Array* type in Java is part of the language; you will find no class description of it in the Java library documentation. We illustrate array object declaration and creation with the following segment of code. It constructs an array that can hold five *String* objects, another array that can hold fifteen *int* objects and an array that can hold thirty-five *Line* objects.

```
String [] strArray = new String[5];
int [] intArray = new int[15];
Line [] lineArray = new Line[35];
```

The "[]" symbol following the base types is used to designate an array of the base type. An array can hold either primitive types or reference types.

The "[]" operators are used to assign or access information at a particular index within an array. For example, to assign the value 25 to index 3 of the *intArray*, one would write *intArray[3] = 25*. If we wish to assign the string "Richard" to the 0th index of the *strArray* we would write *strArray[0] = "Richard"*.

The index range of all arrays is from 0 to one less than the size of the array. Any attempt to write or access an index out of this range causes an *ArrayIndexOutOfBoundsBounds* exception to be thrown.

We can initialize the values of an array at its point of declaration as follows:

```
double [] myArray = {1.2, 1.3, 1.6, -12.8, 16.2};
```

The size of *myArray* will be 5 since we have provided five constants in the initialization expression. The index range for *myArray* is 0 to 4.

Suppose we wish to fill an array of type *int* with the consecutive integers from 1 to 1,000,000. The following code segment demonstrates one way to do this.

```
int myArray = new int [1000000];
for (int i = 0; i < 1000000; i++)
    myArray [i] = i;
```

If the *less than* operator ("<") in the *for* loop were changed to a *less than or equal to* operator ("<="), we would run past the boundaries of the array producing an *ArrayIndexOutOfBoundsBounds* exception.

One can determine the size of an array object, say *myArray*, by directly accessing its *length* field by using *myArray.length*. This is inconsistent with the *length()* function in class *String*. Another unfortunate inconsistency!

Suppose one wishes to copy the contents of one array to another, say *myArray* to *yourArray*. What is wrong with the following?

```
yourArray = myArray;
```

The assignment given above creates two names (references) to the same storage. If later, any elements of *myArray* are changed, *yourArray* will be affected as well. We have not copied information using the above assignment but instead have just created aliasing.

The correct method for copying the values from one array to another is to use the static method *arraycopy* given in class *System*. Function *arraycopy* works as follows:

```
arraycopy (sourceArray, sourcePosition, destinationArray,
           destinationPosition, numberOfEntriesToCopy);
```

Another way of copying *myArray* to *yourArray* is:

```
for (int index = 0; index < myArray.length; index++)
    yourArray[index] = myArray[index];
```

We consider a relatively simple application of arrays. Suppose that we wish to store the grades of students in a class and then determine the following statistics: highest grade, lowest grade, and average grade. Suppose further that the grades are held in an ASCII file, one grade per line. The name of this file is *grades.txt*.

Our task is to write a complete application that reads the input file, stores the information in an array, and computes the various statistics.

Design of Solution

1. Let us assume that we have loaded the raw data values into an array.
2. To compute the highest grade we assume that the first element in the array is the largest (this will probably not be true, but it is just our initial assumption).
3. We iterate through the grades and compare each of the grades found to the largest. If we find a grade (as we most probably shall) that is larger than the current largest grade, we replace the largest grade with the new grade and continue our iteration through the grades. When we have completed this iteration, we should have the largest grade.
4. To compute the smallest grade we assume that the first element in the array is the smallest (again this will probably not be true).
5. We again iterate through the grades and compare each grade found to the smallest. If we find a grade that is smaller than the current smallest, we replace the

current smallest with this new grade that is smaller. When we have completed this iteration we should have the smallest grade.

6. To compute the average grade we must compute the total of all the grades and then divide this total by the number of grades. We initialize a variable *sum* of type double to zero.

Listing 2.9 shows an implementation of the solution.

Listing 2.9 Class *Grades*

```
/** A class that manages the computation of several grading statistics.
*/
import java.io.*;
import java.util.*;

public class Grades {

  // Internal fields
  private int numberGrades;
  private double [] data;

  // Constructor
  public Grades(String fileName) throws IOException {
    data = new double [100];
    BufferedReader diskInput = new BufferedReader (
                        new InputStreamReader (
                        new FileInputStream (
                        new File (fileName))));
    // Load internal array data with grades
    String line;
    line = diskInput.readLine();
    while (line != null) {
      data [numberGrades] = (new Double (line)).doubleValue();
      numberGrades++;
      line = diskInput.readLine();
    }
  }

  // Methods
  public double maximumGrade () {
    double largest = data[0];
    for (int i = 1; i < numberGrades; i++) {
      double nextValue = data [i];
      if ( nextValue > largest)
          largest = nextValue;
    }
    return largest;
  }
```

```
public double minimumGrade () {
  double smallest = data [0];
  for (int i = 1; i < numberGrades; i++) {
    double nextValue = data [i];
    if ( nextValue < smallest)
      smallest = nextValue;
  }
  return smallest;
}

public double averageGrade () {
  double sum = 0.0;
  for (int i = 0; i < numberGrades; i++) {
    double nextValue = data [i];
    sum += nextValue;
  }
  return sum / numberGrades;
}
}
```

2.10 Vector

Class *Vector* is an important container class. It is available in the standard Java class *java.util.Vector*. It can hold any number of elements, is dynamic, and is indexable; that is, one can insert or access information at a specific index. A *Vector* is dynamic and automatically resizes itself if an insertion causes the number of elements to exceed the current capacity.

There are several constructors in class *Vector*. The constructor without parameters, *Vector()*, assigns a default capacity of 10. The constructor *Vector (int capacity)* allows the user to set the initial capacity.

The behavior of a *Vector* is completely defined by its methods. The more widely used methods of class *Vector* are presented in Listing 2.10.

Listing 2.10 A Description of Class *Vector*

```
/**
 * Most of the key methods of this standard Java class are presented.
 * No implementation details are shown.
 */
public class Vector {

  // Constructors
  public Vector () { /* Constructs an empty Vector*/ }

  public Vector (int initialCapacity) {
    /* Empty vector with specified initial capacity */
  }
```

```
public Vector (int initialCapacity,
               int capacityIncrement) {
  /* Constructs an empty vector with the specified initial
   * capacity and capacity increment.
   */
}

  // Methods
public void trimToSize () {
  /* Trims the capacity of this vector to be the vector's current
     size. An application can use this operation to minimize the
     storage of a vector.
   */
}

public void setSize (int newSize) {
  /* Sets the size of this vector. If the new size is greater
     than the current size, new null items are added
     to the end of the vector. If the new size is less
     than the current size, all components at index
     newSize and greater are discarded.
   */
}

public void setElementAt (Object obj, int index) {
  /* Sets the component at the specified index of this vector
     to be the specified object. The previous component
     at that position is discarded.
     The index must be a value greater than or equal to 0
     and less than the current size of the vector.
     Throws: ArrayIndexOutOfBoundsException if the index was
     invalid.
   */
}

public void insertElementAt (Object obj, int index) {
  /* Inserts the specified object as a component in this vector
     at the specified index. Each component in this vector
     with an index greater than or equal to the specified index
     is shifted upward to have an index one greater than
     the value it had previously. The index must be a value
     greater than or equal to 0 and less than or equal to the
     current size of the vector.
     Throws: ArrayIndexOutOfBoundsException if the index was
     invalid.
   */
}

public void addElement (Object obj) {
  /* Adds the specified object to the end of this vector,
```

```
        increasing its size by one. The capacity of this vector
        is increased if its size becomes greater than its capacity.
    */
}

public boolean removeElement (Object obj) {
    /* Removes the first occurrence of the argument from this
       vector. If the object is found in this vector, each
       component in the vector with an index greater than
       or equal to the object's index is shifted downward to have an
       index one smaller than the value it had previously. Returns
       true if the argument was a component of this vector,
       false otherwise.
    */
}

public void removeElementAt (int index) {
    /* Deletes the component at the specified index.
       Each component in this vector with an index
       greater than or equal to the specified index is shifted
       downward to have an index one smaller than the value it
       had previously. The index must be a value greater than or
       equal to 0 and less than the current size of the vector.
       Throws: ArrayIndexOutOfBoundsException if the index was
       invalid.
    */
}

public void removeAllElements () {
    /* Removes all components from this vector and sets its size to
       zero.
    */
}

public int capacity () {
    /* Returns the current capacity of this vector. */
}

public int size () {
    /* Returns the number of components in this vector. */
}

public boolean isEmpty () {
    /* Returns true if the vector has no components. */
}

public Enumeration elements() {
    /* Returns an enumeration of the components of this vector. */
}
```

```
  public boolean contains (Object elem) {
    /* Tests if the specified object is a component in this vector.
    */
  }

  public int indexOf (Object elem) {
    /* Searches for the first occurrence of the given argument
       testing for equality using the equals method.
       Returns -1 if the object is not found, otherwise the index of
       elem.
    */
  }

  public int indexOf (Object elem, int index) {
    /* Searches for the first occurrence of the given argument
       beginning the search at index and testing for equality
       using the equals method.
    */
  }

  public Object elementAt (int index) {
    /* Returns the component at the specified index.
       Throws: ArrayIndexOutOfBoundsException
       if an invalid index was given.
    */
  }

  public Object firstElement () {
    /* Returns the first component of this vector.
       Throws: NoSuchElementException if this vector has no
       components.
    */
  }

  public Object lastElement () {
    /* Returns the last component of the vector.
       Throws: NoSuchElementException
       if this vector is empty.
    */
  }

  public Object clone () {
    /* Returns a clone of this vector. */
  }

  public String toString () {
    /* Returns a string representation of this vector. */
  }
}
```

Comments Related to Listing 2.10

- There are three constructors in this class, each of course with the name *Vector*.

- Commands *trimToSize()* and *setSize()* may be used to explicitly control the size of a *Vector*. It is dangerous to use *setSize()* on a nonempty vector.

- Command *setElementAt* takes a parameter of type *int* and a parameter of type *Object*. This implies that any reference type (nonprimitive type) can be put into a *Vector* at the specified index. *Object* acts as a placeholder for any object type. This command replaces the element that currently occupies that index location. If the index specified is out of range, an exception is raised.

- Command *insertElementAt* also takes a parameter of type *Object* (*Object* again serves as a placeholder for any object type). The command does not replace the element currently at the specified index but pushes it upwards. If the index specified is out of range (larger than size −1), an exception is raised.

- Command *addElement* increases the size of the *Vector* by a factor of two or a user-specified *capacityIncrement*, if the number of elements exceeds the capacity.

2.11 Enumeration

The query *elements()* given in class *Vector* returns an object of type *Enumeration*. An *Enumeration* allows one to traverse through all of the elements of a *Vector*. The following code illustrates how one might do this. Assume that one has constructed a *Vector v*. We also assume that each element of the *Vector* can respond to the *toString()* method so it can be printed.

```
for (Enumeration e = v.elements(); e.hasMoreElements() ; ) {
        System.out.println(e.nextElement());
}
```

Listing 2.11 presents a simple example that exercises some of the protocol of class *Vector* and utilizes the enumeration given above.

Listing 2.11 Class *VectorTest*

```
/** A test program that exercises some of the behavior of class Vector.
*/
import java.util.*;
public class VectorApp {

  // Fields
  private Vector v = new Vector();

  // For internal use
  private void displayVector() {
    System.out.println();
```

```
        for (Enumeration enum = v.elements(); enum.hasMoreElements(); )
            System.out.println (enum.nextElement());
    }

    private void buildVector() {
        v.addElement ("John");
        v.addElement ("Mary");
        v.addElement ("Paul");
        v.addElement ("Cindy");
        System.out.println ("v.capacity() = " + v.capacity());
        v.setElementAt ("Richard" , 1);
        v.insertElementAt ("Mary" , 1);
        v.removeElementAt (0);
        System.out.println ("v.lastElement() = " + v.lastElement());
        System.out.println ("v.size() = " + v.size());
        v.trimToSize();
        System.out.println ("v.capacity() = " + v.capacity());
    }

    public static void main(String[] args) {
        VectorApp app= new VectorApp();
        app.buildVector();
        app.displayVector();
    }
}
```

The output of the program in Listing 2.11 is

```
v.capacity() = 10
v.lastElement() = Cindy
v.size() = 4
v.capacity() = 4

Mary
Richard
Paul
Cindy
```

Suppose we desire to construct a *Vector* of integer primitives (*int*). The formal type specified for a *Vector* is *Object*. This type serves as a placeholder for any reference type (any object type). This allows us to insert elements of type *String* earlier since *String* is a bona fide reference type (it is a class). But what about inserting elements of type *int* or *double* or any other primitive type?

To insert a primitive type into a *Vector* we must wrap the type using one of the standard wrapper classes (*Integer* for *int*, *Double* for *double*, *Float* for *float*, *Boolean* for *boolean*, *Character* for *char*). Listing 2.12 demonstrates how we can accomplish this.

Listing 2.12 Using Wrapper Classes for Primitive Types in a *Vector*

```
/** A test program to show how wrapper objects may be used with Vector.
*/
import java.util.*;

public class VectorWrapperApp {

  public static void main(String[] args) {
    Vector v = new Vector();
    v.addElement (new Integer (10));
    v.addElement (new Boolean (true));
    v.addElement (new Double (-1.95));
    v.addElement ("We are done");
    for (Enumeration enum = v.elements(); enum.hasMoreElements(); )
        System.out.println (enum.nextElement());

    // Suppose we wish to access the element in index 2 and output
    // five times its value
    double value = ((Double) v.elementAt (2)).doubleValue();
    System.out.println ("Five times the value at index 2 = " +
                        5.0 * value);
    System.out.println ("index of -1.95 is " +
                        v.indexOf (new Double (-1.95)));
  }
}
```

Output from Listing 2.12

```
10
true
-1.95
We are done
Five times the value at index 2 = -9.75
index of -1.95 is 2
```

Let us revisit the problem solved in Section 2.9. We wish to store the grades of students in a class and determine the following statistics: highest grade, lowest grade, and average grade. Suppose further that the grades are held in an ASCII file, one grade per line. The name of this file is *grades.txt*. We modify the solution given earlier.

Modified Design of Solution

1. Let us assume that we have loaded the raw data values into a *Vector* using wrapper objects of type *Double* (the raw data will be input as type *String* and converted to *Double*).

2. To compute the highest grade we assume that the first element in the *Vector* is the largest (this will probably not be true but it is just our initial assumption).

3. We iterate through the enumeration of grades and compare each of the grades found to the largest. If we find a grade (as we most probably shall) that is larger than the current largest grade, we replace the largest grade with the new grade and continue our iteration through the enumeration of grades. When we have completed this iteration, we should have the largest grade.

4. To compute the smallest grade we assume that the first element in the *Vector* is the smallest (again this will probably not be true).

5. We again iterate through the grades and compare each grade found to the smallest. If we find a grade that is smaller than the current smallest, we replace the current smallest with this new grade that is smaller. When we have completed this iteration we should have the smallest grade.

6. To compute the average grade we must compute the total of all the grades and then divide this total by the number of grades. We initialize a variable *total* of type double to zero.

7. We iterate through the scores and increment the variable sum. Upon the completion of the iteration we divide the sum by the number of scores and output the mean.

Listing 2.13 presents the solution using *Vector*.

Listing 2.13 Class *Grades*

```
/** A class that manages the computation of several grading statistics
 * using Vector.
 */

import java.io.*;
import java.util.*;

public class Grades {

  // Fields
  private int numberGrades;
  private Vector v;

  // Constructor
  public Grades(String fileName) throws IOException {
    v = new Vector();
    BufferedReader diskInput = new BufferedReader(
                               new InputStreamReader(
                               new FileInputStream(
                               new File (fileName)))) ;
    // Load internal vector v with grades
    String line;
    line = diskInput.readLine();
    while (line != null) {
```

```
      v.addElement (new Double(line));
      numberGrades++;
      line = diskInput.readLine();
    }
  }

  // Methods
  public double maximumGrade () {
    double largest = ((Double) v.firstElement()).doubleValue();
    for (Enumeration enum = v.elements(); enum.hasMoreElements();){
      double nextValue =
              ((Double) enum.nextElement()).doubleValue();
      if ( nextValue > largest)
          largest = nextValue;
    }
    return largest;
  }

  public double minimumGrade () {
    double smallest = ((Double) v.firstElement()).doubleValue();
    for (Enumeration enum = v.elements(); enum.hasMoreElements();){
      double nextValue =
              ((Double) enum.nextElement()).doubleValue();
      if ( nextValue < smallest)
          smallest = nextValue;
    }
    return smallest;
  }

  public double averageGrade () {
    double sum = 0.0;
    for (Enumeration enum = v.elements(); enum.hasMoreElements();){
      double nextValue =
              ((Double) enum.nextElement()).doubleValue();
      sum += nextValue;
    }
    return sum / numberGrades;
  }
}
```

2.12 Summary

❏ An object is associated with a reference type – a class. It is more specifically an instance of a class.

❏ Memory for an object and its contents (field values) is allocated dynamically using the object creation operator *new*.

❏ Before an object can be created it must be declared to be of a reference type.

❏ A class that implements the *Cloneable* interface may redefine the inherited *clone* method from *Object*. Its instances may then be sent the *clone* message.

❏ The predefined equality operator returns *true* if the object references are identical. This is true only if there exist two separate references to the same underlying storage as when aliasing occurs.

❏ Reference types include programmer-defined classes as well as the set of classes provided in the standard Java libraries.

❏ The primitive types are not associated with a class and do not need to be created. They may be initialized at their point of declaration.

❏ One of the most widely used Java classes is class *String*. This reference type is used to represent sequences of characters.

❏ A *StringBuffer* object is not immutable, unlike a *String* object. A string buffer implements a mutable sequence of characters.

❏ In Java, an array is an object and is represented by a reference type. Like all reference types an array must be created before it can be used.

❏ A *Vector* can hold any number of elements, is dynamic, and is indexable; that is, one can insert or access information at a specific index. A *Vector* is dynamic and automatically resizes itself if an insertion causes the number of elements to exceed the current capacity.

❏ An *Enumeration* allows one to traverse through all of the elements of a *Vector*.

2.13 Exercises

1   Write a complete Java application that inserts 100 random numbers, each a double from 0.0 to 100.0, in a *Vector*. Output the second largest value in the vector. Also output the next to smallest value in the vector. Lastly, output all values in the vector that contain numbers between 90 and 95.

2   Repeat Exercise 1 using an array.

3   Write a method *isOrdered* that returns a *boolean* and takes an array of *double* and *size* as inputs. If the values in the input array are ordered from smallest to largest, the function returns true; otherwise it returns false.

4   Write a Java class *TwoDimensionalArray* that has the following properties:

   a. Its constructor takes as its first parameter a two-dimensional array of type *double (data)*, as its second parameter the number of rows *(rows)*, and as its third parameter the number of columns *(cols)*. A two-dimensional array *(data)* should be held as a private field of the class *TwoDimensionalArray*. The number of rows *(rows)* and number of columns *(cols)* should also be held as private fields.

   b. It has a method *rowAverage* that takes as input an *int* that represents the row number (from 0 to *rows* −1) and returns the average value of the numbers in that particular row.

    c. It has a query function *colAverage* that takes as input an *int* that represents the column (from 0 to *cols* −1) and returns the average value of the numbers in that particular column.

    d. It has a query function *overallAverage* that returns the average of all the numbers in the two-dimensional array.

5 Write a test class (class *TwoDimensionalTest*) that:

    a. Loads a two-dimensional array of 20 rows and 6 columns with random double values, each from 0 to 100.0.

    b. Creates an instance of class *TwoDimensionalArray* and invokes the queries developed in Exercises 4b and c to output to the console the average value of the numbers in row 0 and row 17 and the average value in column 0 and column 4 of *TwoDimensionalArray*.

    c. Invokes the query *overallAverage()* to return the average value of all the numbers *n* the two-dimensional array sent in.

6 Given the string

```
String str = "123456789";
```

For the following questions write a single line of code.

    a. Produce a new string by inserting the string "ABC" between the 4 and 5 in the original string.

    b. Produce a new string that is formed by taking all the characters between index 2 and 6, not including position 6, in the string produced in part a.

3

Class Construction

Object-oriented software development is centered on the construction of classes. Classes represent a model of the application domain. Object-oriented software analysis and design are preoccupied with the discovery of classes and the relationships they have to each other. Through composition – in which one class holds one or more objects from other classes – and inheritance, the architecture of a software system is defined. This architecture is ultimately realized at the implementation phase by the construction and definition of classes.

This chapter closely examines the issues related to class construction using Java. Among the important issues to be discussed are:

1. What responsibilities should be vested within a class?
2. What responsibilities should be vested with the user of a class?
3. How can we bind the user's responsibilities with the class's responsibilities?
4. How can we organize the behavior of a class in a systematic manner?
5. What naming conventions and documentation style should be employed in class construction?
6. How can and should one control the visibility and access to various features of a class?

3.1 Responsibilities between a Class and Its Users – Design by Contract

Bertrand Meyer, perhaps more than any other writer, has clarified and influenced our thinking regarding the responsibilities between a class and its users. His ideas are contained in his seminal work *Object-Oriented Software Construction*, Second Edition (Prentice-Hall, 1997) and manifested in the Eiffel programming language and environment. His concept of **design by contract** has become a staple part of the thinking and practice in this field. Support for this concept has been embedded in many UML analysis and design tools. The Eiffel programming language is perhaps the only language that fully implements the ideas associated with this elegant and powerful set of ideas. We shall explore these ideas in this section and see how they may be applied when constructing Java classes.

It was Brad Cox, in his important book *Object-Oriented Programming: An Evolutionary Approach* (Addison-Wesley, 1986), who introduced the terminology of a software producer and consumer. The producer is responsible for constructing the features of a class, whereas the consumer, the user of a class, is responsible for its correct usage. Other names have been used to express the same idea. The terms "client" and "server" have been used to characterize the user of a class (client) and the class itself (server).

Design by contract involves a partnership between the producer and consumer of a class and between the features promised in the class and the responsibility of using these features correctly. If both parties adhere to this contract, the resulting software has the potential to be more understandable and reliable.

Let us first focus on the features and promises in a class. Following the suggestions of Meyer, we classify features into commands and queries. A **command** is a feature that may change the internal state of a class instance. It is typically implemented as a method that does not return information – a function that returns *void* in Java. A **query** is a feature that only returns information regarding the internal state of a class instance without changing this internal state. A query is typically implemented as a method that returns information: a function that has a nonvoid return type in Java.

The totality of a class's commands and queries completely defines its behavior. In terms of design by contract, it is the commands and queries that specify both the producer side and user side of the agreement. More precisely, each command and query must state the requirements that must be met in order to assure the correct outcome of the method. In addition, the command or query must state the conditions that will be guaranteed if the user requirements are met. In short, if the user complies precisely with the requirements of the command or query, it in turn will assure the user that a particular result shall be achieved.

The user requirements are given by a set of preconditions and the producer requirements are given by a set of postconditions. The preconditions are typically provided as one or more constraints on the input parameters to the command or query. The postconditions are usually provided in terms of the values of one or more fields.

In order for a precondition to have any validity it must be testable by the user. For example, if a precondition of popping a stack object is that the stack is not empty, the user must be able to test the stack object for emptiness before invoking a *pop* command. If this were not possible, the specification of a precondition would be quite useless since it is always the responsibility of the user to test each and every precondition before invoking a command or query. This last sentence raises an important organizational principle regarding coding practice.

Let us pursue the example of a stack structure since it provides an excellent example that illustrates these ideas. Although Chapter 11 is devoted entirely to classes *Stack* and *Queue*, at the risk of a small amount of repetition, we shall focus on details of a *Stack* here that pertain to class construction and design by contract in particular.

A *Stack* is a data abstraction that provides an orderly insertion and removal of objects from a container, the *Stack*. Objects in a stack follow first-in, last-out logic so that the first object to be inserted into the *Stack* is the last object that may be removed. The insert operation is specified by a command called *push* and the remove operation is specified by a command called *pop*. In addition to these two commands, a *Stack* also provides a query, *size*, that returns the number of objects currently stored and another query, *top*, that returns the next element that can be removed – the element that is said to reside on the top of the stack.

Let us consider the contract between the *Stack* supplier (producer) and *Stack* user in terms of each of the commands and queries.

Command *push (Object obj)*

There are no constraints on the type of object that can be inserted into a stack. If we assume that the stack has a huge capacity, then we should impose no constraints on the number of objects that can be inserted. So in fact there are no constraints of any kind that need to be met by the user. This is the type of contract that any user desires!

The producer, on the other hand, needs to satisfy an important constraint – namely, that the number of objects stored in the stack after the push operation is exactly one greater than the number of objects stored in the stack before the push operation. We represent this postcondition as follows:

size = old size + 1

Command *pop()*

This command removes the object that is currently on the top of the stack. One might therefore ask why is this a command since a command cannot return anything? The answer is that *pop* is designed only to change the internal state of the stack. If the value to be removed is desired, the *top* query should be invoked before invoking the *pop* command.

There is an important constraint on the user of *pop*, namely that stack is not empty. This is a constraint that can be tested by the user since class *Stack* provides a *size* query. The producer needs to satisfy an important constraint as well – namely, that the number of objects stored in the stack after the *pop* operation is exactly one less than the number of objects stored in the stack before the *pop* operation. We represent this postcondition as:

size = old size − 1

You might be wondering, OK, what if the user fails to meet his or her obligation in ensuring that the stack is not empty before invoking a *pop* command? The same question can be asked of failure to meet any precondition. The design-by-contract answer to this question is that an exception must be thrown by the *pop* method and sent to the user's method that invoked the *pop* command. If this user's method fails to handle the exception, the exception is propagated up the stack call chain and if no method in this call chain handles this exception, the program will be aborted with an error message indicating the source of the problem.

It must be emphasized that <u>it is not</u> the responsibility of the *pop* method to explicitly test for an empty stack before proceeding with the removal of the top element. Many *Stack* classes have been constructed in which a control structure such as:

```
if size() > 0 {
  // Code to remove top element
}
```

is written. This is in complete violation of the design-by-contract principle in which the user, not the producer, is responsible for ensuring that the stack is not empty.

One effect of placing the responsibility for such a test with the user (and this can be generalized to the construction of any class based on design by contract) is the significant simplification of the code within the class. This is most desirable since a well-designed class may serve as a reusable component available and used in a wide variety of applications. Keeping such a class streamlined adds to the overall efficiency of the software development and reuse process. In addition, by requiring the user to comply with one or more preconditions, this promotes a more engaged and intelligent user since the user must better understand the details and function of the class before using it.

Query *Object top()*

The query *top* returns the object that is at the top of the stack. As with command *pop*, there is an important constraint on the user of *top* – namely, that the stack is not empty. It does not make much sense to obtain an object that is not present. We could adopt the protocol that *top()* returns a *null* object if the stack is empty. A possible problem with this approach is that the query *top* may be embedded in a larger expression that attempts to take some action on the object that is returned. For example, suppose that the objects stored in the stack are *String* objects. Consider the following expression:

```
int stringSize = ((String) stackObject.top()).length();
```

Here *stackObject* is an instance of *Stack*. The downcast operator *(String)* is needed since the formal type returned by *top()* is *Object*. If *stackObject* has no elements and returns *null*, a *NullPointerException* shall be generated since *length()* expects a non-null *String* object.

For consistency and adherence to the design-by-contract principle, we shall require a precondition that *size* > 0 for query *top*. As with the other methods that have a precondition, if the user fails to meet the precondition, an exception shall be thrown. There is never a postcondition associated with any query since the internal state of the class instance is not changed by a query. In Java, pre- and postconditions are stated as comments associated with the relevant commands and queries. These are backed up by appropriate exceptions. The details of class *Stack* are presented in the next section.

3.2 Organization of a Class

The features that define a class include **fields** (information content of a class instance), **constructors** (methods for object creation and initialization), **commands, queries**, and **private methods** (methods that are called by the public commands and queries but are not accessible outside the class). Although the sequence of presenting these features is arbitrary, we shall usually follow the sequence given above.

Listing 3.1 presents an implementation of a *Stack*. The implementation closely follows the *LinkedStack* presented in Chapter 11. The data structure details related to this important software component are discussed in Chapter 11. Here we shall focus only on the class organization of *Stack* and not the data structure details.

Listing 3.1 Class *Stack*

```
/** A dynamic implementation of Stack
*/
public class Stack {
  // Fields
  private Node top = null;
  private int numberElements = 0;

  // Commands

  // Postcondition: size = old size + 1
  public void push (Object item) {
    Node newNode = new Node(item, top);
    top = newNode;
    numberElements++;
  }
  // Precondition: size > 0
  // Postcondition: size = old size - 1
  public void pop () {
    if (isEmpty())
        throw new NoSuchElementException("Stack is empty." );
    else {
      Node oldNode = top;
      top = top.next;
      numberElements--;
      oldNode = null;
    }
  }

  // Queries

  // Precondition: size > 0
```

```
public Object top () {
  if (isEmpty())
     throw new NoSuchElementException("Stack is empty." );
  else
    return top.item;
}
public boolean isEmpty () {
  return top == null;
}
public int size () {
  return numberElements;
}
private class Node {

  // Fields
  private Object item;
  private Node next;

  // Constructors
  private Node (Object element, Node link) {
    item = element;
    next = link;
  }
}
```

There are two fields specified in class *Stack*: *top* and *numberElements*. These are both designated as *private*. There are two commands, *push* and *pop*. The pre- and postconditions for each are shown. Finally, there is a private inner class *Node* that is available only inside class *Stack*.

There is no explicit constructor in class *Stack*. The default constructor is sufficient in this case. The explicit initializations shown in the two fields are not required. The default constructor would perform the same initialization.

3.3 Packages

Packages provide a mechanism for physically grouping logically related classes into a common subdirectory. Packages provide a mechanism for resolving name clashes if two or more classes have the same name. And finally, as we shall see in the next section, packages provide controlled accessibility to the features of a class.

The Java class library is organized into a set of packages. Table 3.1 presents the packages not including Common object request broker architecture (CORBA) related packages currently available in Platform 2 (Java 1.2). These may change over time.

Each of the packages in Table 3.1 contains collections of classes related to the task indicated by the package name.

Table 3.1 Packages in Java Version 1.2

java.applet	java.security.acl
java.awt	java.security.cert
java.awt.color	java.security.interfaces
java.awt.datatransfer	java.security.spec
java.awt.dnd	java.sql
java.awt.event	java.text
java.awt.font	java.util
java.awt.geom	java.util.jar
java.awt.im	java.util.zip
java.awt.image	javax.accessibility
java.awt.image.renderable	javax.swing
java.awt.print	javax.swing.border
java.beans	javax.swing.colorchooser
java.beans.beanscontext	javax.swing.event
java.io	javax.swing.filechooser
java.lang	javax.swing.plaf
java.lang.ref	javax.swing.plaf.basic
java.lang.reflect	javax.swing.plaf.metal
java.math	javax.swing.plaf.multi
java.net	javax.swing.table
java.rmi	javax.swing.text
java.rmi.activation	javax.swing.text.html
java.rmi.dgc	javax.swing.text.html.parser
java.rmi.registry	javax.swing.text.rtf
java.rmi.server	javax.swing.tree
java.security	javax.swing.undo

The package name indicates the subdirectory path that holds each collection of classes that define the package. For example, the package *javax.swing.text.html.parser* is located in a subdirectory *javax\swing\text\html\parser* (forward slashes if you are running under Unix). This subdirectory contains a set of classes that define this package.

Let us consider an example of utilizing a class in one of the Java packages, class *Random*. This class is quite important in generating pseudorandom numbers and it will be utilized often in Part Two of the book. How might we access this class and its features? Suppose that we wish to generate 1,000,000 random numbers, each uniformly distributed between 0 and 1, and compute the average value of the numbers generated.

We need to first construct an instance of class *Random* using its constructor. Then each number is obtained using the query method *nextDouble()*. Listing 3.2 presents a simple Java program that computes the average of 1,000,000 random numbers.

Listing 3.2 Class *RandomTest*

```
public class RandomTest {

  public static void main(String[] args) {
    Random rnd = new Random();
    double sum = 0.0;
    for (int index = 0; index < 1000000; index++)
      sum += rnd.nextDouble();
    System.out.println("Average value = " + sum / 1000000.0);
  }
}
```

There is a problem with the code in Listing 3.2: It will not compile. The error message that is generated states: "class Random not found in class RandomTest." Like most Java classes except for those in package *java.lang*, class *Random* must be accessed through its package name. Listing 3.3 shows a modified class *RandomTest* that illustrates qualified access to class *Random*. This class compiles and runs correctly.

Listing 3.3 Class *RandomTest* with Qualified Access

```
public class RandomTest {

  public static void main(String[] args) {
    java.util.Random rnd = new java.util.Random();
    double sum = 0.0;
    for (int index = 0; index < 1000000; index++)
      sum += rnd.nextDouble();
    System.out.println("Average value = " + sum / 1000000.0);
  }
}
```

The qualified name *java.util.Random*, used twice in class *RandomTest*, specifies precisely where the class is found. Suppose that *Random* also existed in package *java.fiction* (such a package does not exist). If we wished to utilize the fictional version of *Random* we could use the name *java.fiction.Random*.

You may now be wondering, "Is it worth having to use a qualified name for a class if only one such class exists in the Java packages?" Before answering, it must be pointed out that you might wish to create your own version of class *Random* and put it into your own package of classes. Then, even though only one version exists among the Java packages, two versions exist in your system.

Java provides a way around the problem of having to use qualified names for a class that exists in only one package. The *import* statement allows you to establish the location of a class once and then make unqualified access to it. Listing 3.4 presents a final version of class *RandomTest* that uses such an *import* statement to allow unqualified access to class *Random*.

Listing 3.4 Class *RandomTest* with Unqualified Access to Class *Random*

```java
import java.util.Random;

public class RandomTest {

  public static void main(String[] args) {
    Random rnd = new Random();
    double sum = 0.0;
    for (int index = 0; index < 1000000; index++)
      sum += rnd.nextDouble();
    System.out.println("Average value = " + sum / 1000000.0);
  }
}
```

The two occurrences of *Random* in Listing 3.4 use the unqualified name.

If we wish to have unqualified access to all of the classes in a package we may use the wildcard "*". An example is:

```java
import java.util.*;
```

When a class is defined as part of a package, the keyword *package* followed by the package name must appear as the first noncomment line in the class definition. We illustrate the mechanics of defining classes as part of a package and then accessing the classes with a simple tutorial example.

Consider the two classes, each named *Greeting*, given in Listings 3.5 and 3.6.

Listing 3.5 Class *Greeting* from Package One

```java
package one;

public class Greeting {

  public static void main(String[] args) {
    System.out.println ("Greetings from package one" );
  }
}
```

Listing 3.6 Class *Greeting* from Package Two

```java
package two;

public class Greeting {

  public static void main(String[] args) {
    System.out.println("Greeting from package two" );
  }
}
```

On the author's computer, the file *Greeting.java* from Listing 3.5 is located in subdirectory *e:\packages\one*. The file *Greeting.java* from Listing 3.6 is located in subdirectory *e:\packages\two*. The directory *e:\packages* is said to be the root directory of the two packages since the subdirectories *one* and *two* are directly under this root directory. The root directory in general is one level back from the package name.

How can we compile and run each of these packages? Compilation is done in the usual way from a command shell. From subdirectory *root\one*, where *root = e:\packages*, invoke *javac Greeting.java*. The byte code file *Greeting.class* is produced as expected. From the subdirectory *root\two*, invoke *javac Greeting.java* and the file *Greeting.class* shall be produced.

To execute the file *Greeting.class* from package one, go to the root directory (*e:\packages*). From a command shell invoke *java one.Greeting*. The program will run and output the appropriate greeting message.

To execute the file *Greeting.class* from package two, go to the root directory (*e:\packages*). From a command shell invoke *java two.Greeting*. The program will run and again output the appropriate greeting message.

In general, to execute the code in a class that is part of a package, go to the subdirectory that is one back from the package name. From a command shell invoke the virtual machine using *java packageName.className*.

As an alternative the user may establish an environment variable called *classpath* that includes the above root directory. It is then possible to execute *java one.Greeting* and *java two.Greeting* from any directory. Still another alternative is to include the classpath in the java command, for example, *java -classpath e:\packages\one.Greeting*.

If one has a set of classes residing in the same subdirectory, each with an unnamed package, a default package is associated with each of the classes and they are considered to be in this same default package. In this case the root directory is the same as the directory containing the classes with unnamed package. All of the rules to be described in the next section pertaining to access modifiers pertain to such a default package.

In Part Two of this book we shall construct a package *foundations* that contains all of our data structure classes. The classes in this package have been archived into a JAR (Java archive) file format and are available for your use. Instructions regarding the installation and use of this JAR file are provided in Appendix C.

For further details regarding the mechanics of package use, the reader is urged to consult a Java programming book, documentation, or reference.

3.4   Access Modifiers

Java provides three explicit access modifiers: *public*, *protected*, and *private*, as well as a default package (blank modifier) access. Each of these shall be described.

Class features (fields and methods) that are designated **public** are directly accessible inside as well as outside the class. Typically only the commands and queries that define the behavior of class instances are declared *public*. These methods form the basis for the messages that will be sent to instances of the class.

Fields and methods that are designated **protected** are accessible inside the class and everywhere within classes in the same package (default or explicit). These features are also accessible inside of all descendent classes. It is this latter feature that typically justifies the use of the *protected* modifier. In most cases it is illogical to deprive a subclass of its parent's features. Therefore it is recommended that fields and methods be designated as *protected* whenever you anticipate that subclasses of the given class shall be defined.

We believe it is unfortunate that the *protected* access modifier provides package access, especially since this is provided by the default package protection mechanism to be described below. We would much prefer that *protected* provide access only to descendent classes and not classes within the same package.

Features that are designated **private** are accessible only inside the class in which these features are defined. This is the most restrictive access modifier. We believe that in most cases *private* should be used only if one does not expect subclasses to be formed from the given class and one wishes to deny other classes in the same package access to the feature.

If no access modifier is specified for a field or method, the feature is said to have package visibility. This implies that the feature is accessible inside of the class and everywhere within classes in the same package (default or explicit). Subclasses (that are not in the same package) do not have access to features with package visibility.

3.5 Naming Conventions

Over the years a de facto standard regarding the naming of classes and their features has evolved. We hasten to say that there is not universal agreement regarding these conventions. There are examples of programming cultures that do not adhere to these conventions.

We strongly recommend the following:

- **Class names should always begin with an upper case character** and be followed by mixed lower and upper case when using a multiple-word identifier such as *LandBasedVehicle*.

- Field and method names should always begin with a lower case character and be followed by mixed lower and upper case when using a multiple-word identifier such as *myLandBasedVehicle*.

- **A command should be named as a verb or verb phrase**. Examples include *push*, *fireRocket*, *performComputation*. Using a verb phrase places the emphasis on the action to be performed.

- **A query should be named as a noun or noun phrase**. Examples include *top*, *speed*, *rocketWeight*. If a query returns a boolean value, a phrase starting with "is" might be considered. Examples include *isEmpty*, *isFull*, and *isCorrect*.

It is noted that a common naming style in Java is to start a query with "get." Examples would include *getSize* or *getRocketWeight*. For Java Beans it is a requirement. Here the focus is on the process of obtaining the information rather than the nature of the information being sought. If all queries start with "get," this action phrase conveys no new information. We prefer putting the focus on the information being sought by using a noun or noun phrase.

3.6 Summary

❏ Object-oriented software development is centered on the construction of classes.

❏ Classes represent a model of the application domain. Object-oriented software analysis and design are preoccupied with the discovery of classes and the relationships they have to each other.

❏ Through composition – in which one class holds one or more objects from other classes – and inheritance, the architecture of a software system is defined. This architecture is ultimately realized at the implementation phase by the construction and definition of classes.

❏ Design by contract involves a partnership between the producer and consumer of a class, and between the features promised in the class and the responsibility of using these features correctly. If both parties adhere to this contract, the resulting software has the potential to be more understandable and reliable.

❏ A command is a feature that may change the internal state of a class instance. It is typically implemented as a method that does not return information – a function that returns *void* in Java.

❏ A query is typically implemented as a method that returns information – a function that has a nonvoid return type in Java.

❏ The totality of a class's commands and queries completely defines its behavior. In terms of design by contract, it is the commands and queries that specify both the producer side and user side of the agreement.

❏ Each command and query must state the requirements that must be met in order to assure the correct outcome of the method. In addition, the command or query must state the conditions that will be guaranteed if the user requirements are met. In short, if the user complies precisely with the requirements of the command or query, it in turn will assure the user that a particular result shall be achieved.

❏ In order for a precondition to have any validity it must be testable by the user.

❏ The features that define a class include commands, queries, and private methods.

❏ Packages provide a mechanism for physically grouping logically related classes into a common subdirectory, a mechanism for resolving name clashes if two or more classes have the same name, and controlled accessibility to the features of a class.

❏ In general, to execute the code in a class that is part of a package, go to the subdirectory that is one back from the package name or use the *classpath* variable to point the virtual machine to your package directory. From a command shell invoke the virtual machine using *java packageName.className*.

3.7   Exercises

1   A *Counter* is a class defined by the following commands and queries:

Commands
reset – sets the Counter's value to zero.
increment – adds one to the current Counter's value.
decrement – subtracts one from the current Counter's value.

Queries
countValue – the current integer value held by the Counter.

   a. State all the preconditions and postconditions for each of the commands and queries if applicable.
   b. Implement class *Counter* in Java.

2   Describe three of the classes in package *java.util* by dividing their methods into constructor, commands, and queries. If possible, write preconditions and postconditions as comments.

3   Do the same as Exercise 2 for package *java.io*.

4   Create a class of your own choosing. State the purpose of the class. Partition the methods of the class into constructors, commands, and queries. For each command and query, state any applicable pre- or postconditions.

4

Relationships between Classes

We examine two important types of relationships between classes in this chapter – namely, **composition** and **inheritance**. We illustrate the concepts by constructing a complete software system in Java that illustrates the use of these two types of relationships.

4.1 Inheritance

Inheritance, as the name implies, involves the transmittal of behavioral characteristics from parent class to child class. Through inheritance one can establish behavior in a base class that is available and directly usable in a hierarchy of descendent classes that extend the base class.

As discussed in Chapter 1, inheritance can be centered on factoring and reusing methods (implementation inheritance) or on extending behavior (behavioral inheritance). It is the latter that we shall utilize in this chapter and throughout this book.

With behavioral inheritance, it is essential that any child class logically be of the same type as its parent. As you recall from Chapter 1, the principle of polymorphic substitution allows a descendent class to be used in place of its ancestor. This would make sense only if each child class can logically be considered to be a kind of its parent.

A child class may extend a parent class by introducing one or more fields or methods not found in the parent or by redefining one or more parent class methods. Although some object-oriented languages provide facilities for a child class to block some of its parent's fields or methods, this violates the logical basis of polymorphic substitution since the child class could no longer be considered to be of the same type as its parent. We shall avoid such usage and encourage you to do the same.

It should be clear from the above description that as one moves down a class hierarchy, behavior becomes more and more refined and fine grained. Classes at the bottom of the hierarchy typically contain more fields and methods than classes near the top of the hierarchy.

It must be emphasized that one does not justify inheritance by simply counting the number of fields or the number of methods and comparing child class to parent class. A classic example of such an error in reasoning would be to argue that class *Rectangle* is a subclass of *Square* because *Rectangle* has two fields, *length* and *width*, whereas *Square* has only one field, *width*. This does not make sense because a *Rectangle* is not a kind of *Square*. It would not make sense to have a *Rectangle* object stand in for a *Square* object under polymorphic substitution. It would also be difficult to explain to a fifteen-year-old that a rectangle is actually a kind of square. It would be easier to justify that the parent of a fifteen-year-old is kind of square!

The challenge in using inheritance properly is to use it wisely. Because a programming language allows you to make any class a subclass of any other class does not justify undisciplined use of this facility. Through inheritance a strong dependency is established between parent class and child class. Strong dependencies need to be carefully justified.

The notation for depicting an inheritance was shown in Figure 1.1. A broad-headed arrow connects the child class (tail) to the parent class (head).

4.2 Composition

A common association between classes is provided by the **composition** relationship. The composition relationship is a whole-part relationship. One class representing the whole defines fields that represent the parts. At the object level this relationship implies the following: A whole object is composed of one or more constituent part objects. If these constituent objects are an essential part of the whole, have a lifetime roughly equivalent to the whole, and are not shared with other objects, we call the association **strong aggregation**. If the constituent objects are essential to the whole but have a lifetime independent of the whole, the association is a **weak** or **reference aggregation**.

Figure 4.1 shows strong and weak aggregation relationships among several classes as well as inheritance relationships. In the UML diagram of Figure 4.1, class *Car* is a subclass of *MotorVehicle*. It acquires the general properties defined in the abstract classes *MotorVehicle*, *LandBased*, and *Vehicle*, as well as introducing specialized properties of its own.

Car is shown as having a strong aggregation relationship to a single instance of class *Engine*. The implication is that an engine is an essential part of a car, is not shared by other cars, and has a lifetime roughly equivalent to that of the car. A solid diamond shows strong aggregation.

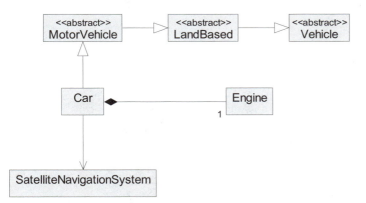

Figure 4.1. Relationships between *Car* and other classes.

Car is also shown as having a weak aggregation or reference relationship with class *SatelliteNavigationSystem*. The implication is that an instance of *Satellite-NavigationSystem* has a lifetime of its own and may be shared by many cars (i.e., many cars may communicate independently using the satellite navigation object).

Association through composition is a natural relationship among classes because there are countless examples of composite objects in the world around us. Inheritance, by its very nature, creates a somewhat artificial model of the real world. For example, although it makes perfect sense for a car to be considered a kind of *MotorVehicle* there is no real object of type *MotorVehicle*. The latter is an intellectual abstraction, albeit a most useful one. Similar statements may be made for the other ancestor classes of *Car*.

Let us examine the skeletal code of class *Car* to see how the two types of relationships shown in Figure 4.1 are represented in Java code. Listing 4.1 shows the skeletal code of class *Car*.

Listing 4.1   Skeletal Code for Class *Car*

```
class Car extends LandBasedVehicle {

  // Fields
  private Engine engine;
  private SatelliteNavigationSystem navigation;

  // Constructors
  public Car (SatelliteNavigationSystem navigate) {
    engine = new Engine();
    navigation = navigate;
    // Other code not shown
  }

  // Other code not shown
}
```

The responsibility for creating an instance of *SatelliteNavigationSystem* lies outside of class *Car*. An instance of this class is passed to the constructor so that an internal reference to such an object is held as a field in class *Car*. This is weak aggregation.

The responsibility for creating an instance of class *Engine* lies totally within class *Car*. This is strong aggregation. This is shown in the constructor.

4.3   Class Relationships in Action – A Case Study

To bring some of these ideas alive, we model and implement a simple simulation game.

4.3.1   Specifications

We wish to simulate a race among four players. The players move in sequence starting with player 1 and ending with player 4. On each "move" a player goes forward or backwards depending on his or her score for the move. A positive score for a move implies a forward move, whereas a negative score implies a backward move. As players move in sequence, the first player to move forward 500 or more units wins and the game is over.

The score a player receives on each move is determined by:

1. The outcome of the throw of a fair die.
2. The relative position of the player that is moving with respect to the other players.
3. The response logic associated with the given player. There are three distinct types of response logic that are possible. Each player is associated with one of the three possible types of response logic. More than one player may have the same type of response logic. At random times, the same or one of the other two types of response logic replaces a player's response logic.

It is the response logic associated with a player that determines how the die outcome and relative position of the other players affects the given player's score and move. The details related to the three types of response logic are given below.

Response Type 1

If a player's move is based on response type 1, its change in position is computed as:

die throw + (position of leading player − player's position) / 2

If the die throw is 3, 4, 5, or 6 the change in position is positive; otherwise it is negative.

Response Type 2

If a player's move is based on response type 2, its change in position is computed as:

3 times the die throw if the dice throw is an even number; otherwise the die throw if the die throw is an odd number

The change in position is always positive.

Response Type 3

If a player's move is based on response type 3, its change in position is computed as:

die throw + (player's position − position of trailing player) / 2

If the die throw is 1 or 2, the change in position is positive; otherwise the change in position is negative.

A player is associated with a particular response type for a random number of moves uniformly distributed between 2 and 5 moves. When the lifetime of a response associated with a given player has expired, a new response type among the three is chosen with an equal likelihood of each. At the same time, a new response life is chosen (between 2 and 5 moves).

As the race between players progresses and after each player's move, a line of output should be sent to the console that specifies the player number and its current position. When the game is over, a final line of output should be written to the console that indicates the winner of the game.

4.3.2 Analysis and Design

From the specifications we identify six classes. These are listed below with a brief description of the responsibilities of each class.

Domain Classes

Game – Owns and controls the four players and random number generator and is responsible for managing their overall play.

Player – Holds a particular response type for a limited lifetime. Each player is responsible for knowledge of its own position.

Response – An abstract class that computes the change in position for a player based on the positions of the other players and the dice throw.

Response Type 1, 2, 3. Concrete response classes that compute the change in position for a player based on rules given in Section 4.3.1.

We discuss more details for each of the classes before attempting to establish the relationships they have to each other.

Class *Game*

Class *Game* owns and is responsible for creating all the *Player* objects. Since the *Game* also requires a random number object, it is responsible for creating this object. Therefore, class *Game* has a strong aggregation relationship with one or more players and a *Random* number object (i.e., strong aggregation with respect to classes *Player* and *Random*).

Game is responsible for assigning a new *Response* object to a player whenever its response life is zero. This action, as well as the control of the game, is established in a *play* method that controls the flow of the game.

Class *Player*

A player must know its response life, its position, and its player number. These become scalar attributes of the class.

A player is always associated with a *Response* object passed to it by the *Game*. Since it does not own the *Response* object, class *Player* has a reference relationship with respect to class *Response*.

A player is responsible for updating its response life whenever it is assigned a new *Response* object. To do this requires the use of a random number. Therefore class *Player* has a reference relationship with class *Random*. An instance of *Random* is passed to *Player* in its constructor and held as a field. This ensures that only one random number object is created and used throughout the application.

One of the important methods of *Player* is *makeMove*. This method determines the new position of the *Player*.

Abstract Class *Response*

Abstract class *Response* holds a reference to an array of *Player* objects. This array is passed to a *Response* object when it is created. A *Response* object must also hold the number of the player associated with it as well as the number of players in the array.

The abstract method *changeInPosition* must be implemented by each of the three concrete *Response* subclasses according to the rules given in the game specification.

Based on the descriptions given above, the UML diagram in Figure 4.2 depicts the relationship among the six classes that define the architecture of this application.

Explanation of Figure 4.2

The associations with a dark diamond attached to *Game* and an arrow attached to *Random* and *Player* indicate strong aggregation relationships with classes *Player* and *Random*. The arrows indicate that *Game* has access to *Random* and *Player* but *Random* and *Player* do not have access to *Game*. A *Game* object (the whole) is responsible for creating *Player* objects and a *Random* object, the parts.

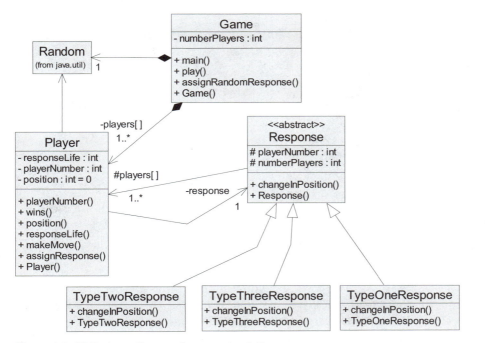

Figure 4.2. UML class diagram for race simulation game.

Class *Player* is shown as having a reference relationship with *Response* and *Random*, each with multiplicity 1. Class *Response* is shown as having a reference relationship with class *Player* of multiplicity 1 or more. This implies that each concrete *Response* object has knowledge of the *Player* objects. This information is provided at initialization time through a constructor.

The three concrete *Response* type classes are shown as subclasses of *Response*. Each has its own *changeInPosition* method. The fields and methods of each class are also shown in Figure 4.2.

4.3.3 Implementation

Abstract class *Response* is presented in Listing 4.2.

Listing 4.2 Abstract Class *Response*

```
/**
  * Abstract class that models change in position
*/
public abstract class Response {

  // Fields
  protected Player [] players;   // The players in the game
  protected int numberPlayers;   // Number of players in the game
  protected int playerNumber;    // Player associated with Response

  // Constructor
  public Response (Player [] players, int numberPlayers,
                   int playerNumber) {
    this.players = players;
    this.numberPlayers = numberPlayers;
    this.playerNumber = playerNumber;
  }

  // Queries
  /**
    * Returns the player's change in position based on move
  */
  public abstract int changeInPosition(int dieThrow);
}
```

Instances of class *Response* are not allowed since it is an abstract class. The abstract method *changeInPosition* is defined in each of the concrete subclasses. All concrete subclasses of *Response* inherit knowledge of the array of players, the number of players, and the particular player number associated with the *Response* object through the fields defined in class *Response*. Listings 4.3, 4.4, and 4.5 present the three concrete subclasses of *Response*.

Listing 4.3 Class *TypeOneResponse*

```
public class TypeOneResponse extends Response {

  // Constructor
  public TypeOneResponse (Player [] players, int numberPlayers,
                          int playerNumber) {
    super (players, numberPlayers, playerNumber);
  }

  // Queries
  public int changeInPosition(int dieThrow) {
    // Compute highest position
    int highest = players[1].position();
    for (int i = 2; i <= numberPlayers; i++)
      if (players[i].position() > highest)
        highest = players[i].position();
    int change = dieThrow + (highest -
                 players[playerNumber].position()) / 2;
    return (dieThrow > 2) ? change : -change;
  }
}
```

In the query *changeInPosition* of class *TypeOneResponse*, the highest position is assumed to be associated with player 1. The loop that follows replaces the highest position with the position of any of the other players if their position is greater than the current highest position. Natural indexing is used in the array of players; therefore the upper limit on the loop is *numberPlayers*, an attribute of abstract class *Response* that is inherited.

The last line of code in query *changeInPosition* returns a positive change in position if the die throw is greater than 2; otherwise it returns a negative change in position as given by the problem specifications.

Listing 4.4 Class *TypeTwoResponse*

```
public class TypeTwoResponse extends Response {

  // Constructor
  public TypeTwoResponse (Player [] players, int numberPlayers,
                          int playerNumber) {
    super (players, numberPlayers, playerNumber);
  }

  // Queries
  public int changeInPosition(int dieThrow) {
    return (dieThrow % 2 == 0) ? 3 * dieThrow : dieThrow;
  }
}
```

The change in position returned by *changeInPosition* in class *TypeTwoResponse* is dependent only on the die throw and is not dependent on the position of the other players.

Listing 4.5   Class *TypeThreeResponse*

```
public class TypeThreeResponse extends Response {

  // Constructor
  public TypeThreeResponse (Player [] players, int numberPlayers,
                            int playerNumber) {
    super (players, numberPlayers, playerNumber);
  }

  // Queries
  public int changeInPosition(int dieThrow) {
    // Compute lowest position
    int lowest = players[1].position();
    for (int i = 2; i <= numberPlayers; i++)
      if (players[i].position() < lowest)
        lowest = players[i].position();
    int change = dieThrow +
                 (players[playerNumber].position() - lowest) / 2;
    return (dieThrow > 2) ? -change : change;
  }
}
```

The logic of method *changeInPosition* in class *TypeThreeResponse* is similar to class *TypeOneResponse*. Here the lowest position is computed. A negative change in position is returned if the die throw exceeds 2; otherwise a positive change in position is returned as required in the specifications.

Listings 4.3, 4.4, and 4.5 demonstrate that each of the concrete *Response* classes provides a specific definition of the query *changeInPosition*. Listing 4.6 presents the details of class *Player*.

Listing 4.6   Class *Player*

```
/**
 * Models each player
 */

public class Player {

  // Fields
  private int position = 0;
```

```java
  private int playerNumber;
  private Response response;
  private int responseLife;
  private java.util.Random rnd;

  // Constructor
  public Player (int number, java.util.Random rnd) {
    this.rnd = rnd;
    playerNumber = number;
  }

  // Commands
  public void assignResponse (Response response) {
    this.response = response;
    responseLife = 2 + rnd.nextInt(4);
  }

  public void makeMove (int dice) {
    responseLife--;
    position += response.changeInPosition(dice);
  }

  // Queries
  public int responseLife () {
    return responseLife;
  }

  public int position () {
    return position;
  }

  public boolean wins() {
    return position >= 500;
  }

  public int playerNumber() {
    return playerNumber;
  }
}
```

The *makeMove* command decrements the attribute *responseLife* and then assigns a change in position based on the query *changeInPosition* sent to the *Response* object associated with the *Player*. This is a form of delegation in which the responsibility for computing a new position is transferred from a *Player* object to the *Response* object associated with the *Player*.

Finally, Listing 4.7 presents the details of class *Game*.

Listing 4.7 Class *Game*

```java
/**
 * Game class that holds the players and initiates action
 */

public class Game {

  // Fields
  private Player [] players = new Player[5]; // Use natural
  indexing private java.util.Random rnd = new java.util.Random();
  private int numberPlayers;

  // Constructor
  public Game (int numberPlayers) {
    this.numberPlayers = numberPlayers;
    // Warm up random number generator
    for (int i = 0; i < 50000; i++)
      rnd.nextDouble();
    // Create four Player objects
    players[1] = new Player(1, rnd);
    players[2] = new Player(2, rnd);
    players[3] = new Player(3, rnd);
    players[4] = new Player(4, rnd);

    // Assign random Response type to each player
    for (int playerNumber = 1; playerNumber <= numberPlayers;
                        playerNumber++)
      assignRandomResponse(players[playerNumber]);
  }

  // Command
  public void assignRandomResponse (Player player) {
    // Assign a random Response object to specified player
    switch (1 + rnd.nextInt(3)) {
      case 1: // Player gets TypeOneResponse
        player.assignResponse(new TypeOneResponse(players,
                        numberPlayers, player.playerNumber()));
        break;
      case 2: // Player gets TypeTwoResponse
        player.assignResponse(new TypeTwoResponse(players,
                        numberPlayers, player.playerNumber()));
        break;
      case 3: // Player gets TypeThreeResponse
        player.assignResponse(new TypeThreeResponse(players,
                        numberPlayers, player.playerNumber()));
        break;
    }
  }
```

```
public void play () {
  int playerNumber = 0;
  do {
    playerNumber++;
    if (playerNumber > numberPlayers)
      playerNumber = 1;

    if (players[playerNumber].responseLife() == 0)
      assignRandomResponse(players[playerNumber]);

    players[playerNumber].makeMove(1 + rnd.nextInt(6));
    System.out.println("Player " + playerNumber +
      " position: " + players[playerNumber].position());
  } while (!players[playerNumber].wins());
  System.out.println("\n\nPlayer " + playerNumber +
                     " wins the game." );
}

public static void main(String[] args) {
  Game game = new Game(4);
  game.play();
}
}
```

Function *main* creates a new *Game* object passing the number of players as a parameter. The constructor in class *Game* warms up a random number generator, creates the four players, and assigns a random response object to each player. Recall that class *Player* has a reference relationship to class *Random*. The *play* command is sent to the *Game* object. A *do-while* loop controls the game and terminates when one of the players returns the value *true* to the query *wins*. Within the loop, *playerNumber* is incremented and is reset to 1 when its value exceeds the number of players. If the response life of a player is 0, it is assigned a new *Response*. The die value is computed and passed as a parameter to the *makeMove* command. The *play* command manages the overall control of the game. A *do-while* loop in this method controls the process. The loop continues until a player returns true to the query *wins()*.

4.4 Summary

❑ Inheritance, as the name implies, involves the transmittal of behavioral characteristics from parent class to child class. Through inheritance one can establish behavior in a base class that is available and directly usable in a hierarchy of descendent classes that extend the base class.

❑ A child class may extend a parent class by introducing one or more fields or methods not found in the parent or by redefining one or more parent class methods.

❑ Through inheritance a strong dependency and association is established between parent class and child class. Strong dependencies need to be carefully justified.

❑ The composition relationship is a whole/part relationship. One class representing the whole defines fields that represent the parts.

❑ A strong aggregation relationship implies that the class representing the whole owns and is responsible for creating each of its aggregate parts. The aggregate parts cannot be shared among other objects.

❑ A weak aggregation or reference relationship implies that the class representing the whole shares its aggregate parts possibly with other objects. These aggregate part objects have a life and identity of their own.

❑ A UML class diagram shows the relationships among the classes that define a system. The fields as well as methods of each class are depicted for each class.

❑ Inheritance is shown on a UML diagram with a broad-headed arrow going from the subclass to its parent.

❑ Strong aggregation is shown on a UML diagram with a diamond attached to the whole and a line connecting to the part class.

❑ A reference relationship is shown on a UML diagram with a line connecting the whole to the part class.

4.5 Exercises

1   Using a UML diagram show the use of inheritance in a problem domain that you should describe briefly. Justify each of the relationships between classes.

2   Using a UML diagram show the use of composition in a problem domain that you should describe briefly. Justify each of the associations between classes.

3   Using a UML diagram show the combined use of inheritance and composition in a problem domain that you should describe briefly. Justify each of the relationships between classes.

4   Modify the *Game* simulation presented in this chapter as follows:

    a. Add two more players. Players continue to move in sequence.

    b. Add one more concrete *Response* class. You are free to invent whatever rule you wish for this new *Response* class. Precisely state the rules for this new class.

    c. Modify the UML diagram so that it shows the changes you have made.

    d. Completely implement the new game.

5

GUIs: Basic Concepts

Most modern software presents a GUI (graphical user interface) for interaction with the user. The GUI typically appears as a window with a variety of widgets (visual components enabling user interaction) in it. These widgets provide information to the user and provide a mechanism for accepting user actions to direct the application. Prior to the Windows revolution, most software was executed from a console using text commands with output in textual format as well. It is our goal to provide the reader with essential knowledge for understanding, designing, and implementing simple GUI applications. In this chapter we present the basic concepts that underlie GUI programming. An overview is given of Java classes that support GUI applications, including those classes that are part of the AWT (abstract windowing toolkit) and the JFC (Java foundation classes). Also in this chapter we present conceptually the design pattern called MVC (model view controller). Implementation in Java of GUI applications and MVC is covered in Chapter 6.

In discussing the operation of a GUI application we may choose one of two points of view: (1) that of the user, or (2) that of the application. As a user we clearly focus on the first point of view; whereas, the developer of a GUI application must focus on both points of view. In that spirit we develop a description of the roles, expectations, and responsibilities of the two major players: user and application.

A GUI application is designed so that most of the actions it performs are directed by the user. It is the role and responsibility of the application to present to the user clear options on possible actions and results of those actions. It is the expectation of the user that all actions are implemented correctly by the application. Verification of the results of an action may also be an expectation.

It is the responsibility of the user to understand what an application can and cannot do and to use the application appropriately. However, many applications are designed to be tolerant of misuse. Through exceptions an application has a number of options on how to respond to misuse. Exception and error handling is covered in more detail in Chapter 7.

5.1 The Graphical Part of a GUI Application

In this section we define the major players that make a graphical user interface graphical. These major players are objects and are well represented by a wide

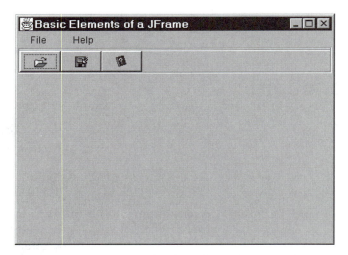

Figure 5.1. An empty top-level window – instance of *javax. swing.JFrame*.

variety of classes in the Java platform.[1] We may identify these graphical objects as: (1) top-level window that contains all graphical elements of the application, (2) widgets (or components) that accept input from the user and/or display information to the user, and (3) a graphics context that is responsible for all drawing within the application window. Each of these graphical objects is described in more detail below with an overview of supporting Java classes.

The Top Window of an Application

Every GUI application needs an identifiable visual boundary. The top-level window provides that boundary. This window contains all the components that are part of the interface with the user. Associated with the top window is a layout manager (may be *null*) that provides methods for positioning and sizing components within the window. If the layout manager is *null*, then the GUI builder may take direct control of the sizing and positioning of components within the top-level window; in many cases this is the best choice.

Top-level windows in Java are instances of *java.awt.Frame* or *javax.swing. JFrame*. These windows have a border, a title bar, and optional components such as a menu bar and toolbars. An example top-level window (instance of *javax.swing. JFrame*) is shown in Figure 5.1. It is a window with a border, a title "Basic Elements of a JFrame," a menu bar with *File* and *Help* menus, and a toolbar with three buttons. Components (widgets) may be added to the blank area of the window below the toolbar.

Class *java.awt.Container* represents generic windows that can contain other AWT, JFC, or custom components (widgets). It has methods that are applicable to all its subclasses. Selected details for top-level window and container classes are shown in Figure 5.2.

---

[1] For a more detailed discussion of the Java AWT, the reader is referred to any of the numerous books on the Java language.

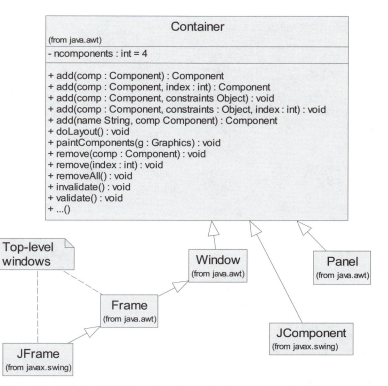

Figure 5.2. Selected details of top-level windows and containers.

Both top-level windows *Frame* and *JFrame* are subclasses of *Container*. A *Panel* is a simple container that may be used inside another container to organize components. *Container* is a direct subclass of *Component* (not shown in the figure). In Part Two we will define a different kind of container (one that contains objects) as an interface.

The Components – Communication between the Application and the User

Most widgets in Java are subclasses of *java.awt.Component*, including all AWT components (except for menus) plus all JFC components. All components have a *parent* field that is a *Container*. The parent may be the top-level window or any other *Container* subclass instance. The JFC components (unlike most AWT components) are instances of *Container* subclasses and may contain other components. Typical components include buttons, text fields, labels, checkboxes, radio buttons, and others. Components respond to messages that set their size and position within their *parent* container. Other selected details for class *Component* (a subclass of *Object*) are shown in Figure 5.3.

The Graphics Context

Drawing is an important function for all user-interface components. For consistency, a separate helper object in Java, which is an instance of class *java.awt. Graphics*, handles all drawing. In an object-oriented design we often delegate responsibility for complex tasks to a new object, called a helper object. Each *Component* has a graphics helper object that may be accessed by using the query

Component
(from java.awt)
- parent : Container
+ getBounds() : Rectangle + getFont() : Font + getFontMetrics() : FontMetrics + getGraphics() : Graphics + getLocation() : Point + getSize() : Dimension + setBounds(r : Rectangle) : void + setBounds(x : int, y : int, width : int, height : int) : void + setFont(f : Font) : void + setLocation(x : int, y : int) : void + setSize(x : int, y : int) : void + setVisible(boolean) : void + paint(g : Graphics) : void + print(g : Graphics) : void + repaint() : void + update(g : Graphics) : void + ...()

Figure 5.3. Selected details of abstract class *Component*.

getGraphics(). Commands may then be sent to this graphics object to draw text, lines, and shapes on the component. Figure 5.4 shows some of the drawing commands supported by the Java *Graphics* class. Examples showing the use of class *Graphics* are given in later chapters.

Graphics
(from java.awt)
+ copyArea(x : int, y : int, width : int, height : int, dx : int, dy : int) : void + drawArc(x : int, y : int, width : int, height : int, startAngle : int, arcAngle : int) : void + drawLine(x1 : int, y1 : int, x2 : int, y2 : int) : void + drawRect(x : int, y : int, width : int, height : int) : void + drawOval(x : int, y : int, width : int, height : int) : void + drawPolygon(xPoints : int[], yPoints : int[], nPoints : int) : void + drawPolyline(xPoints : int[], yPoints : int[], nPoints : int) : void + drawRoundRect(x : int, y : int, width : int, height : int, arcWidth : int, arcHeight : int) : void + drawString(str : String, x : int, y : int) : void + drawImage(img : Image, x : int, y : int, observer : ImageObserver) : + fillArc(x : int, y : int, width : int, height : int, startAngle : int, arcAngle : int) : void + fillRect(x : int, y : int, width : int, height : int) : void + fillOval(x : int, y : int, width : int, height : int) : void + fillPolygon(xPoints : int[], yPoints : int[], nPoints : int) : void + fillRoundRect(x : int, y : int, width : int, height : int, arcWidth : int, arcHeight : int) : void + fillPolygon(p : Polygon) : void + setFont(font : Font) : void + setColor(c : Color) : void + ... ( )

Figure 5.4. Selected details of class *java.awt.Graphics*.

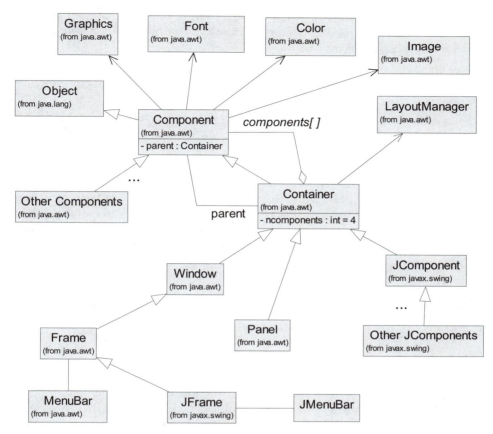

Figure 5.5. Associations among the primary GUI classes in Java.

Associations among the Primary GUI Classes

There are a number of important associations among the classes that are part of the Java model for GUIs. These associations are shown in Figure 5.5.

There are three connections between *Component* and *Container*. *Container* extends *Component* (a container is a component). *Container* has a field called *components[ ]* that is an array of *Component* objects. Finally, *Component* has a field called *parent* that is an instance of *Container*. All components have a *parent* container, except the top-level windows (instances of *Frame* or *JFrame*) which have a *null* value for *parent*. All components have a *Graphics* helper object for drawing and have the ability to be sized and positioned within their parent container.

These circular relationships between *Component* and *Container* can be confusing; however, they are an elegant example of the richness provided by a good object-oriented design. Many of the *Container* subclasses represent objects that can be components in another container. For example, a *Frame* object (*aFrame*) may contain a *Panel* object (*aPanel*) that contains a *Button* object (*aButton*) and a *TextField* object (*aTextField*). From this simple example we get the following hierarchical structure.

- Object *aFrame* contains *aPanel* and is the *parent* of *aPanel*. The *components[ ]* array of object *aFrame* contains object *aPanel*. Object *aFrame* has a *null* value for *parent* (i.e., no *parent*).

- Object *aPanel* has *parent aFrame*. It contains and is the *parent* of objects *aButton* and *aTextField*. The *components[ ]* array of *aPanel* contains objects *aButton* and *aTextField*.

- Objects *aButton* and *aTextField* have the same *parent*, *aPanel*. Neither of these objects can be containers.

The combinations of containers and components that may be designed with the Java AWT and JFC are limited only by one's imagination.

The Java 2 Platform provides a rich variety of components for use in a user interface. Included are classes in the AWT (indicated by *Other Components*, with the ellipsis, in Figure 5.5) and a much larger set of classes in the JFC (indicated by *Other JComponents*, with the ellipsis, in Figure 5.5). Supporting classes such as *Font*, *Color*, and *Image* shown in Figure 5.5 provide useful services for customizing the appearance of a component.

This brief introduction only scratches the surface of the rich collection of classes in the Java platform for supporting graphical user interfaces. An increasing number of third-party components are also available.

5.2   Events – Making Communication Work

Events are the mechanism by which a user directs the actions of a GUI application. A large and increasing number of software applications are event driven. Event-driven applications may be characterized by a need to respond to asynchronous external actions. The timing and sequence of these actions are not known a priori by the application. External actions may be initiated by a person using the application (through a user interface), by another application, by the operating system, or by hardware devices attached to the computer. We need a consistent, logical, and efficient way to capture these external actions so the event-driven application can respond appropriately.

As a starting point we define what is meant by an event. If we check the definition of event in the dictionary[2] we find:

> *event – n.* 1. something that happens or is regarded as happening; an occurrence, esp. one of some importance, 2. the outcome, issue or result of anything; consequence.

So event is a noun and it is something that happens, typically as the result of some action or set of conditions. This leads to our first step in decomposing and understanding events. We distinguish the cause of an event (the source) from the event itself. The event is the result of some behavior by the source. The next step in our decomposition of events is to realize that events are intended to invoke

---

[2] Abstracted from *Webster's College Dictionary*, Random House, New York, 1995.

some response (even if the response is to ignore the event). So we distinguish the event from a response to the event. If an object is to respond to an event it must be notified that the event has occurred. This approach leads to a description of events involving several players with specific roles and responsibilities. In the next section we present a simple example using events. We then correlate the example with and expand upon the features already defined for events – source, event, notification, and response.

5.2.1 Features of Event-Driven Applications

We first illustrate the features of events with a simple nontechnical example. Then we define the terms used to describe events and event handling.

5.2.1.1 A Simple Event-Driven Example

Suppose you are enrolled in a class and the instructor has promised to periodically provide helpful key information for doing well on exams. Based on perceived needs of the students, coupled with goals for the class and progress toward those goals, the instructor will decide the content and timing of any new information made available. The instructor promises to post such information on a Web page and to notify students.

As the term progresses we look at a possible scenario. Based on student performance in completion of a particular homework assignment and questions raised in class, the instructor decides to create supplementary notes, post them on the Web page, and notify students. Students may then access, download, and study the notes.

This simple example has all the features of an event-driven application. If we break down the scenario into a more formal description, we get a better idea of the precise steps involved in this simple task.

1. A set of actions (student performance on homework assignment) and conditions (perceived student misunderstanding of concepts) lead the instructor to create a set of supplementary notes. We may characterize the actions and conditions as a threshold phenomenon that leads to a binary decision to create notes. The act of creating the notes is the event. The instructor is the source of the event.

2. Once completed, the notes are posted on the Web page following a sequence of steps. If these steps are done correctly, the instructor receives confirmation that the notes are in fact on the Web page and available for download. This confirmation may be taken as a signal back to the instructor to notify students about the new notes. Notifying the students of the event (creation of notes) is the responsibility of the instructor (the source).

3. Before we talk about response, it is important to discuss briefly the responsibilities of the instructor and students as part of the notification process. As stated in step 2, it is the responsibility of the instructor to notify students of the event. Making an announcement in class typically does this. A student must be

in class to hear the announcement. The student has an implied contract with the instructor to listen for any new announcements. The actual announcement follows a pattern including a reference to the filename and link information for retrieving the notes. The instructor notifies and passes along key information about the notes to the students. All students must understand and follow this announcement pattern.

4. Response to the event is the responsibility of each student. Each may respond differently to the same event. A student's response may be interpreted as the steps taken as a result of hearing the announcement. Specific steps may include downloading, reading, printing, highlighting, marking, and discussing the notes. The student has access to the details of the notes (created as part of the event) for use in his or her response. The student also knows the source (the instructor) and may query the source for additional information.

5.2.1.2 Terms for Describing Events and Event Handling

Based on the details of the simple example described above, we may extract some terminology for characterizing various players and responsibilities in an event-driven application. The exact details for event handling vary significantly for different programming languages; however, the same work must be done by all. Our terminology will be consistent with object orientation and will (not by accident) map nicely into the event-handling model of Java.

1. *Environment* – The environment consists of all the external conditions and actions that may lead to the source firing an event. Actions and conditions may be from other software components, a person interacting with the source, or hardware devices. In many cases, actions may be the result of some other event. For example, a software "button" fires an event in response to a user-initiated mouse click (another kind of event) on the image of the button.

2. *Source* – A source fires a specific kind of event based on rules for its use. In firing an event, the source creates a new *EventObject* and posts it to an *EventQueue* (a kind of waiting line that follows first-in, first-out logic). A source also maintains an active list of interested listeners who want to be notified when an event occurs. Actual notification of the listeners does not occur until another object, the *EventHandler*, says okay. This adds consistency to event handling. The source must allow listeners to be added or removed from its active list.

3. *EventObject* – An event is an object. It knows its source as well as other information that may be useful to an interested listener. There may be many different kinds of event objects. A hierarchy of subclasses under *EventObject* may represent these kinds of events.

4. *EventHandler* – The event handler is a centralized software component whose only responsibility is to keep track of generated events and dispatch (delegate responsibility for handling) them. The *EventHandler* usually runs in a continuous loop to remove an event from an *EventQueue* and dispatch it (by telling the source to notify all its listeners). This logic guarantees a first-in, first-out handling of events. A variation is made possible by using a priority queue, in which

higher priority events are handled first. The event handler assumes no responsibility for how any object responds. It simply manages all events by dispatching them in an organized fashion. The listeners that are associated with each source determine their own response to the event.

5. *EventQueue* – A normal queue or a priority queue may be used to store a set of *EventObject* instances. These instances are typically inserted into the queue by event sources and then extracted and dispatched by the *EventHandler*.

6. *EventListener Interface* – This is a pattern for notification of event listeners by an event source. In object-oriented terms, an *EventListener* interface defines the messages that may be sent by the source to interested listeners. Each kind of event object has its own *EventListener* interface.

7. *Event Listener* – An event listener will be notified by an event source when a specific fired event is ready for processing. It is the responsibility of the event listener to register with all event sources for which it wishes to receive notification. An event listener must implement the messages defined in a particular *EventListener* interface, corresponding to a specific kind of event. Notification is accomplished by the source, sending the appropriate message to all registered listeners.

We now revisit the example presented earlier, showing how the above defined players and actions map into that example.

Preparation for event handling consists of the following steps. The instructor provides details for notification about significant events to the students. Specifically, the requirements are (1) registration as an interested listener consists of attending class, and (2) notification consists of a class announcement providing details about the Web page and the file that should be downloaded. Step 1 is equivalent to registration with the source (the instructor) by an object (the student) as an interested listener for a specific event (posting of supplemental notes). Step 2 describes precisely how an interested listener (the *EventListener*, the student) will be notified of a new event (posting of supplemental notes).

The following steps characterize the actual event generation, dispatching, notification, and handling.

1. Based on threshold conditions in the environment (described previously) the source (instructor) fires an event (creates a set of supplemental notes).

2. The source posts that *EventObject* (the notes) with the *EventHandler* (his or her Web page).

3. The *EventHandler* (the Web page) *dispatches* the event (confirms the posting).

4. This is a signal to the *source* (the instructor) to notify all registered listeners of the event.

5. All properly registered *EventListener* objects (those students in class) are notified of the event, including details on how to download.

6. Each *EventListener* object (each student in class) then responds to the event according to his or her own wishes.

5.2.2   The Java Delegation Event Model (for Advanced Readers)

The Java delegation event model, introduced with JDK 1.1 and continuing in JDK 1.2 (Platform 2), provides classes representing the seven major players in event-driven applications as described in the previous section. In our discussion we will focus on a simple environment where a person creates the conditions and actions that cause a source to fire an event. This is typical of a user interacting with a graphical user interface. We present selected details of the classes in JDK 1.2 that support the delegation event model and how they map into our seven players.

5.2.2.1   Mapping the Event Players into Java Classes

We present classes in the JDK that correspond to the seven players described in the previous section. The programmer may extend and add classes to those already provided in the JDK. We focus on classes that are part of the AWT (abstract windowing toolkit). There are many other classes in the JFC (Java foundation classes) that also support event handling.

1. **Environment** – The user interacts with a GUI through the mouse and keyboard. Possible actions include movement, clicking, double clicking, and dragging with the mouse plus typing from the keyboard. These hardware devices generate events that are translated into appropriate responses by the software components in the GUI. For now we will skip the details of the hardware-generated events and focus on the events generated by the software components (event generation is part of the response by a software component to the hardware-generated event).

2. **Source** – Many sources in the JDK are subclasses of *java.awt.Component*. Typical sources include buttons, text fields, lists, and other user interface (UI) components that respond to user interaction. Figure 5.6 shows how the environment, event sources, and user interact in a typical GUI application.

   Class *MyGUI* is the application. It is a subclass of *java.awt.Frame*, *Window*, and *Container*. As a container it contains instances of *Component*. The user interacts with various components contained in *MyGUI* to generate events. These components are the event sources. Other potential sources for events not shown in the figure include menu items and all the JFC subclasses of *JComponent* (a subclass of *Container*).

   Actual user interaction with these software components requires the use of some input device such as the mouse or keyboard. In a very real sense, the mouse and the keyboard are the actual sources for most user-generated events. However, semantically we say that clicking a mouse button with the cursor on a *Button* causes the *Button* to generate an event. We call the *Button* the source of the event.

3. **EventObject** – Class *EventObject* in package *java.util* is the parent class of a hierarchy of subclasses representing specific kinds of event objects. It has a field called *source* that represents the source that generated the event. Most events are instances of *AWTEvent* or its subclasses. Figure 5.7 shows a hierarchy of

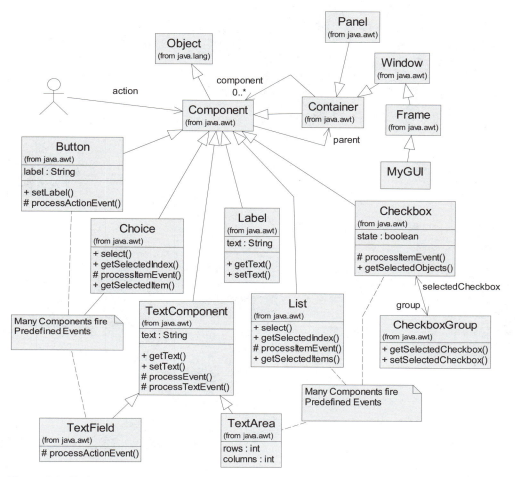

Figure 5.6. Environment and event sources.

the *EventObject* classes that are a part of JDK 1.1, including the *AWTEvent* hierarchy. In JDK 1.2 there are a large number of other event classes (JFC event classes not shown in the figure) with common parent *EventObject*.

AWT events may be grouped into two categories: (1) low-level events and (2) semantic events. Low-level events are those that are typically generated in response to direct interaction with the computer, such as clicking a mouse or pressing a key on the keyboard. Semantic events are those typically generated by some user interface component such as clicking a button. The low-level events make the semantic events possible.

In Figure 5.7, *ComponentEvent* and its subclasses define low-level events.

- *ComponentEvent* (component is resized, moved, shown or hidden)
- *MouseEvent* (mouse button is depressed, released, clicked, dragged, or moved)
- *KeyEvent* (key is pressed or released)
- *ContainerEvent* (a component is added or removed from a container)
- *FocusEvent* (a component gets or loses focus, usually by mouse click)

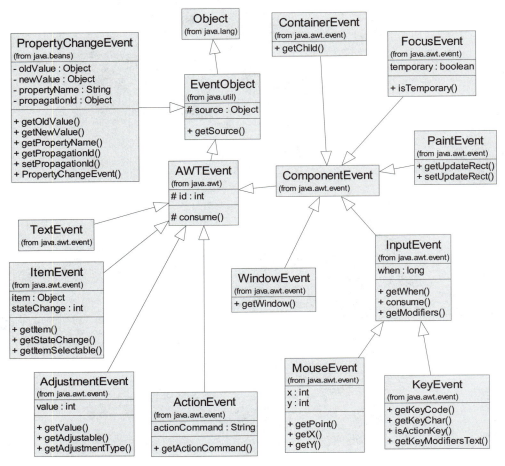

Figure 5.7. The *EventObject* hierarchy.

- *WindowEvent* (a window is iconified, deiconified, activated, deactivated, or closed)
- *PaintEvent* (a component is repainted – redisplayed on the screen)

Semantic events in Figure 5.7 include the following.

- *ActionEvent* (clicking a button, selecting a menu item, double clicking an item in a list, typing *Enter* key in a text field)
- *AdjustmentEvent* (the user modifies a scroll bar)
- *ItemEvent* (the user selects an item from a checkbox, choice, or list)
- *TextEvent* (content of a text component – text field or text area – changes)
- *PropertyChangeEvent* – a property change event may be fired directly by methods in a class as a result of a command to change a particular property (field). A delegate object (an instance of *PropertyChangeSupport*) assumes responsibilities of the source for the property change event.

4. ***Event Handler*** – A package private class called *EventDispatchThread* in package *java.awt* is the event handler. It runs in its own thread (Java supports

multiple threads of execution) and is started whenever any Java program is executed. Its *run()* method is a loop that performs the following steps unless interrupted.

```
AWTEvent event = theQueue.getNextEvent(); // get next event
theQueue.dispatchEvent(event);            // dispatch the event
```

The event handler gets the next event from an event queue and then tells the event queue to dispatch the event. The event queue sends an appropriate dispatch message to the source of the event. The source notifies all its listeners. Each of the listeners takes action to respond to the event.

5. *EventQueue* – Class *EventQueue* in package *java.awt* contains instances of *EventQueueItem* (a package private class). Event queue items are linkable nodes that contain event objects. Sources may post an event with *EventQueue* by sending the message *postEvent(AWTEvent event)* to the system event queue. The following expression shows how to post an action event generated by object *aButton*.

```
EventQueue theQueue = Toolkit.getEventQueue();
theQueue.postEvent(new ActionEvent(aButton));
```

6. *EventListener Interface* – An *EventListener* interface defines the messages that may be sent by the source to interested listeners. Each kind of event object has its own *EventListener* interface. Figure 5.8 shows the event listener interfaces that are part of the *java.awt.event* package and the *java.beans* package (JFC event listeners are not shown). Notice that there is a listener interface for each kind of event object in the AWT (except for *PaintEvent*, which is not designed for use with the event listener model[3]).

7. *Event Listener* – An event listener must register with all event sources for which it has an interest. Secondly, it must implement the methods in the corresponding *EventListener* interface for all those events generated by the selected sources. Having done this initialization properly, the event listener will be notified by the source when an event has occurred; that is, it will be sent a message matching the template in the *EventListener* interface. There are options on how an event listener may choose to meet its obligations. These options, as implemented in Java, are illustrated in Chapter 6.

5.3 The MVC Design Pattern

For many applications, especially those that provide a graphical user interface, the application may be described in terms of three distinct concepts with separate responsibilities. These three concepts are model, view, and controller (MVC).

---

[3] See the Java documentation.

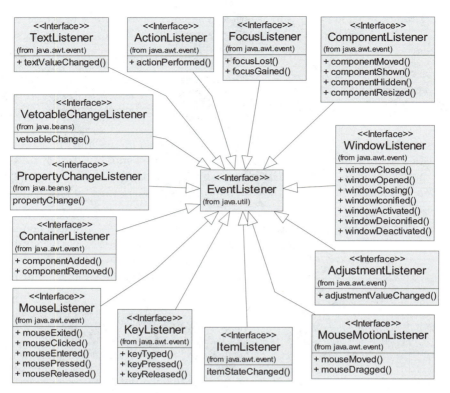

Figure 5.8. AWT *EventListener* interface hierarchy.

The MVC concept, now recognized as a design pattern,[4] was developed as part of the Smalltalk[5] environment in the 1970s and 1980s. MVC assigns the following properties and responsibilities to model, view, and controller.

1. *Model* – Data and computations performed on data comprise the model of a software application. This model may be as simple as an integer counter or as complex as a spreadsheet or database. The model is responsible for maintaining its internal data and for providing commands and queries that allow external objects to access and/or modify its internal data. The model is also responsible for broadcasting change notices to all interested views whenever its internal data change. A helper object to provide consistency across all models often handles this last responsibility. The capabilities of the helper object may be implemented through inheritance or delegation.

2. *View* – View objects are responsible for presenting a view of their associated model or models. Views may range from simple textual display to complex tabular or graphical display. The view depends on queries provided by the model to access

---

[4] See *Design Patterns: Elements of Reusable Object-Oriented Software*, Gamma, et al., Addison-Wesley, 1994, for a discussion of design patterns.
[5] Smalltalk-80 was released as the first commercial product based on the Smalltalk language and was developed at Xerox Palo Alto Research Center.

the data it wishes to display. It is the responsibility of the view to register with its model(s) to be notified of changes. Upon notification of a change in its model(s), the view must update its display. The view needs a reference to its model(s).

3. *Controller* – A controller provides the interface between the model and an initiator (typically a user in a GUI application) of changes in its model(s). It depends on commands provided by the model that allow the model's internal data to be modified. The components (or widgets) along with their event handlers in a GUI application serve as controllers. They present a graphical image for interaction with the user. Actions by the user cause the components to fire events. These events are handled in a way to effect the intended change in the model(s). The event handling part of the controller is typically consistent with a larger and more general concept for event handling. The controller needs a reference to its model(s).

The separation of roles and responsibilities for model, view, and controller is a design pattern that enables the easy addition of views or controllers without adversely affecting those already present. It provides a consistent approach to the storage, modification, and display of data. With the evolution of GUI applications, the user interface has become the software component with responsibility for both view and controller. We often speak of an M-VC design as opposed to an MVC design. Clearly, the graphical components in a GUI represent the controls for modifying data in the model as well as views for displaying the model. Figure 5.9 shows the key players in an M-VC design that uses a graphical user interface.

The interactions in Figure 5.9 represent the M-VC concept. The user initiates an action by using the keyboard or mouse to activate some visual control (component) in the GUI. The component (controller) responds by firing an event. The *eventHandler* part of the controller is assumed to have registered as a listener for that kind of event and is notified of the event firing. It responds by sending a command, *setData(newValue)*, to the model. The model responds by changing its data. It then invokes the helper object, *changeMonitor*, by sending it the message *changed()*. The helper object then notifies all registered views of the change in the model by sending them the message *update(model)*. Using the knowledge of

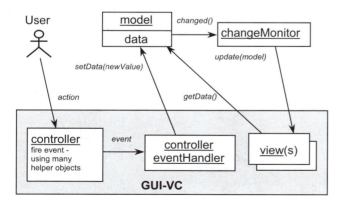

Figure 5.9. Key players in an M-VC design using a GUI.

which model changed, each view then may query, for example, using *getData()*, the model for information required to update itself.

5.3.1   Inheritance Approach to M-VC

The inheritance approach to M-VC requires that all model classes extend a common parent class. The parent class provides all fields and methods for maintaining a list of registered views and for notifying those views of changes in the model. This approach is great from the standpoint of good object-oriented design and maximum reusability. In Java, the common parent class for models is class *java.util.Observable*. Views must register as observers with the model and implement the *java.util.Observer* interface, which defines only one command, *update*. See Figure 5.10. *Observable* uses a *Vector* to store registered observers for the model.

5.3.2   Delegation Approach to M-VC

Primary classes and their relationships are shown in Figure 5.11 for the delegation approach to M-VC in Java.

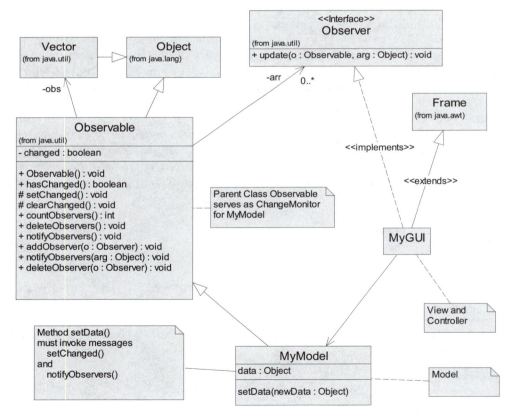

Figure 5.10. Inheritance approach to M-VC in Java.

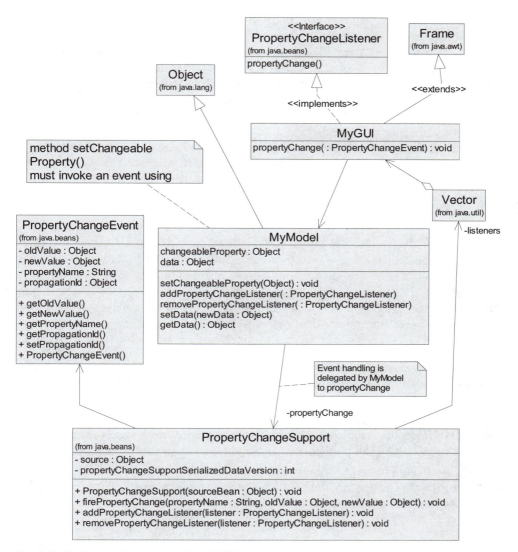

Figure 5.11. Delegation approach to M-VC in Java.

It is not always convenient or even possible for a model class to extend the parent class *java.util.Observable*; then we must use the delegation approach. The delegation approach to M-VC adds a new field to the model class. This field is the delegate object responsible for registering views with the model and for notifying registered views when the model has changed. This approach frees the model to extend any appropriate class (instead of *Observable*). The delegation approach to M-VC in Java is an extension of the property change mechanism in Java beans (see example in Chapter 6). Changing a property of a Java bean causes a *PropertyChangeEvent* to be fired. All objects that wish to be notified of the property change must register (add themselves as listeners) with the bean and implement the *PropertyChangeListener* interface.

A model class may tap into this bean behavior by adding a delegate field that is an instance of class *java.beans.PropertyChangeSupport* (see Figure 5.10). Class *PropertyChangeSupport* provides methods for maintaining a list (using a *Vector*) of interested listeners to be notified of a *PropertyChangeEvent*. The implementations for adding and removing property change listeners in the model simply pass responsibility along to the *propertyChange* field. In a sense, our model is now behaving as a nonvisual Java bean. We present a simple example using this approach in Chapter 6.

The delegate also provides a command that fires the *PropertyChangeEvent*. At least one command in the model class (e.g., *setChangeableProperty* in *My-Model*) must invoke the expression *propertyChange.firePropertyChange()* to fire the event.

5.4 Summary

Graphical user interfaces are event-driven applications. The Java platform provides a rich set of classes representing the essential elements of an event-driven, GUI application. If an application interacts with data then the software developer may take advantage of the MVC design pattern to provide a more object-oriented and elegant design for the application. Java provides classes supporting two approaches to MVC: (1) the inheritance approach and (2) the delegation approach.

❑ Top-level windows (instances of *Frame* or *JFrame*) and other container classes organize and present graphical controls to the user for interaction with a GUI application.

❑ Components or widgets are the graphical controls that allow a user to interact with a GUI application. Interaction with a component causes an event to be fired. Event handling by the application causes desired changes to take effect.

❑ MVC is a design concept that separates responsibilities for (1) maintaining data used by an application (model), (2) allowing the user to modify data (controller), and (3) presenting data to the user (view).

6

Implementing Simple GUIs in Java

In this chapter we extend our discussion of GUI applications, event handling, and MVC to show simple implementation details in Java of the concepts presented in Chapter 5. We limit our implementations to a select few of the available components that are part of the AWT (abstract windowing toolkit) and JFC (Java foundation classes).

6.1 Containers and Essential Components – Building a GUI

6.1.1 The Top-Level Window – Essentials

The top-level window is typically an instance of *Frame* or *JFrame*. Essential and desirable steps in creating a top-level window include the ability to (1) set its size, (2) give it a title, (3) position it on the screen, (4) display it, and (5) close it. These steps are easily accomplished by the source code shown in Listing 6.1. Details for centering the frame on the screen and closing it are a little messy and are done automatically by many development environments. We encounter our first event handler in choosing to enable window closing. For now we present the event-handling code without explanation. It is covered in more detail in Section 6.2. The operations for *Frame* in Listing 6.1 also work correctly for *JFrame*.

Listing 6.1 Essential/Desired Operations for a Top-Level Window

```
/** A simple frame, centered and closeable
*/

import java.awt.*;
import java.awt.event.*;

public class EssentialFrame extends Frame {

  public EssentialFrame () {
    super("A Simple Frame");  // create with title
    setSize(300, 200);
    // enable the window to be closed - event handler
    addWindowListener(new WindowAdapter() {
```

```
     public void windowClosing (WindowEvent evt) {
        System.exit(0);
     }
   });
   center();
   setVisible(true);
}

//Center the window
public void center () {
  Dimension screenSize =
    Toolkit.getDefaultToolkit().getScreenSize();
  Dimension frameSize = this.getSize();
  // set frameSize to smaller of frameSize or screenSize
  if (frameSize.height > screenSize.height)
    frameSize.height = screenSize.height;
  if (frameSize.width > screenSize.width)
    frameSize.width = screenSize.width;
  // center the frame by setting upper left corner location
  this.setLocation((screenSize.width - frameSize.width) / 2,
    (screenSize.height - frameSize.height) / 2);
}

public static void main (String[] args) {
  new EssentialFrame();
}
}
```

The example in Listing 6.1 displays a 300 × 200 pixel, centered, closeable window that has a specified title and is empty. It is pretty boring and useless. The next step in building a useful GUI application is to add components. There are a large number of predefined components in the AWT and JFC. We choose to add only a few selected components that are simple and useful for common user interaction. More specifically, we focus on the following components to illustrate steps in creation, sizing, and positioning of those components supporting text input, text display, and simple controls.

6.1.2 Simple Components

1. *java.awt.Label* – contains a field called *text* of type *String*. The value of *text* may be accessed by query *getText()* and changed by command *setText(aString)* by the program but not the user. There are options for setting the alignment of the text string and for changing font properties. This component is useful for static labeling and for dynamic display of simple textual output that is under program control. The JFC component *javax.swing.JLabel* may be used in the same way.

2. *java.awt.TextField* – contains a single line of text, represented by field *text* of type *String*, that may be editable by the user. The value of *text* may be accessed

by query *getText( )* and changed by command *setText(aString)* by the program. The value of *text* may also be changed directly by the user. This component is useful for user input of simple textual information as well as output display. The JFC component *javax.swing.JTextField* may be used in the same way. The text field components generate a *KeyEvent* while being edited and an *ActionEvent* on pressing the *Enter* key.

3. *java.awt.Button* – a simple control that translates a mouse click over its image into an *ActionEvent*. This provides the user with a simple activating input. The JFC component *javax.swing.JButton* may be used in the same way. Other useful components include the AWT components *List, TextArea, Choice, Checkbox, CheckboxGroup* (a group of *Checkbox* objects behaving as a group of radio buttons), *Dialog*, and *Menu*. The JFC adds many more useful components. Some of these components are used in the GUI laboratories in Part Two of the book.

6.1.3 Organizing and Laying Out Components in a Window

The Java 2 Platform comes with several predefined layout managers that automatically size and position components within a container. Each container has a default layout manager; the default for *Frame* is *BorderLayout* (see Java documentation). For simple applications the predefined layout managers may be suitable; however, for applications with a large number of precisely arranged components a different approach is needed.

The process of sizing and positioning components in a container is one of the most labor-intensive parts of building a GUI application. Fortunately, we have a variety of development environments that allow this to be done graphically. The development environment generates the Java code from the graphical design. Each development environment has its own style for layout coding. A simple, non-cluttering, and understandable style that works well for most GUI applications is to set the layout manager to *null* and use the *Component* method *setBounds* to set the size and position of all components. JBuilder[1] uses this approach. Listing 6.2 shows a simple class, *LayoutExample*, for adding two buttons and a label to a *Frame*. Command *initialize( )* sets the layout to *null*, creates the components, determines their size and position using *setBounds( )*, and then *adds* them to the frame.

Listing 6.2 Simple Layout Example

```
/** Positioning components in a container
*/

import java.awt.*;
import java.awt.event.*;
```

---

[1] JBuilder is a product of Borland, http://www.borland.com/jbuilder/.

```java
public class LayoutExample extends Frame {

  Label valueLabel;
  Button incrementButton;
  Button resetButton;

  public LayoutExample () {
    super("An Incrementer" );
    addWindowListener(new WindowAdapter() {
      public void windowClosing(WindowEvent evt) {
        System.exit(0)
      }
    });
    initialize();
  }

  private void initialize () {
    setSize(200, 100);
    this.setLayout(null);
    incrementButton = new Button("Increment" );
    incrementButton.setBounds(20, 40, 75, 25);
    add(incrementButton);
    resetButton = new Button("Reset" );
    resetButton.setBounds(105, 40, 75, 25);
    add(resetButton);
    valueLabel = new Label("0" , Label.CENTER);
    valueLabel.setBounds(75, 70, 50, 25);
    add(valueLabel);
    setVisible(true);
  }

  public static void main (String[] args) {
    new LayoutExample();
  }
}
```

If we use a *JFrame* instead of *Frame*, the components must be added to the content pane of the *JFrame*. Listing 6.3 shows the details for command *initialize()* if we are using a *JFrame*. Components are contained in the *JFrame*'s content pane. The second parameter of each *setBounds()* message is reduced by 20 because the y-distance is measured from the bottom of the title bar in a *JFrame*. Key changes are shown in boldface.

Listing 6.3   Adding Components to a *JFrame*

```java
...
  private void initialize () {
    setSize(200, 100);
```

```
this.getContentPane().setLayout(null);
incrementButton = new Button("Increment" );
incrementButton.setBounds(20, 20, 75, 25);
getContentPane().add(incrementButton);
resetButton = new Button("Reset" );
resetButton.setBounds(105, 20, 75, 25);
getContentPane().add(resetButton);
valueLabel = new Label("0" , Label.CENTER);
valueLabel.setBounds(75, 50, 50, 25);
getContentPane().add(valueLabel);
setVisible(true);
}
...
```

We have now built a simple GUI with some components (two buttons and a label; other components are used in examples in later chapters) that still does nothing. The next step is to understand and enable event handling, to make the application do some work.

6.2 Implementation of Event Handling in Java

The delegation event model in Java allows any object to register as an event handler by (1) adding itself as a listener to the event source and (2) implementing the appropriate *EventListener* interface for that source.

6.2.1 Options for Implementing an *EventListener* Interface

In a GUI application there are many options for implementing listener interfaces for the variety of events that may be generated by components in the GUI. These options are illustrated in Figure 6.1.

Specific *EventListener* interfaces may be implemented:

- Directly by:
  - *MyGUI*
  - *NamedInnerClass*
  - *AnonymousInnerClass*
  - *ExternalHelper*
- Subclassed under predefined adapter:
  - Difficult for *MyGUI* (usually a subclass of *Frame* or *JFrame*)
  - Possible for *NamedInnerClass*
  - Possible for *AnonymousInnerClass*
  - Possible for *ExternalHelper*

The first option available to an event listener is to decide who implements the *EventListener* interface methods. The event listener may choose to implement

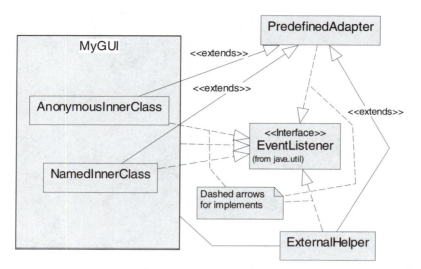

Figure 6.1. Options for implementing *EventListener* interfaces.

these methods itself or to use a helper class. The helper class may be (1) a named inner class, (2) an anonymous inner class, or (3) an external class.

An advantage of using a helper class is that the helper class usually has no constraints on its parent class and may extend one of the predefined *adapter* classes. A GUI application class is typically a subclass of *Frame*. Adapter classes provide "do nothing" implementations of *EventListener* subinterfaces that have more than one method. They satisfy the contract that all methods in the interface must be implemented. In many applications, not all the methods in an *EventListener* are used; the helper class then extends the adapter class and redefines the method or methods that are used. In a roundabout way, adapters save a little effort by providing empty implementations for the methods that are not used. Figure 6.2 shows the predefined adapter classes that are part of the AWT. Each adapter class implements its corresponding event listener interface; for example, class *ComponentAdapter* implements interface *ComponentListener*.

6.2.2   Steps in Processing a Simple Button Click Event

In the AWT, components have peer classes that interface directly with the operating system. Implementations for these peer classes handle details of capturing low-level events and posting semantic (see Chapter 5) events to the *EventQueue*. Figure 6.3 presents a collaboration diagram showing the sequence of steps following the clicking of a *Button* component in a user interface. The *AWT Runtime* is not really an object. It is more precisely a collection of objects and instructions that comprise the Java runtime environment (JRE). Its first role in our example is to recognize that the mouse pointer is over the button and that the mouse button has been clicked, that is, responds to an imagined message, *buttonClicked()*.

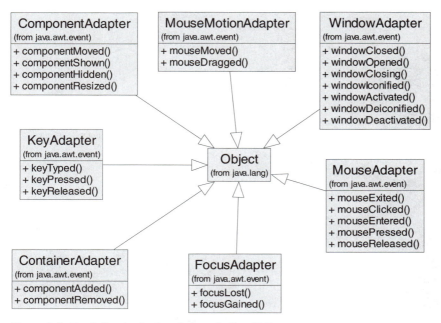

Figure 6.2. Predefined adapter classes in the AWT.

Discussion of the Collaboration Diagram in Figure 6.3

The rectangular boxes are objects with labels identifying their class and optionally the object name; for example, *button* is an instance of *Button* and is the source for the *ActionEvent*. Object *AWT Runtime* represents the peer class object for *Button* plus other supporting communication with the operating system; most of its details are hidden.

The steps are numbered in their sequence of occurrence. Thus step 1 occurs when the user clicks the mouse with its cursor positioned on the *button* object's image in a user interface. The steps show messages sent to an object by another object. The arrows show the direction of communication. A description of the steps in Figure 6.3 is given as:

1. Based on actions by the user, the *AWT Runtime* detects that *button* has been clicked.

2. The peer object (part of the *AWT Runtime*) updates the *button* by making it look as if it has been clicked. It cycles from normal to depressed to normal view. Since this is part of the hidden details of the peer class, the exact sequence and messages of this step are unknown.

3. The peer object for *Button* fires an *ActionEvent*; that is, it creates a new instance, *evt*, of class *ActionEvent* with *button* as the source.

4. The peer object posts the event with the *EventQueue*.

5. The *EventDispatchThread* gets the *ActionEvent, evt*, from the *EventQueue*.

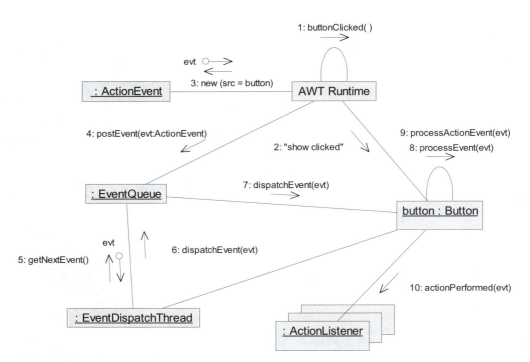

Figure 6.3. Collaboration diagram – generation and handling of an *ActionEvent*.

6. The *EventDispatchThread* sends the message *dispatchEvent(evt)* to the *EventQueue*.

7. The *EventQueue* sends the message *dispatchEvent(evt)* to the *button*.

8. The first response of *button* is to send itself the message *processEvent(evt)*.

9. The *processEvent* method sends the message *processActionEvent(evt)* to *button*.

10. The *processActionEvent* method sends message *actionPerformed(evt)* to all registered listeners.

11. Each registered listener performs the steps in its implementation of *actionPerformed*.

6.2.3   Examples of Events-Handling Options in the Java 2 Platform

A number of options were described in Section 6.2.1 for implementation of the details for event handling. In this section we define a simple GUI application consisting of a frame with two buttons and a label in it. Then we present details for all the available options for handling events generated by this simple application. A screen shot is shown in Figure 6.4 of the application after it is first launched and after a number of button clicks. The name of our application class is *EventExampleUI*.

We need to handle two kinds of events. The first is an *ActionEvent* generated by one of the buttons. The second is a *WindowEvent* generated by clicking the

a) Initial screen shot   b) After using buttons

Figure 6.4. Simple event example in Java.

"close" icon (with an × on it) in the upper right corner of the frame. This allows us to close the frame and application. We begin by letting the UI class handle the action event and delegating the window-closing event to an anonymous adapter class. We will then look at other options for handling the action events.

6.2.3.1   Handling the *WindowEvent* with an Anonymous Adapter Class

Anonymous classes are classes with no specific name that implement an interface or extend an existing class. Anonymous classes can only be inner classes. Therefore, we extend and redefine part of the *WindowAdapter* class (the method for window closing) as an inner class within our application class, *EventExampleUI*. Listing 6.4 shows the details for this part of *EventExampleUI.java*. It is contained in the implementation details for the constructor and shown in boldface in Listing 6.4. Class *EventExampleUI* extends class *java.awt.Frame*.

Listing 6.4   **Details for an Anonymous Window Adapter Inner Class**

```
// constructor
public EventExampleUI() {
  super("An Incrementer" );
  addWindowListener(new WindowAdapter() {
    public void windowClosing (WindowEvent evt) {
      System.exit(0);}});
  initialize();
}
```

We are adding a *WindowListener* to the current object (an instance of *EventExampleUI*) that is created as a new *WindowAdapter* subclass that redefines the *windowClosing* command to *exit* (close the application).

When we compile *EventExampleUI* we get two *.class* files. The first is *EventExampleUI.class* as expected; the second is the compiled version of the anonymous inner class. By default, the Java compiler assigns unique labels to all anonymous classes. In this example, we will observe a class file *EventExampleUI$1.class*. The $ sign attaches the anonymous class designation (1 in this case) to its containing class (*EventExampleUI*). In this way Java maintains unique names for all classes including named or anonymous inner classes.

Since only method *windowClosing* is redefined in our anonymous inner class, we accept the default (null) implementations in *WindowAdapter* for the remaining six methods of interface *WindowListener*. Without the short code segment just described, our application cannot be closed gracefully. The only options would be to use a system interrupt such as the task manager or a control key from within a command window (or of course the time-tested method of pulling the plug out of the wall!).

6.2.3.2 Handling an Action Event – Letting the Application Implement *ActionListener*

As a first option for handling action events we let the application class *implement* the *ActionListener* interface. This is a promise to implement the method defined in *ActionListener*, which is *actionPerformed(ActionEvent evt)*. Complete details for class *EventExampleUI* are given in Listing 6.5. We see the details of the event-handling code as well as details for building the user interface. Statements necessary for handling action events are shown in boldface in the listing.

Listing 6.5 Complete Details for *EventExampleUI.java*

```
import java.awt.*;
import java.awt.event.*;

public class EventExampleUI extends Frame implements ActionListener {

  Label valueLabel;
  Button incrementButton;
  Button resetButton;

  public EventExampleUI () {
    super("An Incrementer" );
    addWindowListener(new WindowAdapter() {
    public void windowClosing(WindowEvent evt)
      System.exit(0);}});
    initialize();
  }

  private void initialize () {
    setSize(200, 100);
    this.setLayout(null);
    incrementButton = new Button("Increment" );
    incrementButton.setBounds(20, 40, 75, 25);
    // register instance of this class as a listener
    incrementButton.addActionListener(this);
    add(incrementButton);
    resetButton = new Button("Reset" );
    resetButton.setBounds(105, 40, 75, 25);
```

```
    resetButton.addActionListener(this);
    add(resetButton);
    valueLabel = new Label("0" , Label.CENTER);
    valueLabel.setBounds(75, 70, 50, 25);
    add(valueLabel);
    setVisible(true);
  }

  public void actionPerformed (ActionEvent evt) {
    if (evt.getSource() == incrementButton) {
      int value = (new Integer(valueLabel.getText())).intValue();
      valueLabel.setText(String.valueOf(value + 1));
    } else if (evt.getSource() == resetButton)
      valueLabel.setText("0");
  }

  public static void main (String[] args) {
    new EventExampleUI();
  }
}
```

Three significant things must happen for *EventExampleUI* to handle the events generated by the two buttons.

1. Class *EventExampleUI* must promise that it **implements ActionListener**.
2. Class *EventExampleUI* must register itself (**this**) with both buttons to receive notification of the action events they generate. This is achieved by sending the message **addActionListener(this)** to each button.
3. Class *EventExampleUI* must implement method *actionPerformed* from interface *ActionListener* to provide its intended response. Details of the response are shown in the listing, either incrementing the *valueLabel* by one or resetting it to zero.

6.2.3.3 Handling an Action Event – Using an Anonymous Inner Class

Listing 6.6 shows significant parts of a revised version of *EventExampleUI2.java* that uses anonymous inner classes to handle action events from the two buttons.

Listing 6.6 Using an Anonymous Inner Class to Handle Action Events

```
import java.awt.*;
import java.awt.event.*;

public class EventExampleUI2 extends Frame {
  ...
  private void initialize () {
    setSize(200, 100);
```

```
    this.setLayout(null);
    incrementButton = new Button("Increment" );
    incrementButton.setBounds(20, 40, 75, 25);
    incrementButton.addActionListener( new ActionListener() {
      public void actionPerformed (ActionEvent evt) {
        int value = (new
          Integer(valueLabel.getText())).intValue();
        valueLabel.setText(String.valueOf(value + 1));
    }});
    add(incrementButton);
    resetButton = new Button("Reset" );
    resetButton.setBounds(105, 40, 75, 25);
    resetButton.addActionListener( new ActionListener() {
      public void actionPerformed (ActionEvent evt) {
        valueLabel.setText("0");
    }});
    ...
    }
    ...
}
```

First, notice that class *EventExampleUI2* does not say it *implements ActionListener* and that method *actionPerformed* is removed as a separate method. The code shown in boldface creates and implements two anonymous inner classes to handle action events from each of the buttons.

When file *EventExampleUI2.java* is compiled it produces four *.class* files: *EventexampleUI2.class, EventExampleUI2$1.class, EventExampleUI2$2.class,* and *EventExampleUI2$3.class.*

6.2.3.4 Handling an Action Event – Using a Named Inner Class

This option is similar to the anonymous inner class except it looks more like our "normal" definition of classes, creation of objects and message sending. Class *EventExampleUI3* adds an action listener to *incrementButton* that is a new instance of the named inner class *IncrementButtonEventHandler*. The named inner class has one responsibility – to implement *actionPerformed* for the *incrementButton* action event. Selected details are shown in Listing 6.7 for this option.

Listing 6.7 Using a Named Inner Class to Handle *incrementButton* Events

```
import java.awt.*;
import java.awt.event.*;

public class EventExampleUI3 extends Frame {

    ...
```

```
private void initialize () {
  setSize(200, 100);
  this.setLayout(null);
  incrementButton = new Button("Increment" );
  incrementButton.setBounds(20, 40, 75, 25);
  incrementButton.addActionListener(
    new IncrementButtonEventHandler());
  add(incrementButton);
  ...
}

class IncrementButtonEventHandler implements ActionListener {
  public void actionPerformed (ActionEvent evt) {
    int value = (new
      Integer(valueLabel.getText())).intValue();
    valueLabel.setText(String.valueOf(value + 1));
  }
}

...
}
```

When file *EventExampleUI3.java* is compiled it produces for the named inner class a file named *EventExampleUI3$IncrementButtonEventHandler.class*. In other words, it is consistent with the naming convention for all inner classes. It just happens to have a specific name instead of a number.

6.2.3.5   Handling an Action Event – Using an External Helper Class

The major disadvantage of an external helper class when compared to the inner classes is that it does not have direct access to the fields of the UI class. Since the event handler method typically needs to interact with those fields, this is a distinct disadvantage. There are several ways to handle this problem. One approach is to let the helper class have a field that is a reference to the UI class. Being in the same package makes direct access to all but private fields of the UI class possible through this contained field. This approach is illustrated in Listing 6.8 for *EventExampleUI4* with external helper class *IncrementButtonEventHandler*.

Listing 6.8   Using an External Helper Class for Handling *incrementButton* Events

```
import java.awt.*;
import java.awt.event.*;

public class EventExampleUI4 extends Frame {

  ...
```

```
private void initialize () {
  setSize(200, 100);
  this.setLayout(null);
  incrementButton = new Button("Increment" );
  incrementButton.setBounds(20, 40, 75, 25);
  incrementButton.addActionListener(
    new IncrementButtonEventHandler(this));
  add(incrementButton);
  ...
}

  ...
}

class IncrementButtonEventHandler implements ActionListener {

  EventExampleUI4 frame;

  public IncrementButtonEventHandler(EventExampleUI4 f) {
    frame = f;
  }

  public void actionPerformed (ActionEvent evt) {
    int value = (new
      Integer(frame.valueLabel.getText())).intValue();
    frame.valueLabel.setText(String.valueOf(value + 1));
  }
}
```

As a separate class, *IncrementButtonEventHandler.java* compiles to *IncrementButtonEventHandler.class*.

We have presented a number of options for implementing the event handling part of a GUI application. All are correct and work as expected. The choice of one option over another is often dependent on the attitudes of the implementer. A number of popular Java development environments all make different choices. We prefer the anonymous inner class that either implements the listener interface or extends the appropriate adapter class (JBuilder also makes this choice). This approach offers the advantage that the response to an event is easily located with the other code that initializes the event source. In other words, we can see the intended response to a button click in the same group of code that sets its size and other properties.

6.3   Implementing MVC in Java

In this section we develop a simple MVC example where the model is a simple counter. The controller includes two buttons to allow the user to increment or reset the counter. The view is a simple text label showing the current value of the

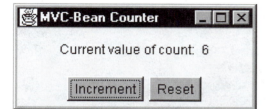

Figure 6.5. A simple MVC GUI application.

counter. This example is implemented using both the inheritance approach and the delegation (beans) approach. Figure 6.5 shows the GUI (bean version) for this application. The inheritance version is identical (in both look and feel) except for its title.

6.3.1 MVC Counter Example Using the Inheritance Approach

The design for this simple example is shown in Figure 6.6. The model class, *CounterModel*, extends *Observable* and the view-controller class, *CounterUI*, implements interfaces *Observer* and *ActionListener*. Recall from Chapter 5 that class *Observable* represents models and interface *Observer* represents view controllers in the inheritance approach to MVC.

Listing 6.9 shows all details of the *CounterModel* class. Key method *setCount(anInt)* changes the internal state and has responsibility for broadcasting any change notifications using inherited methods, *setChanged()* and *notifyObservers()*, from parent class *Observable*.

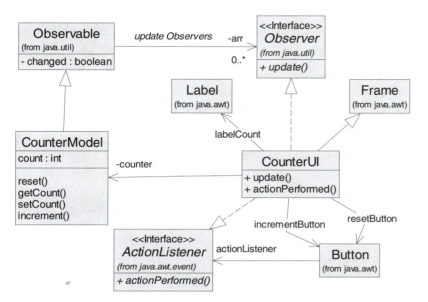

Figure 6.6. Design for MVC implementation using inheritance approach.

Listing 6.9 Details of Class *CounterModel*

```
/* class CounterModel - MVC Inheritance Example
*/
import java.util.*;

public class CounterModel extends Observable {
  protected int count = 0;

  // commands
  public void setCount (int anInt) {
    count = anInt;
    setChanged();
    notifyObservers();
  }

  public void increment () {
    setCount(count + 1);
  }

  public void reset () {
    setCount(0);
  }

  // queries
  public int getCount () {
    return count;
  }
}
```

Listing 6.10 shows selected details of class *CounterUI*. The implementation for method *actionPerformed* shows how the controller function interacts with the model. Method *update* (from interface *Observer*) shows how the view responds to an update message from the model; it queries the model for its *count* and updates the *labelCount* widget in the GUI. The GUI class must register as an observer of the model and a listener for the button events.

Listing 6.10 Selected Details of Class *CounterUI* Showing View-Controller Methods

```
import java.awt.event.*;
import java.awt.*;
import java.util.*;
import javax.swing.*;
```

```java
public class CounterUI extends JFrame
                       implements Observer, ActionListener {

...
  // set a reference to the model
  protected CounterModel counter = new CounterModel();
...

  public void init () {
    ...
    // register with model and controls
    counter.addObserver(this);
    incrementButton.addActionListener(this);
    resetButton.addActionListener(this);
    ...
  }

...

  // View update method
  public void update (Observable o, Object arg) {
    if ( o instanceof CounterModel)
      labelCount.setText("Current value of count: "
        + String.valueOf(counter.getCount()));
  }

  // Controller event handlers
  public void actionPerformed (ActionEvent evt) {
    if (evt.getSource() == resetButton)
      counter.reset();
    else if (evt.getSource() == incrementButton)
      counter.increment();
  }

  /** Invoke this as a stand alone application.
  */
  public static void main (String args[]) {
    new CounterUI("MVC-Counter" );
  }
}
```

6.3.2 MVC Counter Example Using the Delegation (Beans) Approach

The design for this simple example is shown in Figure 6.7. The model class, *Coun-terBean*, extends *Object* and uses a delegate instance of *PropertyChangeSupport* to notify any views of changes in the state of the model. This is accomplished by

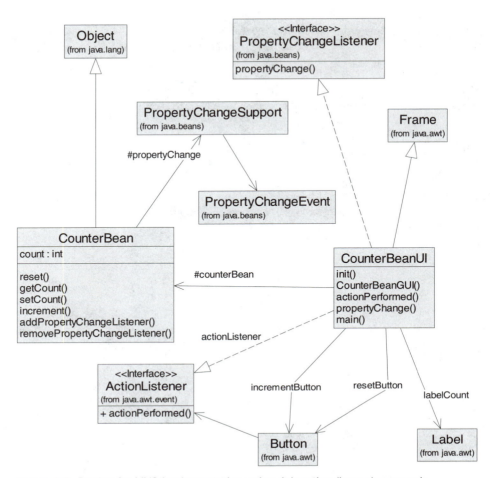

Figure 6.7. Design for MVC implementation using delegation (beans) approach.

directing the delegate to fire a *PropertyChangeEvent*. The view-controller class, *CounterBeanUI*, implements interfaces *PropertyChangeListener* for notification of changes in the model and *ActionListener* for handling controller events.

Since the model is using a delegate for its MVC duties, it may extend any class. In this case, it extends *Object*. The only change in the view-controller class is implementation of a different interface (*PropertyChangeListener* instead of *Observer*) for notification by the model's change monitor.

Listing 6.11 shows details for class *CounterBean*. The key method *setCount* must modify the internal state and then fire a *PropertyChangeEvent* via the delegate object *propertyChange*. Since the view-controller only has a reference to its model, the model must also include methods allowing a view to register as a listener for the property change event. The model implements two registration methods, for adding and removing property change listeners, by invoking the appropriate similar methods on the delegate.

Listing 6.11   Details of Class *CounterBean*

```java
/** class CounterBean - MVC Delegation Example
*/
import java.beans.*;

public class CounterBean extends Object {

  protected PropertyChangeSupport propertyChange
                          = new PropertyChangeSupport(this);
  protected int count = 0;

  // supporting commands for registration of listeners
  public synchronized void addPropertyChangeListener
                          (PropertyChangeListener listener) {
    propertyChange.addPropertyChangeListener(listener);
  }

  public synchronized void removePropertyChangeListener
                          (PropertyChangeListener listener) {
    propertyChange.removePropertyChangeListener(listener);
  }

  // model commands
  public void setCount (int anInt) {
    count = anInt;
    propertyChange.firePropertyChange("count" , null, null);
  }

  public void increment () {
    setCount(count + 1);
  }

  public void reset () {
    setCount(0);
  }

  // queries
  public int getCount () {
    return count;
  }
}
```

Listing 6.12 shows selected details of class *CounterBeanUI* that are important to the beans approach to MVC.

Listing 6.12   Selected Details of *Class CounterBeanUI*

```
import java.awt.event.*;
import java.awt.*;
import java.beans.*;
import javax.swing.*;

public class CounterBeanUI extends JFrame
                  implements PropertyChangeListener, ActionListener {

  protected CounterBean counter = new CounterBean();

...
  public void init () {
    ...
    // register with model and controller event sources
    counter.addPropertyChangeListener(this);
    incrementButton.addActionListener(this);
    resetButton.addActionListener(this);
    ...
  }
...

  // event handling - for model invoked event
  public void propertyChange(PropertyChangeEvent evt) {
    if ((evt.getSource() == counter)
       && (evt.getPropertyName().equals("count"))) {
      labelCount.setText("Current value of count: "
         + String.valueOf(counter.getCount()));
    }
  }

  // event handling - controller generated events
  public void actionPerformed (ActionEvent evt) {
    if (evt.getSource() == resetButton)
      counter.reset();
    else if (evt.getSource() == incrementButton)
      counter.increment();
  }

  public static void main (String args[]) {
    new CounterBeanUI("MVC-Bean Counter");
  }
}
```

A simple walk through is helpful in understanding this example. When the application is launched the constructor in class *CounterBeanUI* (not shown in the listing) invokes the *init* method, which registers the instance of *CounterBeanUI* as a listener with the model, *counter*, and with the two event sources used by the controller, *incrementButton* and *resetButton*. Suppose the user clicks the increment button (with label "Increment"). This causes an *ActionEvent* to be fired. Having registered as a listener for action events, our application is sent the message *actionPerformed*. Based on the details of *actionPerformed* in Listing 6.12, the *increment* message is sent to model *counter*. From Listing 6.11 the *increment* method in class *CounterBean* invokes *setCount*. Method *setCount* updates the value of *count* to be one larger than before and tells its *propertyChange* delegate to fire a *PropertyChangeEvent*. From this point we must look at the source code for *PropertyChangeSupport* to see what happens next. In essence, the *propertyChange* delegate posts the event and then handles it by sending the message *propertyChange* to all registered listeners (including our application object – an instance of *CounterBeanUI*). The steps in method *propertyChange* in Listing 6.12 are then executed to update the value of the *labelCount* widget in our application GUI.

There are many options for either approach to MVC in Java. For example, a model may have multiple views and controllers. These views and controllers may reside in one or more GUIs. A given view controller (GUI) may also have multiple models.

6.4 Summary

Implementation of a graphical user interface (GUI) in Java may be done by using appropriate classes in the abstract windowing toolkit (AWT) and Java foundation classes (JFC) directly or by using one of many available interface development environments (IDEs).

The major requirements for a GUI include:

1. a top-level container (instance of *Frame* or *JFrame*)
2. components for user interaction (instances of subclasses of *Component*)
3. layout of the components in their containers (using default or custom layout options)
4. enabling of components by implementation of event handling (using inner classes or external helper classes).

Java uses a delegation event-handling model. Any object that registers with an event source and implements the required listener interface may be an event handler.

Model, view, and controller (MVC) is a design pattern that organizes and separates responsibilities for storing, viewing, and modifying data that is part of an application.

6.5 Exercises

1   Build a simple GUI application that has two text fields for entering numbers. Place labels above the text fields to indicate Fahrenheit and Celsius.

The behavior of the application should be implemented so that each text field can be edited to change its temperature. The text fields are to be synchronized to show the same equivalent temperature. On each keystroke modifying the value of one temperature, the other temperature should be updated immediately to reflect the change. Hint: Use one of the key events. See class *java.awt.TextField* in the Java documentation.

2   You are to build a simple calculator that performs the basic arithmetic operations $(+, -, *, /)$. A typical layout is shown below. The application is to be built without the use of an interface development environment (IDE) such as JBuilder. You will find it helpful to use panels and a grid layout for the buttons. See classes *java.awt.Panel* and *java.awt.GridLayout* in the Java documentation for details and hints on using these classes.

3   You are to build a GUI application that explores the use of several key AWT components including event handling. The project will require the use of AWT components *Frame, Button, TextField, Panel, Label, Choice, CheckboxGroup*, and *List* as well as supporting classes *Color, Font*, and layouts *(BorderLayout, FlowLayout, GridLayout, null* layout). This project requires that the reader be familiar with many of the AWT classes or to gain that familiarity through independent study.

The project is to be done without the use of any Java IDE. This is to be a Java application (use a centered frame as main window). The frame will contain the following components with the indicated functionality:

* Three buttons labeled "Red," "Green," and "Blue" that set the background color for the frame. Clicking on any one button must disable that button, set the background color, and ensure that the other two buttons are enabled.
* A *Choice* object that also allows the user to set frame background color to red, green, or blue. The three buttons and *Choice* must be synchronized. Selected choice must agree with the current background color.
* Two *TextField* objects with *Labels*. One text field will display a number (labeled "Root") and the other will display the square of that number (labeled "Square"). Both text fields are to be editable. Changing the number in either text field will update the other with each keystroke.
* A *CheckboxGroup* object with options Normal and Reverse. The Normal option (default) is to set the relationship between the two text fields as

"Root"–"Square" corresponding to left–right. The Reverse options sets the relationship between the two text fields as "Square"–"Root" corresponding to right–left. On clicking one of the checkboxes, the labels for "Root" and "Square" will change to be consistent with this logic and the roles of the two text fields will also change.

- A *List* object that will display an event message for each user-initiated event. It must also handle *List* events for selection, deselection, and double clicking.

User Action	Event Message
Click background color button	"Background color set by Red Button"
Set background color with Choice	"Background color set by Choice – Red"
Edit text in "Root" text field	"Edited value of root"
Edit text in "Square" text field	"Edited value of square"
Select Reverse checkbox	"Role of numbers reversed"
Select Normal checkbox	"Role of numbers normal"
List item double clicked	"List item at index 3 double clicked"
List item selected	"List selected at index 2"
List item deselected	"List deselected at index 2"

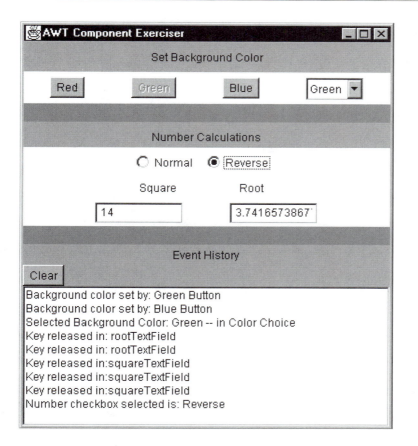

A typical layout is shown above for this application. The background is the area consisting of two thin stripes – one below the buttons and one below the Square and Root text fields. This example was built using only combinations of panels and predefined layout managers.

4   Using the inheritance approach to MVC build an application that displays two views of a two-dimensional point. The actual point may be selected by clicking the mouse within a region of the GUI window. A typical view of this application is shown below. It has the following features.

- Model – contains a single field, which is an instance of *java.awt.Point*.
- View – two views are provided: (1) a text label (instance of *java.awt.Label*) indicating the currently selected point and (2) a line drawn from the upper left corner of the selectable area to the point at which the mouse was clicked. A coordinate label generated using *Graphics* method *drawString* is added to the end of the line as shown in the figure.
- Controller – the controller intercepts mouse-click events in the white area of the GUI shown, capturing the coordinates of the mouse position. The model is updated to have this new value.

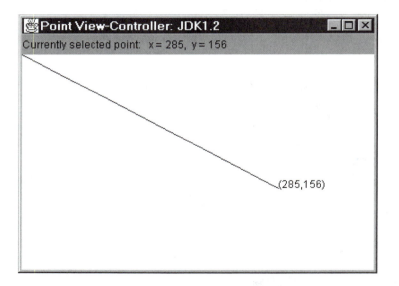

5   Repeat Exercise 4 using the Java beans (delegation) approach to MVC.

7

Errors and Exceptions

In a world with perfect users, perfect programs, and perfect hardware we would not have to concern ourselves with exceptions. Users would never enter incorrect data (e.g., enter an alphabetic character when a number is required). Hardware would never fail. Printers would always be on when our software attempts to access them. A hard drive would never be full when a program attempts to write to it. Such a world does not exist.

Brittle programs do indeed crash because of some failure in the input, the program logic, or the physical system supporting the application. Some crashes occur because of hardware interrupts (failures in a hardware component) or synchronization conflict (two or more segments of code attempting to modify the same data simultaneously). Program crashes may be catastrophic. If the rudder computer control system on an aircraft were to go down or the computer guidance system on a rocket were to fail, a catastrophe of major proportions might occur. Often a program crash results in a loss of input data – not a catastrophe but a profound annoyance to the user. One's confidence in using a program often disappears if such loss of data occurs frequently.

Exception handling involves defensive programming tactics that ensure a more benign outcome if your programming application should fail. Exception handling can ensure that input data are saved before a program is terminated, can notify the user that an input or hardware error has occurred and allow program execution to continue, or can bring the system to a stable and safe state before exiting the application. The context of the application and the nature of the exception determine the appropriate course of action.

In older languages only primitive mechanisms exist for indicating and responding to errors. One technique that has been used is to have a function return an error value (usually an *int*). This enables the caller (the segment of code that invokes the function) to detect that an error has occurred and to take corrective action. This technique is limited by the fact that often the error that occurs within a function disables the software application before being able to return an error value and notify the caller that corrective action must be taken. Examples of such errors include an index-range error in an array (attempting to modify an index location beyond the range in the array), sending a command to an object whose value is null (object not constructed), or assigning a string value to a numeric type. Many other types of errors also disable the software application before the function can return an error value.

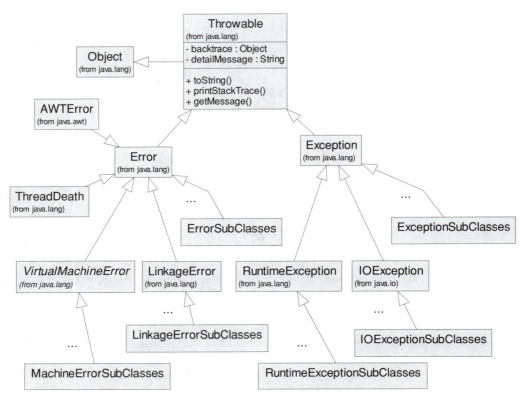

Figure 7.1. *Throwable* – errors and exceptions.

Java provides a powerful mechanism for exception handling that avoids the problems mentioned above. We explore Java's exception and error handling mechanism in this chapter and illustrate its use. Some languages speak of "raising" an exception or error. Consistent with Java terminology, we speak of "throwing" an exception or error.

7.1 Classification of Errors and Exceptions

Errors or exceptions in Java are always an instance of a class derived from *Throwable*. Generally speaking, errors are more serious than exceptions. A program cannot recover from an error (the program terminates); however, it may be able to recover from an exception and continue running. Many exceptions may be avoided through correct programming. There are a large number of predefined exception and error classes in the Java platform. We may also construct our own exception classes for use in an application.

The Java hierarchy of *Throwable* classes that support errors and exceptions is shown in Figure 7.1.

For brevity, additional subclass hierarchies are indicated in the figure with a generic name and an ellipsis (...). There are two major categories of errors: *VirtualMachineError* (an abstract class) and *LinkageError*. A *VirtualMachineError* is thrown whenever the Java virtual machine is broken or has run out of necessary resources (e.g., out of memory or stack overflow). A *LinkageError* indicates that an incompatible change has occurred between two linked classes. An *AWTError* is thrown whenever a serious AWT error occurs. An instance of *ThreadDeath* is thrown whenever an active thread is sent the zero-argument message, *stop()*. Method *stop()* is deprecated (its use is no longer advisable) in JDK 1.2; the reader is referred to the Java documentation for additional information.

There are two major categories of exceptions: *IOException* and *RuntimeException*. A *RuntimeException*[1] is thrown during normal operation of the Java virtual machine indicating an exceptional condition. A runtime exception generally occurs because of a programming error (index range error or sending a command or query to a null object). These programming errors are usually fixed by better programming. There are many kinds of runtime exceptions (more than twenty subclasses in JDK 1.2). An *IOException* is thrown as the result of failed or interrupted I/O operations. An *IOException* may occur because of trying to read past the end of a file, trying to open a malformed URL, or some other error associated with input or output. There are about sixteen subclasses of *IOException* and thirty-three other subclasses of *Exception* in JDK 1.2. Class *Exception* has other subclasses also.

7.2 Advertising Exceptions

If a Java method generates an exception, its header may choose (in some cases it is required) to include a reference to the type of exception that might be generated within the method – that is, advertise the exception using the *throws* keyword.

For example, the *readLine()* method in class *java.io.BufferedReader* has the following signature:

```
public String readLine() throws IOException;
```

The above signature indicates the possibility that things may go wrong and the method may throw an object of type *IOException*. This warns and requires any caller to set up an exception-handling mechanism.

The Java language specification refers to subclasses of *Error* or *RuntimeException* as **unchecked**. A very large number of exceptions in the JDK are subclasses of *RuntimeException*. All other exceptions are called **checked** exceptions. Different rules apply for advertising and/or handling **checked** versus **unchecked** exceptions.

You are not required to advertise every possible exception your method may throw. You are not required to advertise any errors. Only the first two (shown

---

[1] This is a poorly named class since all exceptions are really runtime exceptions.

in boldface type) of the following four situations require you to advertise that an exception may be thrown in your method:

1. **Your method invokes a method that throws a checked exception; and, your method chooses to not handle the exception** (e.g., your method uses *readLine( )* from class *BufferedReader*).
2. **You detect an exception and throw a checked exception with the *throw* statement.** The identifier *throw* is a reserved word in Java.
3. You make a programming error that generates a runtime exception.
4. An internal error occurs in Java.

Sometimes a method may throw several types of checked exceptions. Each must be advertised in the function header using a *throws* clause. An example is the following:

```
class FileApp {

  public Image loadPicture (String fileName)
    throws EOFException, MalformedURLException {
    ...
  }
}
```

As indicated earlier you do not have to advertise an *Error*. Errors are out of control of the programmer. You also do not have to advertise exceptions inheriting from *RuntimeException*. These exceptions are within your control; your program should be designed so they do not occur. The Java virtual machine has a default mechanism for handling all exceptions and errors.

A method must advertise all the checked exceptions it throws. It must also advertise or handle all checked exceptions thrown by any of the methods it invokes. The Java compiler will notify the programmer of any required but missing exception declarations.

Listing 7.1 illustrates a number of methods that throw checked and unchecked exceptions. A simple menu allows the user to choose one of the three commands in class *Advertise* for execution. Each of the three commands illustrates a variation on generation/advertising of checked or unchecked exceptions. For all exceptions in this example, exception handling is done by the runtime system. The runtime system has a default-handling mechanism (described later) for all exceptions and errors.

Command *required( )* invokes method *clone( )*, defined in *Object*. It requires that class *Advertise* implement the *Cloneable* interface (not done in the Listing). If this contract is not honored then method *clone( )* throws a *CloneNotSupportedException*. Since *CloneNotSupportedException* is a checked exception, advertising is required. Notice that both *required( )* and *main* must advertise the exception.

Command *notRequired( )* throws an *ArrayIndexOutOfBounds* exception because of the erroneous attempt to access an invalid index in *array*. This is a runtime exception that is not required to be advertised.

The third command, *mixed()*, is a little more involved. It takes an input class name string and creates a new instance of the indicated class using methods found in *java.lang.Class*. There are a number of ways this operation may fail. The JDK documentation tells us that static method *forName* throws a checked exception, *ClassNotFoundException*. Method *newInstance* throws two checked exceptions (*InstantiationException* and *IllegalAccessException*) plus two unchecked exceptions (*ExceptionInInitializerError* and *SecurityException*). The checked exceptions must be advertised as shown.

Since *required()* and *mixed()* advertise the checked exceptions they may receive, the *main* function must also advertise them (we will show later how any method may choose to handle exceptions as an alternative to advertising). Additionally, *main* advertises an *IOException* as required by method *readLine()* in *java.io.BufferedReader*. As a final touch and an introduction to the next section, we choose to throw a new *java.util.NoSuchElementException* (a runtime exception) if the user enters anything other than 1, 2, or 3 while executing the program options.

The Java compiler is very helpful in letting the programmer know which exceptions must be advertised. Should the programmer fail to advertise a checked exception, the compiler halts with an error that specifically states which exceptions must be advertised by which methods in the program. The Java documentation also provides this information.

Listing 7.1   Advertising Exceptions – The *throws* Clause

```java
/** Advertising exceptions
*/
import java.io.*;
import java.util.*;

public class Advertise {

  int value = 6;

  // cloning - throws checked exception
  public void required () throws CloneNotSupportedException {
    Advertise ad = (Advertise) this.clone();
  }

  // array index - throws unchecked exception
  public void notRequired () {
    int [] array = new int[3];
    array[3] = 25;
  }
  // instantiation - throws both checked and unchecked exceptions
  public void mixed (String name) throws ClassNotFoundException,
                                         InstantiationException,
                                         IllegalAccessException {
```

```
            System.out.println("New instance of" + name + ": "
                             + Class.forName(name).newInstance());
    }
    // main must advertise all checked exceptions
    static public void main (String [] args)
                               throws CloneNotSupportedException,
                               ClassNotFoundException,
                               InstantiationException,
                               IllegalAccessException,
                               IOException {

        BufferedReader keyboard =
                new BufferedReader(new InputStreamReader(System.in));
        Advertise ad = new Advertise();

        System.out.println("Cloning--------- 1" );
        System.out.println("Array index----- 2" );
        System.out.println("Instantiation--- 3" );
        System.out.print("\nEnter number:" );
        String choice = keyboard.readLine();
        System.out.println(choice);

        if (choice.equals("1" ))
          ad.required();
        else if (choice.equals("2" ))
          ad.notRequired();
        else if (choice.equals("3" )) {
          System.out.print("Enter a class name:" );
          String name = keyboard.readLine();
          ad.mixed(name);
        }
        else // throw an unchecked exception - no need to advertise
            throw new NoSuchElementException("No such choice" );
    }
}
```

7.3 Throwing an Exception

Since exceptions are objects, the syntax that must be used is:

```
throw new SomeExceptionClass();
```

In general when throwing an exception:

1. Find an appropriate predefined exception class (or write your own).

2. Construct an object of that exception class.

3. Throw (using reserved word *throw*) the exception object.

All exception classes provide constructors allowing the user to initialize a string parameter, *message* (there is a default message), which describes the problem that caused the exception. This message string may be used to provide useful information to the user. An example is:

```
throw new EOFException("End of file error occurred in method getData" );
```

Once a method throws an exception the method does not return to its caller. Control is transferred to the exception handler, if any (see Section 7.5). If no exception handler has been defined, program execution terminates if the application is a non-GUI application and displays the message in a console window if the application is a GUI application. GUI applications continue running in the presence of an exception (although not always properly). When debugging a GUI application it is advisable to keep a console window open to detect exceptions.

If you redefine a method from a superclass in your subclass, the subclass method cannot throw more checked exceptions than the superclass method that you redefine. If no checked exceptions are thrown by the superclass method, then the subclass must throw none. This is consistent with the constraint that a polymorphically redefined method in a subclass must have exactly the same signature that it has in the parent class.

When a method declares that it throws an exception that is an instance of a particular checked exception class, it may throw an exception of that class or any of its descendent classes. Declaring it to throw *Exception* allows an instance of any exception subclass to be thrown. Declaring it to throw a specific exception subclass provides more precise information on what the exception is.

7.4 Creating Exception Classes

A method that you write may need an exception object not available in the standard *Exception* classes. You must extend your exception class from one in the *Exception* hierarchy. A highly contrived example is shown in Listing 7.2, which throws a *SpecialFileException* on encountering a 'Z' character while reading a file. Notice that the only thing unique about this exception class is its name; this is typical of all exception and error classes. In essence we are cataloging exceptions and errors by unique class names and the value of their contained *message* strings.

Listing 7.2 Creating a Custom Exception Class – Selected Details

```
class SpecialFileException extends IOException {
// Thrown when reading letter 'Z' in a file

  // Constructors
  public SpecialFileException() {}
```

```
  public SpecialFileException (String message) {
    super(message);
  }
}


class SpecialFileReader {
  public String readSpecialData (BufferedReader in) throws
                                        SpecialFileException {
    // Throws exception if file contains letter 'Z'
    ...
    while (...) {
      if (ch == 'Z') // character 'Z' encountered
        throw new SpecialFileException("Z encountered");
      ...
    }
    ...
  }
}
```

7.5   Handling Exceptions

Any method that can receive an exception from one of its statements may choose
to handle the exception rather than pass it along with a *throws* clause (required
only for checked exceptions). The method may choose to handle both checked and
unchecked exceptions. Exception handling in Java is done with *try/catch* blocks.
The structure of these blocks is:

```
try {
  code that may generate an exception
}
catch (ExceptionType1 ex) {
  code that handles an exception of ExceptionType1
}
catch (ExceptionType2 ex) {
  code that handles an exception of ExceptionType2
}
...
```

If any statement inside the *try* block throws an exception, the remainder of
the *try* block is skipped. Control is transferred to the *catch* block that handles
the specific exception. If none of the *catch* blocks handle the type of exception
generated, the method containing the *try/catch* blocks exits and control goes to
the default exception handler. If no statement in the *try* block throws an exception, then the code in the *try* block executes normally and all *catch* clauses are
skipped.

If you declare the *ExceptionType* to be *Exception*, any exception will be trapped since all exception classes are derived from class *Exception*. When using multiple *catch* clauses, it is not advisable to use exception types that are hierarchically related. The result may be a compiler error or cause one or more catch clauses to be unreachable.

In general if the code of your method invokes (calls) one or more functions that throws a checked exception, you must handle the exception with *try/catch* blocks or pass the exception on by advertising that your method throws that type of exception. The choice of whether to handle or throw an exception is best made on an individual basis. A checked exception may be passed all the way to the runtime system using the *throws* clause at each calling level (as done in Listing 7.1). The default handling mechanism is to halt and display a default error message. Although not required, the programmer may optionally choose to handle unchecked exceptions as well by using a *try/catch* block or ignore them and let the runtime use its default-handling mechanism.

7.6 The *finally* Clause

When the code in a method throws an exception it does not execute the remaining code in the *try* block. Since the *try* block did not finish its work, some resources such as opened files or graphics contexts may need to be cleaned up. The optional *finally* clause allows this to be done.

An example is the following:

```
Graphics g = image.getGraphics();
try {
  Some code that might throw exceptions
}
catch (IOException ex) {
  Exception handling code
}
finally {
  g.dispose();
}
```

The *g.dispose()* will be executed after the exception-handling code. You can have a *finally* clause without a *catch* clause. In this case if an exception occurs in the *try* block, all the code in the *finally* block will be executed before the program terminates.

7.7 Putting It All Together – An Example

Listing 7.3 presents details of class *ExceptionGenerator*, designed to illustrate some of the properties of exceptions. This class contains methods that generate several different kinds of standard exceptions in Java. Some are checked and some are unchecked.

Listing 7.3   Class *ExceptionGenerator*

```java
/** Generates various kinds of exceptions
/
import java.io.*;

public class ExceptionGenerator {

  // Fields
  Counter myCounter;

  // Commands
  public void incrementCounter () {
    // Generate a NullPointerException - runtime
    myCounter.increment();
  }

  public void divideByZero () {
    // Generate an ArithmeticException - runtime
    int y = 6, x = 0;
    int z = y / x;
    System.out.println ("z = " + z);
  }

  public void arrayOutOfBounds () {
    // Generate an ArrayIndexOutOfBoundsException - runtime
    int [] data = new int [10];
    data[10] = 16;
    System.out.println ("data[10] = " + data[10]);
  }

  public void badCast () throws IOException {
    // Generate a NumberFormatException - runtime
    BufferedReader keyboard = new BufferedReader (
                         new InputStreamReader (System.in));
    System.out.print ("Enter an integer: " );
    String line = keyboard.readLine();
    int value = (new Integer(line)).intValue();
    System.out.println("value = " + value);
  }

  public void numericInput () {
    try {
      // Have user input a string representing a number
      BufferedReader keyboard = new BufferedReader (
                      new InputStreamReader(System.in));
      System.out.print ("Enter an integer: " );
      String line = keyboard.readLine();
      int value = (new Integer(line)).intValue();
```

```
        System.out.println("value = " + value);
      }
    catch (IOException ex) {
      System.out.println (
             "IO exception in reading user input." );
      }
    catch (NumberFormatException ex) {
        System.out.println ("Invalid integer entered." );
      }
    }


  public void numericInputWithException () {
    try {
        // Have user input a string representing a number
        BufferedReader keyboard = new BufferedReader (
            new InputStreamReader (System.in));
        System.out.print ("Enter an integer: " );
        String line = keyboard.readLine();
        int value = (new Integer(line)).intValue();
        System.out.println("value = " + value);
      }
    catch (IOException ex) {
        System.out.println (
               "IO exception in reading user input." );
      }
    }
  }
```

Method *incrementCounter* attempts to send a message to an uninitialized object, *myCounter*, causing a *NullPointerException* (unchecked) to be thrown. Method *divideByZero* throws an *ArithmeticException* (unchecked) to be thrown. Method *arrayOutOfBounds* throws an *ArrayIndexOutOfBoundsException* (unchecked) when trying to access an invalid index.

Method *badCast* can throw an *IOException* (checked) for serious I/O failure or a *NumberFormatException* (unchecked) for an incorrectly entered number (must be a valid integer string).

Method *numericInput* also invokes methods that can throw an *IOException* (checked) or a *NumberFormatException* (unchecked). It chooses to handle both exceptions by displaying a custom error message in the console.

Method *numericInputWithException* chooses to handle the potential *IOException* but not the *NumberFormatException*. This choice eliminates the need for a *throws* clause and places any exception handling for number format errors on the user.

Listing 7.4 presents an application class that allows the user to select and generate the various exceptions in class *ExceptionGenerator*.

Listing 7.4 Class *ExceptionsApp*

```java
/** Illustrates exception handling
*/
import java.io.*;

public class ExceptionsApp {
  // Fields
  ExceptionGenerator except = new ExceptionGenerator();
  int choice;
  BufferedReader keyboard = new BufferedReader (
                           new InputStreamReader(System.in));

  // Commands
  public void generateExceptions () {
    System.out.println ("1 --> Null pointer");
    System.out.println ("2 --> Divide by zero");
    System.out.println ("3 --> Array index range error");
    System.out.println ("4 --> Bad cast");
    System.out.println ("5 --> Bad numeric input");
    System.out.println ("6 --> Trap bad numeric input");
    System.out.print("Enter choice: ");
    try {
      choice = (new Integer(keyboard.readLine())).intValue();
    }
    catch (IOException ex) { // do nothing
    }
    switch (choice) {
      case 1:
        except.incrementCounter();
        break;
      case 2:
        except.divideByZero();
        break;
      case 3:
        except.arrayOutOfBounds();
        break;
      case 4:
        try {
          except.badCast();
        }
        catch (IOException ex) {} // Unhandled exception
        break;
      case 5:
        except.numericInput ();
        break;
```

```
     case 6:
       try {
         except.numericInputWithException();
       }
       catch (NumberFormatException ex) {
         try {
           // Second and final chance
           except.numericInputWithException ();
         }
         catch (Exception e) { }
       }
       finally {
         System.out.println ("In finally block." );
       }
       break;
     }
   }

  public static void main (String[] args) {
    ExceptionsApp app = new ExceptionsApp ();
    app.generateExceptions();
  }
}
```

Notice that, for *case 6*, in function *main*, we choose to handle the *NumberFormatException* that may be generated by method *numericInputWithException* by allowing the user one additional chance to enter a correct integer. Statements in the *finally* block are executed after a correct input (valid number) or after the second chance is completed (for an invalid numeric input).

The *switch* statement in Listing 7.4 allows the user to experiment with each of the exception conditions in class *ExceptionGenerator*. After each exception, the program terminates so the user may wish to run the program several times.

7.8 Catching Runtime Exceptions – An Example

Instances of *RuntimeException* and its subclasses are unchecked exceptions. Recall that unchecked exceptions always have a default exception handling mechanism in the runtime system without the need for a *throws* statement. The user is not required to catch or advertise these exceptions. However, the user does have the option to catch and handle the exceptions. This option was exercised in the *numericInputWithException* option in *ExceptionsApp*. As a further illustration we examine the difference between the default exception handler and a custom exception handler in the next two listings. Class *StringIndex* shown in Listing 7.5 uses the default exception handler and verifies that execution stops at the point of occurrence of an exception.

Listing 7.5 Class *StringIndex*

```
/** Unchecked exception - no throws statement required in signature
 *   Default exception handler
 */

class StringIndex {

  static public void main (String args[]) {
    String myString = new String("Hello" );
    System.out.println("myString[5] is: " + myString.charAt(5) );
    System.out.println("Execution stops on exception" );
  }
}
```

The *main* function in class *StringIndex* attempts to access index 5 of *myString*, which has index values from 0 to 4. A *StringIndexOutOfBoundsException* in package *java.lang* is thrown and handled by the runtime system as indicated below.

On running the program, we get the following output in the console window. The program terminates.

```
java.lang.StringIndexOutOfBoundsException: String index out of range: 5
Application Exit...
```

The user may optionally choose to catch and handle the exception to provide customized information about its source. The example shown in Listing 7.6 illustrates this option. The program terminates with the indicated output (in the console window) when the exception occurs.

Listing 7.6 Class *StringIndex2*

```
class StringIndex2 {
  static public void main (String args[]) {
    String myString = new String("Hello" );
    try {
      System.out.println("myString[5] is: "
                                    + myString.charAt(5) );
    }
    catch (java.lang.StringIndexOutOfBoundsException ex ) {
      System.out.println("Exception: (index = " + index
                      + ") Max index in myString is: "
                      + (myString.length()- 1) );
    }
  }
}
```

```
// Output in console window
Exception: (index = 5) Max index in myString is: 4
```

Clearly, the attempt to access index 5 of *myString* is a programming error that should be corrected instead of adding all the *try/catch* code to the example. How then can we justify catching exceptions generated by programming errors? If the block of code were large, with a complex algorithm for calculating the value of index, a *try/catch* block could be useful while testing the program. Of course, a good debugger could do the same thing without cluttering the source code. As a general rule, one should use exception-handling code sparingly.

7.9 Summary

Key points to remember about errors and exceptions include the following.

❏ Errors and exceptions may occur because of hardware problems, software glitches, or misuse of a program and may cause a program to crash with dire effects.

❏ Languages that support exception handling allow the software developer to catch and handle exceptions in a graceful way. Java provides a rich hierarchy of exception and error classes under class *Throwable*.

❏ Exceptions in Java come in two flavors – checked and unchecked. Checked exceptions that can be thrown within a calling method require that the calling method either advertise (by passing responsibility up the calling chain) the exception using a *throws* clause in its method header or handle the exception using a *try/catch* clause. There is no need to advertise errors or unchecked exceptions. Unchecked exceptions may be optionally handled with a *try/catch* clause. Errors should not be handled since they represent serious irrecoverable conditions. The best you can do is display a custom message in the console window. The runtime system has a default handling mechanism for all exceptions and errors.

❏ The optional *finally* part of a *try/catch* clause provides a way to clean up unfinished business as a result of an exception being thrown.

7.10 Exercises

1 Test and verify the results of all listings in this chapter. Write a brief description of each kind of exception capable of being generated including its cause and a brief discussion of the pros and cons of attempting to continue program execution after handling the exception. In other words, can the exceptional condition be fixed to allow continuation of the program?

2 Draw a complete hierarchical diagram of all the *Throwable* subclasses. You may use a class diagram tool or a simple indented list. Include a brief description of each class. Details are available in the Java documentation.

3 Currently the *generateExceptions()* method in Listing 7.4 prompts the user to enter a number indicating a choice. The chosen example is then executed and the program terminates. If the user enters other than a digit between 1 and 6, the application crashes with *NumberFormatException*. Modify the code to catch the exception thrown by a bad choice, notify the user of the required inputs, and redisplay the menu of choices. Also modify option 6 to allow an unlimited number of retries.

4 Build a GUI version of *ExceptionsApp* called *ExceptionsUI* that represents each kind of exception by a radio button. Run the program and report on your results.

8

Recursion

An essential and important part of computer problem solving is the development of algorithms – the detailed logic and steps required to solve a problem. All programmers are introduced very early to a number of useful programming constructs for building algorithms. These include assignment, branching, and iteration. Branching provides a means for conditional or alternative execution of steps in an algorithm. Iteration provides a convenient way to perform repetitive steps. Without branching and iteration the algorithms for even simple problem solutions would be either impossible or verbose and cumbersome. Another useful concept for construction of algorithms is recursion. Recursion is a construct that provides an alternative to iteration for repetitive steps. In many problems requiring repetitive steps we may find equivalent iterative and recursive algorithms as solutions.

What is recursion? A recursion may be described as the process of executing the steps in a recursive algorithm. So what is recursive? We sometimes tell our students, "If you look up 'recursive' in the dictionary, its definition is 'see recursive.' " We deduce from this anecdotal definition that a recursive algorithm is defined in terms of itself. The actual definition found in one dictionary,[1] "pertaining to or using a rule or procedure that can be applied repeatedly," is not very helpful.

In developing an understanding for recursion we rely on its use in mathematics, algorithms, and computer programming. From mathematics we find recursive functions defined in terms of themselves. In algorithms we create a specific block of steps (a function), wherein one of the steps in the function invokes the function itself. When the recursive algorithm is implemented in a programming language, we have a function that calls itself. As an example we define a recursive command in Java as

```
public void recursive () {
  recursive();
}
```

This command is recursive; however, it is pretty boring and useless. Additionally, it has the problem of calling itself in an infinite loop. Since computers do not have

---

[1] Abstracted from *Webster's College Dictionary*, Random House, New York 1995.

infinite resources, this method (if invoked) will cause the program to crash with a *StackOverflowException*. This tells us something about the way recursions are processed; they use a *Stack* (an important data structure covered in Chapter 11). In Section 8.1 we develop a list of essential properties for a well-behaved (and useful) recursive algorithm/function/implementation. In other sections we show the relationship between iterative and recursive solutions to the same problem, discuss the relative complexity of recursion, and present examples that illustrate single and double recursion.

8.1   Properties for a Well-Behaved Recursion

8.1.1   Essential Properties and Terminology

From our description and definition of recursion we may deduce the first and most important property of a well-behaved recursion. It must be recursive. Given a function, algorithm, or implementation, it must satisfy the essential property stated as:

> *Recursion essential property #1 – A recursive function, algorithm, or implementation is defined in terms of itself.*

A classic example from mathematics that is easily represented as an algorithm and implementation is the factorial function, n-factorial:

```
n! = n * (n - 1)!
```

where n is a non-negative integer and $0! = 1$.

Alternatively, n! is the cumulative product of all integers from n down to 1:

```
n! = n * (n - 1) * (n - 2) * (n - 3) * ... * (2) * (1).
```

Satisfying property #1, we may implement a Java function for the factorial of n as:

```
public int factorial (int n) {
  return n * factorial(n - 1);
}
```

This implementation has the same problem as our *recursive()* function; it recurses infinitely and causes a stack overflow. Furthermore, factorial is not defined for negative integers. For any input parameter value, *n*, the above implementation will eventually evoke factorial of a negative number. We need a logical way to stop the recursion. This is typically accomplished using a conditional test on the value of a sentinel parameter.

> *Recursion essential property #2 – A recursive function, algorithm, or implementation must have a sentinel parameter. The recursion continues or stops conditional on the value of this sentinel parameter.*

For the factorial example, the condition required for recursion to continue is clearly stated as part of the defining function – n must be a non-negative integer. The parameter n is the sentinel. The recursion continues only if the current value of n is non-negative. We may easily modify our Java implementation to include a test of this sentinel. For $n = 0$ we stop the recursion and return 0!, which is equal to 1 by definition.

By including a test on the value of our sentinel parameter, n, we get an implementation of *factorial* that satisfies properties #1 and #2.

```
public int factorial (int n) {
  if (n > 0)
    return n * factorial(n - 1);
  else
    return 1;
}
```

The third essential property for recursion is closely related to property #2 in that it helps stop the recursion. Suppose, for example, we erroneously implement factorial as:

```
public int error (int n) {
  if (n > 0)
    return n * error(n + 1);
  else
    return 1;
}
```

The typographical error that invokes $error(n + 1)$ drives the value of the sentinel parameter in a direction that never allows it to stop the recursion. We again get an eventual stack overflow. This leads to property #3.

> ***Recursion essential property #3 – A recursive function, algorithm, or implementation must drive the value of its sentinel parameter in a way to eventually stop the recursion.***

Our correct implementation for *factorial* satisfies this property as well. On each recursive invocation of *factorial*, the value of n is decremented by one. It will eventually reach a value of zero and stop the recursion.

The following additional terms for describing a recursion are by no means standard; however, they are useful in describing the steps in a recursion.

Recursive level – Each recursive call has its own level. The first time a recursive method is invoked, we enter the method at level 1. The second call enters the method at level 2 and so on.

Going in / Backing out – On entering a recursive method we talk of "going in" to deeper levels. This continues until the sentinel stops the recursion. We then talk of "backing out" of the recursion. A well-executed recursion goes in *n* levels (one level at a time) and then backs out *n* levels (one level at a time). We also say that the recursion "*bottoms out*" when stopped by the sentinel.

8.1.2   Steps in Executing a Recursion

We give a brief description of what happens while a recursive implementation is executed. It is helpful to use a simple example and show graphically what happens. Using pseudocode we develop a recursive function called *single(int n)*, where *n* is the sentinel parameter. Details for *single* are given in Listing 8.1.

Listing 8.1   A Recursive Function in Pseudocode

```
function single (int n) {
  if (n > 0) {
    statement1;
    single(n - 1);
    statement2;
  }
}
```

An invocation of function *single(2)* causes the sequence of steps shown in Figure 8.1 to occur. At each level, the runtime system stores an independent copy of *n* whose value is one less than at the previous level. The arrows indicate the sequence of steps. When the recursive call is encountered all processing at the current level is stopped and control passes to the next deeper level. On "backing out" of the recursion (after the sentinel stops the recursion), control returns to the precise point at which processing was stopped on "going in." In our example, control returns to *statement2*.

In this simple example, the sequence of execution for the statements that are part of the recursion is given by:

```
statement1; (at level 1; n has value = 2)
statement1; (at level 2; n has value = 1)
  <sentinel stops recursion; n has value = 0>
statement2; (at level 2; n has value = 1)
statement2; (at level 1; n has value = 2)
```

Statements prior to the recursive call are executed on going into the recursion; and, statements after the recursive call are executed on backing out of the recursion. The value of *n* at each level is preserved on going in and on backing out. The same is true for any local parameters that may be part of the recursive function.

8.2   Iteration versus Recursion

As mentioned earlier most problems have both an iterative and recursive solution. In this section we present both solutions for two examples. The first example is

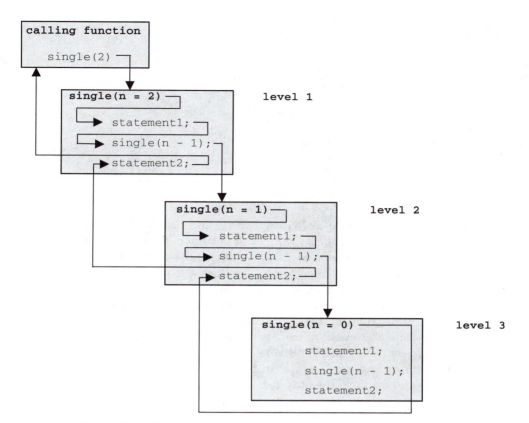

Figure 8.1. Graphical tracking of a simple recursion.

one for which an obvious recursive solution applies. The second example is one for which an obvious iterative solution applies.

8.2.1 Finding an Iterative Solution for a Recursive Problem

As an example of a problem with an obvious recursive solution, suppose we wish to prompt the user for an unspecified number of input strings and display the strings in the reverse order of their entry. How might we do this recursively? Recall from the previous section that statements before a recursive call are executed in order while going into a recursion and statements after a recursive call are executed in reverse order while backing out of the recursion. This maps nicely into the stated problem. A statement before the recursive call will prompt the user and accept an input string. A statement after the recursive call will display the string. The user may enter a special string (the character 'q') as a sentinel to stop the recursion.

Listing 8.2 shows a recursive solution to this problem. Prompting for user input is delegated to a helper method, *promptForString()*, to reduce clutter caused by necessary programming details and to focus on the recursive method logic.

Listing 8.2 Recursive Problem Solution – Example 1

```
public void getString () {
  String str = promptForString();
  if (!str.equals("q")) {
    getString();
    System.out.println(str);
  }
  else
    System.out.println("Reversed list");
}
```

On analyzing the example in Listing 8.2 we find that local parameter *str* is the sentinel parameter. Further its value is determined at each recursive level by the user in responding to *promptForString()*. Notice also that the input statement is outside the sentinel test block, whereas the normal output statement is inside the sentinel test block. This recursive function continues until the user enters *q* as a string. After the user enters *q*, the recursion stops. It executes the *else* clause only one time; then it starts backing out. On backing out it invokes the *System.out.println()* statement at each level, skipping the *else* clause.

As an example of the output obtained with this method, consider the following sequence of prompts and user inputs (in boldface). When the user enters **q**, the recursion stops and displays the output as indicated.

```
Enter string: Hello
Enter string: How are you?
Enter string: Goodbye
Enter string: q
Reversed list
Goodbye
How are you?
Hello
```

One thing we notice about this solution is its compactness. Where are all the different values of *str* stored? They are stored on the system stack (we will learn all about stacks in Chapter 11) and then retrieved on backing out of the recursion.

Now let's build an iterative solution to the same problem. With an iterative solution we must take charge of storing the entered strings in a structure that allows them to be accessed in reverse order for display. There are many options for a solution in Java, including an array or a *Vector*. Since the size of an array is static it is not a good conceptual match to a problem with an undetermined number of entries. After a discussion of *Stack* in Chapter 11, you may wish to revisit this problem. Using our current limited set of tools, we give a solution in Listing 8.3. Parameter *v* is an instance of *java.util.Vector* that is initialized external to method *getString()*.

Listing 8.3 Iterative Problem Solution – Example 1

```
public void getString () {
  String str = promptForString();
  while (!str.equals("q" )) {
    v.addElement(str);
    str = promptForString();
  }
  System.out.println("Reversed list" );
  for (int i = v.size() - 1; i >= 0; i--)
    System.out.println(v.elementAt(i));
}
```

How does the iterative solution compare with the recursive solution? Since the problem is simple, both solutions are simple. We suggest the recursive solution is more elegant; however, one may argue that its elegance comes from the fact that many of the details are being handled by the runtime system. The more important point is that both approaches produce a correct solution. The recursive solution is more compact and has fewer lines of code (a potential advantage for readers of the code).

8.2.2 Finding a Recursive Solution to an Iterative Problem

A problem that seems to be a natural for an iterative solution is one that must find the average of an array of numbers. The solution is to iterate over the array, computing the sum of all numbers, and then divide by the size. A simple solution is presented in Listing 8.4 using this iterative approach. Parameter *reals* is an array of type *double* initialized by the calling program.

Listing 8.4 Iterative Problem Solution – Example 2

```
public double getAverage (double [] reals) {
  double sum = 0.0;
  for (int i = 0; i < reals.length; i++)
    sum += reals[i];
  return sum / reals.length;
}
```

Next we consider a recursive solution to this problem. We must first find a way to express the average of an array of numbers in terms of itself. The only approach is to find the average of an array of n numbers in terms of the average of an array of the first $n-1$ numbers of that array. From the definition of *average* we have:

For an array of numbers, x[i]; $i = 1...n$, the average is

$$\text{Avg}[n] = \sum_{i=1}^{n} \text{x}[i]/n.$$

If we factor out the nth term we get

$$\text{Avg}[n] = \text{x}[n]/n + \sum_{i=1}^{n-1} \text{x}[i]/n.$$

The summation term with a little massaging can be expressed in terms of the average of the first $n-1$ terms in the array, yielding

$$\text{Avg}[n] = \text{x}[n]/n + ((n-1)/n)\,\text{Avg}[n-1].$$

This is our recursive function for finding the average of an array of n numbers. The sentinel parameter is n. For $n = 1$, the recursion stops and returns x[n]. The average of an array of one number is the number. Figure 8.2 shows this algorithm in action.

The figure shows the steps in tracking a recursive algorithm where the recursive call is embedded as a function call within an expression. The value returned at each level is the average of the first n values in the array (based on the value of n at that level).

Listing 8.5 shows implementation in Java of a recursive average computation done by method *getAverage*.

Listing 8.5   Recursive Problem Solution – Example 2

```
public double getAverage (double [] reals, int n) {
  if (n == 1)
    return reals[n - 1];
  else
      return reals[n - 1] / n
                    + ((n - 1.0)/n) * getAverage(reals, n - 1);
}
```

Recursive and iterative solutions are correct and very compact. Notice the concession to Java indexing from 0 to $n-1$ for arrays in both Figure 8.2 and Listing 8.5. Also, the $(n-1.0)$ term in Listing 8.5 is necessary to coerce floating-point division. Without it $(n-1)/n$ is always 0 using division of integers.

8.3   Relative Complexity of a Recursion

Considering that algorithms must lend themselves to both analysis and design, we are interested in how difficult it may be to analyze and design recursive algorithms. So far we have seen two useful recursive algorithms that were not too difficult to analyze or design. With more complex recursive algorithms we find that humans do not find recursive thinking to be natural. In this section we look at some of the options and features that make a recursive algorithm difficult to understand and techniques for managing that difficulty.

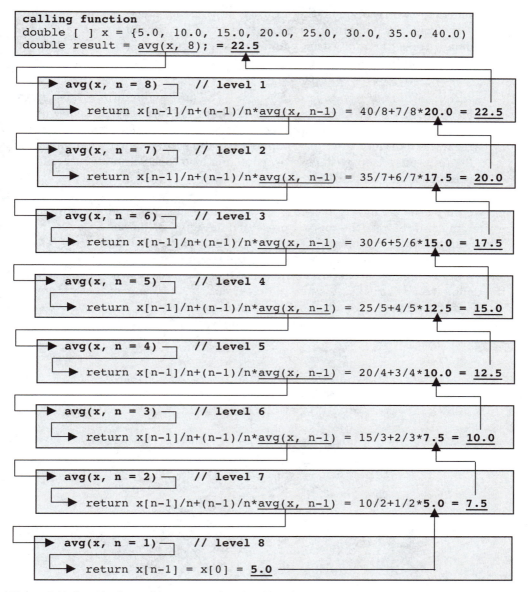

```
calling function
double [ ] x = {5.0, 10.0, 15.0, 20.0, 25.0, 30.0, 35.0, 40.0)
double result = avg(x, 8); = 22.5
```

avg(x, n = 8) ─┐   // level 1
   └► return x[n-1]/n+(n-1)/n*avg(x, n-1) = 40/8+7/8***20.0** = **22.5**

avg(x, n = 7) ─┐   // level 2
   └► return x[n-1]/n+(n-1)/n*avg(x, n-1) = 35/7+6/7***17.5** = **20.0**

avg(x, n = 6) ─┐   // level 3
   └► return x[n-1]/n+(n-1)/n*avg(x, n-1) = 30/6+5/6***15.0** = **17.5**

avg(x, n = 5) ─┐   // level 4
   └► return x[n-1]/n+(n-1)/n*avg(x, n-1) = 25/5+4/5***12.5** = **15.0**

avg(x, n = 4) ─┐   // level 5
   └► return x[n-1]/n+(n-1)/n*avg(x, n-1) = 20/4+3/4***10.0** = **12.5**

avg(x, n = 3) ─┐   // level 6
   └► return x[n-1]/n+(n-1)/n*avg(x, n-1) = 15/3+2/3***7.5** = **10.0**

avg(x, n = 2) ─┐   // level 7
   └► return x[n-1]/n+(n-1)/n*avg(x, n-1) = 10/2+1/2***5.0** = **7.5**

avg(x, n = 1) ─┐   // level 8
   └► return x[n-1] = x[0] = **5.0**

Figure 8.2. Graphically tracking a recursive algorithm for average.

Among the features of a recursive algorithm that impact its perceived complexity are the following.

Degree of recursion – A recursive algorithm may have one or more recursive calls in it. A single recursive call has degree one; an algorithm with two recursive calls has degree two, and so on. The ability to track the steps in a single recursion is usually achieved with a little practice and the use of graphical tools such as illustrated in Figure 8.2.

For degree two recursions, the difficulty of tracking steps goes up by an order of magnitude. After much practice coupled with an understanding of binary trees, the analyst may find tracking of double recursions to be relatively straightforward. There is a natural mapping between the structure of a binary tree and double recursion.

Relative position of recursive statements – The positioning of recursive statements within a recursive algorithm can have an impact on difficulty of understanding. Combinations of executable statements before and/or after the recursive call may add new complexity. If the recursive call(s) is imbedded in an iterative loop, with possibly changing loop constraints, the complexity is increased significantly.

We may use a graphical tool to help track the steps in a double recursion by expanding and refining the concept presented in Figure 8.1 for a single recursion. We distinguish the two recursive calls by going down to the left for the first and down to the right for the second. Consider the simple double recursion algorithm shown in Listing 8.6. All details including the sentinel test are left out except for the double recursive calls. Assume the recursion stops when sentinel parameter i <= 0. If this method is invoked with an initial value of i = 7, the recursive steps are as indicated in Figure 8.3. Additional complexity appears when we add statements before, between, and/or after the recursive calls.

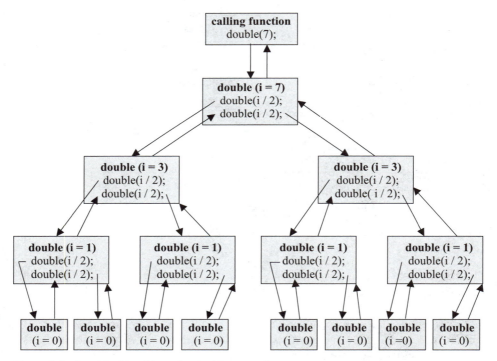

Figure 8.3. Graphical tracking of a double recursion.

Listing 8.6 Doubly Recursive Algorithm

```
double (int i) {
  if ( i > 0 )
    double(i / 2);
    double(i / 2);
}
```

We will learn more about binary trees and double recursion in Chapters 14 and 15.

8.4 Examples of Single and Double Recursion

In this section we present two Java classes that illustrate a number of single and double recursions.

Listing 8.7 provides details for class *Recursion1*, which includes eight single recursion examples. Output produced by each recursive method is included as a comment following the method in the listing. A brief description of the eight recursive methods is given below.

replicator – recursively print a string a specified number of times.

factorial – return the factorial of a number. The type *double* is used to extend the range of computable factorials.

average – compute the average of an array of numbers.

earlycall – a simple example where the recursive call occurs first.

latecall – a simple example where the recursive call occurs last.

findlargest – find the largest value in an array.

binsearch – use binary search algorithm to find an element in an array. This method invokes a private, recursive method *binarysearch* that does the work.

In addition to a *main* function there is a static method *pause* that allows the user to set a time delay between tests of the various recursive methods. This allows viewing of the results before scrolling to the next test.

Listing 8.7 Single Recursion Examples – Class *Recursion1*

```
/** File Recursion1.java - illustrating single recursion examples
*/
import java.io.*;

public class Recursion1 {

  // print string, count times
  public void replicator (String string, int count) {
```

```
      if ( count > 0 ) {
        System.out.println( "Count = " + count
                          + ", string is: " + string);
        replicator( string, count - 1 );
      }
   }
 }
/*
Test of recursive function, replicator
Count = 10, string is: Hello
Count = 9, string is: Hello
Count = 8, string is: Hello
Count = 7, string is: Hello
Count = 6, string is: Hello
Count = 5, string is: Hello
Count = 4, string is: Hello
Count = 3, string is: Hello
Count = 2, string is: Hello
Count = 1, string is: Hello
*/

   // return the factorial of num
   public double factorial (double num) {
     if ( num > 0.0 )
       if ( num == 1 )
         return 1.0;
       else
         return( num * factorial( num - 1 ) );
     else {
       System.out.println(
         "Factorial not defined for negative numbers" );
       return 0.0;
     }
   }
 /*
Test of factorial recursive function
 The factorial of 6 is: 720.0
 */

   // return the average of size numbers in inArray
   public double average (double[] inArray, int size) {
     int index = size - 1;
     if ( size == 1 )
       return inArray[index];
     else
       return inArray[index] / size + (size - 1.0)/size
         * average( inArray, size - 1 );
   }
```

```
/*
Test of recursive average function
The average of 8 numbers in inArray is: 22.5
*/

  // first statement is recursive call
  public void earlycall (int val) {
    if ( val != 0 ){
      earlycall( val / 2 );
      System.out.println( "val = " + val );
    }
  }
/*
Test of recursive call as first statement
val = 1
val = 2
val = 4
val = 8
val = 16
val = 32
val = 64
val = 128
val = 256
*/

  // last statement is recursive call
  public void latecall (int val) {
    if ( val != 0 ) {
      System.out.println( "val = " + val );
      latecall( val / 2 );
    }
  }
/*
Test of recursive call as last statement
val = 256
val = 128
val = 64
val = 32
val = 16
val = 8
val = 4
val = 2
val = 1
*/

  // return largest int in inArray
  public double findlargest (double[] inArray, int size) {
```

```
    double temp;
    int index = size - 1;

    if ( size == 1 )
      return inArray[ 0 ];
    else{
      temp = findlargest( inArray, size - 1 );
      if ( temp > inArray[ index ] )
        return temp;
      else
        return inArray[ index ];
    }
  }
/*
Test of recursive function to find largest in array
The largest of 8 numbers in inArray is: 40.0
*/

  // use binary search to find val in sorted inArray
  // return index in array of val if found; -1 if not found
  public int binsearch (double[] inArray, double val, int size) {
    return binarysearch( inArray, val, 0, size-1 );
  }

  // searches for index of val in inArray between low and high
  private int binarysearch (double[] inArray,
                            double val, int low, int high) {
    int mid;
    if ( low > high )
      return -1;          // val not in inArray
    else {
      mid = ( low + high ) / 2;
      if ( val == inArray[ mid ] )
        return mid;
      else {
        if ( val < inArray[ mid ] )
          return binarysearch(inArray, val, low, mid - 1);
        else
          return binarysearch(inArray, val, mid + 1, high);
      }
    }
  }
/*
Test of binary search for val in a sorted array
Binary search for value = 20.0 gives index = 3 (-1 means not found)
Binary search for value = 12.0 gives index = -1 (-1 means not found)
*/
```

```
public static void main (String[] args) throws IOException {
  String    greeting = "Hello";
  int       count    = 10;
  int       num      = 6;
  int       size     = 8;
  double[]  inArray;
  int       val      = 256;
  double    value;
  Recursion1 recursion = new Recursion1();

  BufferedReader br = new BufferedReader(
                    new InputStreamReader(System.in));
  System.out.print(
        "Enter time delay between experiments (seconds): ");
  int sec = new Integer(br.readLine()).intValue();

  // test of recursive function, replicator
  System.out.println(
        "Test of recursive function, replicator\n");
  recursion.replicator( greeting, count );
  Recursion1.pause(sec);

  // test of recursive function, factorial
  System.out.println(
        "Test of factorial recursive function\n");
  System.out.println( "The factorial of " + num + " is: "
        + recursion.factorial( num ));
  Recursion1.pause(sec);

  // test of recursive function, average
  System.out.println( "Test of recursive average function\n");
  inArray = new double[size];
  for ( int i = 0; i < size; i++ )
    inArray[ i ] = 5.0 * ( i + 1 );
  System.out.println( "The average of " + size
        + " numbers in inArray is: "
+ recursion.average( inArray, size ) );
  Recursion1.pause(sec);

  // Test of recursive function, earlycall
  System.out.println(
        "Test of recursive call as first statement\n");
  recursion.earlycall( val );
  Recursion1.pause(sec);

  // Test of recursive function, latecall
  System.out.println(
```

```
                "Test of recursive call as last statement\n" );
    recursion.latecall( val );
    Recursion1.pause(sec);

    // Test of recursive function for findlargest
    System.out.println(
      "Test of recursive function to find largest in array\n" );
    System.out.println(
        "The largest of " + size + " numbers in inArray is: "
        + recursion.findlargest( inArray, size ) );
    Recursion1.pause(sec);

    // Test of recursive function for binary search
    System.out.println(
        "Test of binary search for val in a sorted array\n" );
    value = 20.0;
    System.out.println( "Binary search for value = "
            + value + " gives index = "
            + recursion.binsearch( inArray, value, size )
            + " (-1 means not found)" );
    value = 12.0;
    System.out.println( "Binary search for value = "
            + value + " gives index = "
            + recursion.binsearch( inArray, value, size )
            + " (-1 means not found)" );
    Recursion1.pause(sec);
}

public static void pause (int seconds) {
    System.out.println("---wait " + seconds + " seconds---" );
    long time = System.currentTimeMillis();
    while(System.currentTimeMillis() - time < 1000 * seconds){}
    System.out.println();
}
}
```

Listing 8.8 shows details for class *Recursion2*, which presents two examples
of double recursion. The first method, *inOrderPrint()*, simply prints the sentinel
value as a statement between the two recursive calls. The second method, *per-
mute()*, accepts an array of characters and prints all permutations of the array.
For an array of size n, there are $n!$ permutations. Method *permute()* is doubly
recursive; however, it is difficult to track because the second recursive call is
embedded in a *for* loop with level-dependent loop parameters. The *main* function prompts for user input to control both recursion examples. The reader is
encouraged to type in details for both *Recursion1* and *Recursion2* and run the
examples.

Listing 8.8 Double Recursion Examples – Class *Recursion2*

```
/** A simple class to illustrate double recursion
*/
import java.io.*;

public class Recursion2 {

  // illustrate double recursion by printing values
  public void inOrderPrint (int index) {
    if (index > 0) {
      inOrderPrint(index/2);
      System.out.println("Index = " + index);
      inOrderPrint(index/2);
    }
  }

  // compute and display all permutations of an array of characters
  // uses a variation of double recursion
  public void permute (char[] inArray, int size) {
    int index = size - 1;
    char temp;

    if (size > 1) {
      permute(inArray, index);
      for (int i = index - 1; i >= 0; i--) {
        temp = inArray[index];
        inArray[index] = inArray[i];
        inArray[i] = temp;
        permute(inArray, index);
        temp = inArray[index];
        inArray[index] = inArray[i];
        inArray[i] = temp;
      }
    }
    else {
      for (int j = 0; j < inArray.length; j++)
        System.out.print(inArray[j]);
      System.out.println();
    }
  }

  public static void main (String[] args) throws IOException {
    char[] inArray;
    int index;
    Recursion2 recurse = new Recursion2();
    BufferedReader br = new BufferedReader(
                        new InputStreamReader(System.in));
```

```
    System.out.print(
            "Enter an index (int) for doubly recursive print: ");
    index = (new Integer(br.readLine())).intValue();
    recurse.inOrderPrint(index);
    System.out.print(
            "Enter a string for permutation (keep it short): ");
    String str = br.readLine();
    inArray = new char[str.length()];
    // copy str into inArray
    str.getChars(0, str.length(), inArray, 0);
    recurse.permute(inArray, inArray.length);
    }
}
```

8.5 Summary

Recursive algorithms provide an alternative way to represent repetitive steps in a problem solution instead of iteration. A well-behaved recursive function, algorithm, or implementation satisfies the following three essential properties.

Recursion essential property #1 – A recursive function, algorithm, or implementation is defined in terms of itself.

Recursion essential property #2 – A recursive function, algorithm, or implementation must have a sentinel parameter. The recursion continues or stops conditional on the value of this sentinel.

Recursion essential property #3 – A recursive function, algorithm, or implementation must use its sentinel parameter in a way to eventually stop the recursion.

The complexity of a recursion depends on the degree (number of recursive calls in its implementation) and, to a lesser extent, on the relative location of the recursive call(s). Single recursions may be tracked using a simple graphical technique. Double recursions may be tracked using a graphical binary tree structure.

Many algorithms have both iterative and recursive solutions.

8.6 Exercises

1   Using a text editor, type in the details for classes *Recursion1* and *Recursion2*. Run both examples for a variety of input choices and report on your results.

2   Write a recursive method that computes the nth Fibonacci number, $F(n)$ where:

$$F(n) = F(n-1) + F(n-2); \quad \text{for } n \geq 2$$

and

$$F(0) = F(1) = 1.$$

3   Implement an iterative solution to the factorial function.

4   Implement an iterative solution to the permutation of characters in an array.

5   Develop a tracking diagram for double recursion (similar to that shown in Figure 8.3), showing the sequence of steps in executing the recursive *permute* method of Listing 8.8. Show the diagram for an array of characters given by the string "abcd."

6   If we estimate the standard deviation (σ_x) of an array of numbers, $x[i]$, $i = 1...n$ using

$$\sigma_x^2 = \sum_{i=1}^{n}(x[i] - \mu_x)^2/(n-1),$$

where the mean value is estimated by

$$\mu_x = \sum_{i=1}^{n} x[i]/n,$$

develop both iterative and recursive algorithms for the standard deviation. Implement and test each in Java. Your test program should prompt the user for the value of n and build an array of n random numbers. It should then compute and display both the mean and standard deviation for the array of numbers.

PART TWO

Data Structures

9

Abstract Data Types

One of the conceptual pillars supporting object-oriented software development is the abstract data type (ADT). David Parnas[1] and others articulated this concept in the 1960s. For many years this concept has formed the basis for software construction, both object oriented and otherwise. All of the data structures to be presented in this book are formulated as abstract data types.

A data type is a program entity holding information that can be manipulated in a disciplined manner through a set of predefined operations. Predefined operations include **commands** that may be used to modify the value of the data type and **queries** that may be used to access the value of the data type. In the Java programming language an abstract data type is implemented using the **class** construct. The information structure (data structure) of the ADT is represented in the internal (usually private or protected) fields of the class. The commands are represented by methods that return type *void*. The queries are represented either by public fields or methods that return a nonvoid type representing field information.

Many software developers have found that ADTs aid in formulating clear and clean software architecture and promote greater understandability of the software and easier software maintenance. In structured programming languages such as C and Pascal the programmer must impose strict protocols in order to utilize ADTs. In the early 1980s two pre–object-oriented languages, Ada and Modula-2, were specifically designed to support and encourage the use of ADTs. With the advent of object-oriented technology during and after the late 1980s, the use of ADTs has become a central feature of software architecture.

In order to illustrate the basic ideas associated with abstract data types and their implementation in Java, this chapter first presents a simple ADT called *Counter* and then focuses on a more complex and useful abstract data type called *Fraction*. We learn about fractions in grade school and use them throughout our lives; however, except for Smalltalk, no programming language provides direct support for a type or class called *Fraction*. The good news is that we can build our own data abstraction and class for *Fraction*. Fractions are also called rational numbers since they may be represented as a ratio of integers. We also introduce in this chapter the concept of a *Laboratory* application that allows the user to test

---

[1] Parnas, David, "On the Criteria to Be Used in Decomposing Systems into Modules," *Communications of the ACM*, Vol. 15, No. 12, pp. 1053–1058, December 1972.

157

the behavior of abstract data types. We present laboratories for both the *Counter* and the *Fraction* abstract data types.

9.1 Counter ADT

Suppose that we wish to count events in various contexts. Each time an event occurs we wish to increment a counter by one. We need to be able to access the current value of a counter at any time. We need to be able to reset its value to zero. That is all.

We do not want to allow a user to set a counter to an arbitrary value (as would be the case with an ordinary integer variable). We do not want to allow a user to increment the internal count value by more than one in a given step. Therefore, the behavior of a counter is defined by the following methods (actions):

Counter ADT

1. **reset** – set internal count value to zero

2. **increment** – increase the internal count value by one

3. **countValue** – access the current count value.

We group this behavior into two categories: commands and queries. As indicated earlier, a **command** is an action that changes the internal state of an abstract data type without returning information. A **query** is an action that returns information about the internal state of the abstract data type without changing this state. The behavior of the ADT is the totality of its commands and queries. Listing 9.1 shows the Counter ADT implemented as a class.

Listing 9.1 Class *Counter*

```
/** Implements the Counter ADT
*/
public class Counter {

  // Fields
  protected int count;

  // Commands
  public void reset () {
    count = 0;
  }

  public void increment () {
    count++;
  }

  // Queries
  public int countValue () {
    return count;
  }
}
```

Since there is no explicit constructor in class *Counter* the default constructor sets the field *count* to its default initial value of zero. The only operations that may be performed on an instance of class *Counter* are *reset*, *increment*, and *countValue*. The first two of these are commands that modify the internal state of the *Counter* object and the third is a query that returns the internal *count*.

Suppose we wish to extend the *Counter* ADT by allowing the user to impose a constraint that limits the count value to a specified maximum. Listing 9.2 presents class *ConstrainedCounter*, which extends class *Counter*.

Listing 9.2   Class *ConstrainedCounter*

```
/** Implements ADT of a Counter with an upper limit on its count value
*/
public class ConstrainedCounter extends Counter {

  // Fields
  protected int upperLimit;

  // Constructor
  public ConstrainedCounter (int upperLimit) {
    this.upperLimit = upperLimit;
  }

  // Commands
  public void increment () {
    if (count ‹ upperLimit)
        count++;
  }
}
```

An explicit constructor is provided in class *ConstrainedCounter*, which sets the value of the new internal field *upperLimit*. A simple application that exercises the two classes *Counter* and *ConstrainedCounter* is presented. Its interface is shown in Figure 9.1.

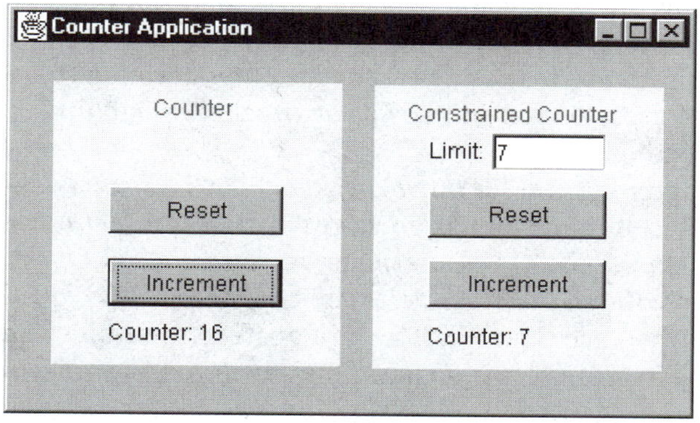

Figure 9.1. Example application using *Counter* and *ConstrainedCounter*.

9.2   General Properties of the *Fraction* ADT

A fraction can represent the number 2/3 precisely. It means that we have exactly two parts out of exactly three. Most computer languages are forced to use a floating-point representation for numbers like 2/3. Many fractions do not have an exact floating-point representation. The best we can do for 2/3 is:

```
2/3 = 0.6666666666666...  // depending on the precision
```

Based on these comments, we now provide a precise definition for a rational number (fraction).

Definition of Rational Number

A rational number, r, is one that can be represented by a ratio of integers:

```
r = numerator / denominator

where:
  - numerator and denominator are positive or negative integers
  - denominator cannot be zero
```

9.3   Requirements for Class *Fraction*

We wish to design a class *Fraction* that correctly represents the properties and definition for rational numbers. Additionally, we wish to provide commands and queries that make instances of class *Fraction* useful. Since this example is not intended as a commercial product we will not add methods for every possible use of fractions. Our *Fraction* class will override some of the methods inherited from its parent class(es) as desired. Table 9.1 gives a general specification of the properties we desire for class *Fraction*. Since the JDK (Java development kit) has an abstract class, *java.lang.Number*, with the wrapper classes for the primitive number types as extensions, it seems logical to let *Fraction* also extend *Number*. A *Fraction* is a kind of *Number*. For consistency, our general specification shows the inclusion and redefinition of methods inherited from *Number* and from *Object*. Class *Fraction* is a *final* class. The access modifier, *final*, designates a Java class as one that cannot be extended. This choice makes sense for *Fraction* because there are no extensions to the concept of a rational number. Other subclasses of *Number* in the Java platform are also specified as *final*.

Figure 9.2 shows a UML design diagram for our *Fraction* class. It directly extends *java.lang.Number*. Selected commands and queries inherited from *Number* and *Object* are shown for each class. The three methods shown in class *Object* should be overridden to satisfy specific requirements for an instance of class *Fraction*. All four methods shown in abstract class *Number* are abstract and must be overridden by *Fraction*. Our class implements interface *Comparable* (a promise to implement query *compareTo*).

Table 9.1 General Specifications for the *Fraction* Class

Property or Feature	Comments
Representation - numerator - denominator	numerator/denominator - an integer - an integer
Create/Initialize Options - default - specify numerator - specify numerator and denominator - from a String	 numerator = 0, denominator = 1 one-parameter set to numerator two parameters specify numerator and denominator String has form numerator / denominator
Store simplest form	Convert 10/15 to 2/3, etc.
Arithmetic operations	Add, subtract, multiply, divide
Conversion to String	Redefine inherited *java.lang.Object* method *toString()*
Equality test	Redefine inherited *java.lang.Object* method *equals()*
Comparison	Implement *java.lang.Comparable* interface
Field commands	Set values of numerator and denominator
Field queries	Get values of numerator and denominator
Equivalent forms	Ensure that 2/3 and −2/−3 are same; −2/3 and 2/−3 are same
Conversion to Numbers	Redefine methods inherited from abstract class *java.lang.Number*
Hashing	Redefine inherited *java.lang.Object* method *hashCode()*

The next step in our design is to add methods (constructors/commands/queries) to class *Fraction*. Table 9.1 gives a general specification of the operations required and/or desired.

When we couple this general specification with details in the Java platform the signatures shown in Listing 9.3 are obtained for our *Fraction* class. The *Comparable* interface is discussed in more detail in Chapter 10.

Listing 9.3 Precise Specification for Class *Fraction*

```
/** Class Fraction specification
*    An instance of Fraction is a rational number.
*/

public final class Fraction extends Number
                         implements Comparable {
```

```
  // Fields
private long numerator;
private long denominator;

// Constructors
public Fraction () {}
public Fraction (long num, long denom) {}
public Fraction (long num) {}
public Fraction (String fString) {}

// Commands
public void setNumerator (long num) {}
public void setDenominator (long denom) {}

// Queries - fields
public long numerator () {}
public long denominator () {}

// Queries - arithmetic operations
public Fraction add (Fraction f) {}
public Fraction subtract (Fraction f) {}
public Fraction multiply (Fraction f) {}
public Fraction divide (Fraction f) {}

// Queries - comparisons
public boolean equals (Object obj) {}
public int compareTo (Object obj) {}
```

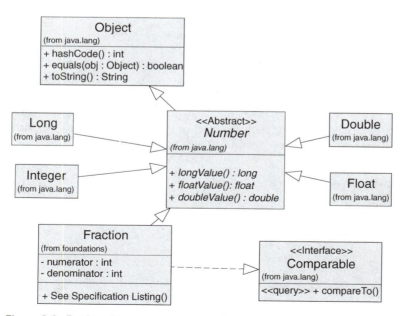

Figure 9.2. Design diagram for class *Fraction*.

```
// Queries - conversions
public int intValue () {}
public long longValue () {}
public float floatValue () {}
public double doubleValue () {}
public String toString () {}
public int hashCode () {}
}
```

Explanation of Listing 9.3

The class header specifies *Fraction* as a *final* class, which means it cannot be extended. *Fraction* extends abstract class *Number* and implements the *Comparable* interface. The fields *numerator* and *denominator* are of type *long* (for a wider range of values) and have *private* accessibility. Since *Fraction* cannot be extended and since it provides commands and queries for field modification/access, the use of *private* is justified.

All the constructors, commands, and queries shown in Listing 9.3 have public visibility. They define the public interface for instances of class *Fraction*.

Four constructors allow creation/initialization options as described in the general specification. Commands and queries for the fields are next. Methods *add, subtract, multiply*, and *divide* are the arithmetic operations. Method *compareTo* is defined as an abstract method in interface *Comparable* and must be implemented in *Fraction* since it *implements Comparable*. Methods *equals, hashCode*, and *toString* are inherited from *java.lang.Object* and overridden. Abstract conversion methods *intValue, longValue, floatValue*, and *doubleValue* in abstract class *java.lang.Number* are to be implemented.

We wish to override the default implementation for *equals* to create our desired result. The default returns true if and only if the fractions being compared are the same objects. We want *equals* to return true if the numerators and denominators of two fractions represent the same numerical valued fraction. We also override *toString* to create a string of the form "<sign>numerator/denominator." We include logic so that: (1) a fraction with numerator = 2 and denominator = −3 will display as "−2/3"; (2) a fraction with numerator = −2 and denominator = −3 (or numerator 2 and denominator 3) will display as "2/3." Method *hashCode* from *Object* returns a unique *int* value for any object. We redefine *hashCode* to depend on the *numerator* and *denominator* field values. The concept and algorithms for hashing are presented in Chapter 16. Conversion methods *intValue* and *longValue* clearly will provide truncated and imprecise values for all fractions except those reducible to whole numbers. Methods *floatValue* and *doubleValue* provide precision based on their internal accuracy.

9.4 Implementation Details for Selected Methods in Class *Fraction*

One of the more interesting constructors for creation and initialization of an instance of *Fraction* is the one that takes a *String* instance as input. Listing 9.4

shows an implementation for two methods in class *Fraction* that enable initialization of an instance from a string.

Listing 9.4   Creation of an Instance of *Fraction* from a *String*

```
// Create an instance of Fraction from a String
// The fString must have form "numerator / denominator".
public Fraction (String fString) {
  try {
    stringToFraction(fString);
  } catch (NumberFormatException ex) {
    throw new NumberFormatException("Error in fraction string" );
  }
}
...

// Internal method - extracts numerator and denominator from fString
private void stringToFraction (String fString) {
  int index = fString.indexOf("/" );
  if (index == -1){ // numerator only specified
    try {
      numerator = (Long.valueOf(fString)).longValue();
      denominator = 1;
    } catch (NumberFormatException ex) {
      throw new NumberFormatException(
                          "Error in fraction string" );
    }
  }
  else { // numerator & denominator specified
    if (index == fString.lastIndexOf("/" )) {
      try {
        setNumerator((Long.valueOf(fString.substring(
          0, index).trim()))).longValue());
        setDenominator((Long.valueOf(fString.
          substring(index + 1, fString.length()).trim())).
          longValue());
      } catch (NumberFormatException ex) {
        throw new NumberFormatException(
                            "Error in fraction string" );
      }
    }
    else // multiple "/" symbols
      throw new NumberFormatException(
                          "Error in fraction string" );
  }
}
```

Clearly, we expect the string to be of the correct form, that is, $-2/3$; however, we must protect against incorrectly formatted input strings. The preferred way to handle exceptional conditions (such as an incorrect input parameter) is to *throw* an exception. We (the developers of the *Fraction* class) may also choose to handle such an exception or we may let it pass to the user of the offending method (the constructor in this case). In our implementation of *Fraction* we choose to modify the message generated by the exception and then throw it to the user.

Explanation of Listing 9.4

The constructor passes the work of initializing a fraction from input parameter, *fString*, to a *private* method, *stringToFraction*. This method is strictly for internal use by class *Fraction* and is justified in having *private* visibility. The conversion process in *stringToFraction* consists of parsing a string of the form *numerator/denominator* to:

1. extract the digits prior to the "/" representing *numerator*,
2. verify that there is no more than one "/" character in the string,
3. extract the remaining characters following the "/" representing *denominator*.

If no "/" character is in the string, it is to be treated as an integer and represented as *numerator = extracted value* and *denominator = 1*. There are three ways an exception may occur in the conversion process. An exception occurs if there is more than one "/" character in the string or if the strings representing *numerator* and *denominator* cannot be converted to valid numbers of type *long*. Static method *Long.valueOf(aString)*, which produces a *Long* from a *String*, may be invoked in three places. If *aString* is not a valid number string, the *valueOf* method throws a *NumberFormatException*. You would have to look at the documentation for class *Long* or its source code to know this. In addition, the last *else* clause specifically throws a *NumberFormatException* if the *fString* contains more than one "/" character (based on the result of the boolean expression (*index ==* *fString.lastIndexOf("/")*). Commands *setNumerator* and *setDenominator* must call method *simplify*, whose purpose is to reduce numerator and denominator to their simplest form (smallest integer values).

Notice that method *stringToFraction* throws all generated exceptions, passing responsibility for throwing or handling to the calling method – the constructor. To make the *Fraction* class friendlier to a user, we choose to rethrow the exception to provide a more specific message in the constructor with a *try catch* clause as shown in Listing 9.4.

Details for method *simplify* are given in Listing 9.5. Since the *Fraction* class takes full responsibility for ensuring that a fraction is always in simplest form, method *simplify* has *private* visibility. The algorithm implemented in Listing 9.5 finds the greatest common denominator *(gcd)* for numerator and denominator, and then divides each by that value. It initializes *gcd* to be the smaller of numerator or denominator, before decrementing *gcd* until division of both numerator and denominator by *gcd* leaves no remainder or until *gcd* equals one. For example, (*f = 12/9*) – *gcd* is initialized to *9*, decremented in the *while* loop until *gcd = 3* (largest value for which the second term in the *&&-clause* is true), and then used to set *numerator = 4* and *denominator = 3*.

Listing 9.5 Details of Private Method *Simplify()*

```
private Fraction simplify () {
  long gcd = 0L;
  // set gcd to smaller of numerator or denominator
  if ( Math.abs( numerator ) > Math.abs( denominator ) )
    gcd = Math.abs( denominator );
  else
    gcd = Math.abs( numerator );
  if ( gcd == 0 )
    return this;
  while ( ( gcd != 1 ) && (( numerator % gcd != 0 )
                      || ( denominator % gcd != 0 )) )
    gcd--;
  numerator /= gcd;
  denominator /= gcd;
  return this;
}
```

9.5 Building a Fraction Laboratory to Test Class *Fraction*

In this section we introduce a concept that will be used to test correct behavior by implementations of abstract data type classes. More specifically, we develop an application called *FractionLab* that provides a graphical interface for testing each method (constructors, commands, and queries) in the public interface of class *Fraction*. The design for the application and how it connects to our *Fraction* class are indicated in the class diagram shown in Figure 9.3. The application uses two instances of class *Fraction*, as indicated by labels *fraction1* (*f1* in Figure 9.4) and *fraction2* (*f2* in Figure 9.4) in the diagram.

FractionLab is the main application class, *FractionLabUI* is the user interface class, and *FractionLabUI* has two instances of class *Fraction*. An initial screen shot of the fraction laboratory is shown in Figure 9.4. Instances *fraction1* and *fraction2* are initialized to 1/1.

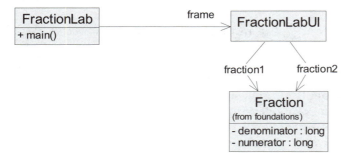

Figure 9.3. Class diagram for the fraction laboratory application.

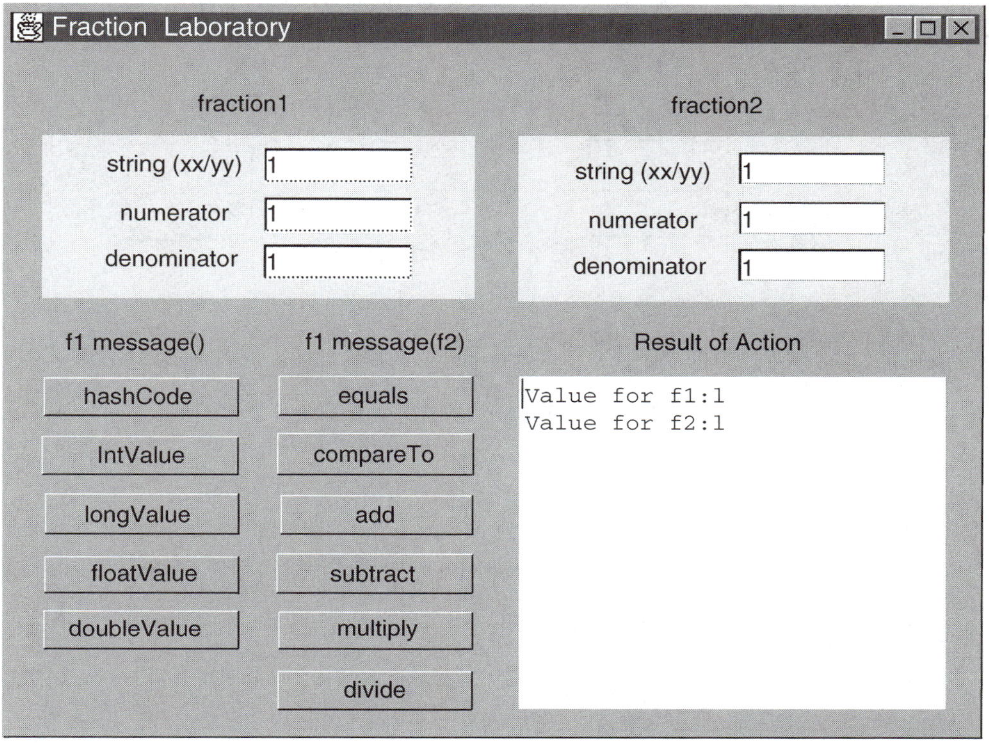

Figure 9.4. Initial screen shot of fraction laboratory application.

The user may enter new values for *fraction1* and *fraction2* by editing the numerator, denominator, or string representations for each followed by a carriage return ("Enter" key). Every action fires an event that is echoed with an appropriate message in the "Result of Action" list. Buttons in the left column enable messages to be sent to *fraction1 (f1)* only. Buttons in the right column enable messages to be sent to *fraction1 (f1)* with *fraction2 (f2)* as a parameter.

Figure 9.5 shows the fraction laboratory after a number of operations on *fraction1* and *fraction2*. The example values chosen in Figure 9.5 illustrate a number of important issues about the correct functioning of a well-designed *Fraction* class as well as some of the limitations of various methods that may be applied to instances of *Fraction*. The following features are of particular interest.

1. The string representation promotes the minus sign to the numerator (although it is really attached to the denominator for *fraction2*).
2. The fractions are equal (again the sign location is compensated).
3. The *intValue* of *fraction1* shows truncation.
4. The *floatValue* of *fraction1* shows round-off error.
5. The values for *fraction2* were actually entered as $4/-6$ (automatically simplified).
6. New value 2/0 entered for *fraction1* is rejected with error message.

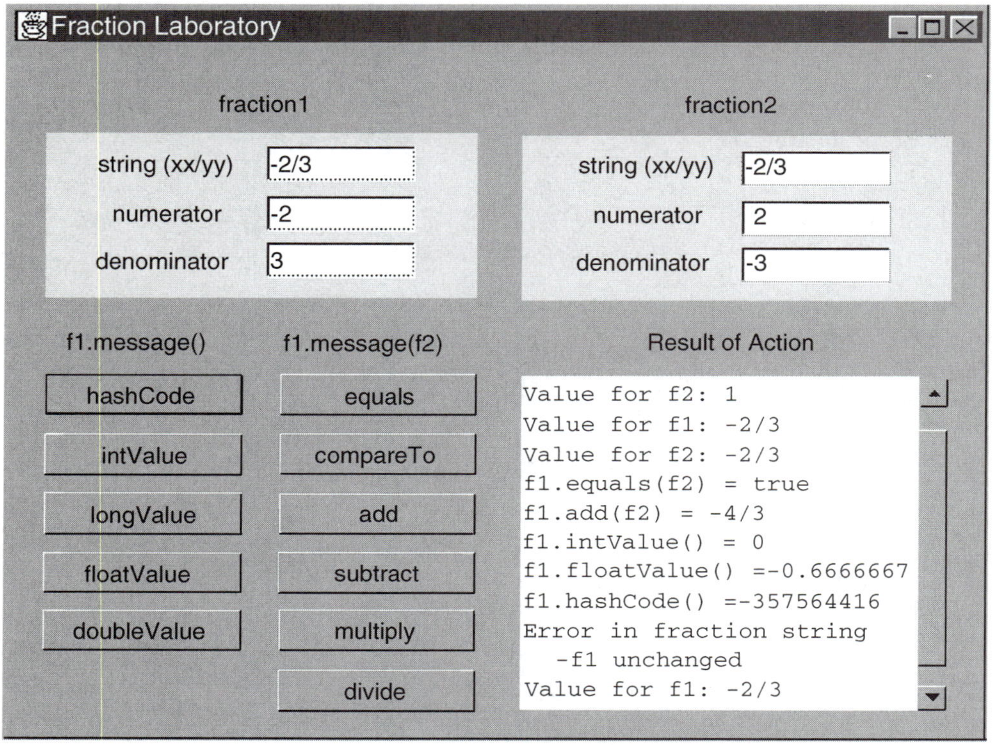

Figure 9.5. Illustration of some operations provided by fraction laboratory.

9.6 Documentation for *Fraction* – Generated by *javadoc*

The JDK comes with a tool called *javadoc* that automatically generates documentation for Java classes. It creates the documentation in HTML format and will read special tags and comments in the source code. This requires considerable extra effort on the part of the developer of a class; however, it provides a uniform way to document Java classes. A fairly complete set of documentation (*javadoc*) comments was added to the *Fraction* source file to illustrate this feature of Java. For details you are referred to the files in the docs folder of the notes for this chapter.

9.7 Summary

❏ In object-oriented languages, the *class* provides an excellent logical unit for encapsulating an abstract data type (ADT) and its operations.

❏ ADTs provide a convenient conceptual framework for data structures that are presented in following chapters.

❏ In this chapter we illustrate two simple abstract data types: *Counter* (including a specialization called *ConstrainedCounter*) and *Fraction*.

❏ GUI-based laboratory applications are introduced as a means of testing the behavior of an ADT. Laboratories are present for both the *Counter* and *Fraction* ADTs.

9.8 Exercises

1   The *Counter* ADT described earlier in this chapter has a very precise but limited specification. Define a new counter that may be decremented by adding a new command, *decrement*, to the specification for *Counter*. Using the source files provided in the *counter* folder of the Chapter 9 notes, modify *Counter.java* to provide a command to decrement. Modify the *CounterUI.java* file to add buttons for decrementing both the *Counter* and *ConstrainedCounter* instances tested by the counter laboratory.

2   The *FractionLab* application may be compiled and executed as is. It imports and uses a fully operational implementation of *Fraction* that is part of the *foundations* package. It may be compiled and launched using the batch file, *Goui.bat*. In the *support* folder in the *FractionLab* folder of the Chapter 9 notes is a file named *Fraction.java*. This file provides a skeletal implementation of *Fraction*. It compiles as is and may be used with the *FractionLab*; however, it does nothing useful. This exercise is a project to complete and test the implementation of this skeletal version of *Fraction*. The following steps are to be followed precisely:

    a. Create a working directory for your project and copy into it the files *FractionLab.java, FractionLabUI.java,* and *Goui.bat* from the *FractionLab* folder. Also copy the skeletal implementation file, *Fraction.java,* from folder *support* into the same directory.

    b. The local copy of *Fraction.java* now preempts the imported class *foundations.Fraction*, allowing the laboratory to be used for testing the new implementation.

    c. Complete the details of all commands and queries in *Fraction.java* and verify correctness using the *FractionLab*.

10

Containers as Abstract Data Types

A **box** of paper clips, a **stack of trays** in a cafeteria, and a **room** full of desks, chairs, lamps, and other furniture are containers. **An array of records**, a **queue** of customers at a movie theatre, a **bag** of groceries, a **set** of lottery tickets, a **dictionary** of words and their definitions, and a **database** of patient records are additional examples of containers. Some of the containers cited above – such as the box of paper clips, set of lottery tickets, and dictionary of words and their definitions – consist of identical types of objects, whereas the other containers consist of a mixture of object types. Each type of container has its own rules for ordering and accessing its entities.

It is important to make a distinction between the container object and the things that it contains. For example, we can distinguish the box that holds paper clips from the paper clips themselves. The box has an identity and existence even if it is empty. It is common to take home empty paper bags from a supermarket that may later be used as garbage bags.

This chapter, as its name implies, focuses on containers. It sets the stage for almost everything that will be done in later chapters. The study of data structures is the study of containers. In this chapter we delineate the behavior of many different container abstract data types. We establish a blueprint that shall form the basis for the concrete data structures that implement the container abstractions defined in this chapter.

Our goals for this chapter are the following:

- Use a combined top-down, bottom-up approach to designing a hierarchy of *Container* classes representing the major classical data structures. A single, final UML diagram is presented of the classes defined in this chapter.

- Use good object-oriented principles in the design.

- Present high-level user interfaces to the *Container* classes using the Java *interface*, a special kind of class that presents the abstract behavior for a kind of object.

- Present clear reasons for the chosen hierarchical relationships among the various *Container* classes.

- Develop a set of logically consistent commands and queries that define the behavior represented by each particular *Container* class.

- Follow good Java design principles when making decisions about exception handling, support for serializability, and redefinition of inherited methods. Consistent with good Java design principles, the *Container* interfaces, plus most supporting or implementing classes, will be in a new *package* called *foundations*.

Among the definitions for container is "anything that contains or can contain something." This leads us to look up the meaning of *contain*, which has a number of definitions. The definition of *contain* that fits our intention for software containers is "to hold or include within itself as constituent parts." In this chapter, we seek to develop a hierarchy of classes representing containers. The hierarchy is designed to include a wide variety of known classical containers used in computer problem solving and provide a framework for possible extensions. Our containers contain only reference types (objects). Containers of primitive types may also be constructed.

We separate the concepts and properties of a container from the details for implementing those concepts and properties. In fact, there are often a number of implementation choices for bringing to life the concepts and properties of any specific container. As a result of this separation of concept and properties from implementation details, we use the Java interface (a special kind of class) for building the container hierarchy. We focus on what you can do with a container and its objects and its behavior, not on the details of how those objects may be stored in the container.

We may distinguish different kinds of containers by considering the following properties:

1. Objects in the container may be ordered or unordered.
   - Order may depend on an inherent property of the container.
   - Order may depend on a property of the contained objects.
2. Duplicate objects may be allowed or disallowed.
3. Objects in the container may be restricted to a particular type.
4. Objects in the container may be accessible by an index.
5. Objects in the container may be accessible based on relative position.
6. Objects in the container may be accessible based on their value.
7. Containers may be distinguished by their connectivity (linear, nonlinear, etc.).

Consistent with the principle that the root of an inheritance tree represents the most general kind of object, we will develop a hierarchy of subinterfaces under a root interface called *Container*. Interface *Container* represents the most general of all containers.

10.1 The *Container* Hierarchy – Top Level

In developing a hierarchy of containers we begin at the top and define properties that are common to all containers. In developing new Java classes we should also consider if serializability is desired. A serializable object is one that can easily be written to or read from a file stream as an object (preserving all details of its fields). Support for serializability was added to the 1.1 release of Java. Since the need for serializability is dependent on the application, we make serializability available to all implementing classes for containers by letting *Container* extend interface *Serializable*. Since interface *Serializable* defines no methods it is simply a flag that enables serialization by the appropriate *Stream* classes. It is thus available if the application chooses to use it. Consideration of exceptions to be thrown is added to the interfaces as comments and deferred to the implementing classes.

The most general kind of container has the following properties:

1. does not care what kind of objects it contains
2. has no requirements about the order of the objects it contains
3. accepts duplicate objects
4. supports serializability
5. accepts commands to:
   - make itself empty
6. accepts queries that:
   - return the number of contained objects
   - answer true if the container is empty.

To represent this most general kind of container, we define the Java interface *Container* as shown in Listing 10.1.

Listing 10.1 Interface *Container*

```
/** Interface Container - top level container
*/
package foundations;
import java.io.Serializable;

public interface Container extends Serializable {

  // Commands - see subinterfaces

  /** Remove all objects from the container if found
  */
  public void makeEmpty ();

  // Queries

  /** Return true if the container is empty
  */
  public boolean isEmpty ();
```

```
/** Return the number of objects in the container
 */
 public int size ();
}
```

10.2 The Simplest Containers – *Stack* and *Queue*

Our approach to defining the container classes is a mixture of top-down and bottom-up logic. We began by defining the top-level interface *Container*. Next we consider the simplest of all containers, *Stack* and *Queue*.

A stack is a container with the following properties:

1. A stack has order that is a property of the stack itself, independent of the objects it contains. Order of the objects in a stack depends on the sequence in which they are inserted or removed. The ordering relationship is characterized as first in, last out or last in, first out.

2. Access to the stack is restricted to one location called the *top*. We may *push* (add) a new object onto the top, *pop* (remove) the object on the top, or query the *top* object without removing it.

3. We may command the stack to *makeEmpty* and we may query the stack to tell us if it *isEmpty* or return its *size*.

The *Stack* interface is an extension of *Container* so it inherits all methods in *Container* and adds only the new commands *push* and *pop* plus the query *top* as shown in Listing 10.2.

Listing 10.2 Interface *Stack*

```
/** Interface Stack - a first-in last-out container
 */
package foundations;

public interface Stack extends Container {

  // Commands

  /** Add an object onto the top of the stack
   */
  public void push (Object obj);

  /** Remove an object from the top of the stack
   *    Throw NoSuchElementException if stack is empty
   */
  public void pop ();
```

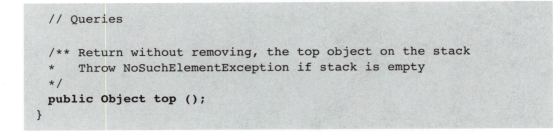

```
// Queries

/** Return without removing, the top object on the stack
 *    Throw NoSuchElementException if stack is empty
 */
public Object top ();
}
```

A *queue* is a container with the following properties:

1. A queue has order that is a property of the queue itself, independent of the objects it contains. Order of the objects in a queue depends on the sequence in which they are inserted or removed. The ordering relationship is characterized as first in, first out or last in, last out.
2. Access to the queue is restricted to two locations called the *front* and *rear*. We may *add* a new object at the rear, *remove* the object at the front, or query the *front* object without removing it.
3. We may command the queue to *makeEmpty* and we may query the queue to tell us if it *isEmpty* or return its *size*.

The *Queue* interface is an extension of *Container* so it inherits all methods in *Container* and adds only the new commands *add* and *remove* plus the query *front* as shown in Listing 10.3.

Listing 10.3   Interface *Queue*

```
/** Interface Queue
 */
public interface Queue extends Container {

// Commands

/** Add an object at the rear of the queue
 */
public void add (Object obj);

/** Remove an object from the front of the queue
 *    Throws NoSuchElementException if queue is empty
 */
public void remove ();

// Queries
```

```
/** Return without removing, the front object in the queue
 *   Throws NoSuchElementException if queue is empty
 */
public Object front ();
}
```

10.3 Supporting Interface and Classes

Before continuing our presentation of the hierarchy of container abstractions (interfaces), we discuss two important supporting abstractions: *Comparable* and *Association*. These abstractions are used to support some of the containers that are
defined in the following sections.

Ordered containers contain elements whose position within the container is
based on the magnitude of some feature of the contained objects. More precisely,
the objects in an ordered container must be comparable. Requiring the class of the
object to implement interface *Comparable* enforces this property. The details of
interface *Comparable* are shown in Listing 10.4, abstracted from the Java source
file for *Comparable* in package *java.lang*. *Comparable* contains a single query,
compareTo.

The *compareTo* query returns an *int* whose value depends on the relative magnitudes of the object receiving the message (receiver) and the parameter object
(obj). It returns −1 if the receiver is less than *obj*, 0 if the receiver is equal to *obj*,
and 1 if the receiver is greater than *obj*.

Listing 10.4 Interface *Comparable*

```
/** Interface Comparable
 */
public interface Comparable {

  // Queries

  /** Return -1 if the receiver is less than obj,
   *    0 if the receiver equals obj and
   *    1 if the receiver is greater than obj
   */
  public int compareTo (Object obj);
}
```

Class *Association* allows us to group a key with a value. There is an association
between a key and its value. Class *Association* plays an important support role in
our study of data structures where we need a container of associated key-value
pairs.

Dictionaries contain instances of *Association*. Keys organize the dictionary;
that is, we typically search for an object in the dictionary by looking up its key.

Lookup requires a test for equality. If the dictionary is ordered (based on the relative magnitude of contained keys), then we must ensure that the keys in any associations entered into the *OrderedDictionary* also be *Comparable*. We also choose to require that associations be serializable to be consistent with our choice that all containers be serializable. Listing 10.5 gives the details for class *Association*. It is a regular class, not an *interface*.

Listing 10.5 Class *Association*

```
/** Class Association
 *    An instance must initialize a key on creation.
 *    If used as a comparable Association, keys must be comparable and
 *       comparison is based on keys only.
 *    Note that equals() does not enforce the comparable feature and
 *       requires equality of both key and value.
 */
package foundations;
import java.io.Serializable;

public class Association extends Object
                        implements Comparable, Serializable {

  // Fields

  private Object key;
  private Object value;

  // Constructors

  /** Create an instance with specified key and null value
   */
  public Association (Object key) {
    this(key, null);
  }

  /** Create an instance with specified key and value
   */
  public Association (Object key, Object value) {
    this.key = key;
    this.value = value;
  }

  // Commands

  /** Set the value
   */
  public void setValue (Object value) {
    this.value = value;
  }
```

```
// Queries

/** return key
 */
public Object key () {
  return key;
}


/** Return value
 */
public Object value () {
  return value;
}


/** Return a String representation.
 *    Return a String of the form <key:value>
 */
public String toString () {
  return " < " + key + ":" + value + " > ";
}


/** Override inherited Object method equals()
 */
public boolean equals (Object obj) {
  if (obj instanceof Association)
    return (key.equals(((Association)obj).key)
            && value.equals(((Association)obj).value));
  else
    return false;
}


/** Implement Comparable method compareTo
 *    Compare based only on key; key must be Comparable
 */
public int compareTo (Object obj) {
  return ((Comparable)key).compareTo(((Association)obj).key());
}


/** Override inherited Object method hashCode().
 *    Return a unique int representing this object
 */
public int hashCode () {
  int bits1 = key.hashCode();
  int bits2 = value.hashCode();
  return (bits1 << 8)^(bits2 >> 8);
}
}
```

10.4   The *Container* Hierarchy

We next consider logic for partitioning our *Container* hierarchy to represent more specific kinds of containers. There are numerous potential criteria for creating a hierarchy of container abstractions. These criteria include ordered versus unordered, order based on container rules (e.g., position, index) versus contained object properties (e.g., relative magnitude), duplicates allowed or disallowed, or contained objects restricted to specific types (e.g., *Comparable, Association* instead of *Object*). In some cases the specific methods for a container are dependent on the internal structure of the container – for example, trees.

As with any good inheritance hierarchy, we are guided and constrained by the principle that methods defined in ancestor classes must make sense in all descendent classes.

We define additional interfaces that directly extend *Container*. They are *List, BinaryTree, SearchTable, Dictionary, Heap,* and *Set*. The distinguishing characteristics of each are given below. Figure 10.1 shows a class diagram for *Container* and its direct descendant interfaces.

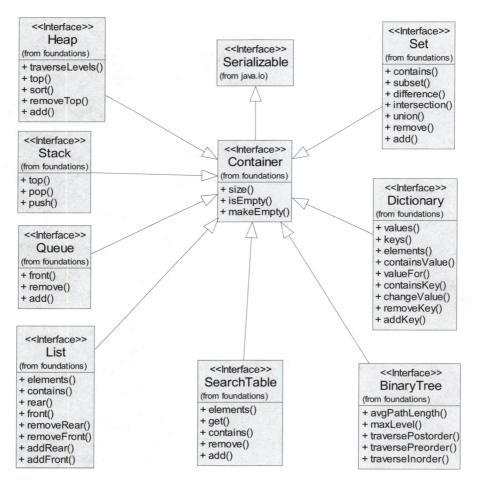

Figure 10.1. Top-level interface *Container* and its direct *descendants*.

List – A list has a linear structure. As a minimum requirement, we may access both ends of a list. Its contained objects have no particular order except as a result of the history of adding and removing objects at either end. The ends of the list may be characterized as *front* and *rear*. The list has some shared features with a queue; however, it has more. Variations on a list may be represented as extensions. These variations include **indexable** (allowing access at an index) and **positionable** (allowing access before or after a contained object). An ordered list (based on some property of the contained objects) is a special list that has fewer methods than *List*. It is implemented as a container whose methods enforce order (i.e., contained objects must be *Comparable*).

BinaryTree – A binary tree is a nonlinear structure consisting of binary nodes. Each node may have at most two offspring nodes (left and right). A tree is generally accessed at one location, a special node known as its *root*. A tree has commands and queries unique to its structure. There are several options for iteration over the objects in a tree. The objects in a tree may be ordered (represented by an implementation based on order of its contained objects) or not. An ordered binary tree (called a *BinarySearchTree*) is implemented as a *SearchTable* that enforces order based on properties of its contained elements (its elements must be *Comparable*).

SearchTable – The elements of this container must implement *Comparable*. An *OrderedDictionary* contains associations and is a kind of *SearchTable*. A special queue called *PriorityQueue* is also a kind of *SearchTable*. Classes *BinarySearchTree* and *OrderedList* implement *SearchTable*.

Dictionary – A dictionary contains *key-value* pairs (instances of *Association*). Commands and queries for a dictionary are centered on the keys. The keys must implement the *equals* query inherited from *Object*. A dictionary may also be ordered (on the keys). Interface *OrderedDictionary* requires that its keys be comparable. Thus *OrderedDictionary* extends interface *SearchTable* (instead of *Dictionary*), which enforces the comparable property. This design choice was not easily made. An *OrderedDictionary* is a kind of *Dictionary* (implying that it should extend interface *Dictionary*). However, Java provides no mechanism for enforcing a type constraint (e.g., forcing an *Object* to be *Comparable*) for parameters in redefined methods in a subclass. We choose the design that allows us to enforce comparability of keys for the elements of an ordered dictionary.

Set – A set is an unordered container with the constraint that no duplicate copies of contained objects are allowed. This is the only container, considered so far, that strictly disallows duplicates. A set includes methods applicable to mathematical sets.

Heap – A heap is a special binary tree (called a *complete* binary tree) whose contained objects obey the heap-ordering property. The heap-ordering property states that the object contained in a node in the tree is smaller than the contents of any node in its left and right subtrees. No other ordering relationship is implied or required.

In the following sections we present additional logic for various interfaces extended from *Container*. Please note that methods inherited from *Container* or other ancestor classes are not repeated in the listings. This allows us to focus on what is new in the subinterfaces and is consistent with inheritance rules of object orientation and of Java.

10.4.1   The *List* Interface and Its Descendants

Interface *List* extends *Container*. It is a linear structure with access to its *front* and *rear*. It adds several new commands and queries. The details of interface *List* are given in Listing 10.6.

Listing 10.6   Interface *List*

```
/** Interface List
*/
package foundations;
import java.util.*;

public interface List extends Container {

  // Commands

  /** Add obj at the front of the list.
  */
  public void addFront (Object obj);

  /** Add obj at the rear of the list
  */
  public void addRear (Object obj);

  /** Remove object from the front of the list if found.
  */
  public void removeFront ();

  /** Remove object from the rear of the list if found.
  */
  public void removeRear ();

  // Queries

  /** Return without removing the front object in the list
  *    Throw NoSuchElementException if list is empty
  */
  public Object front ();

  /** Return without removing the rear object in the list
  *    Throw NoSuchElementException if list is empty
  */
  public Object rear ();
```

```
    /** return true if the list contains obj
     */
    public boolean contains (Object obj);

    /** return an iterator on the elements in the list
     */
    public Iterator elements ();
}
```

Notice that method *elements* in Listing 10.6 has a return type of *Iterator*. Iterators provide sequential access to the user of each element in a container using the messages shown in interface *Iterator* in Listing 10.7. The user may send appropriate messages to each contained object during the iteration. Iterators will be used in several of our container classes. They allow the user to access each element in the container. Listing 10.7 is abstracted from *Iterator.java* in the Java package *java.util*.

Listing 10.7   Interface *Iterator*

```
/** Interface Iterator
 */

public interface Iterator {

    // Commands

    /** Remove the last element returned by next()
     *    Use only once after a call to next()
     */
    public void remove ();

    // Queries

    /** Return true if the container has an unvisited element
     */
    public boolean hasNext ();

    /** Return next element in the container
     *    Use only after hasNext() returns true
     *    Throws NoSuchElementException if no more elements
     */
    public Object next ();
}
```

Interface *List* has a number of potential subinterfaces representing specific kinds of lists. Included are *IndexableList* and *PositionableList*. Figure 10.2 shows the hierarchy of interfaces for lists.

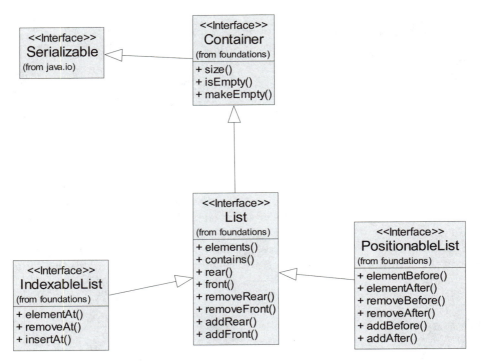

Figure 10.2. The *List* interface hierarchy.

Listing 10.8 gives details for interface *IndexableList*. An indexable list is a list whose elements may be accessed via an index. The index is of type *int*. This interface adds commands for adding and removing an object at a specified index and a query for accessing an object at a specified index without removing it.

Listing 10.8 Interface *IndexableList*

```
/** Interface IndexableList
*/
package foundations;

public interface IndexableList extends List {

  // Commands

  /** Replace object at index with obj
  *    Throws ArrayIndexOutOfBoundsException if index error
  */
  public void insertAt (Object obj, int index);
```

```
/** Remove an object at specified index
 *    Throws ArrayIndexOutOfBoundsException if index error
 */
public void removeAt (int index);

// Queries

/** Return the object at index without removing
 *    Throws ArrayIndexOutOfBoundsException if index error
 */
public Object elementAt (int index);
}
```

Listing 10.9 gives details for interface *PositionableList*. A positionable list is a list whose elements may be accessed relative to an object in the list, such as before or after. It adds commands for adding and removing an object before or after a specified object. The interface adds queries for accessing, without removing, an object before or after a specified object in the list.

Listing 10.9   Interface *PositionableList*

```
/** Interface PositionableList
 *    Objects in PositionableList must override equals() from Object
 */
package foundations;

public interface PositionableList extends List {

  // Commands

  /** Insert obj after target object in the list
   *    Throw NoSuchElementException if target not in the list.
   */
  public void addAfter (Object obj, Object target);

  /** Insert obj before target object in the list
   *    Throw NoSuchElementException if target not in the list.
   */
  public void addBefore (Object obj, Object target);

  /** Delete object after target object in the list
   *    Throw NoSuchElementException if target not in the list.
   *    Throw NoSuchElementException if target is last in the list.
   */
  public void removeAfter (Object target);
```

```
/** Delete object before target object in the list
*    Throw NoSuchElementException if target not in the list.
*    Throw NoSuchElementException if target is first in the list.
*/
public void removeBefore (Object target);


// Queries


/** Return object after target object in the list
*    Throw NoSuchElementException if target not in the list.
*    Throw NoSuchElementException if target is last in the list.
*/
public Object elementAfter (Object target);


/** Return object before target object in the list
*    Throw NoSuchElementException if target not in the list.
*    Throw NoSuchElementException if target is first in the list.
*/
public Object elementBefore (Object target);
}
```

10.4.2 The *BinaryTree* Interface

Listing 10.10 gives details for interface *BinaryTree*. A binary tree generally does
not require that its contained objects be ordered. Objects in the binary tree must
respond to the *equals* method inherited from *Object*. Interface *BinaryTree* adds no
new commands because the actual commands needed depend on the kind of binary
tree. Almost all binary trees have need for the five queries added by interface
BinaryTree. These new queries allow the user to know the maximum level or
average path length of the tree and to return three varieties of iterators. The
iterators allow the user to traverse (visit every node of) the binary tree using
preorder, in-order, or postorder traversal algorithms.

Listing 10.10   Interface *BinaryTree*

```
/** Interface BinaryTree
*    Contained objects must override equals() from Object
/
package foundations;
import java.util.*;


public interface BinaryTree extends Container {
    // Commands


    // Queries
```

```
    /** Return an in-order iterator on elements in the tree
    */
    public Iterator traverseInorder ();

    /** return a preorder iterator on elements in the tree
    */
    public Iterator traversePreorder ();

    /** Return a postorder iterator on elements in the tree
    */
    public Iterator traversePostorder ();

    /** return the maximum level in the tree, root is at level 1
    */
    public int maxLevel ();

    /** Return average path length for the tree
    */
    public double avgPathLength ();
}
```

10.4.3   The *SearchTable* Interface and Its Descendants

A *SearchTable* extends *Container* and holds elements that are of type *Comparable*. Duplicates are allowed. *SearchTable* has two subinterfaces: *OrderedDictionary* and *PriorityQueue*. Figure 10.3 shows the *SearchTable* hierarchy of interfaces.

In addition to the commands and queries inherited from *Container*, a *Search Table* adds commands to *add* and *remove* a comparable object. It also adds queries

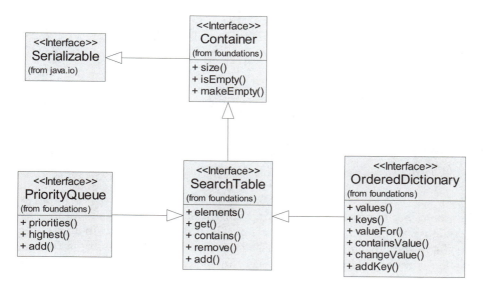

Figure 10.3. *SearchTable* interface hierarchy.

that allow the user to *get* a contained object, check to see if the search table *contains* an object, or return an iterator on all *elements* in the search table. Details for interface *SearchTable* are given in Listing 10.11.

```
/** Interface SearchTable
 *    The elements in this container must be of type Comparable.
 *    Duplicates are allowed for contained objects.
 */
package foundations;
import java.util.*;

public interface SearchTable extends Container {

  // Commands

  /** Add obj to the table; must be Comparable
   */
  public void add (Comparable obj);

  /** Remove obj from table, if found
   */
  public void remove (Comparable obj);

  // Queries

  /** Return true if the table contains obj
   */
  public boolean contains (Comparable obj);

  /** Return obj if in table, else return null
   *    useful when obj is a key & returns an Association
   */
  public Comparable get (Comparable obj);

  /** Return an iterator on all elements
   */
  public Iterator elements ();
}
```

An *OrderedDictionary* is a special kind of *SearchTable* that restricts its contained elements to be instances of *Association*. The order of elements in an ordered dictionary is based on the *key* of each association. One might also argue that an *OrderedDictionary* is a kind of *Dictionary*. Since Java does not support generic typing, we choose to let *OrderedDictionary* extend *SearchTable* instead of *Dictionary* to enforce the constraint that an ordered dictionary may contain only

Comparable objects. Recall that a *Dictionary* can contain any *Object*. Details for *OrderedDictionary* are given in Listing 10.12.

OrderedDictionary adds two new commands *(addKey, changeValue)* and four new queries *(containsValue, valueFor, keys, values)* to support dictionary operations while making use of inherited methods from *SearchTable* and *Container*. As a result, the user may iterate over the keys, values, and elements (contained associations) of an *OrderedDictionary*.

Listing 10.12   Interface *OrderedDictionary*

```
/** Interface OrderedDictionary
 *   A dictionary contains instances of Association: key-value pairs
 *   A class for a key must implement equals() from class Object
 *      AND interface Comparable for an ordered dictionary
 */
package foundations;
import java.util.*;

public interface OrderedDictionary extends SearchTable {

  // Commands

  /** Add an association <key-value>
   */
  public void addKey (Comparable key, Object value);

  /** Changes value for specified key
   *   Throw NoSuchElementException if key not found.
   */
  public void changeValue (Comparable key, Object value);

  // Queries

  /** Return true if key is in dictionary
   */
  public boolean containsValue (Object value);

  /** Return value for specified key
   *   Throw NoSuchElementException if key not found
   */
  public Object valueFor (Comparable key);

  /** Return an iterator on the keys
   */
  public Iterator keys ();

  /** Return an iterator on the values
   */
  public Iterator values ();
}
```

A *PriorityQueue* is a kind of *SearchTable* with the property that the order of contained elements is based on a *priority*. From its name, we might also assume that a priority queue is also a kind of *Queue*. While this may be true, its behavior is more closely aligned with the behavior of a *SearchTable*. Like the *OrderedDictionary*, a *PriorityQueue* must contain only *Comparable* objects. We choose to let *PriorityQueue* extend *SearchTable*. Details of interface *PriorityQueue* are given in Listing 10.13. It provides a new command to *add* an element to the priority queue plus two new queries. Query *highest* returns the contained element with the highest priority. The *remove* command inherited from *SearchTable* is interpreted to always remove the element with the highest priority. Query *priorities* returns an iterator over the priorities of contained elements, from highest to lowest.

Listing 10.13   Interface *PriorityQueue*

```
/** Interface PriorityQueue
*    Contained objects must implement Comparable
*/
package foundations;
import java.util.*;

public interface PriorityQueue extends SearchTable {

  // Commands

  /** Add an Association as key-value pair; priority is key
  */
  public void add (Comparable key, Object value);

  // Queries

  /** Return the object with highest priority
  *    Throw NoSuchElementException if priority queue is empty
  */
  public Comparable highest ();

  /** Return an iterator on the priorities
  */
  public Iterator priorities ();
}
```

10.4.4   The *Dictionary* Interface

A *Dictionary* contains associations and provides behavior that allows user interaction primarily through the keys. Although we think of a dictionary as a large book of words and definitions that happen to be in alphabetical order, there is no constraint that a dictionary is ordered. We typically require only the ability to add, remove, or look up elements based on knowledge of a key. There are ways to store the elements electronically and achieve this behavior without requiring the elements to be stored in order. *Dictionary* extends *Container* and adds three new commands and six new queries. Commands *addKey, removeKey*, and *changeValue* allow us to add or remove a key or change the value associated with a key in the dictionary. Queries allow us to check if the dictionary *containsKey* or *containsValue* or to get the *valueFor* a key. There are queries to return iterators *(keys, values, elements)* respectively on the keys, values, or elements in the dictionary. Listing 10.14 gives details for interface *Dictionary*.

Listing 10.14   Interface *Dictionary*

```
/** Interface Dictionary
 *   A dictionary contains instances of Association: key-value pairs
 *   A class for a key must implement equals() from class Object
 */
package foundations;
import java.util.*;


public interface Dictionary extends Container {

  // Commands

  /** Add an association <key-value>
   *   If the key already exists, set its value
   */
  public void addKey (Object key, Object value);

  /** Remove association with key if found
   */
  public void removeKey (Object key);

  /** Change value for specified key
   *   Throw NoSuchElementException if key not found.
   */
  public void changeValue (Object key, Object value);

  // Queries

  /** Return true if key is in dictionary
   */
  public boolean containsKey (Object key);

  /** Return value for specified key
   *   Throw NoSuchElementException if key not found
   */
  public Object valueFor (Object key);
```

```
/** Return true if the dictionary contains value
*/
public boolean containsValue (Object value);

/** Return iterator over the entries - Associations
*/
public Iterator elements ();

/** Return iterator over all keys
*/
public Iterator keys ();

/** Return iterator over all values
*/
public Iterator values ();
}
```

10.4.5 The *Set* Interface

A *Set* is a container that specifically disallows duplicate objects. Further, it supports typical mathematical operations on sets such as union, difference, and others. Interface *Set* extends *Container* and adds two new commands (*add, remove*) for adding and removing objects plus five new queries. Three of the new queries represent set operations (*union, intersection, difference*). One may test to see if the current set is a *subSet* of another set and check if the set *contains* an object. No iterator is provided for *Set*. Listing 10.15 gives details for interface *Set*.

Listing 10.15   Interface *Set*

```
/** Interface Set
*/
package foundations;

public interface Set extends Container {

    // Commands

    /** Add obj to the set
    */
    public void add (Object obj);

    /** Remove obj from the set
    */
    public void remove (Object obj);
```

```
// Queries

/** Return the union of receiver with s
*/
public Set union (Set s);

/** Return intersection of receiver with s
*/
public Set intersection (Set s);

/** Return difference of receiver with s
*/
public Set difference (Set s);

/** Return true if receiver is a subset of s
*/
public boolean subset (Set s);

/** return true if obj is in the set
*/
public boolean contains (Object obj);
}
```

10.4.6 The *Heap* Interface

A *Heap* is a special kind of binary tree satisfying the heap-ordering property. It typically may be implemented using a binary tree; however, the interface does not extend *BinaryTree* for several reasons. First, we add commands for adding *(add)* and removing *(removeTop)* elements (specific to a heap). A heap is one binary tree for which we do not much care about average path length, or the maximum level. It always satisfies the shape property of a *complete* binary tree. And finally, we usually are interested in only one kind of traversal called a level-order traversal. Interface *Heap* extends *Container* and adds three new commands and two new queries. In addition to *add* and *removeTop*, we have a new command to *sort* the elements in the heap. A sorted heap is still a heap. Query *top* allows us to access the top of the heap and *traverseLevels* returns a level-order iterator on the elements of the heap. Listing 10.16 gives details for the *Heap* interface.

Listing 10.16 Interface *Heap*

```
/** Interface Heap - contained objects must implement Comparable
*    root contains minimum value
*/
package foundations;
import java.util.*;
```

```
public interface Heap extends Container {

  // Commands

  /** Add obj to the heap, maintaining a heap
   */
  public void add (Comparable obj);

  /** Remove top obj from the heap, maintaining a heap
   *   throw NoSuchElementException if empty
   */
  public void removeTop ();

  /** Sort the elements in the heap, maintaining a heap
   *   use level-order heapsort algorithm
   */
  public void sort ();

  // Queries

  /** Return contents of the root - top of the heap
   *   throw NoSuchElementException if heap is empty
   */
  public Comparable top ();

  /** Return a level-order iterator
   */
  public Iterator traverseLevels ();
}
```

10.5   UML Description of Container Hierarchy

The relationships among the various *Container* interfaces, plus supporting interfaces and classes, are easily visualized by a class diagram. We present in Figure 10.4 a class diagram of all the interfaces in the *foundations* package with supporting class *Association* and supporting interfaces (*Iterator, Comparable, Comparator*) from the Java 2 Platform. Interfaces are identified by the stereotype ⟨⟨interface⟩⟩ appearing in the class name partition (the top part of each class icon).

Interface *Comparator* is part of the Java 2 Platform and is included for that reason. It provides a single method for comparing objects that do not implement the *Comparable* interface. We will not use *Comparator* in our implementations of the *Container* interfaces.

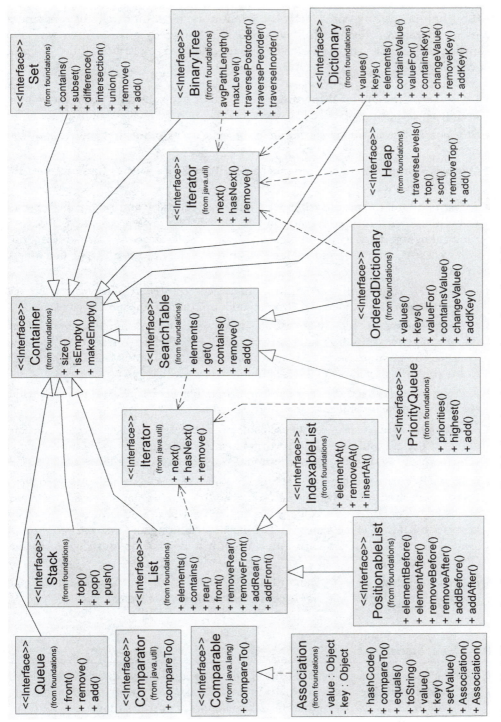

Figure 10.4. The core interfaces (plus supporting interfaces) and classes in package *foundations*.

10.6 Summary

In this chapter we have presented the framework for a hierarchy of containers by using the Java interface. In developing the hierarchy of interfaces we have followed the guideline that inherited behavior and type constraints must be valid at every level.

❏ *Container* is the top-level container interface. It provides only those commands and queries that may be used without modification by all container types.

❏ *Stack* is a simple linear container of objects. It exhibits first-in, last-out behavior.

❏ *Queue* is a simple linear container of objects. It models a waiting line with first-in, first-out behavior.

❏ A *List* is a linear container that allows access, addition, and removal of objects at both ends. An *IndexableList* is a *List* that also allows access, addition, and removal of objects at a specified index location. A *PositionableList* is a *List* that allows access, addition, and removal of objects before or after a specified object in the list.

❏ A *BinaryTree* is a nonlinear container of objects. Its structure consists of binary nodes that may have, at most, two descendants that are also binary trees.

❏ A *Heap* is a special binary tree that shares none of the specific behavior that applies to general *BinaryTree* containers. It is a "complete" binary tree that also satisfies the heap property (the object contained in a node is less than or equal to the contents of nodes in its descendants).

❏ A *PriorityQueue* is a container of *Comparable* objects. It has the property that the highest priority object is always removed next.

❏ A *SearchTable* is a container whose contained objects must be *Comparable*. The ability to test for containership and to get a contained object is part of the behavior of a *SearchTable*. Duplicates are optionally disallowed in our *SearchTable*.

❏ A *Dictionary* is a container of <key-value> pairs, that is, instances of *Association*. Its behavior is characterized by accessing, adding, and removing elements based on the keys. An *OrderedDictionary* is a dictionary whose elements are ordered by keys. Its contained objects must be *Comparable*, making an *OrderedDictionary* a kind of *SearchTable*. Duplicates are optionally disallowed in our *Dictionary* and *OrderedDictionary*.

❏ A *Set* is a container of objects with the strict behavior that duplicates are not allowed. The behavior of a *Set* is consistent with mathematical sets.

10.7 Exercises

1   Given that containers contain data (objects) and that the structure and form of how a container organizes these data are important, explain as clearly as possible why the Java interface (which specifically disallows fields except for static constants) is a valid construct for representing the container hierarchy.

2 Instances of class *Association* are used as contained objects in *Dictionary* and *OrderedDictionary* as well as other containers. Class *Association* overrides the *equals* query inherited from *Object* and implements *compareTo* from interface *Comparable*. Both *equals* and *compareTo* test for equality between two instances of *Association*. Each defines a different test for equality. Explain the difference and why it is desirable.

3 Of all the containers, *Set* is the only one that strictly disallows duplicates; however, other containers may optionally disallow duplicates. Specifically, dictionaries and search tables may disallow duplicates. For each container interface, describe briefly the pros and cons or desirability for allowing/disallowing duplicates.

4 Using your knowledge of the behavior of a *Queue* and of a *PriorityQueue*, explain how a *PriorityQueue* (where objects are removed based on priority) has anything in common with a *Queue*.

5 A *Heap* is defined as a special kind of *BinaryTree* and a *BinarySearchTree* is a kind of *BinaryTree*, yet neither of these two containers is an extension of *BinaryTree*. Explain why.

6 For any container to be useful, we must be able to add and remove objects, yet *Container* does not define any commands for adding and removing. Why?

7 In terms of accessing all the elements in a container, how does an *Iterator* object offer an advantage over simple query methods that actually iterate through all objects in the container for you? When is it better to use a simple query as opposed to returning an *Iterator*?

8 In implementing a container abstract data type, we are constrained to use the features of the programming language of choice. Arrays have been a part of most modern programming languages and provide one choice for the underlying data structure in a container implementation. What other choice(s) are provided by the Java programming language (independently of its predefined classes such as *Vector*, etc.)? List all options and justify your answer. Do other object-oriented languages provide the same choice(s)? Do non–object-oriented languages provide the same choice(s)?

9 If Java provided the capability for generic types, how would the *Container* hierarchy be affected? Specifically, how would interface *Container* change?

10 Given that elements in a *SearchTable* or any of its subinterfaces must be *Comparable*, how would we place objects into a search table whose classes are already defined and do not implement interface *Comparable*?

11 Present arguments for and against placing the container interfaces in a package. We clearly have chosen to place them in a package called *foundations*. What advantages have we gained and what compromises have been made as a result of this decision?

12   There are numerous examples (the Java collections classes, the Java generic library, libraries defined by other authors of CS 2 books, standard libraries in other languages) of "container" classes. Each uses its own logic for organizing, naming, and defining the interfaces/classes representing the containers. Make a list of specific containers and their properties, showing similarities and differences. You may optionally choose from containers in one or more of the above examples and contrast your results with those presented in this chapter.

11

Stack and Queue

11.1 The Stack

A stack is one of the simplest and perhaps most widely used container types. Many software applications require the logical equivalent of piling objects on top of each other. The only object that may be accessed from a stack is the most recent object placed onto the stack. We refer to this ordering as last in, first out.

A stack's commands and queries define its behavior. These methods specify what one can do with a stack object. The interface for *Stack* given in Listing 10.2 and repeated in Listing 11.1 provides a precise specification of the behavior of a stack.

The *push* command is used to add a new object to a stack. The *pop* command is used to remove the object on the top of the stack. The *top* query returns the object on top of the stack without removing it. A command for removing all objects from the stack *(makeEmpty)* and queries for determining whether the stack is empty *(isEmpty)* and the number of elements on the stack *(size)* are inherited from class *Container.*

Listing 11.1 Interface *Stack*

```
/** Interface Stack
*/
package foundations;
public interface Stack extends Container {

  // Commands

  /** Add an object onto the top of the stack
  */
  public void push (Object obj);

  /** Remove an object from the top of the stack
  *    Throws NoSuchElementException if stack is empty
  */
  public void pop ();

  // Queries
```

```
/** Return without removing, the top object on the stack
 *   Throws NoSuchElementException if stack is empty
 */
 public Object top ();
}
```

We consider two implementations of a stack in this chapter. The first, *ArrayStack*, is a fixed implementation of specified size. Once this size is set, it cannot be changed. Any insertions that exceed the capacity of this fixed size will result in an error. The second implementation presented in this chapter, *LinkedStack*, is a dynamic implementation. The size of the stack grows on demand as items are inserted. As we shall see later, accessing fixed structures is generally faster than accessing dynamic structures. We consider each type of stack in the sections that follow.

11.2 *ArrayStack*

In the fixed stack implementation *ArrayStack*, an internal array field *data* is used to hold the objects that comprise the stack.

Figure 11.1 depicts the internal structure of the *ArrayStack* when the capacity is set to 5 and the stack contains 3 objects (in indices 1, 2, and 3). In the interest of making the algorithms easier to understand, we use "natural" indexing starting at index 1. The first index, index 0, is not used at all. Objects *obj1*, *obj2*, and *obj3* are pushed (inserted) successively onto the stack.

We examine the algorithmic details of the commands *push* and *pop* and the query *top*.

push
- Increment *top*.
- Insert the new element into the index position *top* in the array.

pop
- Decrement *top*.

top
- Return the element in index *top*.

Listing 11.2 presents the details of class *ArrayStack*.

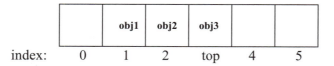

index: 0   1   2   top   4   5

Figure 11.1. Internal structure of *ArrayStack*.

Listing 11.2 Class *ArrayStack*

```java
/** A fixed stack implementation
*/
package foundations;
import java.util.*;
public class ArrayStack implements Stack {

  // Fields

  private int capacity = 101;    // Default value
  private Object [] data;         // Holds the information in the stack
  private int top = 0;           // Tracks last element inserted

  // Constructors

  public ArrayStack () {
    this(101);
  }

  public ArrayStack (int capacity) {
    this.capacity = capacity;
    data = new Object[capacity + 1];
  }

  // Commands

  public void push (Object item) {
    top++;
    try {
      data[top] = item;
    }
    catch (ArrayIndexOutOfBoundsException ex) {
      top--;
      throw new ArrayIndexOutOfBoundsException(
                              "Stack capacity exceeded." );
    }
  }

  public void pop () {
    if (isEmpty())
      throw new NoSuchElementException("Stack is empty." );
    else {
      data[top] = null;
      top--;
    }
  }
```

```
public void makeEmpty () {
  top = 0;
}

// Queries

public Object top () {
  if (isEmpty())
    throw new NoSuchElementException("Stack is empty.");
  else
    return data[top];
  }

public boolean isEmpty () {
  return top == 0;
}

public int size () {
  return top;
}

static public void main(String[] args) {
  ArrayStack myStack = new ArrayStack(5);
  myStack.push(new Integer(1)); // obj1 in Figure 11.1
  myStack.push(new Integer(2)); // obj2 in Figure 11.1
  myStack.push(new Integer(3)); // obj3 in Figure 11.1
  System.out.println("myStack.size() = " + myStack.size());
  myStack.pop();
  System.out.println("myStack.size() = " + myStack.size());
  System.out.println ("myStack.top() = " + myStack.top());
  }
}
```

Output of Listing 11.2

```
myStack.size() = 3
myStack.size() = 2
myStack.top() = 2
```

Explanation of Listing 11.2

Two constructors are provided. The first constructor with no parameters sets capacity to allow 100 objects in the stack by default (index 0 does not store an object). It does this by invoking the second constructor with *capacity* as its parameter. The second constructor is the key constructor and allows the caller to determine the fixed size of the stack.

In command *push* an attempt to write a value into *data[index]* where *index* is not between 0 and *capacity -1* causes an *ArrayIndexOutOfBoundsException* to be thrown. This exception is trapped and rethrown with a new message indicating that the capacity of the stack has been exceeded. Otherwise, the index top is incremented by one and the item being added is put at position *top*.

In command *pop*, a *NoSuchElementException* is thrown if an attempt is made to remove an element from an empty stack. Otherwise, the datum stored at index *top* is set to *null* and *top* is decremented by one. Setting *data [top]* to null enables the automatic garbage collector to reclaim the storage at this array position. We note that *pop* is implemented as a command since it changes the internal state of a stack without returning any information.

The query *top* throws a *NoSuchElementException* if an attempt is made to access information that does not exist. Otherwise, the function returns the object stored at index *top*.

Function *main* is included as a short test stub. In this function, a stack object, *myStack*, is created of fixed size 5. Three integer objects that correspond to *obj1*, *obj2*, and *obj3* in Figure 11.1 are inserted using the *push* command. The query *size* is invoked, the stack is popped, and the query *size* is again invoked. Test stubs of this kind are often embedded as a function *main* in a class not intended to serve as a main application class. Such test stubs provide a "quick and dirty" mechanism or sanity check to verify major aspects of the reusable class.

Later in the chapter a complete stack laboratory is constructed to enable more extensive testing and examination of the *Stack* abstraction.

11.3   *LinkedStack*

The *LinkedStack* implementation of *Stack* is a dynamic stack implementation. The storage associated with such a stack grows and shrinks as objects are added and removed from the stack. This is in contrast to the *ArrayStack* presented in Section 11.2. The storage associated with *ArrayStack* is determined when the stack is constructed and, once chosen, remains constant.

Dynamic structures offer more flexibility since their capacity does not have to be known in advance. The price that must usually be paid for this flexibility is speed. Fixed structures generally perform faster than dynamic structures.

The information contained in a *LinkedStack* is contained within a *Node* class. This class may be defined as a stand-alone class or as an inner class within class *LinkedStack*. We choose to make *Node* an inner class since it is dedicated exclusively to serve class *LinkedStack*.

Inner class *Node* contains two fields, *item* (which contains the object being stored) and *next* (a reference to the next *Node* in the stack).

Listing 11.3 presents inner class *Node*, which is contained in *LinkedStack.java*.

Listing 11.3   Class *Node*

```
private class Node {

    // Fields

    private Object item;
    private Node next;
```

```
// Constructor

private Node (Object element, Node link) {
  item = element;
  next = link;
}
}
```

Class *Node* is designated as *private* to ensure that it cannot be accessed outside of class *LinkedStack*. The two fields and constructor are also *private* to further enforce internal use only. Everything in class *Node* is accessible within *LinkedStack* since all the features of class *LinkedStack* (public, protected, and private) are accessible within the class.

We shall use a linked-list structure to implement *LinkedStack* (thus the name *LinkedStack*). A linked-list structure consists of a sequence of nodes with each node containing a reference or pointer to the next node in the sequence. If we draw such a linked-list structure from left to right, the most recent object pushed onto the stack would be the leftmost node and the oldest object to have been pushed onto the stack would be the rightmost node. Each time we add a node (command *push*) to the *LinkedStack* this node becomes the first node in the linked-list structure. The oldest node is linked to *null*, which serves as a terminator of the linked list. We illustrate this in Figure 11.2. The arrows in Figure 11.2 represent the values of fields (*top* and *next*). The last node in this sequence has a *next* field with the value *null*. This is why the final arrow is shown with value *null*.

The *LinkedStack* must be connected to the linked list of nodes. This is accomplished by defining a *top* field within class *LinkedStack* that holds a reference to the top node of the linked list of nodes.

Whenever an object is pushed onto the *LinkedStack*, a new *Node* is created and linked to the previous top node. This is illustrated in Figure 11.3.

When the *LinkedStack* is popped, its pointer to top is modified and assigned to the second node in the linked list or *null* if there is no second node.

The implementation of *LinkedStack* is presented in Listing 11.4.

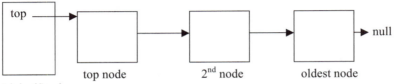

top node   2nd node   oldest node

LinkedStack

Figure 11.2. Linked-list structure.

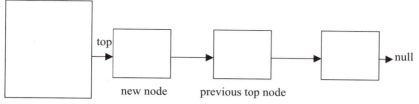

LinkedStack

Figure 11.3. *LinkedStack.*

Listing 11.4 Class *LinkedStack*

```java
/** A dynamic implementation of Stack
*/
package foundations;
import java.util.*;

public class LinkedStack implements Stack {

  // Fields

  private Node top = null;
  private int numberElements = 0;

  // Commands

  public void push (Object item) {
    Node newNode = new Node(item, top);
    top = newNode;
    numberElements++;
  }

  public void pop () {
    if (isEmpty())
      throw new NoSuchElementException("Stack is empty." );
    else {
      Node oldNode = top;
      top = top.next;
      numberElements--;
      oldNode = null;
    }
  }

  public void makeEmpty () {
    while (top != null) {
      Node previous = top;
```

```
      top = top.next;
      previous = null;
    }
    numberElements = 0;
  }

  // Queries

  public Object top () {
    if (isEmpty())
      throw new NoSuchElementException("Stack is empty.");
    else
      return top.item;
  }

  public boolean isEmpty () {
    return top == null;
  }

  public int size () {
    return numberElements;
  }

  private class Node {

    // Fields

    private Object item;
    private Node next;

    // Constructors

    private Node (Object element, Node link) {
      item = element;
      next = link;
    }
  }

  static public void main(String[] args) {
    LinkedStack myStack = new LinkedStack();
    myStack.push(new Integer(1));
    myStack.push(new Integer(2));
    myStack.push(new Integer(3));
    System.out.println("myStack.size() = " + myStack.size());
    myStack.pop();
    System.out.println("myStack.size() = " + myStack.size());
    System.out.println ("myStack.top() = " + myStack.top());
  }
}
```

The output is the same as for Listing 11.2. Let us examine some of the commands and queries of Listing 11.4.

Command *push*

The statement

```
Node newNode = new Node(item, top)
```

constructs a new node initializing it with *item* and having it point to what is currently node *top*.

The next line of code assigns *top* to the *newNode*. Finally, the number of elements is incremented by one.

Command *pop*

The field *top* is assigned to *top.next*. The number of elements is decremented by one and the previous *top* node is assigned to *null*.

Command *makeEmpty*

A *while* loop traverses through all the nodes in the linked list, setting each to *null*. The *top* field is used in this loop so that when the loop is terminated, *top* has the value *null*.

11.4 Comparing the Efficiency of *ArrayStack* with *LinkedStack*

To compare the efficiency of the fixed stack versus the dynamic stack we shall determine the time that it takes to push and then pop a large number of items using each stack type. To do this we need a timer. Listing 11.5 presents the code for a *TimeInterval* class.

Although timing is a useful and common method for determining the relative efficiency of two implementations (fixed and dynamic stack in this case), it is subject to some variability that is sometimes out of the control of the programmer. Timing results may be influenced by the operating system that may cache segments of code after repeated use, the quantity of available RAM, the granularity of the clock, and the number of users accessing the computer in a multiuser system. Appendix B introduces algorithm complexity analysis. Using such methods one can often determine the relative efficiency of implementations in a machine/operating system–independent manner.

In the case of *ArrayStack* and *LinkedStack*, the *push* and *pop* commands are faster using the internal array in the fixed stack compared to the linked nodes in the dynamic stack. Inserting (pushing) a stack element in the fixed stack takes fixed time – namely, the time required to insert an element into a particular index in the array. Pushing a stack element in the dynamic stack requires creating a new node (dynamic storage allocation is generally a relatively slow operation), assigning to its fields, and linking the new node to the previous first node. This requires more computational effort (more CPU cycles).

Listing 11.5   Class *TimeInterval*

```java
/**
 * A timing utility class useful for timing code segments.
 */
public class TimeInterval {

  private long startTime, endTime;
  private long elapsedTime; // Time interval in milliseconds

  // Commands
  public void startTiming () {
    elapsedTime = 0;
    startTime = System.currentTimeMillis();
  }

  public void endTiming () {
    endTime = System.currentTimeMillis();
    elapsedTime = endTime - startTime;
  }

  // Queries
  public double getElapsedTime () {
    // Return time in seconds
    return (double) elapsedTime / 1000.0;
  }
}
```

We construct an application that allows the user to input the number of pushes and pops. The application outputs the processing time for each type of stack.

A Windows application was written in which 100,000 *Integer* objects were pushed and then popped from an *ArrayStack* and from a *LinkedStack*. The GUI is shown below.

It can be seen from these results that the *ArrayStack* is about twice as fast as the *LinkedStack*. Building this application is left as an exercise for the reader.

11.5 *Queue*

A queue is an information structure in which the first item that is inserted is the first that is available (first in, first out). This is in contrast to a stack in which the first item that is available is the last item inserted (first in, last out). Many software applications require the logical equivalent of accessing "things" in the same order as inserted. This is true in traffic systems in which vehicles line up at a traffic light or airplanes hold to land in the order in which they arrive at an airport. It is also true in many service-based systems, such as a bank or supermarket, in which customers line up in front of a server (teller or checkout person).

A queue's commands and queries define its behavior. These methods specify what one can do with a queue object. The interface for *Queue* given in Listing 10.3 and repeated in Listing 11.6 provides a precise specification of the behavior of a queue.

Listing 11.6 Interface *Queue*

```
/** Interface Queue
*/
package foundations;
public interface Queue extends Container {

  // Commands

  /** Add an object at the rear of the queue
  */
  public void add (Object obj);

  /** Remove an object from the front of the queue
  *   Throws NoSuchElementException if queue is empty
  */
  public void remove ();

  // Queries

  /** Return without removing, the front object in the queue
  *   Throws NoSuchElementException if queue is empty
  */
  public Object front ();
}
```

In addition to the commands and queries inherited from *Container*, a queue provides the commands *add* and *remove* and the query *front*.

We shall present only a dynamic implementation of *Queue*, called *LinkedQueue*, and leave the fixed implementation as an exercise for the reader.

11.6 *LinkedQueue*

The *LinkedQueue* also requires the services of an inner class *Node*. This class holds the information that is stored in the queue. It has the same properties as inner class *Node* used in the *LinkedStack*. Its implementation is given in Listing 11.3 and is reused in *LinkedQueue.java*.

We shall employ the same type of linked-list node structure that was used for the *LinkedStack*. The details of *add* and *remove* will of course be changed to accommodate the different ordering rule of a queue: last in, last out (or first in, first out).

The implementation of class *LinkedQueue* is given in Listing 11.7.

Listing 11.7 Class *LinkedQueue*

```
/**
 * Dynamic queue implementation
 */
package foundations;
import java.util.*;

public class LinkedQueue implements Queue {

  // Fields

  private Node first = null;
  private int numberElements = 0;

  // Commands

  public void add (Object item) {
    Node newNode;
    if (numberElements == 0) {
      newNode = new Node(item, null);
      first = newNode;
    }
    else {
      Node currentNode = first;
      Node previousNode = null;
      while (currentNode != null) {
        previousNode = currentNode;
        currentNode = currentNode.next;
      }
      newNode = new Node(item, null);
      previousNode.next = newNode;
    }
    numberElements++;
  }
```

```
public void remove () {
  if (isEmpty())
    throw new NoSuchElementException("Queue is empty.");
  else {
    Node oldNode = first;
    first = first.next;
    numberElements—;
    oldNode = null;
  }
}


public void makeEmpty () {
    while (first != null) {
      Node previous = first;
      first = first.next;
      previous = null;
    }
    numberElements = 0;
}

// Queries

public Object front () {
  if (isEmpty())
    throw new NoSuchElementException("Queue is empty.");
  else
    return first.item;
}

public boolean isEmpty () {
  return first == null;
}

public int size () {
  return numberElements;
}

private class Node {

  // Fields

  private Object item;
  private Node next;

  // Constructors
```

```
    private Node (Object element, Node link) {
      item = element;
      next = link;
    }
  }

  public static void main (String [] args) {
    LinkedQueue myQueue = new LinkedQueue();
    myQueue.add(new Integer(1));
    myQueue.add(new Integer(2));
    myQueue.add(new Integer(3));
    System.out.println("myQueue.size() = " + myQueue.size());
    myQueue.remove();
    System.out.println("myQueue.size() = " + myQueue.size());
    System.out.println("myQueue.front() = " + myQueue.front());
  }
}
```

Output of Listing 11.7

```
    myQueue.size() = 3
    myQueue.size() = 2
    myQueue.front() = 2
```

We examine some of the interesting methods of Listing 11.7.

Command *add*

If the number of elements is 0, a new node is created and linked to *null*. The field *first* of *LinkedQueue* is assigned to the new node.

If the number of elements is greater than 0, a *while* loop is used to determine the last node in the linked list. A new node is created and linked to *null*. The last node in the linked list *(previousNode)* is linked to the new node.

Command *remove*

If the number of elements is 0, *NoSuchElementException* is thrown.

If the number of elements is greater than 0, the field *first* is assigned to *first.next*. The old *first* node *(oldNode)* is set to *null*.

A test stub is provided in function *main* that is similar to the test stub in class *LinkedStack*. These test stubs are not very interesting.

In the next section we develop a full-featured stack/queue laboratory GUI application that allows all of the features of *Stack* and *Queue* to be exercised.

11.7   Stack/Queue Laboratory

A stack/queue laboratory has been written to test and exercise the stack-and-queue behavior. A screen shot of the program in action is shown in Figure 11.4. You

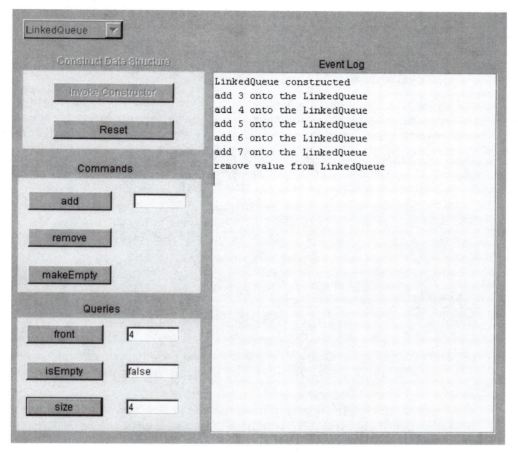

Figure 11.4. The *StackQueueLab* application.

are encouraged to copy the files for this lab from *foundations.zip* and experiment with each data structure.

The combo box at the top left allows the user to choose "ArrayStack," "LinkedStack," or "LinkedQueue" (choice made above). When the program is launched only the "Construct Data Structure" panel is visible. When the "Invoke Constructor" button is clicked, the "Commands" panel and the "Queries" panel are both made visible. The "Construct Data Structure" panel and combo box are disabled and the "Reset" button is enabled. If the user selects "LinkedQueue," the buttons "push," "pop," and "top" get labeled "add," "remove," and "front," as shown.

11.8 Summary

❑ A stack is one of the simplest and perhaps most widely used container types. Many software applications require the logical equivalent of piling objects on top of each other.

❑ The *push* command is used to add a new object to a stack. The *pop* command is used to remove the object on the top of the stack. The *top* query returns the object on top of the stack without removing it.

❑ In the fixed stack implementation *ArrayStack*, an array field *data* is used to hold the objects that comprise the stack.

❑ The *LinkedStack* implementation of *Stack* is a dynamic stack implementation. The storage associated with such a stack grows and shrinks as objects are added and removed from the stack.

❑ Dynamic structures offer more flexibility since their capacity does not have to be known in advance. The price that must usually be paid for this flexibility is efficiency. Fixed structures generally perform faster than dynamic structures.

❑ A *queue* is an information structure in which the first item that is inserted is the first that is available (first in, first out). This is in contrast to a *stack*, in which the first item that is available is the last item inserted (first in, last out).

11.9 Exercises

1 Construct a GUI application as described in Section 11.4 that compares the efficiency of an *ArrayStack* to a *LinkedStack*.

2 Implement class *ArrayQueue*. Include some test code in function *main* that inserts the values 3, 4, 5, 6, 7, and 8, does a remove, and outputs the front of the queue and its size.

3 Construct a GUI application similar to the one in Exercise 1 that compares the efficiency of the *ArrayQueue* built in Exercise 2 with the *LinkedQueue* presented in this chapter.

4 List three specific applications in which you believe it would be useful to utilize a stack. Explain the purpose of the stack in each of these applications.

5 List three specific applications in which you believe it would be useful to utilize a queue. Explain the purpose of the queue in each of these applications.

6 Suppose we add an internal field to the implementation of class *LinkedQueue* as follows (new field shown in boldface):

```
// Internal fields
private Node first;
private Node last;
int numElements;
```

This new field *last* is always a reference to the last node in the list representing the queue. The command *add* is expected to be much more efficient. Explain why.

Reimplement all the methods of class *LinkedQueue* making sure to correctly use and update the *last* field. Include some test code in function *main* that performs the same operations as given in the test function of Exercise 2.

7 Implement a class *InefficientQueue* in terms of two internal stacks. All the methods required in a *Queue* are to be fully implemented. You are not to use class *Node* explicitly. The goal of this problem is to get you to use the *Stack* abstraction while implementing a *Queue* abstraction. Include some test code in function *main* that performs the same operations as given in the test function of Exercise 2.

Explain why this method for implementing a *Queue* is quite inefficient (thus the name of the class).

```
public class InefficientQueue implements Queue {

  // Fields
  LinkedStack stack1, stack2;

  // No other fields should be used
}
```

8 Implement a class *InefficientStack* in terms of two internal queues in a manner similar to Exercise 7. The only two fields that you may use in this class are *queue1* and *queue2*. Include a test function *main* that pushes the values 5, 4, 3, 2, and 1 onto the stack, pops the stack once, and outputs the top of the stack and its size.

9 Implement a *VectorStack*, another dynamic stack, using an internal field of type *java.util.Vector* to hold the data. Include a test function *main* that performs the same operations as those given in Exercise 8.

10 Implement a *VectorQueue*, another dynamic queue, using an internal field of type *java.util.Vector* to hold the data. Include some test code in function *main* that performs the same operations as given in the test function of Exercise 2.

11 Add a query with signature *public VectorStack copy()* in your class *VectorStack* (from Exercise 9) that creates and returns a new stack and fills it with the elements contained in the receiver (the stack object sent the message).

12

Application of Stack

The main application of this chapter is algebraic expression evaluation. This is a classic and important problem. An algebraic expression containing single character operands and the four arithmetic operators is input as a string. When numeric values are assigned to each operand our goal is to be able to evaluate the arithmetic expression on the fly. The *String* representing the arithmetic expression is not known until runtime.

What makes this problem particularly interesting is that the core of the solution requires two stacks, each holding different types of data. The solution illustrates how abstractions (the stack in this case) may be utilized to provide an effective underpinning for the solution to a complex problem.

12.1 Algebraic Expression Evaluation

Problem: Develop a Java software application that takes an algebraic expression as an input string. An example of such an algebraic expression is $(a + b) * c - d + e * f$. After numeric values are assigned to each operand (values for a, b, c, d, e, and f), the algorithm must compute the value of the algebraic expression.

Input: A string representing an algebraic expression involving n operands and an n-tuple representing the values for the operands (i.e., numeric values for each operand).

Output: The value of the expression for the particular n-tuple of input operand values.

Solution of Problem:

1. Conversion from infix to postfix

The first step in solving this problem involves a transformation of the input algebraic expression from infix to postfix representation. Infix is the format normally used in representing an algebraic expression. Postfix is a format that places an operator directly after its two operands.

The infix expression $a * b$ converts to the postfix expression $ab*$ (the way you would perform this computation on most Hewlett-Packard (HP) scientific calculators). One can interpret the postfix representation by reading from right to left. For example, "multiply the previous two operands by each other."

Let us convert the algebraic expression $a * (b + c)$ to postfix. The result is $abc+ *$. This postfix representation may be interpreted by finding the first operator symbol, "+". This operates on the previous two operands, b and c. The "$*$" operator then operates on its previous two operands, $(b + c)$ and a, by forming the product of these two operands.

What about the conversion of the algebraic expression $a + b * c$ to postfix form? The result is $abc*+$. The first operator (reading from left to right) "$*$" operates on its two previous operands b and c and performs the product of these. Then the "+" operator finds the sum of its two previous operands, a and $b * c$.

Now what about the conversion from infix to postfix of the algebraic expression given above, $(a + b) * c - d + e * f$? The postfix representation is: $ab + c * d - ef*+$.

We observe that none of the above postfix expressions contain any parentheses. The precedence of operations is uniquely encapsulated in the postfix expression.

2. Evaluation of postfix expression

Once the postfix representation of the input algebraic expression has been accomplished, it is relatively easy to evaluate the postfix expression when the numeric values of the operands are given. We illustrate the process with an actual example before expressing the solution in algorithmic terms.

Example. Consider the postfix expression $ab + c * d - ef*+$ representing the algebraic expression $(a + b) * c - d + e * f$. We initialize a stack of base-type *Double*. We push the real values of the first two operand symbols a and b onto the stack in the order in which they appear in the postfix expression (from left to right). Each primitive value is wrapped as a *Double* before pushing the values onto the stack. When we encounter our first operator symbol, "+", we pop the operand stack twice and perform the indicated operation and push the result back onto the operand stack, in this case the numeric value of $(a + b)$, wrapped as a *Double*. The numeric value of the next operand, c, is pushed onto the operand stack (on top of $(a + b)$). When we encounter the operator "$*$", we again pop the operand stack twice and perform the multiplication of the two operands getting $(a + b) * c$ as a result. We push its value onto the operand stack. Continuing, we push the numeric value of the operand d onto the stack. When we next encounter the operator "$-$", we pop the operand stack twice and perform the subtraction on the two real values coming off the stack producing the result $(a + b) * c - d$. This value is then pushed onto the operand stack. The two real values for e and f are next pushed onto the stack (on top of the previous value $(a + b) * c - d$). When the second "$*$" operator symbol is encountered, the stack is popped twice and the operation of multiplication is performed on the two values obtained from the stack. This represents the multiplication of e and f. This product value is then pushed onto

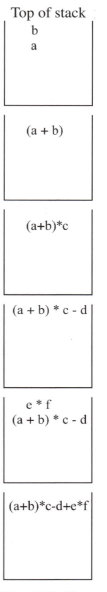

Figure 12.1. Steps in evaluating postfix expression using stack.

the stack. Finally, when the last operator symbol "+" is encountered, the stack is popped twice and the sum of the two values is computed and then pushed onto the stack. This value equals $(a + b) * c - d + e * f$. When it is detected that there are no further input symbols to be processed, the "answer" to the problem (i.e., the value that represents the expression evaluation) is popped from the stack and returned to the user.

Figure 12.1 shows the sequence of operations involved in evaluating the postfix expression.

We more formally encapsulate the process just described and illustrated in the following algorithm.

Algorithm for Postfix Expression Evaluation

Initialize an operand stack.

Read the sequence of symbols in the postfix expression from left to right.

If an operand symbol is read, push its real value (supplied as input) onto the operand stack (we must convert the double scalar to a Double *wrapper object since the stack specifies* Object *as its type).*

If an operator symbol is read, pop the stack twice (obtaining two numeric values) and then perform the operation indicated by the operator symbol. Push the resulting numeric value onto the operand stack (again, properly wrapped as a Double).

After all symbols have been read, the expression value is obtained by popping the stack one last time and returning the value to the user.

Clearly the key to the success of this algorithm is based on the manipulations of the operand stack.

This raises the obvious question, how do we write a procedure that converts the input string representing the algebraic expression to be evaluated (always in infix form) to the postfix representation that may be used in the manner described above for expression evaluation?

12.2   Algorithm for Converting from Infix to Postfix Representation

A stack shall once again play a key role in performing the desired conversion from infix to postfix representation. We define an operator stack of base-type *Character*.

1. Initialize an operator stack.

2. Read the sequence of symbols in the infix expression from left to right passing through white space (ignoring spaces, tabs, and new lines).

3. If the symbol read is an operand symbol (upper or lower case letters of the alphabet), insert the symbol directly into the output postfix string.

4. If the symbol read is an operator symbol and the operator stack is empty, push the operator symbol onto the stack, wrapping it as a *Character*.

5. If the symbol read is an operator symbol and the operator stack is nonempty, obtain the *top* of the stack (using the *top* query defined in the stack class) and compare the precedence of this *top* symbol with the newly read operator symbol

(e.g., * and / have higher precedence than + and −). If *top* has lower or equal precedence to the symbol just read, leave the stack alone; otherwise, append the *top* symbol to the postfix string and then pop the stack.

6. Push the newly read operator symbol onto the operator stack.
7. When all symbols in the infix string have been read, pop the operator stack and add the symbols directly to the postfix string.

Note: This algorithm does not take parentheses into account. This will be done at the implementation level.

Example Application of Algorithm

Let us use the infix-to-postfix algorithm to convert the infix string $a * b + c$ to postfix format.

The symbol a is appended to the postfix string. The operator symbol "*" is pushed onto the operator stack. The symbol b is appended to the postfix string. The operator symbol "*" representing *top* is compared in precedence to the newly read operator symbol "+". Since the "*" is not of lower or equal precedence, it is popped from the stack and appended to the postfix string (which is now $ab*$). The "+" is pushed onto the operator stack. The final symbol c is appended to the postfix string (since it is an operand symbol). With all symbols read, the operator stack

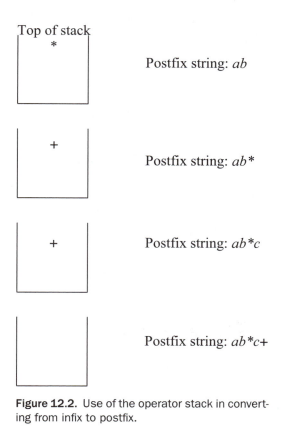

Top of stack

Postfix string: ab

Postfix string: $ab*$

Postfix string: $ab*c$

Postfix string: $ab*c+$

Figure 12.2. Use of the operator stack in converting from infix to postfix.

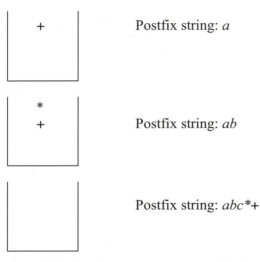

Postfix string: a

Postfix string: ab

Postfix string: $abc*+$

Figure 12.3. Another operator stack used in the conversion from infix to postfix.

is popped (until empty) and in this case only the operator symbol "+" is appended to the postfix string producing the final result $ab * c+$.

Figure 12.2 shows the operator stack as it evolves in the process of converting the infix expression to postfix form.

Another Application of the Algorithm

Let us use the infix-to-postfix algorithm to convert the infix string $a + b * c$ to postfix format.

The symbol a is appended to the postfix string (since it's not an operator symbol). The "+" operator is pushed onto the operator stack since that stack is initially empty. The symbol b is next appended to the postfix string. When the operator symbol "*" is encountered, the top symbol "+" is found to be of lower precedence than the newly read operator symbol "*". The algorithm specifies that this newly read symbol "*" is pushed onto the operator stack (which now has "*" on top and "+" directly beneath it). Finally, the last symbol c is appended to the postfix string (which is now abc). The stack is repeatedly popped until empty and the two operator symbols "*" and "+" are appended in turn to the postfix string, which ends up as $abc * +$.

Figure 12.3 depicts the evolution of the operator stack for the example given above.

12.3   Implementation of Algebraic Function Evaluation

12.3.1   Infix to Postfix Conversion

In Listing 12.1 we show most of class *FunctionEvaluation* focusing only on the details that support infix-to-postfix representation. This is one of the key steps in the process of algebraic expression evaluation. The class has a field called *operands* that is a *Vector* implementation of *Dictionary*. The command *infixToPostfix* contains logic for handling parentheses in the infix expression. We include a test stub in function *main*.

Listing 12.1   Class *FunctionEvaluation*

```
/** Defines the methods needed to evaluate an algebraic expression
 *     represented as an infix String
 */
package foundations;
import java.util.*;

public class FunctionEvaluation {

  // Fields
  private String infix, postfix;
  private Dictionary operands = new VectorDictionary();

  // Constructor
  public FunctionEvaluation (String infixExpression) {
    infix = infixExpression.trim().toLowerCase();
    infixToPostfix();
  }

  // Commands

  /*
   * Converts infix producing postfix
   */
  public void infixToPostfix () {
    int infixIndex;
    char ch, topSymbol;
    LinkedStack opStack = new LinkedStack();
    postfix = "";
    for (infixIndex = 0; infixIndex < infix.length();
      infixIndex++) {
      // Get character from the infix String
      ch = infix.charAt (infixIndex);

      if (ch == ' ') // Skip white space
        continue;      // Skip back to bottom of loop

      if (ch >= 'a' && ch <= 'z') // operand
        postfix = postfix + ch;

      if (ch == '+' || ch == '-' || ch == '*' || ch == '/' ||
        ch == '(' || ch == ')') { // operator
        if (opStack.size() > 0) {
```

```
        topSymbol = ((Character)opStack.top()).charValue();
        if (topSymbol == '(' && ch == ')')
          continue;
        if (precedence (topSymbol, ch) == true) {
          if (topSymbol != '(')
            postfix = postfix + topSymbol;
          opStack.pop();
        }
      }
    if (ch != ')')
      opStack.push (new Character(ch));
    else { // ch == ')'
      char c;
      // pop operator stack down to first left paren
      do {
        c = ((Character) opStack.top()).charValue();
        if (c != '(')
          postfix = postfix + c;
        opStack.pop();
      } while (c != '(');
    }
  }
}
// Pop leftover operands
while (opStack.size() > 0) {
  if ((Character) opStack.top()).charValue() != '(')
    postfix = postfix +
              ((Character)opStack.top()).charValue();
  opStack.pop();
}
}

/** Sets the value associated with an operand */
public void setKeyValue (char ch, double value) {
  operands.addKey(new Character(ch), new Double(value));
}

// Queries

/** Returns the postfix string */
public String postfix () {
  return postfix;
}

/** Returns the infix string */
public String infix () {
  return infix;
}
```

```java
/** Returns a Dictionary containing the operands and their values
*/
public Dictionary operands () {
  return operands;
}

/** Returns true if operator symb1 has higher
/*  precedence than operator symb2 */
private boolean precedence (char symb1, char symb2) {
  if ( (symb1 == '+' || symb1 == '-') &&
       (symb2 == '*' || symb2 == '/'))
    return false;
  else if ( (symb1 == '(' && symb2 != ')') ||
            symb2 == '(')
    return false;
  else
    return true;
}

double evaluate () { /* Details to be added later */ }

// Test stub for algebraic function evaluation
public static void main (String [] args) {
  FunctionEvaluation f;

  f = new FunctionEvaluation ("a + b * c");
  System.out.println ("Infix expression = " + f.infix() +
                      "\nPostfix expression = " + f.postfix());
  f.setKeyValue('a', 2.0);
  f.setKeyValue('b', 3.0);
  f.setKeyValue('c', 4.0);
  System.out.println ("When a = 2.0, b = 3.0, and c = 4.0, f = " +
                      f.evaluate());

  f = new FunctionEvaluation ("(a + b) * c");
  System.out.println ("\nInfix expression = " + f.infix() +
                      "\nPostfix expression = " + f.postfix());
  f.setKeyValue('a', 2.0);
  f.setKeyValue('b', 3.0);
  f.setKeyValue('c', 4.0);
  System.out.println ("\nWhen a = 2.0, b = 3.0, and c = 4.0,
                      f = " + f.evaluate());

  f = new FunctionEvaluation ("a / (b + c)");
  System.out.println ("\nInfix expression = " + f.infix() +
                      "\nPostfix expression = " + f.postfix());
  f.setKeyValue('a', 2.0);
  f.setKeyValue('b', 3.0);
```

```
        f.setKeyValue('c', 4.0);
        System.out.println ("\nWhen a = 2.0, b = 3.0, and c = 4.0,
                            f = "+ f.evaluate());


        f = new FunctionEvaluation ("a / b + c");
        System.out.println ("\nInfix expression = " + f.infix() +
                            "\nPostfix expression = " + f.postfix());
        f.setKeyValue('a', 2.0);
        f.setKeyValue('b', 3.0);
        f.setKeyValue('c', 4.0);
        System.out.println ("\nWhen a = 2.0, b = 3.0, and c = 4.0,
                            f = "+ f.evaluate());


        f = new FunctionEvaluation ("(a + b)/c + d * (e + h)");
        System.out.println ("\nInfix expression = " + f.infix() +
                            "\nPostfix expression = " + f.postfix());
        f.setKeyValue('a', 2.0);
        f.setKeyValue('b', 3.0);
        f.setKeyValue('c', 4.0);
        f.setKeyValue('d', 5.0);
        f.setKeyValue('e', 6.0);
        f.setKeyValue('h', 7.0);
        System.out.println ("\nWhen a = 2.0, b = 3.0, and c = 4.0, "
                            "d = 5.0, ... f = "+ f.evaluate());
    }
}
```

Explanation of Listing 12.1

- The constructor strips out leading and trailing blank characters and converts the input string to lower case before assigning the string to the internal field *infix*. Then the constructor invokes the function *infixToPostfix()*.

- A local *opStack* (of type *LinkedStack*) is constructed inside the method *infixToPostfix()*. This stack holds operator symbols as they are encountered in the infix string.

- Since the formal type for the items stored in a *LinkedStack* is *Object*, we cannot insert elements of type *char* since *char* is a scalar (primitive) type and is not a subclass of *Object*. We must therefore wrap the *char* to a *Character*. The code that accomplishes this is:

```
opStack.push(new Character(ch));
```

- When we send the query *top()* to the *opStack* we receive an object whose formal type is *Object*. We must therefore downcast this to *Character* and then use the method *charValue()* to obtain the *char* that is wrapped in the *Character*.

Specifically, the code that accomplishes this is:

```
topSymbol = ((Character) opStack.top()).charValue();
```

- Although later we shall construct a laboratory-type Windows application that enables us to fully test the functionality of algebraic expression evaluation, we include a test stub through function *main()*. Here we "hard-wire" several test cases. We create several different instances of class *FunctionEvaluation* (objects of type *FunctionEvaluation*) and send the command *infixToPostFix()* to each and then through a query obtain the resulting postfix expression.
- The field *operands* is defined as type *Dictionary*. An instance of class *VectorDictionary* is used in creating an instance of this abstraction. The details of this class shall be presented and discussed in Chapter 17, which deals with dictionary data structures.

12.3.2 Evaluation of Postfix Expression

In order to evaluate the postfix expression, we must be able to associate a numeric value with each operand character that we encounter in the infix expression. This is accomplished using the command *setKeyValue* given in Listing 12.1.

The only missing element in class *FunctionEvaluation* is the query *evaluate()*. This function is presented in Listing 12.2.

Listing 12.2 Function *evaluate*

```
/**
  * Evaluates postfix string to produce numerical answer
  */
public double evaluate () {
  int postfixIndex;
  char ch;
  double operand1, operand2;
  LinkedStack valStack = new LinkedStack();

  for (postfixIndex = 0; postfixIndex < postfix.length();
    postfixIndex++) {
    ch = postfix.charAt (postfixIndex);
    if (ch >= 'a' && ch <= 'z') { // operand
      if (operands.containsKey(new Character(ch)))
        valStack.push (operands.value(new Character(ch)));
      else
        throw new NoSuchElementException(
                  "No value for character " + ch +"." );
    }
```

```
    if (ch == '+' || ch == '-' || ch == '*' || ch == '/' ||
      ch == '(' || ch == ')') { // operator
      operand1 = ((Double) valStack.top()).doubleValue();
      valStack.pop();
      operand2 = ((Double) valStack.top()).doubleValue();
      valStack.pop();
      switch (ch) {
        case '+':
          valStack.push(
                    new Double (operand2 + operand1));
          break;
        case '-':
          valStack.push(
                    new Double (operand2 - operand1));
          break;
        case '*':
          valStack.push(
                    new Double (operand2 * operand1));
          break;
        case '/':
          if (operand1 != 0.0)
            valStack.push(
                    new Double (operand2 / operand1));
          else
            valStack.push(
                    new Double (Double.MAX_VALUE));
      }
    }
  }
  double valueToReturn = ((Double) valStack.top()).doubleValue();
  valStack.pop();
  return valueToReturn;
}
```

Explanation of Listing 12.2
- A local *LinkedStack valStack* is declared.
- If the user has entered an operand symbol and associated value (using *setKeyValue*), this value is pushed onto the *valStack* by sending the query *value with new Character(ch)* as a parameter. An object of type *Double* is returned by this query.

```
valStack.push (operands.value(new Character(ch)));
```

- If the operand symbol is not found in the *operands* dictionary a *NoSuch-ElementException* is thrown.

- If during division the denominator is zero, the largest double value is returned (simulation of the value infinity).

12.4 Function Evaluation Laboratory

A complete Windows application that allows the user to experiment with the important aspects of algebraic function evaluation is included in the downloadable *foundations.zip*. You are strongly encouraged to experiment with this GUI application and study its source code.

The user interface in the function evaluation laboratory is given below.

12.5 Summary

❏ The process of evaluating an algebraic function is accomplished in two steps:

  1. Convert the expression *String* from ordinary infix to postfix form since it is relatively easy to evaluate the postfix expression.
  2. Evaluate the postfix expression.

❏ The algorithm for evaluating a postfix expression is given as follows:

  (1) *Initialize an operand stack.*
  (2) *Read the sequence of symbols in the postfix expression from left to right.*
  (3) *If an operand symbol is read, push its real value (supplied as input) onto the operand stack (we must convert the double scalar to a* Double *wrapper object since the stack specifies* Object *as its type).*

(4) *If an operator symbol is read, pop the stack twice (obtaining two numeric values) and then perform the operation indicated by the operator symbol. Push the resulting numeric value onto the operand stack (again properly wrapped as a* Double*).*

(5) *After all symbols have been read, the expression value is obtained by popping the stack one last time and returning the value to the user.*

12.6 Exercises

1   Convert the following expressions from infix to postfix:

   a. $(a + b)/(c + d) * e$
   b. $((a + b) * c) * ((c + d) * e)$
   c. $(a + b)/(c + d) - (e * f + g)/(h + i)$

2   Convert the following expressions from postfix to infix:

   a. $ab + c/d*$
   b. $abcd + /+$

3   Develop an algorithm for converting an infix expression with parentheses to prefix form and evaluating the resulting expression. (Hint: Prefix expressions should be evaluated from left to right).

   Note: In a prefix expression the operator precedes the two operands (e.g., the infix expression $a * b$ is equivalent to the prefix expression $*ab$).

4   Suppose we define the symbol $ to denote exponentiation (e.g., 2 $ 4 = 16). We assign a higher precedence to exponentiation than any other arithmetic operation. Exponentiation is performed from right to left (e.g., 4 $ 2 $ 2 = 4 $ (2 $ 2) = 256). Modify the algorithm for converting infix expressions to postfix form to include exponentiation. Your solution should still require only one pass of the input infix string. Code and test your algorithm.

5   Extend the code in this chapter to accept strings as operands, not just single characters.

13

Lists

A list is a widely used container abstraction. Lists come in various flavors, so we really have a family of list abstractions. In real life, lists are used to hold information stored in a particular sequence. This information may be ordered as in a telephone directory or unordered as in a grocery shopping list.

Some lists allow items to be stored in any order whereas others require a sequential ordering of their data. The simplest list allows the addition of objects, removal of objects, and access to objects only at two ends, front and rear. An "indexable" list extends a simple list by allowing the insertion of objects, removal of objects, and access of objects at a particular index. A "positionable" list extends a simple list by allowing the addition of objects, removal of objects, and access to objects before or after a specified object in the list. Finally, an "ordered" list extends *SearchTable* (see Chapter 10) and requires that its elements be comparable. A strict ordering relationship is maintained among the elements of an ordered list. This is true in a search table.

Lists may be implemented in many ways, both fixed and dynamic. Perhaps the simplest implementation is a singly linked dynamic implementation. Here links flow in only one direction: from the start of the list to its end. One may move quite easily in a singly linked list from a given node to its successor but not to its predecessor. A more complex but efficient dynamic implementation is a doubly linked list. Here links flow in both directions so that one may move from any node in the list to its successor or to its predecessor. Other implementation variations exist as well, including dynamic circularly linked lists and fixed implementations. Implementing classes for interface *List* and its subinterfaces allows duplicate entries. Class *OrderedList*, which implements interface *SearchTable*, does not allow duplicate entries.

In this chapter, we examine a variety of concrete implementations for the various list abstractions.

13.1 *Dequeue* – An Implementation of *List*

A *Dequeue* is an implementation of a simple *List*. Objects may be added, removed, or accessed at the front or the rear of such a list. As a review, Listing 13.1 presents the interface to *Container* and Listing 13.2 the interface to *List*. These two abstractions provide the required commands and queries for our *Dequeue*.

Listing 13.1 Interface *Container*

```
/** Interface Container - top level container
*/
package foundations;
import java.io.Serializable;

public interface Container extends Serializable {

  // Commands - see subinterfaces

  /** Remove all objects from the container if found
  */
  public void makeEmpty ();

  // Queries

  /** Return true if the container is empty
  */
  public boolean isEmpty ();

  /** Return the number of objects in the container
  */
  public int size ();
}
```

Listing 13.2 Interface *List*

```
/** Interface List
*/
package foundations;
import java.util.*;

public interface List extends Container {

  // Commands

  /** Add obj at the front of the list.
  */
  public void addFront (Object obj);

  /** Add obj at the rear of the list
  */
  public void addRear (Object obj);
```

```
/** Remove object from the front of the list if found.
 */
public void removeFront ();

/** Remove object from the rear of the list if found.
 */
public void removeRear ();

// Queries

/** Return without removing the front object in the list
 *   Throw NoSuchElementException if list is empty
 */
public Object front ();

/** Return without removing the rear object in the list
 *   Throw NoSuchElementException if list is empty
 */
public Object rear ();

/** return true if the list contains obj
 */
public boolean contains (Object obj);

/** return an iterator on the elements in the list
 */
public Iterator elements ();
}
```

Our *Dequeue* class shall implement *List*. It must provide concrete implementations of the commands *makeEmpty* (from *Container*) plus commands *addFront*, *addRear*, *removeRear* (from *List*), and the queries *size* and *isEmpty* (from *Container*) plus queries *front*, *rear*, *contains*, and *elements* (from *List*).

As with all our list implementations, we must first decide whether we want a fixed or dynamic implementation. As discussed in Chapter 11, a fixed implementation requires that the user specify the size of the list in advance and, once specified, the size cannot be changed. The advantage of such an implementation is efficiency. A dynamic implementation provides more flexibility since memory is allocated on demand as more objects are added.

We present only dynamic implementations of all the list structures in this chapter, leaving fixed implementations as exercises for the reader.

13.1.1 Singly Linked *Dequeue*

Figure 13.1 depicts the internal structure of a *SinglyLinkedDequeue*.

A singly linked list of nodes holds the objects of our *Dequeue*. Fields *front* and *rear* "point" to the beginning and end of the singly linked list. These

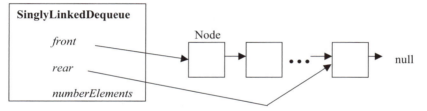

Figure 13.1. *Dequeue* structure.

fields make it relatively easy to add, remove, or access objects at the front and rear of the *Dequeue*. Listing 13.3 presents implementation details of class *SinglyLinkedDequeue*.

Listing 13.3   Class *SinglyLinkedDequeue*

```
/** A singly linked implementation of a Dequeue with duplicates.
*/
package foundations;
import java.util.*;
import java.io.Serializable;

public class SinglyLinkedDequeue implements List {

  // Fields

  protected Node front, rear;
  protected int numberElements;

  // Commands

  /** Remove all objects from the Dequeue, if any */
  public void makeEmpty () {
    while (front != null) {
      Node previous = front;
      front = front.next;
      previous = null;
    }
    numberElements = 0;
    rear = null;
  }

  /** Add obj at the front of the Dequeue */
  public void addFront (Object obj) {
    Node newNode = new Node(obj, front);
    front = newNode;
    if (numberElements == 0)
      rear = front;
    numberElements++;
  }
```

```java
/** Add obj at the rear of the Dequeue */
public void addRear (Object obj) {
  Node newNode = new Node(obj, null);
  if (numberElements == 0) {
    front = newNode;
    rear = newNode;
  }
  else {
    rear.next = newNode;
    rear = newNode;
  }
  numberElements++;
}


/** Remove object from the front of the Dequeue, if found */
public void removeFront () {
  if (isEmpty())
    throw new NoSuchElementException("Dequeue is empty.");
  else {
    front = front.next;
    numberElements--;
    if (numberElements == 0)
      rear = null;
  }
}


/** Remove object from the rear of the Dequeue, if found */
public void removeRear () {
  if (isEmpty())
    throw new NoSuchElementException("Queue is empty.");
  else if (numberElements == 1) {
    front = null;
    rear = null;
  }
  else { // 2 or more elements
    // Find the node just in front of rear
    Node previous = front;
    while (previous.next != rear)
      previous = previous.next;
    previous.next = null;
    rear = previous;
  }
  numberElements--;
}


// Queries
```

```java
/** Return true if the Dequeue is empty */
public boolean isEmpty () {
  return numberElements == 0;
}


/** Return the number of objects in the Dequeue */
public int size () {
  return numberElements;
}


/** Return without removing the front object in the Dequeue */
public Object front () {
  if (isEmpty())
    throw new NoSuchElementException("Dequeue is empty.");
  else
    return front.item;
}


/** Return the rear object in the Dequeue without removing it */
public Object rear () {
  if (isEmpty())
    throw new NoSuchElementException("Dequeue is empty.");
  else
    return rear.item;
}


/** Returns true if the Dequeue contains obj otherwise returns
  * false */
public boolean contains (Object obj) {
  Node current = front;
  while (current != null && !current.item.equals(obj))
    current = current.next;
  return current != null;
}


/** Return an iterator on the elements in the Dequeue */
public Iterator elements () {
  // Load the objects of the Dequeue into a Vector
  Vector v = new Vector();
  Node current = front;
  while (current != null) {
    v.addElement(current.item);
    current = current.next;
  }
  return v.iterator(); // Only valid in Platform 2
}
```

```java
/** Models an internal node of dequeue */
protected class Node implements Serializable {

  // Fields

  protected Object item;
  protected Node next;

  // Constructors

  protected Node (Object element, Node link) {
    item = element;
    next = link;
  }
}

public static void main (String[] args) {
  SinglyLinkedDequeue myDequeue = new SinglyLinkedDequeue();
  // Add three Integer objects to the front of the Dequeue
  myDequeue.addFront(new Integer(5));
  myDequeue.addFront(new Integer(4));
  myDequeue.addFront(new Integer(3));

  // Add three Integer objects to the rear of the Dequeue
  myDequeue.addRear(new Integer(6));
  myDequeue.addRear(new Integer(7));
  myDequeue.addRear(new Integer(8));

  // Remove the front and rear objects
  myDequeue.removeFront();
  myDequeue.removeRear();

  // Obtain an iterator for the Dequeue
  Iterator iter = myDequeue.elements();

  while (iter.hasNext())
    System.out.println (iter.next());

  // Test for the presence of 5 and 8
  if (myDequeue.contains(new Integer(5)))
    System.out.println("5 is in the Dequeue." );
  else
    System.out.println("5 is not in the Dequeue." );
  if (myDequeue.contains(new Integer(8)))
    System.out.println("8 is in the Dequeue." );
  else
    System.out.println("8 is not in the Dequeue." );

  }
}
```

Output of Listing 13.3

```
4
5
6
7
5 is in the Dequeue.
8 is not in the Dequeue.
```

Explanation of Listing 13.3

There are many methods in class *SinglyLinkedDequeue*. These represent implementations of the promises made in interfaces *Container* and *List*. Protected inner class *Node* defines the linkable nodes that hold the objects in this container.

Since the complexities of the methods are roughly equivalent, we shall dissect a few here and leave the rest of the analysis as an exercise for the reader.

Let us examine command *makeEmpty*.

```
public void makeEmpty () {
  while (front != null) {
    Node previous = front;
    front = front.next;
    previous = null;
  }
  numberElements = 0;
  rear = null;
}
```

The reference *front* is used directly. As the list is traversed, each element is visited and set to *null*. This allows the Java automatic garbage collector to recycle the storage associated with each node. Upon the completion of the loop the field *numberElements* is assigned to 0 and the field *rear* is assigned to *null*. The field *front* has already been assigned to *null* in the loop.

Next we examine command *addRear*.

```
public void addRear (Object obj) {
  Node newNode = new Node(obj, null);
  if (numberElements == 0) {
    front = newNode;
    rear = newNode;
  }
  else {
    rear.next = newNode;
    rear = newNode;
  }
  numberElements++;
}
```

The node *newNode* is constructed using *obj* with a link to *null*. If the *Dequeue* is empty both *front* and *rear* are assigned to the reference *newNode*. If the *Dequeue* is not empty the object *rear* is linked to *newNode* and then reassigned to *newNode*.

Next we examine the command *removeRear*.

```
public void removeRear () {
  if (isEmpty())
    throw new NoSuchElementException("Queue is empty.");
  else if (numberElements == 1) {
    front = null;
    rear = null;
  }
  else { // 2 or more elements
    // Find the node just in front of rear
    Node previous = front;
    while (previous.next != rear)
      previous = previous.next;
    previous.next = null;
    rear = previous;
  }
  numberElements--;
}
```

If the *Dequeue* is empty, a *NoSuchElementException* is generated. If the number of elements equals 1, references *front* and *rear* are assigned to *null*. If the number of elements is 2 or greater, a *while* loop is used to determine the node just in front of *rear*, node *previous*. This previous node's value is assigned to *null*. The value of *rear* is reassigned to *previous* and the field *numberElements* is reduced by one.

Lastly, we examine the query *elements*.

```
public Iterator elements () {
  // Load the objects of the Dequeue into a Vector
  Vector v = new Vector(numberElements);
  Node current = front;
  while (current != null) {
    v.addElement(current.item);
    current = current.next;
  }
  return v.iterator();
}
```

A local *Vector* instance *v* is declared and constructed with an initial capacity equal to *numberElements*. Using a *while* loop, all the elements in the *Dequeue* are added to the *Vector v*. Finally the query *iterator* from class *Vector* is invoked returning

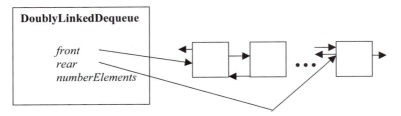

Figure 13.2. *DoublyLinkedDequeue.*

an iterator over elements of the *Vector*. It is noted that *iterator* is a new method of class *Vector* in Java 2 Platform. This code will not compile using Java Version 1.1.x.

A main function is defined as a quick test stub. This is no substitute for the list laboratory test suite that will be presented later in this chapter.

13.1.2 Doubly Linked *Dequeue*

As an alternative to the singly linked *Dequeue* discussed in Section 13.1.1 we may implement a doubly linked *Dequeue*. Its structure is shown in Figure 13.2

Each node has two references, one forward and one backward. The implementation of class *DoublyLinkedDequeue* is given in Listing 13.4.

Listing 13.4   Class *DoublyLinkedDequeue*

```
/** Implements Dequeue with forward and backwards links with duplicates
*/
package foundations;
import java.util.*;
import java.io.Serializable;

public class DoublyLinkedDequeue implements List {

  // Fields

  protected Node front, rear;
  protected int numberElements;

  // Commands

  /** Remove all objects from the Dequeue, if any */
  public void makeEmpty () {
    while (front != null) {
      Node previous = front;
      front = front.next;
      previous = null;
    }
```

```
    numberElements = 0;
    rear = null;
  }

  /** Add obj at the front of the Dequeue */
  public void addFront (Object obj) {
    Node newNode = new Node(obj, front, null);
    if (numberElements == 0)
      rear = newNode;
    else
      front.before = newNode;
    front = newNode;
    numberElements++;
  }

  /** Add obj at the rear of the Dequeue */
  public void addRear (Object obj) {
    Node newNode = new Node(obj, null, rear);
    if (numberElements == 0)
      front = newNode;
    else
      rear.next = newNode;
    rear = newNode;
    numberElements++;
  }

  /** Remove object from the front of the Dequeue, if found */
  public void removeFront () {
    if (isEmpty())
      throw new NoSuchElementException("Dequeue is empty." );
    else {
      if (front.next != null)
        front.next.before = null;
      front = front.next;
      numberElements--;
      if (numberElements == 0)
        rear = null;
    }
  }

  /** Remove object from the rear of the Dequeue, if found */
  public void removeRear () {
    if (isEmpty())
      throw new NoSuchElementException("Queue is empty." );
    else if (numberElements == 1) {
      front = null;
      rear = null;
    }
```

```
  else { // 2 or more elements
    // Find the node just in front of rear
    Node previous = rear.before;
    previous.next = null;
    rear = previous;
  }
  numberElements--;
}

// Queries
/** Return true if the Dequeue is empty */
public boolean isEmpty () {
  return numberElements == 0;
}

/** Return the number of objects in the Dequeue */
public int size () {
  return numberElements;
}

/** Return front item without removing it */
public Object front () {
  if (isEmpty())
    throw new NoSuchElementException("Dequeue is empty." );
  else
    return front.item;
}

/** Return the rear object in the Dequeue without removing it */
public Object rear () {
  if (isEmpty())
    throw new NoSuchElementException("Dequeue is empty." );
  else
    return rear.item;
}

/** Returns true if the Dequeue contains obj otherwise returns
  * false */
public boolean contains (Object obj) {
  Node current = front;
  while (current != null && !current.item.equals(obj))
    current = current.next;
  return current != null;
}

/** Return an iterator on the elements in the Dequeue */
public Iterator elements () {
  // Load the objects of the Dequeue into a Vector
  Vector v = new Vector();
```

```
      Node current = front;
      while (current != null) {
        v.addElement(current.item);
        current = current.next;
      }
      return v.iterator(); // Only valid in Platform 2
    }

    /** Models internal node for DoublyLinkedDequeue */
    protected class Node implements Serializable {
      protected Object item;
      protected Node next;
      protected Node before;

      public Node (Object element, Node link, Node backLink) {
        item = element;
        next = link;
        before = backLink;
      }
    }

    public static void main (String[] args) {
      DoublyLinkedDequeue myDequeue = new DoublyLinkedDequeue();
      // Add three Integer objects to the front of the Dequeue
      myDequeue.addFront(new Integer(5));
      myDequeue.addFront(new Integer(4));
      myDequeue.addFront(new Integer(3));

      // Add three Integer objects to the rear of the Dequeue
      myDequeue.addRear(new Integer(6));
      myDequeue.addRear(new Integer(7));
      myDequeue.addRear(new Integer(8));

      // Remove the front and rear objects
      myDequeue.removeFront();
      myDequeue.removeRear();

      // Obtain an iterator for the Dequeue
      Iterator iter = myDequeue.elements();

      while (iter.hasNext())
        System.out.println (iter.next());

      // Test for the presence of 5 and 8
      if (myDequeue.contains(new Integer(5)))
        System.out.println("5 is in the Dequeue." );
      else
        System.out.println("5 is not in the Dequeue." );
```

```
    if (myDequeue.contains(new Integer(8)))
      System.out.println("8 is in the Dequeue." );
    else
      System.out.println("8 is not in the Dequeue." );
  }
}
```

Output for Listing 13.4

```
    4
    5
    6
    7
    5 is in the Dequeue.
    8 is not in the Dequeue.
```

13.2 Positionable List

We shall present two dynamic implementations of positionable lists: *SinglyLinked-List* and *DoublyLinkedList*. Each implements the interface *PositionableList*. Recall that a positionable list allows insertions at the front or rear of the list as well as before or after a specified element in the list.

Because of the common protocol between a linked list and a *Dequeue* (commands *addFront*, *addRear*, *removeFront*, and *removeRear* and queries *front* and *rear*), class *SinglyLinkedList* extends *SinglyLinkedDequeue* and class *Doubly-LinkedList* extends *DoublyLinkedDequeue*. This allows us to focus on the new commands and queries provided by a linked list.

13.2.1 Singly Linked List

The structure of a singly linked list is the same as a singly linked *Dequeue* (see Figure 13.1). Listing 13.5 presents the details of class *SinglyLinkedList*.

Listing 13.5 Class *SinglyLinkedList*

```java
/** Implements a positionable list with duplicates.
*/
package foundations;
import java.util.*;

public class SinglyLinkedList extends SinglyLinkedDequeue
                              implements PositionableList {

  // Fields are inherited from SinglyLinkedDequeue

  // Commands
```

```java
/** Insert obj after target object in the list
*/
public void addAfter (Object obj, Object target) {
  Node itemNode = getNode (target);
  if (itemNode == null)
    throw new NoSuchElementException(
                  "addAfter::target does not exist" );
  else {
    Node newNode = new Node (obj, itemNode.next);
    itemNode.next = newNode;
    numberElements++;
    if (this.rear == itemNode)
      rear = newNode;
  }
}


/** Insert obj before target object in the list
*/
public void addBefore (Object obj, Object target) {
  Node itemNode = getNode (target);
  if (itemNode == null)
    throw new NoSuchElementException(
                  "addBefore::target does not exist" );
  else {
    Node newNode = new Node (obj, itemNode);
    if (this.front == itemNode)
      this.front = newNode;
    else {
      Node beforeNode = nodeBefore(itemNode);
      beforeNode.next = newNode;
    }
    numberElements++;
  }
}


/** Delete object after target object in the list
*    Throw NoSuchElementException if target not in the list.
*    Throw NoSuchElementException if target is last in the list.
*/
public void removeAfter (Object target) {
  // Exercise
}


/** Delete object before target object in the list
*    Throw NoSuchElementException if target not in the list.
*    Throw NoSuchElementException if target is first in the list.
*/
```

```
public void removeBefore (Object target) {
  // Exercise
}

// Queries

/** Return object after target object in the list
 *    Throw NoSuchElementException if target not in the list.
 *    Throw NoSuchElementException if target is last in the list.
 */
public Object elementAfter (Object target) {
  Node targetNode = getNode(target);
  if (!this.contains(target) || targetNode == this.rear)
    throw new NoSuchElementException(
    "removeAfter::obj does not exist or is last in list" );
  else
    return targetNode.next.item;
}

/** Return object before target object in the list
 *    Throw NoSuchElementException if target not in the list.
 *    Throw NoSuchElementException if target is first in the list.
 */
public Object elementBefore (Object target) {
  if (!this.contains(target) || getNode(target) == this.front)
    throw new NoSuchElementException(
      "removeBefore::obj does not exist or is first in list" );
  else
    return nodeBefore(getNode(target)).item;
}

// Internal methods

/**
  * For internal use only.
  * This function, available only within this class
  * returns the node associated with value. If value is
  * not present in the list getNode returns null
 */
protected Node getNode (Object value) {
  Node frontNode = front;
  Node result = null;
  while (frontNode != null) {
    if (frontNode.item.equals(value)) {
      result = frontNode;
      break;
    }
    frontNode = frontNode.next;
  }
  return result;
}
```

```
/**
 * For internal use only.
 * This function, available only within the class
 * returns the node just before someNode. If someNode is null or
 * the only node present in the list, this function returns null.
 */
protected Node nodeBefore (Node someNode) {
  if (someNode != null && someNode != front) {
    Node previous = front;
    while (previous.next != someNode)
      previous = previous.next;
    return previous;
  }
  else
    return null;
}

static public void main (String[] args) {
  SinglyLinkedList myList = new SinglyLinkedList();
  myList.addFront(new Integer(3));
  myList.addFront(new Integer(2));
  myList.addFront(new Integer(1));
  myList.addRear(new Integer(4));
  myList.addRear(new Integer(6));
  myList.addRear(new Integer(8));
  myList.addBefore(new Integer(5), new Integer(6));
  myList.addAfter(new Integer(7), new Integer(6));
  Iterator iter = myList.elements();
  while (iter.hasNext())
    System.out.println(iter.next());
  System.out.println("Element before 6 is " +
      myList.elementBefore(new Integer(6)));
  System.out.println("Element after 6 is " +
      myList.elementAfter(new Integer(6)));
}
}
```

Output for Listing 13.5

```
1
2
3
4
5
6
7
8
Element before 6 is 5
Element after 6 is 7
```

Explanation of Listing 13.5

The methods *removeAfter* and *removeBefore* are left as exercises for the reader.
Let us examine command *addAfter*.

```
public void addAfter (Object obj, Object target) {
  Node itemNode = getNode (target);
  if (itemNode == null)
    throw new NoSuchElementException(
                "addAfter::target does not exist" );
  else {
    Node newNode = new Node (obj, itemNode.next);
    itemNode.next = newNode;
    numberElements++;
    if (this.rear == itemNode)
      rear = newNode;
  }
}
```

Node *itemNode* associated with *target* is obtained by invoking the protected (internal) method *getNode*. Node *newNode* is constructed using *obj* and it is set to point to *itemNode.next*. The next field of *itemNode* is linked to *newNode*. The field *numberElements* is increased by one. Finally, if the field *rear* equals *itemNode*, then *rear* is reassigned to *newNode*.

Finally, we examine command *addBefore*.

```
public void addBefore (Object obj, Object target) {
  Node itemNode = getNode (target);
  if (itemNode == null)
    throw new NoSuchElementException(
                "addBefore::target does not exist" );
  else {
    Node newNode = new Node (obj, itemNode);
    if (this.front == itemNode)
      this.front = newNode;
    else {
      Node beforeNode = nodeBefore(itemNode);
      beforeNode.next = newNode;
    }
    numberElements++;
  }
}
```

Node *itemNode* is again determined using *getNode*. Node *newNode* is constructed using *obj* and is set to point to *itemNode*. If *front* equals *itemNode*, *front* is reassigned to *newNode*. If *front* does not equal *itemNode*, *beforeNode* is computed using *nodeBefore(itemNode)*. The field *next* of *beforeNode* is linked to *newNode*. Finally, the field *numberElements* is increased by one.

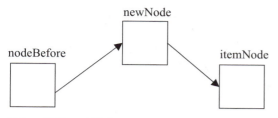

Figure 13.3. *addBefore.*

Figure 13.3 depicts the nodes used in the logic associated with *addBefore*.

13.2.2   Doubly Linked List

The structure of a doubly linked list is the same as a doubly linked *Dequeue* (see Figure 13.2). Listing 13.6 presents the details of class *DoublyLinkedList*.

Listing 13.6   Class *DoublyLinkedList*

```
/** Implements PositionableList with duplicates and links pointing
 * forwards and backwards
 */
package foundations;
import java.util.*;

public class DoublyLinkedList extends DoublyLinkedDequeue
                          implements PositionableList {

  // Fields are inherited from DoublyLinkedDequeue

  /** Insert obj after target object in the list
   */
  public void addAfter (Object obj, Object target) {
    Node itemNode = getNode (target);
    if (itemNode == null)
      throw new NoSuchElementException(
          "addAfter::target does not exist" );
    else {
      // Backlink to itemNode and forward link to itemNode.next
      Node newNode = new Node (obj, itemNode.next, itemNode);
      if (itemNode.next != null)
        itemNode.next.before = newNode;
      else
        rear = newNode;
      itemNode.next = newNode;
      numberElements++;
    }
  }
```

```
/** Insert obj before target object in the list
*/
public void addBefore (Object obj, Object target) {
  Node itemNode = getNode(target);
  if (itemNode == null)
    throw new NoSuchElementException(
                "addBefore::target does not exist" );
  else {
    Node beforeNode = itemNode.before;
    // Backlink to beforeNode forward link to itemNode
    Node newNode = new Node (obj, itemNode, beforeNode);
    if (front == itemNode)
      front = newNode;
    else
      beforeNode.next = newNode;
    itemNode.before = newNode;
    numberElements++;
  }
}

/** Delete object after target object in the list
*    Throw NoSuchElementException if target not in the list.
*    Throw NoSuchElementException if target is last in the list.
*/
public void removeAfter (Object target) {
  // Exercise
}

/** Delete object before target object in the list
*    Throw NoSuchElementException if target not in the list.
*    Throw NoSuchElementException if target is first in the list.
*/
public void removeBefore (Object target) {
  // Exercise
}

// Queries

/** Return object after target object in the list
*    Throw NoSuchElementException if target not in the list.
*    Throw NoSuchElementException if target is last in the list.
*/
public Object elementAfter (Object target) {
  if (!this.contains(target) || getNode(target) == this.rear)
    throw new NoSuchElementException(
      "removeAfter::obj does not exist or is last in list" );
  else
    return getNode(target).next.item;
}
```

```
/** Return object before target object in the list
 *    Throw NoSuchElementException if target not in the list.
 *    Throw NoSuchElementException if target is first in the list.
 */
public Object elementBefore (Object target) {
  if (!this.contains(target) || getNode(target) == this.front)
    throw new NoSuchElementException(
      "removeBefore::obj does not exist or is first in list" );
  else
    return getNode(target).before.item;
}


// Internal methods


/**
  * For internal use only.
  * This function, available only within this class
  * returns the node associated with value. If value is
  * not present in the list, getNode returns null
 */
protected Node getNode (Object value) {
  Node node = front;
  Node result = null;
  while (node != null) {
    if (node.item.equals(value)) {
      result = node;
      break;
    }
    node = node.next;
  }
  return result;
}


static public void main (String[] args) {
  DoublyLinkedList myList = new DoublyLinkedList();
  myList.addFront(new Integer(3));
  myList.addFront(new Integer(2));
  myList.addFront(new Integer(1));
  myList.addRear(new Integer(4));
  myList.addRear(new Integer(6));
  myList.addRear(new Integer(8));
  myList.addBefore(new Integer(5), new Integer(6));
  myList.addAfter(new Integer(7), new Integer(6));
  Iterator iter = myList.elements();
  while (iter.hasNext())
    System.out.println(iter.next());
```

```
    System.out.println("Element before 6 is " +
        myList.elementBefore(new Integer(6)));
    System.out.println("Elment after 6 is " +
        myList.elementAfter(new Integer(6)));
  }
}
```

The output for Listing 13.6 is the same as for Listing 13.5.

Explanation of Listing 13.6

The methods *removeAfter* and *removeBefore* are again left as exercises for the reader. As before, we shall dissect methods *addAfter* and *addBefore*. Let us examine command *addAfter*.

```
public void addAfter (Object obj, Object target) {
  Node itemNode = getNode(target);
  if (itemNode == null)
      throw new NoSuchElementException(
          "addAfter::target does not exist" );
  else {
     // Backlink to itemNode and forward link to itemNode.next
     Node newNode = new Node(obj, itemNode.next, itemNode);
     if (itemNode.next != null)
       itemNode.next.before = newNode;
     else
       rear = newNode;
     itemNode.next = newNode;
     numberElements++;
  }
}
```

Node *itemNode* is found using *getNode(target)*. Node *newNode* is constructed using the *obj* so that it is forward linked to *itemNode.next* and back linked to *itemNode*. If *itemNode* is not at the end of the list, *itemNode.next.before* is linked to *newNode*; otherwise the field *rear* is reassigned to *newNode*. The *next* field of *itemNode* is assigned to *newNode* and the field *numberElements* is increased by one.

Finally, we examine command *addBefore*.

```
public void addBefore (Object obj, Object target) {
  Node itemNode = getNode(target);
  if (itemNode == null)
      throw new NoSuchElementException(
                "addBefore::target does not exist" );
```

```
  else {
     Node beforeNode = itemNode.before;
     // Backlink to beforeNode forward link to itemNode
     Node newNode = new Node (obj, itemNode, beforeNode);
     if (front == itemNode)
       front = newNode;
     else
       beforeNode.next = newNode;
     itemNode.before = newNode;
     numberElements++;
  }
}
```

The Node *itemNode* is computed using *getNode(target)*. The Node *beforeNode* is assigned to *itemNode.before*. The Node *newNode* is constructed using *target* so that it is forward linked to *itemNode* and back linked to *beforeNode*. If *itemNode* is the first element in the list, *front* is reassigned to *newNode*; otherwise *beforeNode* is linked to *newNode*. The *before* field of *itemNode* is linked to *newNode* and the field *numberElements* is increased by one.

13.3 Vector List

Class *VectorList* implements the interface *IndexableList*. Its skeletal structure is given in Listing 13.7. Recall that an indexable list allows insertion or removal at a specified index in the list.

Listing 13.7 Skeletal Structure of Class *VectorList*

```
/** An implementation of IndexableList
*/
package foundations;
import java.util.*;

public class VectorList implements IndexableList {

  // Fields
  Vector data = new Vector();

  // Commands

  /** Remove all objects from the container if found */
  public void makeEmpty () {
    // Exercise for reader
  }

  /** Add obj at the front */
  public void addFront (Object obj) {
    // Exercise for reader
  }
```

```java
/** Add obj at the rear */
public void addRear (Object obj) {
  // Exercise for reader
}

/** Remove object from the front if found. */
public void removeFront () {
  // Exercise for reader
}

/** Remove object from the rear if found. */
public void removeRear () {
  // Exercise for reader
}

/** Replace object at index with obj
 *    Throws ArrayIndexOutOfBoundsException if index error
 */
public void insertAt (Object obj, int index) {
  // Exercise for reader
}

/** Remove an object at specified index
 *    Throws ArrayIndexOutOfBoundsException if index error
 */
public void removeAt (int index) {
  // Exercise for reader
}

// Queries

/** Return without removing the front object
 *    Throws NoSuchElementException if list is empty
 */
public Object front () {
  // Exercise for reader
}

/** Return without removing the rear object
 *    Throws NoSuchElementException if list is empty
 */
public Object rear() {
  // Exercise for reader
}

/** Return true if the list contains obj
 */
public boolean contains (Object obj) {
  // Exercise for reader
}
```

```
/** Return true if the list is empty */
public boolean isEmpty () {
  // Exercise for reader
}

/** Return the number of objects in the list */
public int size () {
  // Exercise for reader
}

/** Return the object at index without removing
 *  Throws ArrayIndexOutOfBoundsException if index error
 */
public Object elementAt (int index) {
  return data.elementAt(index);
}

/** Iterator */
public Iterator elements () {
  return data.iterator();
}

static public void main (String[] args) {
  VectorList myVectorList = new VectorList();
  myVectorList.addRear(new Integer(4));
  myVectorList.addRear(new Integer(5));
  myVectorList.addRear(new Integer(6));
  myVectorList.addFront(new Integer(3));
  myVectorList.addFront(new Integer(2));
  myVectorList.addFront(new Integer(1));
  System.out.println ("The element at index 1 = " +
                          myVectorList.elementAt(1));
  System.out.println ("The element at index 5 = " +
                          myVectorList.elementAt(5));
  myVectorList.insertAt(new Integer(20), 2);
  System.out.println ("The element at index 2 = " +
                          myVectorList.elementAt(2));
  myVectorList.removeRear();
  System.out.println ("The element at the rear = " +
                          myVectorList.rear());
  myVectorList.removeFront();
  System.out.println ("The element at the front = " +
                          myVectorList.front());
  Iterator iter = myVectorList.elements();
  while (iter.hasNext())
    System.out.println (iter.next());
}
}
```

The implementation of all the methods are left as an exercise for the reader.

Output for Listing 13.7

```
The element at index 1 = 2
The element at index 5 = 6
The element at index 2 = 20
The element at the rear = 5
The element at the front = 2
2
20
4
5
```

13.4   Ordered List

An ordered list implements the interface *SearchTable*. Its elements are ordered (therefore the need to implement a search table) and therefore must be of type *Comparable*. No duplicates are allowed in an *OrderedList*.

In Java 2 Platform, all wrapper classes are of type *Comparable*. Class *String* is also of type *Comparable*.

Listing 13.8 presents the details of class *OrderedList*.

Listing 13.8   Class *OrderedList*

```java
/** Implements SearchTable with singly linked list without duplicates.
*/
package foundations;
import java.util.*;
import java.io.Serializable;

public class OrderedList implements SearchTable {

  // Fields
  protected Node first;
  int numberElements;

  // Commands

  /** Remove all objects from the container if found */
  public void makeEmpty () {
    while (first != null) {
      Node previous = first;
      first = first.next;
      previous = null;
    }
    numberElements = 0;
  }
```

```
/** Add obj to the table; must be Comparable */
public void add (Comparable obj) {
  if (numberElements == 0)
    first = new Node(obj, null);
  else {
    Node current = first;
    Node previous = null;
    if (current.item.compareTo(obj) == 0)
      throw new NoSuchElementException(
              "add::obj already in list" );
    // Search for first node in list that is greater than obj
    while (current != null &&
        current.item.compareTo (obj) < 0) {
      previous = current;
      if (current.item.compareTo(obj) == 0)
        throw new NoSuchElementException(
                "add::obj already in list" );
      current = current.next;
    }
    Node newNode = new Node(obj, current);
    if (previous != null)
      previous.next = newNode;
    else
      first = newNode;
  }
  numberElements++;
}

/** Remove obj from table, if found */
public void remove (Comparable obj) {
  // Exercise
}

// Queries

/** Return true if the container is empty */
public boolean isEmpty () {
  return numberElements == 0;
}

/** Return the number of objects in the container */
public int size () {
  return numberElements;
}

/** Return true if the table contains obj */
public boolean contains (Comparable obj) {
  Node current = first;
```

```java
    while (current != null && current.item.compareTo(obj) != 0)
      current = current.next;
    return current != null;
}

/** Return obj if in table otherwise returns null
 *    useful when obj is a key & returns an Association
 */
public Comparable get (Comparable obj) {
  Node current = first;
  while (current != null && current.item.compareTo(obj) != 0)
    current = current.next;
  if (current != null)
    return current.item;
  else
    return null;
}

/** Return an iterator on all elements */
public Iterator elements () {
  // Load the objects of the Dequeue into a Vector
  Vector v = new Vector();
  Node current = first;
  while (current != null) {
    v.addElement(current.item);
    current = current.next;
  }
  return v.iterator(); // Only valid in Platform 2
}

/** Models internal node for OrderedList */
protected class Node implements Serializable {
  protected Comparable item;
  protected Node next;

  public Node (Comparable value, Node lnk) {
    item = value;
    next = lnk;
  }
}

// Internal methods

/**
  * For internal use only.
  * This function, available only within this class,
  * returns the node associated with value. If value is
  * not present in the list, getNode returns null
  */
```

```
private Node getNode (Comparable value) {
  Node node = first;
  Node result = null;
  while (node != null) {
    if (node.item.compareTo(value) == 0) {
      result = node;
      break;
    }
    node = node.next;
  }
  return result;
}

/**
 * For internal use only.
 * This function, available only within the class,
 * returns the node just before someNode. If someNode is null or
 * the only node present in the list, this function returns null.
 */
private Node nodeBefore (Node someNode) {
  if (someNode != null && someNode != first) {
    Node previous = first;
    while (previous.next != someNode)
      previous = previous.next;
    return previous;
  }
  else
    return null;
}

static public void main (String[] args) {
  OrderedList strList = new OrderedList();
  strList.add(new String("Erik" ));
  strList.add(new String("Adam" ));
  strList.add(new String("Charlie" ));
  strList.add(new String("Peter" ));
  strList.add(new String("Marc" ));
  strList.remove(new String("Charlie" ));
  Iterator iter = strList.elements();
  while (iter.hasNext())
    System.out.println(iter.next());

  OrderedList intList = new OrderedList();
  intList.add(new Integer(12));
  intList.add(new Integer(10));
  intList.add(new Integer(11));
  intList.add(new Integer(17));
  intList.add(new Integer(13));
```

```
    intList.remove(new Integer(12));
    iter = intList.elements();
    while (iter.hasNext())
      System.out.println(iter.next());
  }
}
```

Output for Listing 13.8

```
Adam
Erik
Marc
Peter
10
11
13
17
```

13.5 List Laboratory

A GUI application that provides a test suite for all six list classes is constructed. A screen shot of the laboratory in action is shown in Figure 13.4.

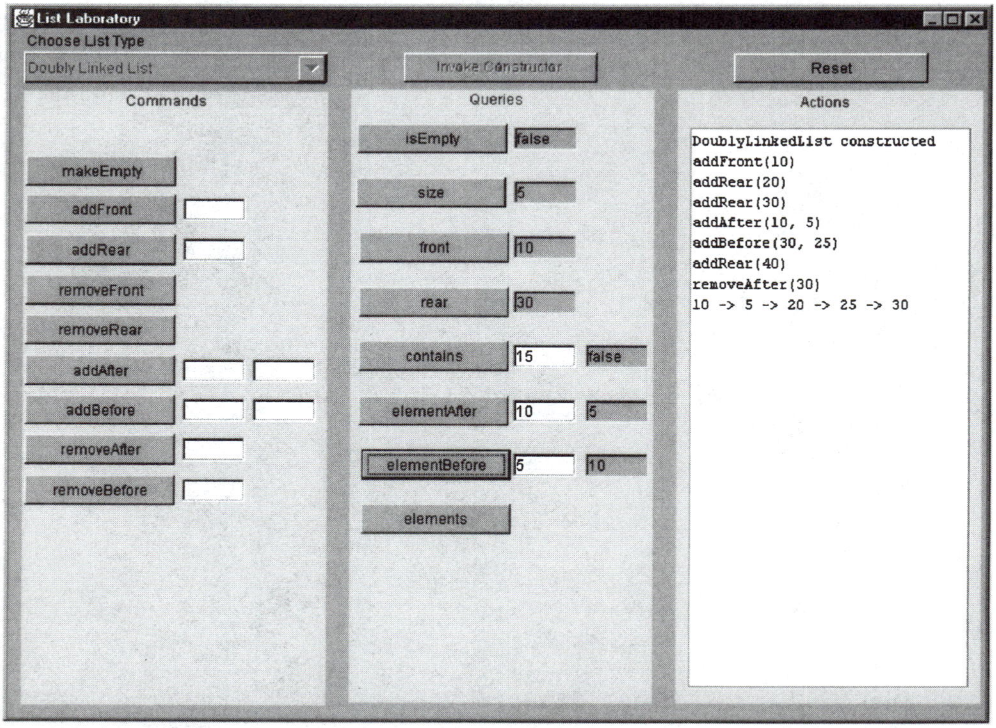

Figure 13.4. Screen shot of list laboratory.

The *ListLabUI* class utilizes two internal fields:

```
// Fields
foundations.List aList;    // Qualified reference needed
OrderedList orderedList;
```

The qualified reference to *List* is needed since *List* classes already exist in the standard *java.awt* and *java.util* packages.

The user is given the choice of choosing one of eight possible list types:

1. SinglyLinkedDequeue
2. DoublyLinkedDequeue
3. SinglyLinkedList
4. SinglyLinkedListE
5. DoublyLinkedList
6. DoublyLinkedListE
7. VectorList
8. OrderedList

The *SinglyLinkedListE* and *DoublyLinkedListE* classes are partially implemented with the *remove* commands left as exercises for the reader to implement.

If the user chooses items 1 through 7 (*SinglyLinkedDequeue* to *VectorList*), the list is constructed using the appropriate concrete class type. For example, if the user chooses *DoublyLinkedList* (as in the screen shot of Figure 13.4), the list would be set as follows:

```
list = new DoublyLinkedList();
```

The principle of **polymorphic substitution** allows a descendant type to be substituted for an ancestor type.

Some downcasting must be done in order to allow operations specific to a given type to be accepted by the compiler. This is illustrated with the line of code below (taken from class *ListLabUI*).

```
((PositionableList) aList).addAfter(item, value);
```

The command *addAfter* is not defined in interface *List*. The downcast shown above forces the compiler to accept the usage.

Depending on which list type the user chooses, a different array of command and query buttons are made visible. If the user clicks the "Reset" button, all panels are made invisible, each list is made empty, and the system is restored to its initial state.

13.6 *Stack* and *Queue* Revisited

We presented static and dynamic implementations of *stack* in Chapter 11 (*ArrayStack* and *LinkedStack*) and a dynamic implementation of *queue* (*LinkedQueue*).

Having completed our presentation of lists it is useful to briefly revisit the issue of stack and queue implementation. Both a stack and queue may be implemented by encapsulating an internal *Dequeue* (or internal *PositionableList* such as *SinglyLinkedList* or *DoublyLinkedList*).

The external operations of a stack or queue are a subset of the operations available in a list such as *Dequeue*. For this reason, we avoid using inheritance as many authors have done in the past because we believe that extension implies added features, not reduced features.

Listing 13.9 shows the implementation of *ListStack* using class *SinglyLinkedList* internally.

Listing 13.9   Class *ListStack*

```
/** A Stack implemented with an internal list
*/
package foundations;
import java.util.*;

public class ListStack {

  // Fields
  SinglyLinkedList list = new SinglyLinkedList();

  // Commands

  public void push (Object item) {
    list.addFront(item);
  }

  public void pop () {
    if (isEmpty())
      throw new NoSuchElementException("Stack is empty.");
    else
      list.removeFront();
  }

  public void makeEmpty () {
    list.makeEmpty();
  }

  // Queries

  public Object top () {
    return list.front();
  }
```

```
public boolean isEmpty () {
  return list.isEmpty();
}


public int size () {
  return list.size();
}


static public void main (String[] args) {
  ListStack myStack = new ListStack();
  myStack.push(new Integer(1));
  myStack.push(new Integer(2));
  myStack.push(new Integer(3));
  System.out.println("myStack.size() = " + myStack.size());
  myStack.pop();
  System.out.println("myStack.size() = " + myStack.size());
  System.out.println("myStack.top() = " + myStack.top());
}
}
```

Output for Listing 13.9

```
myStack.size() = 3
myStack.size() = 2
myStack.top() = 2
```

It is left as an exercise for the reader to implement *ListQueue* using an approach similar to Listing 13.9.

13.7 Summary

❏ A list is a useful and widely used container abstraction. Lists come in various flavors so we really have a family of list abstractions.

❏ The simplest list allows the addition of objects, removal of objects, and access to objects only at two ends, front and rear.

❏ An indexable list extends a simple list by allowing the insertion of objects, removal of objects, and access of objects at a particular index.

❏ A positionable list extends a simple list by allowing the addition of objects, removal of objects, and access to objects before or after a specified object in the list.

❏ An ordered list extends *SearchTable* and requires that its elements be comparable. A strict ordering relationship is maintained among the elements of an ordered list.

❏ A *Dequeue* is an implementation of a simple *List*. Objects may be added, removed, or accessed at the front or the rear of such a list.

❏ A static implementation of a list requires that the user specify the size of the list in advance and, once specified, the size cannot be changed. The advantage of such an implementation is efficiency. A dynamic implementation provides more flexibility, since memory is allocated on demand as more objects are added.

❏ Because of the common protocol between a linked list and a *Dequeue* (commands *addFront*, *addRear*, *removeFront*, and *removeRear* and queries *front* and *rear*), class *SinglyLinkedList* extends *SinglyLinkedDequeue* and class *DoublyLinked-List* extends *DoublyLinkedDequeue*.

13.8 Exercises

1 Implement *removeAfter* and *removeBefore* for class *SinglyLinkedListE*. This partially completed class is located in the *foundations* folder in a subdirectory of the *ListLab*.

2 Implement *removeAfter* and *removeBefore* for class *DoublyLinkedListE*. This partially completed class is located in the *foundations* folder in a subdirectory of the *ListLab*.

3 Implement the complete class *ListQueue* using class *SinglyLinkedList* internally. Your queue implementation should not use *class Node* explicitly (it is used in implementing *SinglyLinkedList*) but only the internally defined instance of *SinglyLinkedList*.

   Write a short test stub in a function main to be included with your class *ListQueue*.

4 Implement all of the methods of class *VectorList* that are specified as "Exercise for reader" in Listing 13.6. The test stub given in function *main* should serve as your *VectorList* test.

5 Implement a static version of a positionable list. Call your class *ArrayList*. Test your list using function *main*. Your new class must be declared to be in package *foundations*.

6 Implement a static version of an ordered list. Call your class *ArrayOrdered-List*. Test your list using function *main*. Your new class must be declared to be in package *foundations*.

   Note: For all the following exercises that require you to add methods to *SinglyLinkedList*, construct a class *SpecialSinglyLinkedList* that extends *SinglyLinkedList* and is declared to be in package *foundations*. You will have access to the protected fields *front* and *rear* inherited from *SinglyLinked-Dequeue*.

7 Add a method *shallowCopy* to class *SinglyLinkedList* with signature:

```
SinglyLinkedList shallowCopy();
```

This method returns a new list that contains the same nodes as the receiver.

8   Add a method *deepCopy* to class *SinglyLinkedList* with signature:

```
SinglyLinkedList deepCopy();
```

This class returns a new list that contains copies of the nodes of the receiver.

9   Design a method for inserting an object into the middle of a *SinglyLinkedList* with signature:

```
void insertMiddle (Object obj);
```

10   Implement a recursive version of the *contains* query for class *SinglyLinked-List*. This method (in your class *SpecialSinglyLinkedList*) should override the method given in *SinglyLinkedList*.

11   Add the method *addAfterSecondOccurrence* to class *SinglyLinkedList*. The signature of this method is:

```
public void addAfterSecondOccurrence (Object obj,
                            Object target);
```

This method searches for the second occurrence of the target object and adds *obj* after this target. If a second occurrence of *target* does not exist, an exception must be thrown. Write test code in function *main*.

12   Add the method *addBeforeSecondOccurrence* to class *SinglyLinkedList*. The signature of this method is:

```
public void addBeforeSecondOccurrence (Object obj,
                            Object target);
```

This method searches for the second occurrence of the target object and adds *obj* before this target. If a second occurrence of *target* does not exist, an exception must be thrown. Write test code in function *main*.

13   Add the method *removeAfterSecondOccurrence* to class *SinglyLinkedList*. The signature of this method is:

```
public void removeAfterSecondOccurrence (Object obj,
                            Object target);
```

This method searches for the second occurrence of the target object and removes *obj* after this target. If a second occurrence of *target* does not exist, an exception must be thrown. Write test code in function *main*.

14   Add the method *removeBeforeSecondOccurrence* to class *SinglyLinkedList*. The signature of this method is:

```
public void removeBeforeSecondOccurrence (Object obj,
                                          Object target);
```

This method searches for the second occurrence of the target object and removes *obj* before this target. If a second occurrence of *target* does not exist, an exception must be thrown. Write test code in function *main*.

15   Compare the list abstractions presented in this chapter to the list abstractions provided in the standard Java libraries.

Trees, Heaps, and Priority Queues

This chapter groups together three important data structures: trees, heaps, and priority queues. Trees are our first example of a nonlinear structure for containing objects. Although conceptually more complex than linear data structures, trees offer the opportunity for improved efficiency in operations such as inserting, removing, and searching for contained objects. Heaps are also nonlinear in structure and contained objects must be organized in agreement with an order relationship between each node and its descendants. A heap may be efficiently implemented using a binary tree. A priority queue is a special kind of queue that contains prioritized objects (usually based on a key) in a way that the objects are removed based on their priority (highest priority first). Priority queues may be implemented using a heap. There is a nonessential but beneficial relationship among these three data structures; that is why they are grouped together in this chapter. Additional variations on binary trees are covered in later chapters.

14.1 Trees

A tree is a nonlinear data structure that derives its name from a similarity between its defining terminology and our friends in the forest, real trees. A tree data structure is considerably more constrained in its variety than a real tree and is typically viewed upside down, with its root at the top and leaves on the bottom. A tree is usually accessed from its *root*, then down through its branches to the leaves.

A tree may be described as a nonlinear container of nodes. The nodes provide storage for contained objects as well as references to other nodes for connectivity. Nodes are connected by edges. A simple tree structure is shown in Figure 14.1.

We use the simple tree in Figure 14.1 to illustrate the defining terminology of trees.

- Node A is the *root* of the tree. It contains the object A (a character) and references to three other nodes: B, C, and D. It has no parent.
- The *degree* of node A is 3 (it has three references to other nodes).
- Nodes B, C, and D are the direct descendants or *children* of node A.
- Node A is the *parent* of nodes B, C, and D.
- Nodes E and F are *siblings* (children of the same parent).
- Nodes A, B, and D are *internal* nodes since they have at least one child.

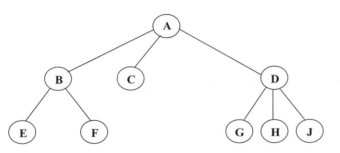

Figure 14.1. A simple tree structure.

- Nodes E, F, C, G, H, and J are *leaf* (or *external*) nodes since they have no children. The degree of a leaf node is 0.
- The *level* (or *depth*) of the root node is 0; node E is at level 2. The *pathLength* (number of edges traversed from the root) to a node is equal to its depth or level.
- The *height* of the tree is 2 (also the maximum level or depth of any node).

In general, the commands and queries required of a tree include those in interface *Container* plus methods for adding and removing objects, iterating over all contained objects, and testing/returning contained objects. There are many variations on kinds of trees with significant conceptual differences in the meaning of add, remove, iterate and other commands/queries. Thus we defer creation of a tree abstract data type to discussions of specific kinds of trees.

14.1.1 *BinaryTree* Abstract Data Type

Our first specialization of a tree is one that constrains the degree of any node in the tree to be no more than two, producing a *BinaryTree* abstraction. More precisely, we define a binary tree as:

- an abstract data type
- a tree whose nodes have degree equal to 0, 1, or 2

A *BinaryTree* is defined recursively by:

- *null* is a *BinaryTree* (an empty tree).
- A *node* is a *BinaryTree* with exactly two children (*left* and *right*) that are binary trees.
- An *external* (leaf) node has 2 null offspring.
- An *internal* node has 1 or 2 non-null offspring.
- Nothing else is a *BinaryTree*.

The recursive definition should make it clear that the children of any node in a tree are also trees. In terms of the overall structure of the tree, we may characterize these children (or offspring) as subtrees. Thus a binary tree is a tree whose nodes

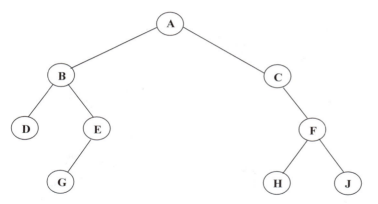

Figure 14.2. A simple binary tree structure.

have a left subtree and a right subtree, either of which may be null. An example binary tree is shown in Figure 14.2.

As with other containers, a tree or binary tree may have a structure with order based on insertion/removal history, insertion/removal rules, or on some ordering relationship of its contained objects. In this section we focus on the conceptual properties shared by most, if not all, binary trees and defer specialization of binary trees to later sections and chapters.

Listing 14.1 repeats the interface for *BinaryTree* presented in Chapter 10. It shows the addition of five queries that are considered to be generally useful for binary trees. Three of these return iterators over the elements in the binary tree; the other two return the maximum level and average path length for the binary tree.

Listing 14.1 Interface *BinaryTree*

```
/** Interface BinaryTree
*    Contained objects must override equals() from Object
*/
package foundations;
import java.util.*;


public interface BinaryTree extends Container {

  // Queries

  /** Return an in-order iterator on elements in the tree
  */
  public Iterator traverseInorder ();

  /** return a preorder iterator on elements in the tree
  */
  public Iterator traversePreorder ();
```

```
/** Return a postorder iterator on elements in the tree
*/
public Iterator traversePostorder ();

/** return the maximum level in the tree, root is at level 0
*/
public int maxLevel ();

/** Return average path length for the tree
*/
public double avgPathLength ();
}
```

14.1.1.1 Traversal of a Binary Tree

In traversing the elements of a binary tree we typically want to visit each node exactly one time (there are variations on this, as we will see in our discussion of expression trees). The meaning of "visit" is considered to be independent of the traversal process as it is for iteration. In other words, the three traversal queries in Listing 14.1 return an *Iterator* that allows the user to get a reference to the next element and visit it as desired.

Traversal of the nodes in a binary tree is easily achieved using double recursion: one recursive call to the left subtree and one recursive call to the right subtree. The recursion sentinel is when a node is *null*. The *visit* operation may occur in three places in the recursion, leading to the three traversal queries. In pseudocode we present the three traversal algorithms with results when applied to the binary tree in Figure 14.2. For the example results, we interpret "visit" to mean "display the contained object."

In-Order Traversal Algorithm – In-Order Visit (between Recursive Calls)

```
traverseInorder(left child)
visit (current node)
traverseInorder(right child)
```

When applied to the binary tree in Figure 14.2, we get:

```
D B G E A C H F J
```

Postorder Traversal Algorithm – Postorder Visit (after the Recursive Calls)

```
traversePostorder(left child)
traversePostorder(right child)
visit (current node)
```

When applied to the binary tree in Figure 14.2, we get:

```
D  G  E  B  H  J  F  C  A
```

Preorder Traversal Algorithm – Preorder Visit (before the Recursive Calls)

visit (current node)
traversePreorder(left child)
traversePreorder(right child)

When applied to the binary tree in Figure 14.2, we get:

```
A  B  D  E  G  C  F  H  J
```

14.1.1.2 Mapping the Traversals into an Iterator

We now consider implementation options to satisfy the desired behavior that the traversal queries return iterators, which allows the user to define "visit." We find it convenient to use a linear container whose elements are in the order implied by a preorder, in-order, or postorder traversal. The next element is then returned from the next index starting with the first element in the linear container. The supporting linear container may be a list or a stack. For purposes of illustration we will use an instance of *java.util.Vector* (a kind of list) for the linear container.

The key method in using a linear container for traversal of a binary tree is a command for building the container – for example, recursively traversing the tree and inserting items into the container so that their order represents the desired traversal order. We currently have three versions of this process using preorder, in-order, and postorder traversal. Here we have an opportunity to develop a solution based on good object-oriented design principles. Figure 14.3 shows a class diagram for a solution using *java.util.Vector*. The new classes are part of the *foundations* package.

Class *TreeIterator* is an abstract class that *implements* interface *Iterator*. It contains an instance of *java.util.Vector* as the linear storage for traversed elements of the binary tree. Implementers of the *BinaryTree* interface may choose to use *TreeIterator* and its subclasses for implementing the three traversal methods. The three subclasses shown for *TreeIterator* need only implement the key method *buildVector*, which is abstract in parent class *TreeIterator*. The details of *buildVector* in each subclass will follow the traversal algorithms for in-order, preorder, and postorder as given above for adding elements to the vector *v*. The promised implementations in interface *Iterator* are all implemented in abstract class *TreeIterator* and useable by subclass instances, unchanged.

Class *SearchTreeNode* shown in Figure 14.3 represents tree nodes with *Comparable* contents, plus references to *left* and *right* instances of *SearchTreeNode*. In the most general sense a *BinaryTree* does not require that its nodes contain *Comparable* objects; however, all the binary tree application classes in this book are compatible with or do require nodes with *Comparable* contents. For that reason we implement the *TreeIterator* classes using instances of *SearchTreeNode*.

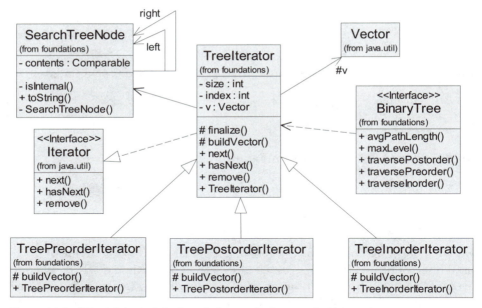

Figure 14.3. Object-Oriented design of classes for traversal of binary trees.

Listing 14.2 shows details for classes *TreeIterator*, *TreeInorderIterator*, and *SearchTreeNode*. Other *TreeIterator* subclasses implement the appropriate *buildVector* algorithm. The tree iterator classes and *SearchTreeNode* have package visibility with a public interface.

Listing 14.2   Details of Classes *TreeIterator, TreeInorderIterator,* and *SearchTreeNode*

```
** Abstract Iterator for traversal of binary search tree
*  Has package visibility
*/
package foundations;
import java.util.*;

abstract class TreeIterator implements Iterator {

  // Fields

  protected Vector v;
  protected int index;
  protected int size;

  // Initialize by building Vector v with elements in desired order
  public TreeIterator (SearchTreeNode root) {
    v = new Vector();
```

```
    buildVector(root);
    v.trimToSize();
    index = 0;
    size = v.size();
  }

  // Commands

  public void remove () {
    // not used - null implementation
  }

  // Queries

  // Return true if last element has not been visited.
  public boolean hasNext () {
    return index < size;
  }

  // Return a reference to the next object.
  public Object next () {
    Object obj = v.elementAt(index);
    index++;
    return obj;
  }

  // Key method - subclass responsibility

  protected abstract void buildVector (SearchTreeNode node);

  protected void finalize () {
    v.removeAllElements(); // prep for garbage collection
  }
}

//------------------------------------------------------------------
/** Iterator for in-order traversal of binary search tree
*/
package foundations;
import java.util.*;

class TreeInorderIterator extends TreeIterator { // package visibility

  // Constructors

  public TreeInorderIterator (SearchTreeNode root) {
    super(root);
  }
```

```
    // Internal command - key method
    // Build Vector v while doing in-order traversal of tree.
    protected void buildVector (SearchTreeNode node) {
      if (node != null) {
        buildVector(node.left);
        v.addElement(node.contents);
        buildVector(node.right);
      }
    }
}


//-------------------------------------------------------------------
/** Node for binary search tree
*/
package foundations;
import java.util.*;
import java.io.Serializable;

class SearchTreeNode implements Serializable { // package visibility

  // Fields

  Comparable contents;
  SearchTreeNode left;
  SearchTreeNode right;

  // Constructors

  SearchTreeNode (Comparable obj) {
    contents = obj;
    left = null;
    right = null;
  }

  // Queries

  public String toString () {
    return contents.toString();
  }

  boolean isInternal () {
    return (left != null) || (right != null);
  }
}
```

14.1.1.3   Average Path Length for Binary Trees

An important quantitative measure of the complexity of a binary tree is its average path length. It provides a measure of the average depth of all nodes in the tree. This may be compared with the number of nodes in the tree and related to time complexity in using the tree. Interface *BinaryTree* includes a query for returning the average path length specified by the signature *public double avgPathLength( )*.

We define average path length, APL[n], for a binary tree with n nodes to be

$$APL[n] = TPL[n]/n,$$

where TPL[n] is the total path length of all nodes in the tree

$$TPL[n] = \sum_{i=1}^{n} d[i],$$

where d [i] = depth of node i.

This formula is always true and is the best we can do without knowing the actual structure of a particular tree. In order to acquire a better understanding of the significance of average path length we may look at several special binary trees. We define two special cases: (1) a perfectly balanced binary tree (PBBT) and (2) a complete or optimally balanced binary tree.

A perfectly balanced binary tree may be defined as follows:

- All leaf nodes are at the same level.
- Required: $height = \log_2 (n + 1) - 1$; conversely: $n = 2^{(height+1)} - 1$.
- Form of the tree is completely specified by either *height* or n.

Figure 14.4 shows an example of a perfectly balanced binary tree.

In calculating the APL for a PBBT we may take advantage of the required relationship (given by the second bullet above) between the height of the tree and

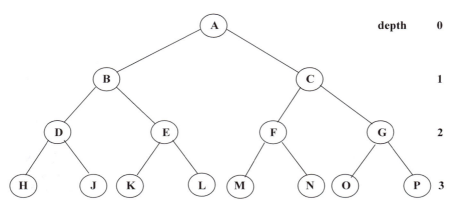

Figure 14.4. A perfectly balanced binary tree.

Table 14.1 APL for Small PBBT Sizes			
n	Height	APL calculation details	APL: $a\frac{b}{c}$
1	0	$(0 * 1) / 1 = 0$	0
3	1	$(0 * 1 + 1 * 2)/3 = 2/3$	$\frac{2}{3}$
7	2	$(0 * 1 + 1 * 2 + 2 * 4) / 7 = 10/7$	$1\frac{3}{7}$
15	3	$(0 * 1 + 1 * 2 + 2 * 4 + 3 * 8)/15 = 34/15$	$2\frac{4}{15}$
31	4	$(0 * 1 + 1 * 2 + 2 * 4 + 3 * 8 + 4 * 16)/31 = 98/31$	$3\frac{5}{31}$

the number of nodes. Furthermore, every level in the tree is full (containing the maximum number of nodes for that level).

For level ℓ the number of nodes in a PBBT is given by:

$$n_\ell = 2^\ell$$

and the APL is given by:

$$APL_{PBBT}[n] = \sum_{\ell=0}^{height} \ell \cdot 2^\ell /n.$$

We now have a parameterized result for computing the APL of a PBBT of size n. We gain additional insights about the average path length of a perfectly balanced binary tree by calculating the result for the first few smallest trees. Table 14.1 shows the result for PBBT sizes of n from 1 to 31 (heights from 0 to 4).

The resulting APL in fraction form given in Table 14.1 shows a distinct pattern for the result with increasing values of n. We find that the parametric values a, b, and c are related to tree parameters in the following way (for $height > 0$):

$a = height - 1$,

$b = height + 1$,

$c = n$.

So an equivalent expression for the APL of a perfectly balanced binary tree is:

$$APL_{PBBT}[n] = \frac{(height - 1)^{(height+1)}}{n}$$
where: $height = \log_2(n + 1) - 1$.

In the limit as the tree gets large, n grows exponentially and $height$ grows linearly, so the fraction term approaches zero. For example, if we have a tree with a $height$ of ten, n equals 2,047. The fraction part is 0.00489. When compared with the integral part of the APL, $a = 9$, the fractional part is only about 0.05 percent of the total. As a general guideline we make the following approximation for the APL of a PBBT:

$$APL_{PBBT}[n] \approx (height - 1); \text{ within maximum error of } 0.05\% \text{ for } height \geq 9.$$

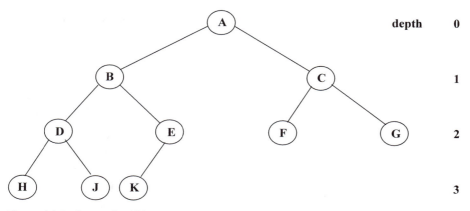

Figure 14.5. A complete binary tree.

A complete binary tree may be defined as follows:

- It is a perfectly balanced binary tree whose maximum level may not be full.
- All leaf nodes are at depth of *height* or *height* − 1.
- Any node that has a right descendant also has a left descendant.

A complete binary tree is shown in Figure 14.5 as a modification to the PBBT in Figure 14.4. Visually, the nodes at the maximum level are complete in a left-to-right sense. This condition is stated above (last bullet) as the requirement that any node with a right descendant must have a left descendant also.

An optimally balanced binary tree may be defined as follows:

- It is a perfectly balanced binary tree whose maximum level is not full.
- All leaf nodes are at depth of *height* or *height* − 1.
- There are no constraints on the ordering of nodes at the maximum level.

An optimally balanced binary tree is shown in Figure 14.6 as a modification to the PBBT in Figure 14.4.

Notice how the optimally balanced binary tree differs from the complete binary tree shown in Figure 14.5 only in the ordering of nodes at the maximum level. From the standpoint of average path length, a complete binary tree with *n* nodes is no different than an optimally balanced binary tree that also has *n* nodes. It is left as an exercise to find a formula for computing the exact APL for both the complete binary tree and optimally balanced binary trees of size *n* nodes.

14.1.2 Binary Expression Trees

A binary expression tree is a special binary tree that represents binary expressions. We already have experience with binary expressions from Chapter 12 where

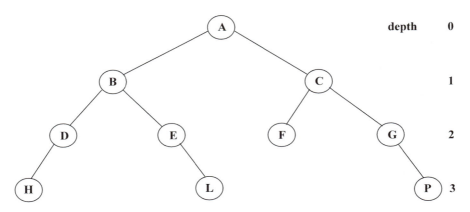

Figure 14.6. An optimally balanced binary tree.

we use a stack coupled with complex precedence logic to convert from infix to post-fix form and then evaluate the postfix expression using another stack.

Using the symbols that are part of a binary expression (without parentheses) we may build an expression tree that represents all three forms (prefix, infix, and postfix) of the expression. The expression tree is most easily built from the postfix expression, again using a stack for intermediate storage. Figure 14.7 shows a simple binary expression tree representing the infix expression, $(a + b) * c - d * e$.

A preorder traversal of the tree gives the prefix form of the expression. A postorder traversal gives the postfix form. An in-order traversal gives the in-order form but without parentheses, so forced precedence is lost. We present a modified version of an Euler traversal that gives us the correct infix form of the expression. It is based on visiting each node three times. The node is visited in preorder, in-order, and postorder during a single traversal.

Modified Euler Traversal Algorithm – for Generating the Infix Form of the Expression

```
If (current node is internal and not the root)
  visit ( '(' )              // prepend open parenthesis to internal node
traverseInorder(left child)
visit (current node){    // append character in the node
traverseInorder(right child)
If (current node is internal and not the root)
  visit ( ')' )              // append close parenthesis to internal node
```

When applied to the binary tree in Figure 14.7, we get:

```
Infix:  ( ( a + b ) * c ) - ( d * e )
```

Although it has unnecessary parentheses, the result is correct. The corresponding results of preorder and postorder traversals of the expression tree in

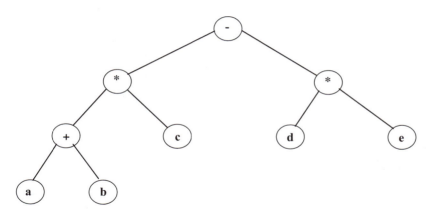

Figure 14.7. An expression binary tree representing $(a + b) * c - d * e$.

Figure 14.7 produce the following expressions:

```
Prefix:  - * + a b c * d e

Postfix: a b + c * d e * -
```

14.1.2.1   Design of a Class for Representing Binary Expression Trees

We design a class called *ExpressionBinaryTree* that has the behavior listed in Table 14.2. It has two constructors, three commands, and six queries. It represents a kind of binary tree.

Based on the desired public interface for class *ExpressionBinaryTree*, we next decide where to place it in our *Container* hierarchy. It is a kind of binary tree, yet it has almost nothing in common with the general concept of a binary tree presented by interface *BinaryTree*. An expression tree is typically used only to represent and return infix, prefix, and postfix strings for its binary expression. Traversals of an expression tree attach a predetermined meaning to "visit." Visit means to append a character to a string. This is simpler and more constrained than the traversals in *BinaryTree* that returned iterators. Further, there is no need for an expression tree to be concerned with average path length or even maximum level. Thus none of the queries in *BinaryTree* are applicable to the expression tree class. However, class *ExpressionBinaryTree* is still a container and does implement the commands and queries in interface *Container*. It also takes advantage of the *TreeIterator* hierarchy described in Section 14.1.1.2 and shown in Figure 14.3.

Instances of the *ExpressionBinaryTree* class may accept as input either an infix string (by constructor or command) or a postfix string (by command). It then builds the expression tree from the postfix string. This may require that an infix string be converted to an equivalent postfix string. The *FunctionEvaluation* class developed in Chapter 12 provides this capability and is to be used by class *ExpressionBinaryTree*. Figure 14.8 shows a class diagram for class *ExpressionBinaryTree* and how it fits within the *foundations* package.

Table 14.2   Public Interface to Class *ExpressionBinaryTree*

Constructors

public ExpressionBinaryTree( )	Create an empty expression tree
public ExpressionBinaryTree(String infix)	Create an expression tree from an infix string

Commands

public void setInfixString(String infix)	Rebuild the tree for the specified infix string
public void setPostfixString(String postfix)	Rebuild the tree for the specified postfix string
public void makeEmpty( )	Make the expression tree empty

Queries

public SearchTreeNode root( )	Return a reference to the root node
public boolean isEmpty( )	Return true if tree is empty
public int size( )	Return the number of nodes in the tree
public String traverseInorder( )	Return the infix expression
public String traversePreorder( )	Return the prefix expression
public String traversePostorder( )	Return the postfix expression

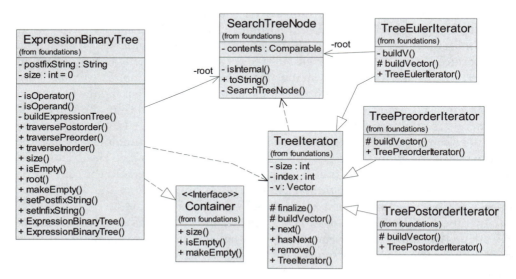

Figure 14.8. Object-oriented design – class diagram for *ExpressionBinaryTree*.

We use the new supporting class called *SearchTreeNode* with the significant feature that it contains a *Comparable* object and has two self-references representing its left and right subtrees (not shown in the diagram). Our expression tree contains instances of *SearchTreeNode*. Nodes in the expression tree will contain instances of *Character*. Although class *Character* implements *Comparable*, the comparable feature is not used in the logic for building an expression tree. Only a test for equality is required. Also not shown in Figure 14.8 is a using relationship from class *ExpressionBinaryTree* to class *FunctionEvaluation* for its infix-to-postfix conversion. Class *ExpressionBinaryTree* has three private internal methods (*isOperator*, *isOperand*, and *buildExpressionTree*) that support its public interface. Notice that the *TreeEulerIterator* needs a persistent reference to the *root* of the tree. This is used as shown in the modified Euler algorithm given earlier.

14.1.2.2 Implementing Class *ExpressionBinaryTree*

Three private fields represent the internal state of an expression tree: *postfixString*, *root*, and *size*. An instance may be created without initialization or from an infix expression string. Commands allow the instance to be modified by sending in a new infix or postfix expression.

Initialization of an instance of *ExpressionBinaryTree* is accomplished by building an expression tree from a postfix expression given by *postfixString*. The algorithm for the private command *buildExpressionTree* uses a stack of nodes to build the tree.

Algorithm for *buildExpressionTree( )*

```
nodeStack = new LinkedStack();
for (ch = next character in postfixString) {
  node = new SearchTreeNode(new Character(ch));
  if (ch == operand)
    nodeStack.push(node);
  else {    // ch is an operator
    node.setRight(nodeStack.top());
    nodeStack.pop();
    node.setLeft(nodeStack.top());
    nodeStack.pop();
    nodeStack.push(node);
  }
}
root = nodeStack.top();
nodeStack = null; // set for gc
```

Logic for *buildExpressionTree* is as follows. We iterate from left to right over the characters in *postfixString*. Each character in *postfixString* is assigned to *ch*.

Character *ch* is either an operand or an operator as verified by supporting internal queries *isOperand()* and *isOperator()*. Operands are encapsulated in instances of *SearchTreeNode* (nodes) and pushed onto the *nodeStack*. Left and right subtrees of operand nodes are *null*. Operators are encapsulated in nodes with right and left subtrees set sequentially to the top two nodes popped from *nodeStack*. The operator node is then pushed back onto *nodeStack*. This algorithm requires that *postfixString* be a valid postfix expression with no blank spaces. Successful completion of the algorithm leaves only a reference to the root node of a valid expression tree on *nodeStack*. This node initializes the *root* field. A simple example follows.

Consider the postfix expression:

```
ab+c*
```

The following steps are completed by algorithm *BuildExpressionTree*.

1. Read symbol *a*; create a new *node* with contents equal to character 'a'.
2. Push *node* containing 'a' onto *nodeStack*.
3. Read symbol *b*; create a new *node* with contents equal to character 'b'.
4. Push *node* containing 'b' onto *nodeStack*.
5. Read symbol +; create a new *node* with contents equal to character '+'.
6. Get topnode with 'b' from stack and make it the *right* child of *node*.
7. Pop topnode with 'b' from stack.
8. Get topnode with 'a' from stack and make it the *left* child of *node*.
9. Pop topnode with 'a' from stack.
10. Push *node* onto *nodeStack*.
11. Read symbol *c*; create a new *node* with contents equal to character 'c'.
12. Push *node* containing 'c' onto *nodeStack*.
13. Read symbol *; create a new *node* with contents equal to character '*'.
14. Get topnode with 'c' from stack and make it the *right* child of *node*.
15. Pop topnode with 'c' from stack.
16. Get topnode with '+' from stack and make it the *left* child of node.
17. Pop topnode with '+' from stack.
18. Push *node* onto *nodeStack*.

The *nodeStack* is shown in Figure 14.9 for completion of selected steps in the example.

Listing 14.3 shows a partial implementation for class *ExpressionBinaryTree*. Details for commands *setPostfixString*, *buildExpressionTree* and queries *traversePreorder*, *traversePostOrder*, *isOperand*, *isOperator* are left as an exercise for the reader.

After step: 4   10   12   18

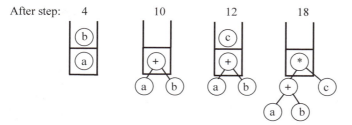

Figure 14.9. The steps in *buildExpressionTree* for postfix string $ab + c*$.

Listing 14.3 Class *BinaryExpressionTree*

```
/** class ExpressionBinaryTree
 *   uses a binary tree to represent binary expressions
 *   does not implement BinaryTree - all iterators return String
 /
package foundations;
import java.util.*;

public class ExpressionBinaryTree implements Container {

  // Fields

  private SearchTreeNode root = null;
  private int size = 0;
  private String postfixString;

  // Constructors

  /** Create an empty expression tree
  */
  public ExpressionBinaryTree () {
  }

  /** Create and initialize an expression tree on infix
  */
  public ExpressionBinaryTree (String infix) {
    postfixString = (new FunctionEvaluation(infix)).postfix();
    buildExpressionTree();
  }

  // Commands

  /** Set a new value for infix
  *    updates postfixString and rebuilds expression tree
  */
  public void setInfixString (String infix) {
    postfixString = (new FunctionEvaluation(infix)).postfix();
    buildExpressionTree();
  }
```

```
/** Set a new value for postfixString
*/
public void setPostfixString (String postfix) {
  // remove blanks then build expression tree
  // left as an exercise
}

/** Remove all objects from the container if found
*/
public void makeEmpty () {
  root = null;
}

// Queries

/** Return a reference to the root
*/
public SearchTreeNode root () {
  return root;
}

/** Return true if the container is empty
*/
public boolean isEmpty () {
  return root == null;
}

/** Return the number of objects in the container
*   postfixString has been trimmed
*/
public int size () {
  return size;
}

/** Return the infix string on elements in the tree
*/
public String traverseInorder () {
  String str = "";
  for (Iterator i = new TreeEulerIterator(root); i.hasNext(); )
    str = str + ((Character)i.next()).charValue();
  return str;
}

/** return the prefix string on elements in the tree
*/
public String traversePreorder () {
  // left as an exercise
}
```

```
/** Return the postfix on elements in the tree
 */
public String traversePostorder () {
  //left as an exercise
}


// Internal methods

/** Build an expression tree from postfixString
 *    - use a Stack of SearchTreeNode
 *    throw NoSuchElementException for caught Stack error
 */
private void buildExpressionTree () {
  // left as an exercise
}


private boolean isOperand (char ch) {
  // left as an exercise
}


private boolean isOperator (char ch) {
  //left as an exercise
}
}
```

Discussion of Listing 14.3

Private command *buildExpressionTree* is clearly a key method that has primary responsibility for initializing (with help from supporting private queries *isOperand* and *isOperator*) the internal state of an instance of *ExpressionBinaryTree*. Public methods for creation or modification of an instance, constructor *ExpressionBinaryTree(String infix)* plus commands *setInfixString(String infix)* and *setPostfixString(String postfix)* must invoke *buildExpressionTree*. Placing state modification instructions in a small number of key methods is a good design choice for object-oriented software.

14.1.3   Binary Expression Tree Laboratory

We present a binary expression tree laboratory that uses methods in class *ExpressionBinaryTree*. The laboratory also uses a utility class named *DrawTree* from package *foundations*. Class *DrawTree*, discussed in Chapter 15, provides methods for displaying graphically a binary tree in a panel. Figure 14.10 shows a UML class diagram for the laboratory. *ExprTreeApp* is the main application class and *ExprTreeUI* is the user interface class.

A screen shot of the expression tree laboratory is shown in Figure 14.11 after clicking the "Construct" button and entering the infix string expression

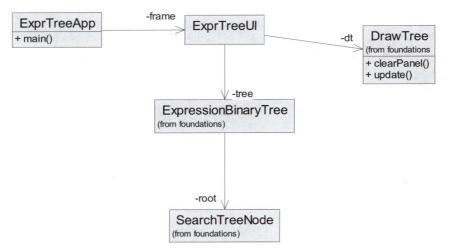

Figure 14.10. UML diagram for binary expression tree laboratory.

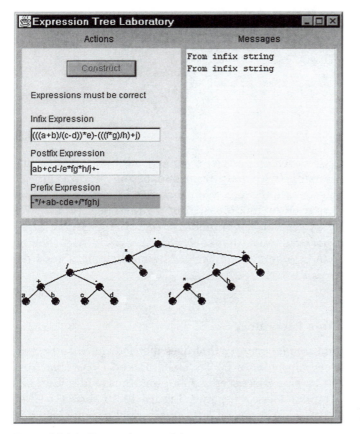

Figure 14.11. Expression tree laboratory.

```
(a+b)/(c-d)*e-f*g/h+j
```

After pressing "Enter," the laboratory automatically displays the prefix, postfix, and traversed infix forms of the expression, plus the tree diagram. The user may also enter a valid postfix expression and observe all the forms. The prefix expression text field is grayed out to prevent input since the laboratory does not support prefix-to-postfix conversion.

14.2 Heaps

14.2.1 The *Heap* Abstract Data Type

A *heap* is a nonlinear data structure that is easily implemented as a **complete** binary tree whose nodes contain elements satisfying two additional properties:

1. The contents of a node in a heap must implement interface *Comparable*.
2. A heap satisfies the following ordering property: For every node in the heap, the contents of the node must be less than or equal to the contents of all its descendants.

   The contained objects may be instances of *Association*, where the *Comparable* and ordering properties must be satisfied for the keys. We defined a complete binary tree in Section 14.1.1.3 with an example in Figure 14.5. Figure 14.12 shows an example of a heap with simple characters as the contained objects. The heap allows duplicates. The exact location of elements in a heap depends on the history of insertions and removals constrained by the ordering property. The root is called the *top* of the heap.
   As an alternative to the binary tree we may also represent a heap as an array. Using the numbering scheme for nodes as shown in Figure 14.12 (left to right, down the tree), we may map the nodes into sequential indices of an array as

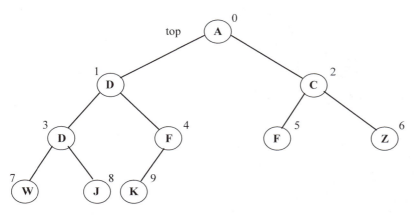

Figure 14.12. A heap as a binary tree.

index: i   0   1   2   3   4   5   6   7   8   9

| array [i] | A | D | C | D | F | F | Z | W | J | K |

Figure 14.13. A heap as an array.

shown in Figure 14.13. The ordering property of the heap is easily verified by visual inspection of the binary tree representation, but it is quite difficult to discern from the array representation. The array representation is, however, convenient for iteration over elements in a heap.

Using integer arithmetic, the following relationships exist among indices for a node and its offspring or parent in the array representation for a heap.

```
left child of array[i] is array[2i + 1]

right child of array[i] is array[2(i + 1)]

parent of array[i] is array[(i - 1)/2]
```

These conceptual views of a heap provide two possibilities for implementation of a heap data structure: a binary tree and a linear list (or array). But first we continue our discussion of the behavior for a heap data structure by revisiting the interface for the *Heap* abstract data type presented in Chapter 10 and repeated in Listing 14.4.

Listing 14.4 Interface *Heap*

```
/** Interface Heap - contained objects must implement Comparable
 *    root contains minimum value
 */
package foundations;
import java.util.*;

public interface Heap extends Container {

    // Commands

    /** Add obj to the heap, maintaining a heap
     */
    public void add (Comparable obj);

    /** Remove top obj from the heap, maintaining a heap
     *    throw NoSuchElementException if empty
     */
    public void removeTop ();
```

```
/** Sort the elements in the heap, maintaining a heap
 *    use level-order heapsort algorithm
 */
public void sort ();
// Queries

/** Return contents of the root - top of the heap
 *    throw NoSuchElementException if heap is empty
 */
public Comparable top ();

/** Return a level-order iterator
 */
public Iterator traverseLevels ();
}
```

Discussion of Listing 14.4

Although our definition for the *Heap* data structure was given in terms of a binary tree, the heap does not need any of the queries in the *BinaryTree* interface. Interface *Heap* extends *Container*, not *BinaryTree*. Like the *ExpressionBinary-Tree*, *Heap* is a special kind of binary tree with its own special behavior and at least two options for its implementation.

In addition to methods inherited from *Container*, the *Heap* interface adds three new commands (*add, removeTop, sort*) and two new queries (*top, traverseLevels*).

As is true for most containers, we need commands that allow us to add or remove objects from a heap. The *add* command takes a single parameter of type *Comparable* and adds it to the heap. The object is added to the heap at the next available location. The next available location is either

1. the next empty position at the maximum depth in the tree (e.g., as right offspring of node **F**, node 4, in Figure 14.12) or
2. the left offspring of the leftmost node in the tree at maximum depth (i.e., when all positions at maximum depth are full we go one level deeper).

As a side effect, adding a new node may break the ordering property of the heap. We must check for this condition and correct it in the algorithm for *add*.

The only object that may be removed from a heap is the *top* object. In essence we are removing the root node of a binary tree, a step that is guaranteed to break the heap. The algorithm for *removeTop* must include steps for rebuilding the heap after removal of the *top* object.

A third command allows us to *sort* the objects in a heap in ascending order based on the node-numbering scheme introduced in Figure 14.12. If we are using an array representation for the heap, then *sort* rearranges the elements in ascending order in the array. **A sorted heap is still a heap.**

We add a query to access the *top* object on the heap without removing it and a new kind of traversal characterized as a "level-order" traversal. Its behavior may be described as a raster-like traversal of the binary tree. It is also a traversal of the tree nodes that follows the numbering sequence in Figure 14.12, or a sequential traversal of the objects in the array representation from index = 0 to size - 1. If the heap is sorted, a level-order traversal visits the nodes in ascending order of the contained objects or keys.

14.2.2   Implementation of Interface *Heap*

In this section we examine details of selected algorithms for implementing the behavior of a heap and look at two specific representations of the heap data structure. The first representation uses a custom-built binary tree to store the heap. The second representation uses an instance of *java.util.Vector* to store the heap elements.

A general algorithm for the *add* command is shown below. It adds a new object to the next available position in the heap and then checks for and corrects violations of the ordering property. Details of the algorithm are implemented differently depending on the chosen representation for the heap data structure (referred to as *data*) in the algorithm.

Algorithm for Heap Command *add(Comparable obj)*

```
// get location and add new obj to heap
location = getLocation()    // another algorithm
node = new HeapNode(obj)    // subclass of SearchTreeNode
data.add(node) at location
size++

// check if heap is broken and repair
child = node
parent = child.parent
// while child < parent and child !root - swap parent and child
while (child != root
              && parent.contents > child.contents) {
  swap(child, parent)
  // move up the tree
  child = parent
  parent = child.parent
}
```

The part of the algorithm that repairs the heap starts at the bottom of the heap (where a new node was added) and works its way up the tree. It uses a "restore up" approach to repairing the broken heap.

As an example of how the *add* command works, consider the heap in Figure 14.12 if we add **B**. The first step is shown in Figure 14.14 after **B** (position 10) is added as the right offspring of **F** (position 4). The heap-ordering property is broken because **B** is smaller than its parent **F**. The algorithm detects this and swaps **B** (to position 4) with **F** (to position 10). In a second pass through the *while* loop,

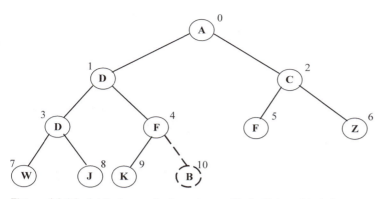

Figure 14.14. Adding a node to a heap: Node **B** is added; heap is broken.

B (position 4) is smaller than its new parent **D** (position 1). We swap **B** (to position 1) with **D** (to position 4). The last pass through the *while* loop detects that **B** is larger than its parent, **A**, and the algorithm is complete. The final result is shown in Figure 14.15

The *removeTop* command has the goal of removing the root node of the heap, which would leave a severely broken data structure if it were simply cut from the tree. The root node cannot be missing from a binary tree. Further, we know that the size of the heap will be one less than it was and that we must preserve the completeness property of the heap as a binary tree. Given these constraints, a solution that avoids most of the difficulties is to replace the root node with the last node in the tree. Implementing classes may find it convenient to maintain a reference to the last node.

Replacing the root with the last node eliminates the problem of a missing root, but probably breaks the ordering property of the heap. In most cases, the last node in the heap has a value that is larger than one or more of its ancestors. Moving it to the root would then violate the ordering property. An algorithm for *removeTop* must check for and restore breaks in the ordering property from the root down

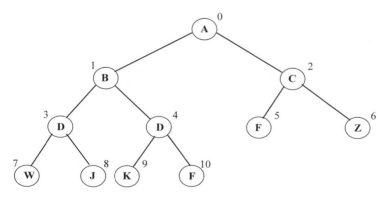

Figure 14.15. Adding a node to a heap: Node **B** is added; heap property is restored.

to the bottom of the tree. It thus uses a "restore down" approach to repairing the broken heap.

Algorithm for Heap Command *removeTop( )*

```
// locate newLast node based on current last node
// replace root with last
newLast = getLast()    // another algorithm
root.contents = last.contents
size-
last = newLast

// for size > 1, check if heap broken and repair
parent = root
// get smaller of children as next
next = parent.left
right = parent.right
if ( right != null && next.contents > right.contents)
  next = right
while (next != null && next.contents < parent.contents){
  swap(next, parent)
  // move down the tree to smaller of children
  parent = next
  next = parent.left
  right = parent.right
  if ( right != null && next.contents > right.contents)
    next = right
}
```

The parameter *next* in the algorithm is always the left or right offspring of node *parent* with the smaller contents. The contents field of parent (if larger) is swapped with the contents field of *next*. This process continues down the tree until the parent contents is equal to or smaller than the smaller of the contents of its offspring or until the bottom of the tree is reached.

If we remove the top element from the heap in Figure 14.15, the result of removing the root and replacing it with the last node is as shown in Figure 14.16. Node **F** (former position 10) is now in position 0, causing a break in the ordering property. Our first iteration through the *while* loop of the *removeTop* algorithm sets *next* to node **B** (the smaller of **F**'s offspring. It then swaps **F** (to position 1, step 1) with **B** (to position 0, step 2). The next iteration of the *while* loop sets *next* to node **D** (position 3) because the default is the left offspring. It then swaps **F** (to position 3, step 3) with **D** (to position 1, step 4). This is the last iteration since **F** (position 3) is smaller than either of its offspring, **W** (position 7) and **J** (position 8).

The resulting heap is shown in Figure 14.17 after completion of the *removeTop* algorithm.

Details for *getLocation* in the *add* algorithm and for *getLast* in the *removeTop* algorithm are strongly dependent on the choice of data structure representation

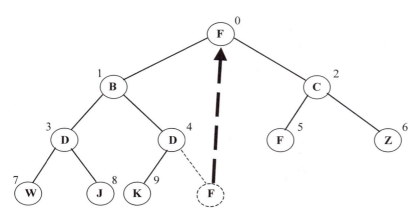

Figure 14.16. Removing top node **A** from a heap: Heap property is broken.

for the heap. Thus details are deferred to the following sections that use two different representations – a binary tree and a *Vector* – for the heap data structure.

14.2.2.1 Binary Tree Implementation of the *Heap* Interface

A design diagram is shown in Figure 14.18 for class *BinaryTreeHeap* that implements interface *Heap* using a binary tree and supporting classes.

Class *BinaryTreeHeap* maintains internal state including *size*, a reference to the root of the binary tree *(root)*, and a reference to the last node in the binary tree *(last)*. In addition to the promised implementations from *Heap* and *Container*, *BinaryTreeHeap* uses six private internal methods to accomplish its work. The algorithms for heap operations using a binary tree require that a node know its parent and which child it is (left or right). We accomplish this by extending *SearchTreeNode* with a new class called *HeapNode* that adds a field *parent* and a new query *isLeftChild*.

An important part of the *add* algorithm is finding the "location" for adding a node. For the binary tree implementation, this means finding the parent node for

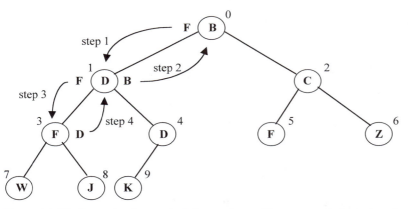

Figure 14.17. Removing top node **A** from a heap: Heap property is restored.

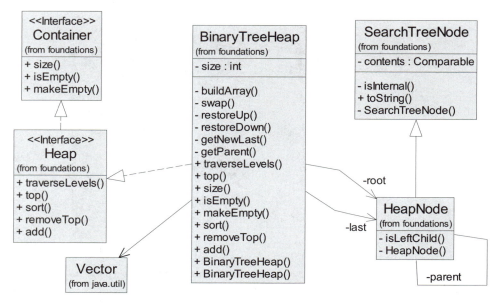

Figure 14.18. UML diagram for binary tree implementation of *Heap*.

which the new node will be a child. Starting with the current *last* node there are two possibilities. The first possibility is that the next location is at the same level as *last* and the next position to its right. The second possibility is that *last* is the node that fills its level (*maxLevel*), causing the next position to be the leftmost position at *maxLevel + 1*.

An algorithm for finding the parent for the next available position that handles both cases is given below. The *add* command then makes the new node the left offspring of *parent* (if *parent* is external) or the right offspring of *parent* (if *parent* is internal).

Algorithm for Private Query *getParent( )*

```
// return the parent for new node to add
node = last
while (node != root && node not LeftChild)
  node = node.parent
if (node != root)
  if (node.parent.right == null)
    return node.parent
  else
    node = node.parent.right
while (node.left != null)
  node = node.left
return node
```

Figure 14.19 illustrates how *parent* is found for Case 1. Case 1 occurs when the new node is added at the current *maxLevel*. The *getParent* algorithm returns node **5** as the parent for the next node being added.

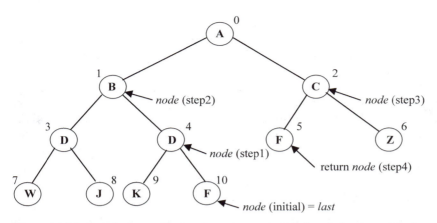

Figure 14.19. Details for *getParent*, Case 1 – next added node is at *maxLevel*.

Discussion of Case 1 Example for *getParent*

Initially we have *node* = *last* = node **10**. The first *while* loop replaces *node* with its *parent* until *node* is either the *root* or a left child. In this example we exit the *while* loop (after two steps) with *node* = node **1** (it is the left child of node **0**). In the compound *if* statement (*node* is not the *root*) we go to the *else* clause of the *if-else* (since the right offspring of *node*'s parent is not null). Statement *node* = *node.parent.right* sets *node* = node **2** (step3). The final *while* loop finds the leftmost child of node **0** (step4), which is node **5**. Node **5** is returned.

Figure 14.20 illustrates how *parent* is found for Case 2. Case 2 occurs when the new node is added at the current *maxLevel* + *1*. The *getParent* algorithm returns node **3** as the *parent* for the next node being added.

Discussion of Case 2 Example for *getParent*

Initially we have *node* = *last* = node **6**. The first *while* loop replaces *node* with its *parent* until *node* is either the *root* or a left child. In this example we exit the *while* loop (after two steps) with *node* = node **0** (it is the root). We skip the compound *if* statement (*node* is the *root*). The final *while* loop finds the leftmost child of node **0** (after two steps), which is node **3**. Node **3** is returned.

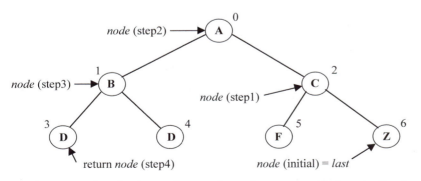

Figure 14.20. Details for *getParent*, Case 2 – next added node is at *maxLevel* + 1.

An important part of the *removeTop* command is updating the reference to *last* before moving the current *last* node to the root position. Starting from the current *last* node there are again two possibilities. The first possibility is that the new *last* location is at the same level as *last* and the previous position is to its left. The second possibility is that *last* is the only node at its level (*maxLevel*), causing the previous position to be the rightmost position at *maxLevel* − 1.

An algorithm for finding the previous position from *last* that handles both cases is given below. The *removeTop* command then reassigns *last* to the *newLast* position after it replaces *root* with the old *last*. It then restores the heap property using *restoreDown*.

Algorithm for Private Query *getNewLast( )*

```
node = last
while (node isLeftChild)
  node = node.parent
if (node != root)
  node = node.parent.left
while (node.right != null)
  node = node.right
return node
```

Figure 14.21 illustrates how *newLast* is found for Case 1. Case 1 occurs when the new *last* node is at the current *maxLevel*. The *getNewLast* algorithm returns node **10** as the new *last* node after node **11** is removed.

Discussion of Case 1 Example for *getNewLast*

Initially we have *node* = *last* = node **11**. The first *while* loop replaces *node* with its *parent* while *node* is a left child. In this example we exit the *while* loop (after two steps) with *node* = node **2** (it is the first nonleft child). The *if* statement (*node*

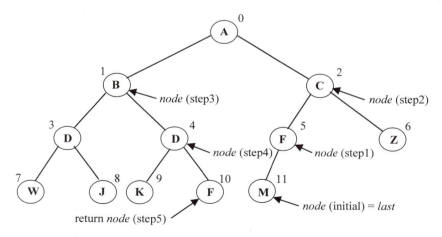

Figure 14.21. Details for *getNewLast*, Case 1 − new *last* node is at *maxLevel*.

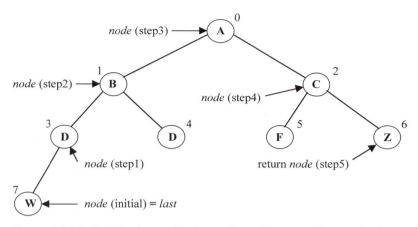

Figure 14.22. Details for *getNewLast*, Case 2 – new *last* node is at *maxLevel* − 1.

is not the *root*) is executed. Statement *node* = *node.parent.left* sets *node* = node **1** (step3). The final *while* loop finds the rightmost child of node **1** (after two steps), which is node **10**. Node **10** is returned.

Figure 14.22 illustrates how *parent* is found for Case 2. Case 1 occurs when the new last node is at the current *maxLevel* − 1. The *getNewLast* algorithm returns node **6** as the new *last* node after node **7** is removed.

Discussion of Case 2 Example for *getNewLast*

Initially we have *node* = *last* = node **7**. The first *while* loop replaces *node* with its *parent* while *node* is a left child. In this example we exit the *while* loop (after three steps) with *node* = node **2** (it is the first nonleft child). The *if* statement (*node* is the *root*) is skipped. The final *while* loop finds the rightmost child of node **0** (after two steps), which is node **6**. Node **6** is returned.

Listing 14.5 provides full details for the class *BinaryTreeHeap*. It has two constructors, one for creating an empty heap and one that creates a heap from an input array of *Comparable* objects. A number of *private* methods are used in class *BinaryTreeHeap* to encapsulate details for various algorithms. Method *getParent* is a *private* method supporting public method *add*. Rebuilding a broken heap after adding a new node is handled by *private* method *restoreUp*. Public method *removeTop* uses *private* method *getNewLast*. After removal of the top element, a heap must be restored using *private* method *restoreDown*.

Listing 14.5   Binary Tree Implementation of Interface *Heap*

```
/** class BinaryTreeHeap
 *    uses a special binary tree to represent the heap
 *    NOTE: equal keys do not maintain FIFO relationship
 */
package foundations;
import java.util.*;
```

```
public class BinaryTreeHeap implements Heap {

  // Fields

  private HeapNode root;
  private HeapNode last;
  private int size;

  // Constructors

  /** Create an empty heap
  */
  public BinaryTreeHeap () {
  }

  /** Create a heap from elements in obj[]
  *    objects must be Comparable
  */
  public BinaryTreeHeap (Object[] obj) {
    for (int i = 0; i < obj.length; i++)
      add((Comparable)obj[i]);
  }

  // Commands

  /** Add obj to the heap, maintaining a heap
  */
  public void add (Comparable obj) {
    HeapNode newNode = new HeapNode(obj);
    if (size == 0){
      root = newNode;
      last = newNode;
    }
    else {
      HeapNode parent = getParent();
      newNode.parent = parent;
      if (parent.isInternal())
        parent.right = newNode;
      else
        parent.left = newNode;
      last = newNode;
    }
    size++;
    if (size > 1)
      restoreUp(last);
  }

  /** Remove top obj from the heap, maintaining a heap
  */
```

```java
public void removeTop () {
  if (size > 1){
    HeapNode newLast = getNewLast();
    if (last.isLeftChild())
      ((HeapNode)last).parent.left = null;
    else
      ((HeapNode)last).parent.right = null;
    root.contents = last.contents;
    last = newLast;
    size--;
    restoreDown(root);
  }
  else{
    root = last = null;
    size = 0;
  }
}

/** Sort the elements in the heap, maintaining a heap
*    use level-order heapsort algorithm
*/
public void sort () {
  if (size > 1){
    int num = size;
    Vector temp = new Vector(size);
    for (int i = 0; i < num; i++){
      temp.add(top());
      removeTop();
    }
    for (int j = 0; j < temp.size(); j++)
      add((Comparable)temp.elementAt(j));
  }
}

/** Remove all objects from the container if found
*/
public void makeEmpty () {
  root = null;
  last = null;
  size = 0;
}

// Queries

/** Return true if the container is empty
*/
public boolean isEmpty () {
  return size == 0;
}
```

```java
/** Return the number of objects in the container
*/
public int size () {
  return size;
}
/** Return contents of the root - top of the heap
 *    throw NoSuchElementException if heap is empty
*/
public Comparable top () {
  if (!isEmpty())
    return root.contents;
  else
    throw new NoSuchElementException("Heap is empty");
}


/** Return a level-order iterator
*/
public Iterator traverseLevels () {
  Comparable [] data = new Comparable[size];
  buildArray(data, root, 0);
  Vector elements = new Vector(size);
  for (int i = 0; i < size; i++)
    elements.add(data[i]);
  return elements.iterator();
}


// Internal methods

/** Return the parent for next insertion
*/
private HeapNode getParent () {
  HeapNode node = last;
  while (node != root && !node.isLeftChild())
    node = node.parent;
  if (node != root)
    if ((HeapNode)node.parent.right == null)
      return node.parent;
    else
      node = (HeapNode)node.parent.right;
  while (node.left != null)
    node = (HeapNode)node.left;
  return node;
}


/** Return new last node if current last to be removed
*/
private HeapNode getNewLast () {
  HeapNode node = last;
```

```
  while (node.isLeftChild())
    node = node.parent;
  if (node != root)
    node = (HeapNode)node.parent.left;
  while (node.right != null)
    node = (HeapNode)node.right;
  return node;
}


/** After call to remove - restore heap property
*/
private void restoreDown (HeapNode parent) {
  HeapNode next = (HeapNode)parent.left;
  HeapNode right = (HeapNode)parent.right;
  if ( right != null
            && next.contents.compareTo(right.contents) > 0)
    next = right;
  while (next != null
            && next.contents.compareTo(parent.contents) < 0){
    swap(next, parent);
    parent = next;
    next = (HeapNode)parent.left;
    right = (HeapNode)parent.right;
    if ( right != null
            && next.contents.compareTo(right.contents) > 0)
      next = right;
  }
}


/** After add a single item - restore heap property
*/
private void restoreUp (HeapNode child) {
  HeapNode parent = child.parent;
  while (child != root
            && parent.contents.compareTo(child.contents) > 0){
    swap(child, parent);
    child = parent;
    parent = child.parent;
  }
}


/** Swap contents of two nodes
*/
private void swap (HeapNode n1, HeapNode n2) {
  Comparable temp = n1.contents;
  n1.contents = n2.contents;
  n2.contents = temp;
}
```

```
/** Recursively build data array in level-order
 */
private void buildArray (Comparable[] data,
                         HeapNode node, int index) {
  if (node != null){
    data[index] = node.contents;
    buildArray(data, (HeapNode)node.left, 2*index + 1);
    buildArray(data, (HeapNode)node.right, 2*(index+1));
  }
 }
}
```

Discussion of Listing 14.5

The *sort* command builds a temporary *Vector* called *temp* by sequentially re-moving the top element from the heap and adding it to *temp*. The elements in *temp* are thus in ascending order. The heap is then rebuilt by iterating through the vector and adding each element to the heap. The result is a sorted heap. The approach used in Listing 14.5 has performance $O(n \log_2 n)$. The *remove* operation is done $O(n)$ times. Each removal invokes *restoreDown* with $O(\log_2 n)$ steps. This gives a total number of steps for removing all elements that is $O(n \log_2 n)$. The rebuild operation requires no swaps during the restore operation and has $O(n)$ steps. The total performance is then $O(n \log_2 n) + O(n)$, which is equivalent to $O(n \log_2 n)$. There are other algorithms for sorting a heap using in-place swapping logic that also perform as $O(n \log_2 n)$.

The query *traverseLevels* starts by building a level-ordered array (using *private* method *buildArray*) from the binary tree structure using a doubly recursive traversal of the tree. It manages the array indexing recursively based on relation-ships between the index of a node and its left and right children. The array is then used to build a *Vector* so that *traverseLevels* simply returns an iterator on the vector. An alternative would have been to encapsulate the array in a special *HeapIterator* class and implement the required *Iterator* methods.

14.2.2.2   Vector Implementation of Interface *Heap*

Based on our earlier discussion of an array representation for the heap data struc-ture, it is clear that we may implement the *Heap* interface using a *vector* or other linear list. Class *VectorHeap* is fully implemented and part of the *foundations* package. It is left as an exercise for the reader to use a vector or linear list to develop his or her own equivalent implementation using class *VectorHeapE*.

14.2.3   Heap Laboratory

A heap laboratory is provided that uses implementations *BinaryTreeHeap* and *VectorHeap* to illustrate the properties of a heap, plus three skeleton exercise implementations. It allows construction of each kind of heap implementation by choosing from a pull-down combo box. The laboratory is designed to accept strings

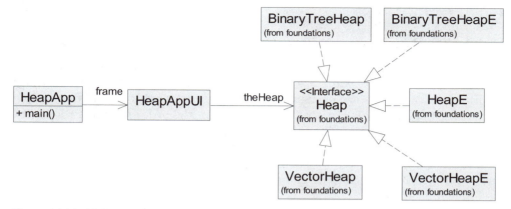

Figure 14.23. UML class diagram for the heap laboratory.

as the contents of nodes in the heap. The laboratory tests all four commands and all four queries.

Figure 14.23 shows the major classes that are required for the heap laboratory to work.

Figure 14.24 shows a screen shot of the heap laboratory after exercising several options. Three strings (*ddd*, *bbb*, and *aaa*) are added. We then verify queries *size*, *traverseLevels*, *isEmpty*, and *top*. Next we *sort* the heap and verify using *traverseLevels*. Next we test *removeTop* and verify using *size* and *traverseLevels*. Finally, we test *makeEmpty* and verify using *size*.

```
┌─────────────────────────────────────────────────────────────┐
│ 🐟 Heap Laboratory                                 _ □ ×      │
├─────────────────────────────────────────────────────────────┤
│        Actions                          Messages             │
│                                                               │
│  ┌──────────────────────────┐  BinaryTreeHeap created        │
│  │ BinaryTreeHeap        ▼ │  ddd - added to the heap        │
│  └──────────────────────────┘  bbb - added to the heap       │
│       ┌─────────────┐          aaa - added to the heap       │
│       │  Construct  │          Heap size: 3                  │
│       └─────────────┘          aaa->ddd->bbb                 │
│    Commands        Queries     Heap is not empty             │
│  ┌─────────────┐               Top of the heap: aaa          │
│  │     Add     │               Heap elements are sorted      │
│  └─────────────┘               aaa->bbb->ddd                 │
│  ┌─────────┐   ┌─────────────┐ Top removed                   │
│  │ aaa     │   │     Top     │ Heap size: 2                  │
│  └─────────┘   └─────────────┘ bbb->ddd                      │
│  ┌─────────────┐┌─────────────┐Heap is now empty             │
│  │  RemoveTop  ││   IsEmpty   │Heap size: 0                  │
│  └─────────────┘└─────────────┘                              │
│  ┌─────────────┐┌─────────────┐                              │
│  │    Sort     ││    Size     │                              │
│  └─────────────┘└─────────────┘                              │
│  ┌─────────────┐┌─────────────┐                              │
│  │  MakeEmpty  ││  Traverse   │                              │
│  └─────────────┘└─────────────┘                              │
└─────────────────────────────────────────────────────────────┘
```

Figure 14.24. Heap laboratory screen shot.

14.3 Priority Queues

14.3.1 The *PriorityQueue* Abstract Data Type

A *priority queue* is a special kind of queue that removes elements based on priorities. Highest priority elements are removed first. Elements with a higher priority are always removed before elements with a lower priority. If there are multiple items with the same priority, they are removed in the order in which they were added to the priority queue. The elements in a priority queue must be comparable. Highest priority may be chosen as the smallest value (e.g., highest $= 0$) or the maximum value (lowest $= 0$) of an *Integer* wrapped *int* field in implementing classes for priority queue. Other comparable keys may also be used dependent on the implementation.

Generally the elements stored in a priority queue consist of (1) a priority (key) and (2) information to be stored. We may easily use our *Association* class to represent the elements in a priority queue, where the key is the priority and the value is the stored information. In this case only the key needs to be comparable. In this chapter and in implementations for priority queue, the highest priority is defined by the lower comparative value (e.g., 0 if an *int*, alphabetically first for strings or characters). More precisely, *key2* has lower priority than *key1* if

```
key1.compareTo(key2) < 0.
```

As a simple example of a priority queue, students with the fewest number of hours remaining before graduation (fewer options on courses) may be given earlier registration time slots.

A *PriorityQueue* behaves differently than a *Queue*. Its contained objects must be *Comparable*, whereas a *Queue* may contain any object. The ordering of a priority queue is based on priorities (a property of the contained objects). A queue has order based on the history of additions and removals of objects. On close examination we find that a priority queue has properties defined by interface *SearchTable* with only one additional command *(add)* and two additional queries *(priorities, highest)* added for convenience. Thus interface *PriorityQueue* extends interface *SearchTable*.

Interface *PriorityQueue* is given in Listing 14.6 (repeated from Chapter 10). The command *add* is a convenient method for adding an *Association* to a priority queue by specifying the *key* and *value*. Query *highest* returns the highest priority object without removing it from the priority queue. Query *priorities* returns an *Iterator* on the priorities (keys) in the priority queue.

Listing 14.6 Interface *PriorityQueue*

```
/** Interface PriorityQueue
 *    Contained objects must implement Comparable
 */
package foundations;
import java.util.*;
```

```
public interface PriorityQueue extends SearchTable {

  // Commands

  /** Add an Association as key-value pair; priority is key
  */
  public void add (Comparable key, Object value);

  // Queries

  /** Return the object with highest priority
  *    Throw NoSuchElementException if priority queue is empty
  */
  public Comparable highest ();

  /** Return an iterator on the priorities
  */
  public Iterator priorities ();
}
```

Table 14.3 lists all the required commands and queries for implementation by classes that *implement* the *PriorityQueue* interface.

Command *remove* inherited from *SearchTable* is usable if we ignore the parameter. Removal from a *PriorityQueue* is restricted to always be the top element

Table 14.3 Public Interface to *PriorityQueue*

Commands	
public void add(Comparable key, Object value);	Add a new association with <key:value>
public void add(Comparable obj);	From SearchTable
public void remove(Comparable obj);	From SearchTable – use null for parameter since the object removed is always the one with highest priority.
public void makeEmpty( )	From Container
Queries	
public Comparable highest( )	Return object with highest priority
public Iterator priorities( )	Return an iterator on the keys (priorities)
public boolean contains(Comparable obj)	From SearchTable
public Comparable get(Comparable obj)	From SearchTable
public Iterator elements( )	From SearchTable
public boolean isEmpty( )	From Container
public int size( )	From Container

(no parameter is needed). An alternative design could implement the inherited *remove* method to do nothing and define a new *remove* method with no parameters to do the removal of the top element.

14.3.2 Implementation of *PriorityQueue* Using a *Vector* of *Queues*

One implementation for *PriorityQueue* uses a *vector* of queues. This implementation is very useful for applications wherein a large number of objects may exist over a limited range of priorities. Many of the objects will have duplicate priorities. A typical example is given by a large number of Java threads running at the same time. Thread priorities range from one to ten (ten is maximum priority) and there may be many more than ten threads executing at the same time. This is an example in which highest values have highest priority. Priorities may be mapped into indices in the vector using a simple translation, $index = 10 - priority$, to place highest priorities at index 0. Each index position in the vector contains a queue. This allows the priority queue to grow and shrink dynamically and preserve the first-in, first-out property for equal priorities.

We define a class called *QueuesPriorityQueue* that implements *PriorityQueue* using a vector of queues. In our implementation, zero represents the highest priority. This maps nicely into index position 0 of the vector. A typical snapshot of the vector of queues might look as shown in Figure 14.25.

In the priority queue in Figure 14.25, we have three objects with priority 0, inserted in the order a, c, k. There is one object, g, with priority 1. There are two objects with priority 3 inserted in order d, e. Queues in positions 2 and 4 through 9 of the vector are empty.

Objects in the priority queue will be removed in an order determined by priority first, and then first in, first out. Object ⟨0, a⟩ will be the first to be removed, object ⟨0, c⟩ second, and so on. After all objects in the queue at $index = 0$ have been removed, objects at $index = 1$ are removed, and so on, until all objects have been removed.

The data structure for our implementation of *QueuesPriorityQueue* may be described as a vector of queues. The elements in an instance of class *java.util.Vector*

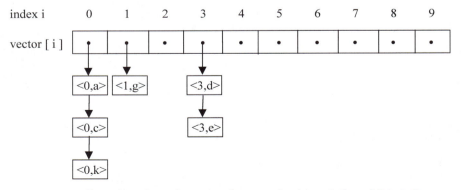

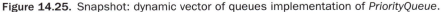

Figure 14.25. Snapshot: dynamic vector of queues implementation of *PriorityQueue*.

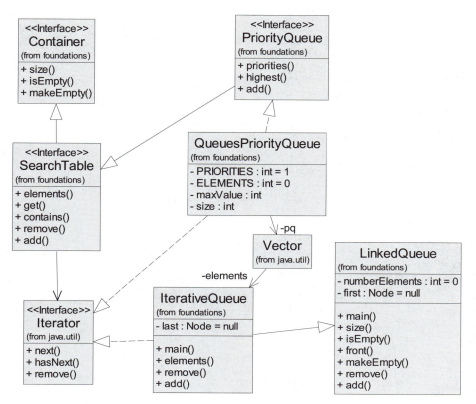

Figure 14.26. Design for implementation of *PriorityQueue* using a *vector* of queues.

will be instances of a queue class. Can we use one of the implementations for interface *Queue* developed in Chapter 11? Since we want the queues to be dynamically sized, *LinkedQueue* is our first candidate. All the commands and queries provided by *LinkedQueue* are useful; however, it is inefficient for adding new nodes (we must always start at the front) and it has no support for iteration (and we need iteration). As a possible design choice we may create a subclass of *LinkedQueue* called *IterativeQueue* that is more efficient (adds a field for the *last* element of the queue) and supports iteration (using an inner class). This is the choice made in our implementation of *QueuesPriorityQueue*. The design is shown in Figure 14.26.

IterativeQueue is part of the *foundations* package and is available for use by the reader. We present only its public interface in Listing 14.7 as a guide to its use.

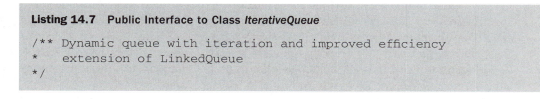

Listing 14.7 Public Interface to Class *IterativeQueue*

```
/** Dynamic queue with iteration and improved efficiency
 *    extension of LinkedQueue
 */
```

```
package foundations;
import java.util.*;

public class IterativeQueue extends LinkedQueue {

  // Commands

  /** Override from parent class to increase efficiency using last
  */
  public void add (Object item);

  /** Override from parent class - must add update for last
  */
  public void remove ();

  // Queries

  /** Return an iterator over all elements in the queue
  */
  public Iterator elements ();

  // Inner class for iteration

  class QueueIterator implements Iterator {

    // Commands

    public void remove ();

    // Queries

    public boolean hasNext ();

    public Object next ();
  }
}
```

A full implementation for *QueuesPriorityQueue* is included in the *foundations* package. Listing 14.8 gives limited details for the implementation of *QueuesPriorityQueue*, including selected private methods and the inner class *PQIterator*.

Two constructors are provided for creating vectors of default size ten or some specifiable size. The size of the vector is the range of possible priorities. Details are given for query *highest*, showing how to return the highest priority object in the priority queue. If the priority queue is empty, *highest* throws a *NoSuchElementException*. The user of this class should test if the priority queue is empty before invoking *highest* or catch and handle the exception.

Private method *validate* ensures that the priorities of any entered objects are of type *Integer* and within the required range of

```
0 = priority < maxValue.
```

Inner class *PQIterator* implements *Iterator* and provides iteration over the contained elements of the priority queue or over the priorities by using a value of *ELEMENTS* or *PRIORITIES* for parameter *type* in the constructor for *PQIterator*.

Listing 14.8 **Selected Details of Class** *QueuesPriorityQueue*

```
/** Class QueuesPriorityQueue
 *    - array of Queues implementation of PriorityQueue
 *    good for many duplicates of a few priorities, e.g., threads
 *    Priorities must be Integer in range: 0 <= priority < maxValue
 *    Elements are automatically sorted by (1) priority, then (2) FIFO
 */
package foundations;
import java.util.*;

public class QueuesPriorityQueue implements PriorityQueue {

  // Fields

  Vector pq;                      // dynamic array of Queues
  int size;
  int maxValue;                   // highest value = lowest priority
  static int ELEMENTS = 0;    // support iteration
  static int PRIORITIES = 1; // support iteration

  // Constructors

  /** Default constructor for 0 <= priority < 10
   */
  public QueuesPriorityQueue () {
    this(10);
  }

  public QueuesPriorityQueue (int max) {
    maxValue = max;
    pq = new Vector(maxValue);
    for (int i = 0; i < maxValue; i++)
      pq.add(new IterativeQueue());
  }

  // Commands

    /** All commands left as an exercise */

  // Queries

  /** Most queries left as an exercise */
```

```java
/** Return the highest priority element in the pq.
 *    Search all indices for nonempty queue.
 *    Throw NoSuchElementException if pq is empty.
 */
public Comparable highest () {
  try {
    for (int j = 0; j < maxValue; j++){
    Queue q = (Queue)pq.elementAt(j);
    if (!q.isEmpty())
      return (Comparable)q.front();
    }
  } catch(Exception ex) {
    throw new NoSuchElementException(
                               "Priority Queue is empty" );
  }
  return null;
}


// Internal methods

/** Validate that obj is Integer or Association
 *    and 0 <= val < maxValue
 */
private int validate (Comparable obj) {
  int val;
  if ( !(obj instanceof Integer)
                  && !(obj instanceof Association))
    throw new IllegalArgumentException(
      "Argument to add() must be Integer or Association" );
  else if (obj instanceof Integer)
    val = ((Integer)obj).intValue();
  else
    val = ((Integer)((Association)obj).key()).intValue();
  if ( val < 0 || val >= maxValue)
      throw new IllegalArgumentException(
        "Integer out of range" );
  return val;
}


// Inner class PQIterator

class PQIterator implements Iterator {

  // Fields

  Comparable [] data;
```

```
    int type;
    int index = 0;

    // Constructor

    PQIterator (int type) {
      int i = 0;
      data = new Comparable[size];
      for (Iterator it1 = pq.iterator(); it1.hasNext();) {
        IterativeQueue q = (IterativeQueue)it1.next();
        for (Iterator it2 = q.elements(); it2.hasNext();)
          data[i++] = (Comparable)it2.next();
      }
      this.type = type;
    }


    // Commands

    public void remove() { // null implementation
    }


    // Queries

    public Object next () {
      Comparable obj = data[index++];
      if (type == PRIORITIES && obj instanceof Association)
        return ((Association)obj).key();
      else
        return obj;
    }
    public boolean hasNext () {
      return index < size;;
    }
  }
}
```

14.3.3 Implementation of *PriorityQueue* Using a *Heap*

A heap has the same structure as a priority queue. It is a binary tree with the highest priority item at the *top* or root node. Using a heap to implement a priority queue is a natural and obvious choice. There is one small variation in the behavior of a heap that is not consistent with our stated behavior for a priority queue. A heap does enforce removal of the highest priority items first; however, it does not ensure a first-in, first-out (FIFO) order for items of equal priority. At least this is true for our implemented behavior of a heap. This anomaly is illustrated by a simple example.

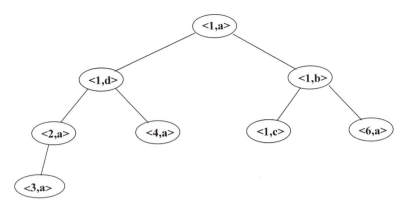

Figure 14.27. Implementing a priority queue with a heap: FIFO anomaly.

Suppose we build a priority queue using a heap by adding sequentially the following associations:

Add: $\langle 1, a \rangle$ $\langle 2, a \rangle$ $\langle 1, b \rangle$ $\langle 3, a \rangle$ $\langle 4, a \rangle$ $\langle 1, c \rangle$ $\langle 6, a \rangle$ $\langle 1, d \rangle$

Following the logic for command *add* in building the heap, we get the result shown in Figure 14.27. It should be clear that the removal order for items with priority 1 is changed from: **a - b - c - d** to: **a - d - b - c**. Correction of this anomaly requires storage of an extra ordering factor and additional logic in the comparison of keys in the heap-implementing class. This is left as an advanced exercise.

On a positive note, the heap implementation for priority queue can easily handle a large number of wide-ranging priorities. There is no implied desirability for the priorities to be mapped into low indices of an array as was true for the array of queues implementation.

A design diagram for implementing interface *PriorityQueue* using a heap (specifically class *BinaryTreeHeap*) is shown in Figure 14.28 as a UML class diagram.

Inner class *PQIterator* implements the iterator of query *priorities*. The iterator for *elements* is implemented as a call to the *traverseLevels* query in class *BinaryTreeHeap*, which returns a level-order iterator on the elements in the heap. The implementation for most commands and queries in *HeapPriorityQueue* uses simple commands and queries sent to field *theHeap* (instance of *BinaryTree-Heap*). Two notable exceptions are queries *get* and *contains*. These queries have no equivalent implementation for a heap and must be created for the priority queue.

Listing 14.9 shows selected implementation details for class *HeapPriority-Queue*. A complete implementation (as a *HeapPriorityQueue.class* file) is provided as part of the *foundations* package. Details are included for the *get*, *contains*, *elements*, and *highest* queries.

Queries *get* and *contains* must iterate over the elements in the heap by sending query *traverseLevels* to field *theHeap* and testing for the *Comparable* parameter of each.

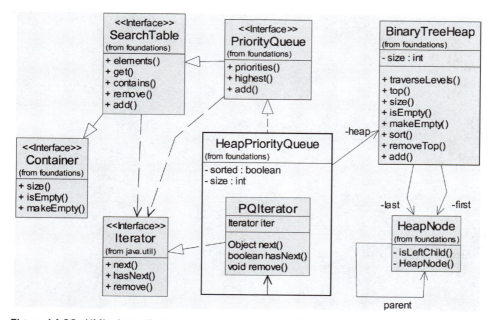

Figure 14.28. UML class diagram for heap implementation of *PriorityQueue*.

An important feature of the heap is that its elements satisfy the heap-ordering property but are not necessarily sorted. In implementing the *elements* query of *PriorityQueue* we must return an iterator over a sorted list of items. It is thus necessary to *sort* the heap before doing a traversal in the implementation of query *elements* as shown in Listing 14.9.

In the *highest* query we normally expect to return the *top* of the heap; however, if the heap is empty we throw a *NoSuchElementException*.

Listing 14.9 **Selected Implementation Details for Class *HeapPriorityQueue***

```
/** Class HeapPriorityQueue - Heap implementation of PriorityQueue
 *    good for many priorities - Priorities must be Comparable
 *    higherPriority.compareTo(lowerPriority) < 0
 */
package foundations;
import java.util.*;


public class HeapPriorityQueue implements PriorityQueue {

  // Fields

  private Heap theHeap = new BinaryTreeHeap();
  private int size;
```

```
private boolean sorted;    // sort only when necessary

// Constructors - use default

// Commands

  /** Send appropriate commands to field heap
   *   Details left as an exercise
   */

// Queries

  /** Where appropriate send queries to field theHeap
   *   Details left as an exercise
   */

/** Return true if the priority queue contains obj
 *   no direct support by Heap - iterate to find
 */
public boolean contains (Comparable obj) {
  for (Iterator i = theHeap.traverseLevels(); i.hasNext();)
    if (((Comparable)i.next()).compareTo(obj) == 0)
      return true;
  return false;
}

/** Return without removing obj if in table
 *   useful when obj is a key & returns an Association
 *   no direct support by Heap - iterate to find
 */
public Comparable get (Comparable obj) {
  for (Iterator i = theHeap.traverseLevels(); i.hasNext();) {
    Comparable o = (Comparable)i.next();
    if (o.compareTo(obj) == 0)
      return o;
  }
  return null;
}

/** Return an iterator on all elements
 *   sort them first
 */
public Iterator elements () {
  if (!sorted)
    theHeap.sort();
  sorted = true;
  return theHeap.traverseLevels();
}
```

```
/** Return the object with highest priority
 *     Throw NoSuchElementException if priority queue is empty
 */
public Comparable highest () {
  try{
    return theHeap.top();
  } catch (Exception ex) {
    throw new NoSuchElementException(
            "PriorityQueue is empty" );
  }
}


  /** Other details left as an exercise */
}
```

14.3.4 *Priority Queue* Laboratory

We provide a priority queue laboratory for testing the commands and queries of classes implementing interface *PriorityQueue*. It is designed to include both the array of queues implementation and the heap implementation. Figure 14.29 shows a UML class diagram for classes used by the priority queue laboratory.

Class *PQAppUI* uses a generic field *PriorityQueue pq* to represent the selected implementation for *PriorityQueue*. This field may be instantiated as an instance of class *HeapPriorityQueue* or *QueuesPriorityQueue*.

A screen shot of the priority queue laboratory is shown in Figure 14.30 after several options have been exercised. The user selects *Comparable* objects or *Associations* for insertion into the priority queue on first use of the *Add(key)* or *Add(key,value)* buttons. The user in Figure 14.30 has selected *Associations*. The iterators return key-ordered results as expected.

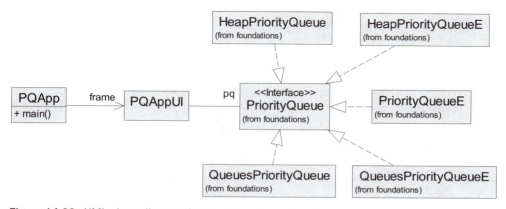

Figure 14.29. UML class diagram for priority queue laboratory.

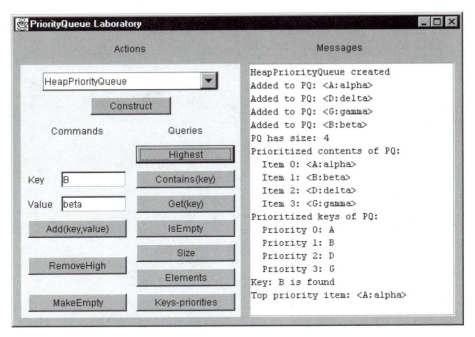

Figure 14.30. Screen shot of the priority queue laboratory.

14.4 Summary

This chapter covers *Tree*, *Heap*, and *PriorityQueue* containers, all of which may be implemented as nonlinear structures.

❏ A *tree* is a nonlinear structure composed of nodes. A tree is accessible only through a special node called the *root*.

❏ A *BinaryTree* is a tree whose nodes have at most two descendant trees as offspring. A *BinaryTree* is characterized by queries for traversing its nodes and for measuring average path length.

❏ A perfectly balanced binary tree has a unique logarithmic relation of its height to the number of nodes it contains. The average path length for a perfectly balanced binary tree is approximately equal to one less than its height.

❏ A *binary expression tree* is a binary tree that represents binary expressions. An expression tree is easily built from a postfix form of the expression it represents. Traversals of an expression tree produce the prefix, infix, and postfix strings for the represented expression.

❏ A *heap* is a complete binary tree whose nodes satisfy the heap-ordering property, that the contents of any node is no larger than the contents of any of its descendant nodes. A heap may also be designed as a linear indexable list. A heap also has the property that it may be used for efficient sorting.

❏ A *priority queue* is a special queue that contains prioritized objects. Since its objects *must be Comparable*, a *PriorityQueue* has behavior consistent with a *SearchTable*. It has the property that the next value removed is always highest priority. A priority queue may be implemented using a heap or a linear structure.

14.5 Exercises

1 Calculate precisely the average path length (APL) of an optimally balanced binary tree with 10,000 nodes. Compare this value with the APL of a perfectly balanced binary tree that has the same height.

2 In Section 14.1.2.2 we define an algorithm, *buildExpressionTree( )*, that builds an expression tree from the postfix string of a binary expression. The algorithm uses a stack of nodes. Define a new algorithm, *buildExpressionTree( )*, for building an expression tree from the prefix form of an algebraic expression.

3 A complete solution to class *ExpressionBinaryTree* (shown partially in Listing 14.3) is provided in the *foundations* package and works with the expression tree laboratory (found in the *ExpressionTree* folder as part of the downloadable notes). Verify that the expression tree laboratory works as expected. You may copy the entire *ExpressionTree* folder into a directory of your choice and run the batch file named *Goui.bat*

4 File *ExpressionBinaryTree.java* in the *ExpressionTree\support* folder is a copy of Listing 14.3 (which gives only a partial implementation for the expression tree) with small changes to make it compilable. File *SearchTreeNode.java* is a supporting class for *ExpressionBinaryTree*. File *ExpressionTest.java* is a simple test class. Note that these classes are not part of package *foundations* nor do they require any classes in package *foundations* except the *Container* interface and class *FunctionEvaluation*. Batch file *Go.bat* compiles all source files and runs the test class. You are required to complete the details for class *ExpressionBinaryTree*. Additional statements may be added to class *ExpressionTest* to expand on the testing performed.

5 Repeat Exercise 4 using the prefix version of *buildExpressionTree( )* developed in Exercise 2. This requires consideration of what field(s) should be part of class *ExpressionBinaryTree*.

6 A complete solution to class *BinaryTreeHeap* (shown in Listing 14.5) is provided in the *foundations* package and works with the heap laboratory (found in the *Heap* folder as part of downloadable notes in *foundations.zip*).

   a. Verify that the heap laboratory works as expected for the binary tree implementation in class *BinaryTreeHeap*. You may copy the entire *Heap* folder into a directory of your choice and run the batch file named *Goui.bat*.

   b. Folder *Heap\foundations* contains a skeletal implementation for *Heap* called *BinaryTreeHeapE* that compiles and runs but does little else. Complete all details for class *BinaryTreeHeapE* and verify that it works using the heap laboratory. In your implementation of *BinaryTreeHeapE*, use a binary tree as the data structure that contains the heap elements. This implementation is to obey the rules of a heap and is to provide first-in, first-out (FIFO) behavior for all duplicate keys. Recall that implementation *BinaryTreeHeap* did not preserve FIFO for duplicate keys.

7   Using the skeletal implementation in *Heap\foundations\VectorHeapE.java*, develop a complete implementation for *Heap*, using a *Vector* as the element container. A complete working solution is already contained in class *Vector-Heap* in the *foundations* package. Verify that the implementation, *Vector-Heap*, works properly and that your implementation, *VectorHeapE*, works properly. Both implementations may be tested using the heap laboratory.

8   Using the skeletal implementation in *Heap\foundations\HeapE.java*, develop a complete implementation for *Heap*, using your choice of data structure as the element container. Your implementation may be tested using the heap laboratory.

9   Listing 14.8 shows a partial implementation for class *QueuesPriorityQueue* that uses a *Vector of Queue* to store the elements of a *PriorityQueue*. Using the file *QueuesPriorityQueueE.java* (similar to Listing 14.8) in folder *PriorityQueue\foundations*, complete the implementation details. Package *foundations* has a complete solution in class *QueuesPriorityQueue*. Test both implementations using the priority queue laboratory. The laboratory may be launched by running batch file *Goui.bat* in the *PriorityQueue* folder.

10   Listing 14.9 provides a partial implementation for *PriorityQueue* using a heap. Package *foundations* provides a complete solution in class *HeapPriorityQueue* that uses *BinaryTreeHeap*. File *PriorityQueue\foundations\Heap-PriorityQueueE.java* provides a skeletal implementation of *PriorityQueue* (similar to Listing 14.9). Complete the details of class *HeapPriorityQueueE* using *BinaryTreeHeapE*, developed in Exercise 6b. Your implementation will preserve the FIFO property for equal priorities. Test your implementation using the priority queue laboratory.

11   File *PriorityQueue\foundations\PriorityQueueE.java* is a skeletal implementation for *PriorityQueue*. Add details to this class using a data structure of your choice for containing elements in the priority queue. Test your implementation with the priority queue laboratory.

15

Search Trees

Binary trees were introduced in the previous chapter. A binary tree holds the generic *Object* type that serves as a placeholder for any reference type. This combined with its nonlinear structure makes it suitable for representing a diversity of information.

This chapter focuses on a specialized but extremely important tree type – the search tree. Such a binary tree holds elements of type *Comparable*. That is, the elements stored in a search tree may be compared to one another by answering to the query *compareTo*. The goal of a search table is to provide efficient access to information while allowing the information to be output in an ordered sequence. The order of elements in a binary search tree is based on a comparable property of the elements themselves.

In Chapter 13 we examined the *OrderedList* as a concrete implementation of a *SearchTable*. Here we shall examine three concrete search tree classes, each providing an implementation of the interface *SearchTable*. These concrete classes are *BinarySearchTree*, *AVLTree*, and *SplayTree*. In addition, we shall investigate another interesting and recent implementation of *SearchTable*, given by class *SkipList*.

15.1 Review of Search Table Abstraction

Recall from Chapter 10 that a search table is a compact abstraction that extends *Container* and provides the commands *add* and *remove* in addition to the command *makeEmpty* in class *Container*. The queries *contains*, *get*, and *iterator* are provided by *SearchTable* in addition to the queries *isEmpty* and *size* inherited from *Container*.

The commands *add* and *remove* and the queries *get* and *contains* have a parameter, *obj*, of type *Comparable*.

The interface *SearchTable* is given in Listing 15.1.

Listing 15.1 Interface *SearchTable*

```
/** Interface SearchTable
 *    The elements in this container must be of type Comparable.
 */
```

```
package foundations;
import java.util.*;

public interface SearchTable extends Container {

  // Commands

  /** Add obj to the table; must be Comparable
  */
  public void add (Comparable obj);

  /** Remove obj from table, if found
  */
  public void remove (Comparable obj);

  // Queries

  /** Return true if the table contains obj
  */
  public boolean contains (Comparable obj);

  /** Return obj if in table
  *    useful when obj is a key & returns an Association
  */
  public Comparable get (Comparable obj);

  /** Return an iterator on all elements
  */
  public Iterator elements ();
}
```

15.2 Binary Search Tree

A **binary search tree** is a specialized type of binary tree. In order for the tree to qualify as a binary search tree, each of its nodes must satisfy the following two conditions:

1. All elements in its left subtree must have key values smaller than the key value of the node.

2. All elements in its right subtree must have key values larger than the key value of the node.

We may compare key values of two nodes by using the query *compareTo* on the key values (the elements in the tree are of type *Comparable*).

In Figure 15.1 we examine a binary search tree.

Suppose we were to change the value of node 750 to 450. This would violate the search tree property since all the elements in the right subtree of 500 must have values greater than 500. A value of 450 to the left of 800 would

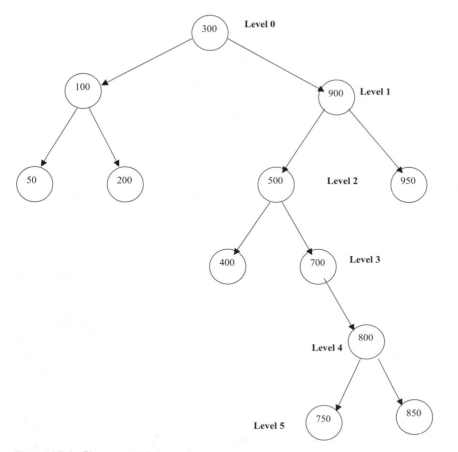

Figure 15.1. Binary search tree.

violate this condition. Likewise, suppose we were to change the value of node 200 to 350. This would also violate the search tree property. All the elements in the left subtree of 300 must be smaller than 300, and 350 would violate this condition.

There are six levels shown in the binary search tree of Figure 15.1. As indicated in Chapter 14, the root node is always at level 0. Each of its children, if any, is at level 1. Its grandchildren, if any, are at level 2. The height of the tree is given by the deepest level of any node in the tree.

Leaf nodes are defined as nodes with no children. In Figure 15.1 the leaf nodes are 50, 200, 950, 750, 850, and 400.

15.3 Searching for an Element in a Search Tree

Suppose we wish to determine whether the element 750 is present in the search tree of Figure 15.1.

We start by comparing 750 to the element in the root node. Since 750 is larger than 300 we can eliminate the left subtree of the root node from further consideration. Next we compare 750 to the right child of the root. Since 750 is smaller than 900 we can eliminate the right subtree of 900 from further consideration. Next we compare 750 to the left child of 900. Since 750 is larger than 500 we descend to the right, eliminating the left subtree of 500 from further consideration. We next compare 750 with 700, again descending to the right because 750 is larger than 700. We next compare 750 with 800, descending to the left since 750 is smaller. Finally, we compare 750 with 750, discovering the presence of 750 in the binary search tree.

The algorithm used above for searching may be summarized as follows if the object we are searching for is defined as the search key:

1. Starting with the root node, compare the search key with the key in the root node.
2. Descend to the left if the search key is smaller than the key in the root.
3. Descend to the right if the search key is larger than the key in the root.
4. Recursively continue this process of comparison and descent until either the search key is found or the bottom of the tree is encountered.

The efficiency of our search may be measured in terms of the number of comparison operations that are required. This depends of course on the particular element being sought. The best case occurs when the search key is found in the root node. If the search key is present, the worst case occurs when the search key is found at a leaf node furthest from the root (either node 750 or 850 in the tree of Figure 15.1). If the search key is not present, the worst case occurs if the search key would have been directly below a leaf node furthest from the root (either below node 750 or 850 in Figure 15.1). So if we were searching for node 775, it would require six comparison operations before descending to the bottom of the tree.

It is important for us to know the **maximum level** (height) of a search tree. This represents the level of the deepest leaf node (the leaf node furthest from the root). In Figure 15.1, the maximum level is 5. This metric provides a bound on the worst case search performance (i.e., *maximum level* + 1 comparison operations in worst case for any tree).

Another important metric is the balance of a search tree.

15.4 Balance of Search Tree

The search tree of Figure 15.1 contains twelve nodes. How much computational effort would be required to search for a node in this tree? Again, it depends on which node we are searching for. Suppose we form the sum of the number of comparison operations required for all the nodes and divide by the number of nodes. This would represent the "average" effort required to search for an arbitrary node in the tree. We define this metric as **ACE** (average comparison effort). The smaller this value, the smaller the computational effort required to locate a search key in the tree or determine that a search key is not present. The ACE is equal to the average path length plus 1.

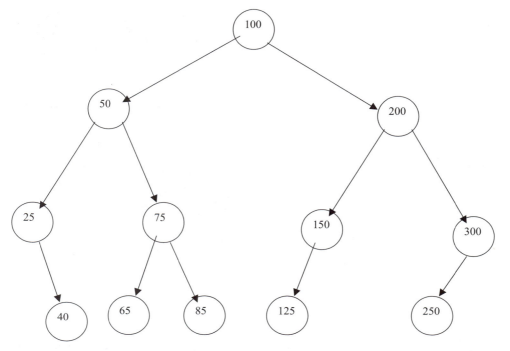

Figure 15.2. Optimally balanced search tree.

Let us compute the ACE for the tree of Figure 15.1. Summing the comparison operations over all the nodes gives us:

$$1 + 2 * 2 + 4 * 3 + 2 * 4 + 1 * 5 + 2 * 6 = 42.$$

Taking the ratio of this sum with the number of nodes gives us the result $42/12 = $ **3.5**. On the average, it takes 3.5 comparison operations to locate a randomly selected node.

Clearly, if the tree were more balanced we could reduce this average search effort. Figure 15.2 shows a tree with twelve nodes that is optimally balanced. The ACE of this tree is:

$$(1 * 1 + 2 * 2 + 4 * 3 + 5 * 4)/12 = \textbf{3.08}.$$

Therefore, the average search effort to locate a search key in the tree of Figure 15.2 is 88 percent of that required to locate a search key in the tree of Figure 15.1.

In general, the ACE of a binary search tree may be computed as follows:

ACE $= \sum$**(#nodes at level$_j$)** $*$ **(j + 1)/n**, for **n** nodes in the tree, as j varies from 0 to the maximum level in the tree.

As seen in Chapter 14, a search tree is **perfectly balanced** if and only if:

1. The tree contains $2^n - 1$ nodes where n is the tree height +1.

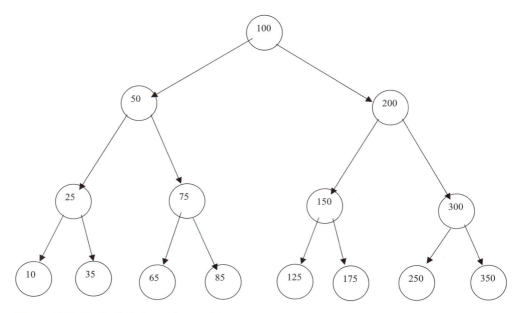

Figure 15.3. Perfectly balanced search tree.

2. The number of nodes at each level in the tree equals twice the number of nodes at the previous level, for all levels from 1 to the maximum level in the tree.

Figure 15.3 shows a perfectly balanced tree with fifteen nodes ($2^4 - 1$). Its ACE equals $(1 + 2 * 2 + 4 * 3 + 8 * 4)/15$. There is no search tree of fifteen nodes with a smaller value for ACE.

15.5 Adding an Element to a Binary Search Tree

The process of adding an element to a binary search tree is similar to searching for an element. Starting at the root node we descend either left or right through a sequence of nodes based on the same criteria as for searching. That is, descend left if the node you are adding is less than the contents of a given node, descend right if the node you are adding is greater than the contents of a given node. Eventually the bottom of the tree will be reached at some leaf node. The node to be added is placed either to the left or the right of this leaf node (based on whether the element being inserted is smaller or larger than the contents of the leaf node). In short, the node to be added is placed in the tree at the exact location where it would be found (using search logic) if it were already in the tree.

As an example, consider the addition of element 70 to the tree of Figure 15.3. It would be placed under and to the right of node 65.

15.6 Removing an Element in a Binary Search Tree

There are three cases to consider when removing an element from a search tree.

The simplest case is associated with the removal of a leaf node. In this case the node is simply clipped from the tree.

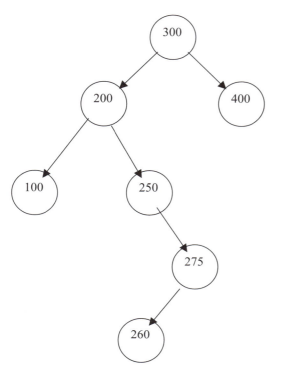

Figure 15.4. Removing a node from a search tree.

The second simplest case is that in which the node to be removed has exactly one child. In this case a linked-list–like remove is performed. The parent of the node being removed is relinked to the only child of the node being removed.

The most complex case is that in which the node being removed has two children. We illustrate this case with the search tree in Figure 15.4.

Suppose we wish to remove the root node 300 from the tree of Figure 15.4. We must first identify the node just smaller than node 300 that is closest in value to node 300 (the in-order predecessor). We can see by inspection that this node is 275. In general the node closest in value to the node that we are removing, but smaller than this node, would be found by descending left one level and then descending as far to the right as possible. This node shall replace the node we are removing. More precisely, we replace the contents of the root node with the contents of the "replacement" node. Then we remove the replacement node from the tree. This latter removal is simple because the replacement node will either have no children (be a leaf node) or have at most one child, as in Figure 15.4. We have already seen that it is relatively easy to handle a leaf or one-child node removal. The result of applying this strategy is shown in Figure 15.5 after node 300 is removed.

As an alternative, we could have replaced node 300 by the node just larger than 300 (the in-order successor). We shall utilize the in-order predecessor in this chapter.

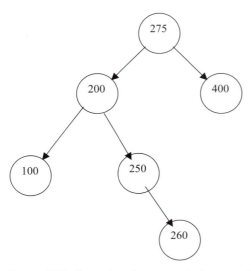

Figure 15.5. Tree after the removal of root node.

With the basic strategies for adding and removing nodes established we must formulate precise algorithms for accomplishing these tasks. These algorithms shall be expressed in the implementation of *add* and *remove* methods presented in the next sections.

15.7 Method *add* for Binary Search Tree

Listing 15.2 presents the public method *add* supported by an internal (private) method *insertNode*.

Listing 15.2 Method *add* in Class *BinarySearchTree*

```
/** Add obj to the table; must be Comparable */
public void add (Comparable obj) {
  root = insertNode(root, obj);
  numberElements++;
}


// Internal methods

private SearchTreeNode insertNode (SearchTreeNode node,
                                       Comparable item) {
  if (node == null)
    return new SearchTreeNode(item);
  else if (item.compareTo(node.contents) < 0) {
    node.left = insertNode(node.left, item);
    return node;
  }
```

```
    else if (item.compareTo(node.contents) > 0) {
      node.right = insertNode(node.right, item);
      return node;
    }
    else // Attempt to insert a duplicate
      throw new UnsupportedOperationException(
                  "add::obj already in binary search tree." );
}
```

Most of the work of *add* is handled by the private method *insertNode*. This method is invoked with the root node as the first parameter and the object being added as the second parameter. If the object *(obj)* being inserted is already present, this triggers an *UnsupportedOperationException* to be thrown.

Let us walk through the recursive function *insertNode* using the tree of Figure 15.5, assuming that we wish to insert the element 225.

Starting at the root, since *item* is less than the root (275) we assign the left child of the root to the return value after invoking *insertNode* recursively with node 200 as the first parameter. This recursive descent continues by descending to node 250. Since *item* is smaller than 250 we invoke *insertNode* again with *null* as the first parameter (since we are at the bottom of the tree). The "if" clause is executed when the node equals *null*. A new *SearchTreeNode* is constructed and assigned to the left of node 250. This completes the process of adding node 225.

15.8 Method *remove* for Binary Search Tree

Listing 15.3 presents the details of the public method *remove* and supporting private methods *deleteNode*, *rightMost*, and *deleteRightMost*.

Listing 15.3 Method *remove* in Class *BinarySearchTree*

```
/** Remove obj from table, if found */
public void remove (Comparable obj) {
  root = deleteNode(root, obj);
  numberElements--;
  if (numberElements == 0)
    root = null;
}

private SearchTreeNode deleteNode (SearchTreeNode node,
                                        Comparable item) {
  if (node == null)
    throw new NoSuchElementException(
                "remove::obj not in binary search tree." );
  if (item.compareTo(node.contents) < 0)
    node.left = deleteNode(node.left, item);
```

```
    else if (item.compareTo(node.contents) > 0)
      node.right = deleteNode(node.right, item);
    else if (item.compareTo(node.contents) == 0) { // item found
      if (node.left == null) // no children or only a right child
        node = node.right;
      else if (node.right == null) // only a left child
        node = node.left;
      else { // two children
        // deletes using the rightmost node of the left subtree
        Comparable replaceWithValue = rightMost(node.left);
        node.contents = replaceWithValue;
        node.left = deleteRightMost(node.left);
      }
    }
    return node;
}

private Comparable rightMost(SearchTreeNode node) {
  if (node.right == null)
    return node.contents;
  else
    return rightMost(node.right);
}

private SearchTreeNode deleteRightMost(SearchTreeNode node) {
  if (node.right == null)
    return node.left;
  else {
    node.right = deleteRightMost(node.right);
    return node;
  }
}
```

Let us again walk through an example exercising the code in Listing 15.3. We show the process of deleting node 300 from the tree of Figure 15.4.

Method *remove* requires that the *obj* being removed be in the tree. The root is assigned the return value of the recursive function *deleteNode*.

Starting at node 300, the final *else* clause (with the comment "two children") is executed. The *replaceWithValue* is computed using the recursive private function *rightMost*. The function returns a value of 275. The contents of *node* (the root node) are assigned 275. The left child of the root is assigned the return value of *deleteRightMost*.

The recursive protected function *deleteRightMost* descends to the right until *node.right* is *null* (node 275 satisfies this condition). It then returns node 260, which is then linked to the right of node 250 (since *node.right = deleteRight-Most(node.right)*).

The remaining commands and queries of class *BinarySearchTree* are presented in Listing 15.4.

Listing 15.4 Class *BinarySearchTree*

```
/** A binary search tree implementation without duplicates.
*/
package foundations;
import java.util.*;

public class BinarySearchTree implements SearchTable, BinaryTree {

  // Fields
  protected SearchTreeNode root = null;
  protected int numberElements = 0;
  protected int maxLevel;

  // Constructor - use default BinarySearchTree()

  // Commands

  /** Add obj to the table; must be Comparable */
  public void add (Comparable obj) {
    // See Listing 15.2
  }

  /** Remove obj from table, if found */
  public void remove (Comparable obj) {
    // See Listing 15.3
  }

  /** Remove all objects from the container if found */
  public void makeEmpty () {
    destroy(root);
    root = null;
    numberElements = 0;
  }

  // Queries

  public boolean isEmpty () {
    return root == null;
  }

  public int size () {
    return numberElements;
  }
```

```java
/** Return true if the table contains obj */
public boolean contains (Comparable obj) {
  if (numberElements == 0)
    return false;
  SearchTreeNode current = root;
  while (current != null) {
    if (obj.compareTo (current.contents) < 0)
      current = current.left;
    else if (obj.compareTo(current.contents) > 0)
      current = current.right;
    else
      break;
  }
  return current != null;
}

/** Return obj if in table
 *    useful when obj is a key & returns an Association
 */
public Comparable get (Comparable obj) {
  if (numberElements == 0)
    return null;
  SearchTreeNode current = root;
  boolean found = false;
  while (current != null && !found) {
    if (obj.compareTo (current.contents) == 0)
      found = true;
    else {
      if (obj.compareTo (current.contents) < 0)
        current = current.left;
      else
        current = current.right;
    }
  }
  return current.contents;
}

public Iterator elements () {
  return traverseInorder();
}

public Iterator traverseInorder () {
  return new TreeInorderIterator(root);
}

public Iterator traversePreorder () {
  return new TreePreorderIterator(root);
}
```

```
public Iterator traversePostorder () {
  return new TreePostorderIterator(root);
}

public int maxLevel () {
  maxLevel = 0;
  computeMaxLevel(root, 0);
  return maxLevel;
}

public double avgPathLength () {
  if (numberElements == 0)
    return 0;
  else
    return computePathLength(root, 0) / numberElements;
}

public SearchTreeNode root () {
  return root;
}

// Internal methods

private SearchTreeNode insertNode (SearchTreeNode node,
                                   Comparable item) {
  // See Listing 15.2
}

private SearchTreeNode deleteNode (SearchTreeNode node,
                                   Comparable item) {
  // See Listing 15.3
}

private Comparable rightMost (SearchTreeNode node) {
  if (node.right == null)
    return node.contents;
  else
    return rightMost(node.right);
}

private SearchTreeNode deleteRightMost (SearchTreeNode node) {
  if (node.right == null)
    return node.left;
  else {
    node.right = deleteRightMost(node.right);
    return node;
  }
}
```

```
private void destroy (SearchTreeNode node) {
  // Postorder traversal that sets each node to null
  if (node != null) {
    destroy (node.left);
    destroy (node.right);
    node.contents = null;
    node = null;
  }
}

private double computePathLength (SearchTreeNode node,
                                  double pathLength) {
if (node != null)
  return pathLength +
    computePathLength(node.left, pathLength + 1) +
    computePathLength(node.right, pathLength + 1);
else
  return 0;
}

private void computeMaxLevel (SearchTreeNode node, int level) {
  if (node != null) {
    computeMaxLevel(node.left, level + 1);
    computeMaxLevel(node.right, level + 1);
    if (node.right == null && node.left == null &&
          level > maxLevel)
      maxLevel = level;
  }
}

public static void main (String[] args) {
  BinarySearchTree myTree = new BinarySearchTree();
  myTree.add(new Double(10));
  myTree.add(new Double(12));
  myTree.add(new Double(5));
  myTree.add(new Double(7.5));
  myTree.add(new Double(15));
  myTree.add(new Double(18));
  myTree.add(new Double(16));
  myTree.add(new Double(20));
  System.out.println ("average path length = " +
                      myTree.avgPathLength());
  System.out.println ("maximum level = " + myTree.maxLevel());

  for (Iterator iter = myTree.elements() ; iter.hasNext() ;) {
      System.out.println(iter.next());
  }
```

```
    System.out.println ("Deleted 10, 15, and 16./n" );
    myTree.remove (new Double(15));
    myTree.remove (new Double(16));
    myTree.remove (new Double(10));
    System.out.println ("average path length = " +
                        myTree.avgPathLength());
    System.out.println ("maximum level = " + myTree.maxLevel());

    for (Iterator iter = myTree.elements() ; iter.hasNext() ;) {
        System.out.println(iter.next());
    }
  }
}
```

Output of Listing 15.4

```
average path length = 2.125
maximum level = 4
5.0
7.5
10.0
12.0
15.0
16.0
18.0
20.0
Deleted 10, 15, and 16.

average path length = 1.4
maximum level = 3
5.0
7.5
12.0
18.0
20.0
```

Explanation of Listing 15.4

Class *BinarySearchTree* implements *SearchTable* and *BinaryTree*. From *BinaryTree* the queries *traversePreorder*, *traverseInorder*, *traversePostorder*, *maxLevel*, and *avgPathLength* must be implemented. From *SearchTable* the commands *add* and *remove* and the queries *contains*, *get*, and *elements* must be implemented. From *Container* the command *makeEmpty* and the queries *isEmpty* and *size* must be implemented.

There are three protected fields defined. The *root* field is of type *SearchTree-Node* and is initialized to *null*. The *numberElements* and *maxLevel* fields describe the size and depth of the tree.

The internal methods *destroy* and *computeMaxLevel* both employ a postorder traversal to do their work. Method *destroy* sets the content of each node to *null* as well as the node itself to *null*. Method *computeMaxLevel* sets the field *maxLevel* to the current level if it is a leaf node whose current level exceeds the previous value of *maxLevel*.

The query *contains* performs an iterative descent down the tree returning true if a matchup occurs and false if the bottom of the tree is reached.

Method *main* provides simple testing of selected commands and queries for the class.

15.9   Performance of Binary Search Tree

The computational effort required to add, remove, or search for an element in a binary search tree is dependent on the relative degree of balance in the tree. As we have seen earlier, the ACE (average comparison effort) measures this. When a tree is optimally or near optimally balanced, the number of comparison operations for any of the above operations is approximately equal to the maximum level in the tree. This is approximately given by (for large n):

$$maximum\ level = \log_2 n,\ \text{where } n \text{ represents the number of nodes in the tree.}$$

Let us consider a tree with 2,047 nodes. Since this number of nodes is equal to $2^{11} - 1$, it is possible for such a tree to be perfectly balanced. In this case the ACE is equal to $(1 + 2 * 2 + 4 * 3 + \cdots + 2^{10} * 11)/2{,}047 = \mathbf{10.01}$. This represents the best performance possible for a tree of size 2,047 nodes (an average of about 10 comparison operations to find an arbitrary node that is present).

The worst performance for such a tree is associated with a linked-list–type tree in which the nodes all fall linearly in either the left or right subtree of the root. The ACE for such a worst-performance tree is:

$$(1 + 2 + 3 + \cdots + 2{,}047)/2{,}047 = 2{,}047 * 2{,}048/(2 * 2{,}047) = \mathbf{1{,}024}.$$

There is therefore approximately a ratio of 100 to 1 between the best and worst performance in a search tree with 2,047 nodes. Suppose we insert elements into a search tree with values provided by a random number generator. What is the performance of such a random search tree?

It is easy to perform a simulation experiment that estimates the ACE of a random search tree. For a tree of 2,047 nodes such a simulation returns an ACE of 13.6. Since for each node in a random search tree the likelihood of having subtrees of approximately equal depth is high, it is not surprising that the ACE of such a tree is close to optimal.

15.10   AVL Tree

In 1962 two Russian mathematicians, **A**delson-**V**elskii and **L**andis, invented an important kind of search tree later named "AVL tree" in their honor. These AVL trees are near optimally balanced and remain balanced after add and remove operations have been applied.

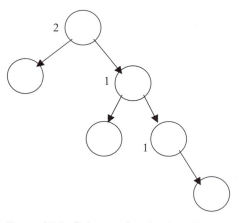

Figure 15.6. Balance of nodes in a binary search tree.

AVL trees are sometimes referred to as "height-balanced trees" since their definition of balance is based on the relative heights of right and left subtrees for each node. More formally, an AVL tree is defined as follows:

A binary search tree is an AVL tree if and only if the maximum depth of the right subtree is within one of the maximum depth of the left subtree for each node.

We define the balance of a search tree node as the maximum right depth minus the maximum left depth. Then a binary search tree is an AVL tree if the balance of each of its nodes is −1, 0, or 1. If a single node violates this condition, the tree in question is not an AVL tree.

Consider the tree in Figure 15.6. The values of each node are not shown and are immaterial. The balance of each node is shown next to the node, except when its value is zero. The tree violates the AVL condition and is not an AVL tree.

Consider the AVL tree with twelve nodes shown in Figure 15.7.

We saw earlier that the optimal ACE for a tree with twelve nodes is 3.08. The ACE of the AVL tree in Figure 15.7 is 3.17, only 3 percent larger than the optimal. AVL trees are attractive because their performance is so close to optimal.

15.11 Tree Rotation

The basis for many balanced tree algorithms, including AVL tree algorithms, is tree rotation. The operations of right rotation and left rotation may be applied to any node of a binary search tree to restore balance to the tree.

Consider the tree given in Figure 15.8. We demonstrate how to perform a right rotation about node 25. The result is shown in Figure 15.9. We twist the tree clockwise at node 25.

Node 20 becomes an orphan after twisting the tree clockwise with respect to node 25. The new right child of 15 is 25. So where does node 20 belong? It is smaller than 25 and larger than 15. It must therefore be placed to the left of 25

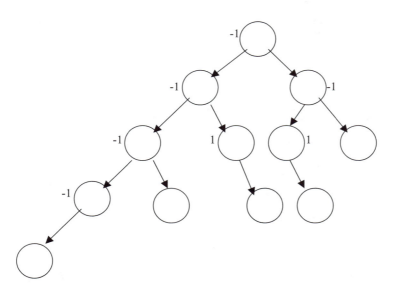

Figure 15.7. AVL tree.

as shown in Figure 15.9. The search tree property is preserved after this and all rotations.

If we were to perform one further right rotation, this time on node 15, the tree of Figure 15.10 would result.

We consider the methods that perform right and left rotation. These are given in Listing 15.5. Each of these methods returns a new subroot node that replaces the node that was the pivot of the rotation.

Two assignment statements that provide relinking are evident in each of the rotation methods. It is important to observe that regardless of the size of the tree or the location of the pivot node, the algorithmic complexity associated with rotation is constant (the cost of two relink operations).

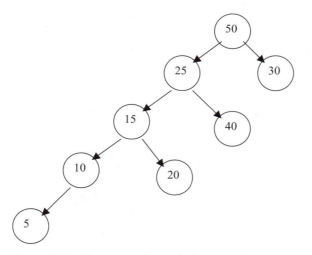

Figure 15.8. Binary search tree before rotation.

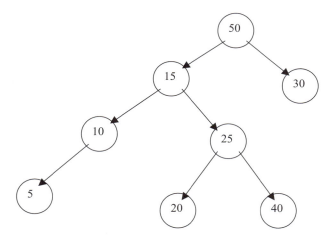

Figure 15.9. Binary search tree after rotation.

Listing 15.5 **Methods For Left and Right Rotation**

```
protected SearchTreeNode rightRotate (SearchTreeNode t) {
  SearchTreeNode returnNode;
  SearchTreeNode temp;
  temp = t;
  returnNode = t.left;
  temp.left = returnNode.right;
  returnNode.right = temp;
  return returnNode;
}

protected SearchTreeNode leftRotate (SearchTreeNode t) {
  SearchTreeNode returnNode;
  SearchTreeNode temp;
  temp = t;
  returnNode = t.right;
  temp.right = returnNode.left;
  returnNode.left = temp;
  return returnNode;
}
```

15.12 AVL *add*

We consider the algorithm for AVL insertion. It is given as follows.

Algorithm for AVL Insertion

1. Perform an ordinary insertion into a search tree. If the resulting search tree is AVL, exit. This will be the case roughly 50 percent of the time.
2. Backtrack up the search path from the newly inserted node to the root. In this path, search for a combination of nodes in which the parent has balance 2

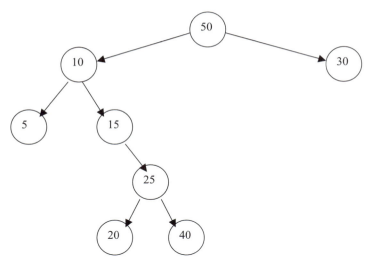

Figure 15.10. Tree after one further rotation on node 15 (from Figure 15.9).

(or minus 2) and the child has balance 1 (or minus 1). If the signs of the balance for parent and child are the same, we define this as a type 1 configuration, otherwise, a type 2 configuration.

3. If the configuration is type 1, perform a single rotation on the parent node in a direction to restore balance. This will guarantee that the tree is restored to an AVL tree. Type 1 configurations occur during roughly 25 percent of insertions.

4. If the configuration is type 2, perform a rotation on the child node in a direction to restore balance with respect to this child node immediately followed by a rotation on the parent node in the opposite direction. This sequence of two rotations is guaranteed to restore the tree to an AVL tree. Type 2 configurations occur during roughly 25 percent of insertions.

We illustrate the insertion algorithm with two examples. In Figures 15.11 and 15.12 we demonstrate a type 1 insertion and in Figures 15.13, 15.14, and 15.15, a type 2 insertion.

In Figure 15.11 we insert node 3.

After performing a single right rotation using node 8 as a pivot node, we achieve an AVL tree as shown in Figure 15.12.

Figure 15.13 shows a type 2 configuration when node 5 is inserted.

To restore AVL balance we must perform a left rotation on node 4 followed by a right rotation on node 8. The results of these two rotations are shown in Figures 15.14 and 15.15.

The coding details for method *add* are quite complex. This method is presented in Listing 15.6 for the interested reader without explanation. This listing presents the details of class *AVLTree*. Since all the methods except *add* and *remove* are the same as in class *BinarySearchTree*, class *AVLTree* extends class *BinarySearchTree*. *AVLTreeNode* is a class extended from *SearchTreeNode* with the additional field *balance*.

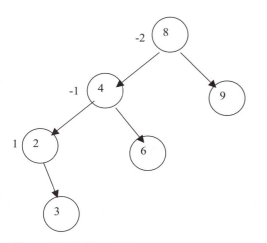

Figure 15.11. Type 1 AVL configuration.

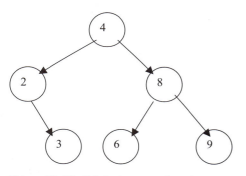

Figure 15.12. AVL balance restored.

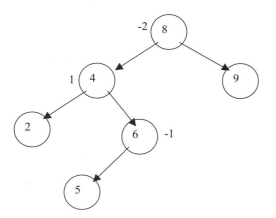

Figure 15.13. Type 2 AVL configuration.

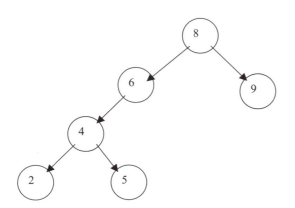

Figure 15.14. First of two type 2 AVL rotations.

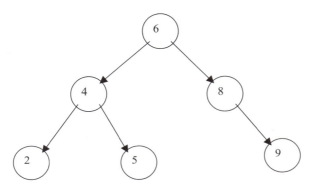

Figure 15.15. Second of two type 2 AVL rotations restoring AVL balance.

Listing 15.6 Class *AVLTree* with Method *add* Implemented

```
/** Implementation of AVL tree.
*/
package foundations;
import java.util.*;

public class AVLTree extends BinarySearchTree {

  // Fields inherited from BinarySearchTree

  // Commands

  /** Add obj to the table; must be Comparable */
  public void add (Comparable obj) {
    if (root == null)
      root = new AVLTreeNode(obj);
```

```
  else {
    SearchTreeNode parent = insertNode (root, null, obj);
  }
  numberElements++;
}

/** Remove obj from table, if found */
public void remove (Comparable obj) {
  // Not implemented
}

// Internal methods and fields

boolean stopRecursion; // For computational support only

private SearchTreeNode insertNode (SearchTreeNode node,
                     SearchTreeNode parent, Comparable item) {
  SearchTreeNode returnNode, newNode;

  if (node != null) {
    if (item.compareTo (node.contents) < 0) {
      returnNode = insertNode (node.left, node, item);
      if (!stopRecursion)
        restructureLeft(returnNode, parent, item);
    }
    else if (item.compareTo (node.contents) > 0) {
      returnNode = insertNode (node.right, node, item);
      if (!stopRecursion) {
        restructureRight(returnNode, parent, item);
      }
    }
    else if (item.compareTo(node.contents) == 0)
      throw new UnsupportedOperationException(
                  "add::obj already in AVL tree." );
  }
  else {
    stopRecursion = false;
    newNode = new AVLTreeNode (item);
    if (item.compareTo (parent.contents) < 0)
      parent.left = newNode;
    else
      parent.right = newNode;
  }
  return parent;
}

private void restructureLeft (SearchTreeNode returnNode,
                     SearchTreeNode parent, Comparable item) {
  SearchTreeNode p1, p2, res1, res2;
```

```
switch (((AVLTreeNode) returnNode).balance) {
  case 1:
    ((AVLTreeNode) returnNode).balance = 0;
    stopRecursion = true;
    break;
  case 0:
    ((AVLTreeNode)returnNode).balance = -1;
    break;
  case -1:
    p1 = returnNode.left;
    if (((AVLTreeNode) p1).balance == -1) {
      ((AVLTreeNode) returnNode).balance = 0;
      res2 = rightRotate (returnNode);
      if (parent != null) {
        if (res2.contents.
          compareTo(parent.contents) < 0)
          parent.left = res2;
        else
          parent.right = res2;
      }
      else
        root = res2;
    }
    else {
      p2 = p1.right;
      if (((AVLTreeNode) p2).balance == -1)
        ((AVLTreeNode) returnNode).balance = 1;
      else
        ((AVLTreeNode) returnNode).balance = 0;
      if (((AVLTreeNode) p2).balance == 1)
        ((AVLTreeNode) p1).balance = -1;
      else
        ((AVLTreeNode) p1).balance = 0;
      res1 = leftRotate (p1);
      ptreturnNode.left = res1;
      ptres2 = rightRotate (returnNode);
      ptif (parent != null) {
        if (res2.contents.
                compareTo (parent.contents) < 0)
                parent.left = res2;
        else
          parent.right = res2;
      }
      else
        root = res2;
    }
    ((AVLTreeNode) res2).balance = 0;
```

```
        stopRecursion = true;
        break;
    }
}


private void restructureRight (SearchTreeNode returnNode,
                    SearchTreeNode parent, Comparable item) {
    SearchTreeNode p1, p2, res1, res2;
    switch (((AVLTreeNode) returnNode).balance) {
      case -1:
        ((AVLTreeNode) returnNode).balance = 0;
        stopRecursion = true;
        break;
      case 0:
        ((AVLTreeNode) returnNode).balance = 1;
        break;
      case 1:
        p1 = returnNode.right;
        if (((AVLTreeNode) p1).balance == 1) {
          ((AVLTreeNode) returnNode).balance = 0;
          res2 = leftRotate (returnNode);
          if (parent != null) {
            if (res2.contents.
              compareTo(parent.contents) < 0)
              parent.left = res2;
            else
              parent.right = res2;
          }
          else
            root = res2;
        }
        else {
          p2 = p1.left;
          if (((AVLTreeNode) p2).balance == 1)
            ((AVLTreeNode) returnNode).balance = -1;
          else
            ((AVLTreeNode) returnNode).balance = 0;
          if (((AVLTreeNode) p2).balance == -1)
            ((AVLTreeNode) p1).balance = 1;
          else
            ((AVLTreeNode) p1).balance = 0;
          res1 = rightRotate (p1);
          returnNode.right = res1;
          res2 = leftRotate (returnNode);
          if (parent != null) {
            if (res2.contents.
              compareTo(parent.contents) < 0)
```

```
            parent.left = res2;
          else
            parent.right = res2;
        }
        else
          root = res2;
      }
      ((AVLTreeNode) res2).balance = 0;
      stopRecursion = true;
      break;
    }
  }
}

protected SearchTreeNode rightRotate (SearchTreeNode t) {
  // See Listing 15.15
}

protected SearchTreeNode leftRotate (SearchTreeNode t) {
  // See Listing 15.15
}
}
```

15.13 AVL Deletion

The algorithm for removing an element from an AVL tree is similar to the insertion algorithm. The only difference is that rotations may be necessary at nodes along the search path from root to the initial pivot node. This is illustrated by the example in Figure 15.16.

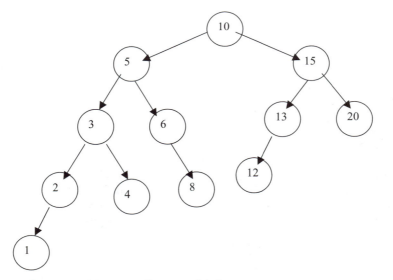

Figure 15.16. AVL tree to illustrate deletion.

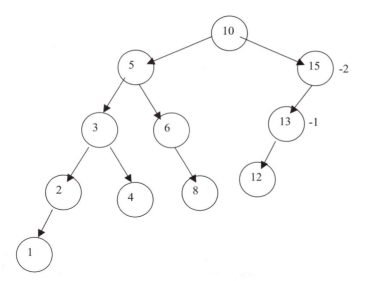

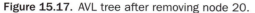

Figure 15.17. AVL tree after removing node 20.

We wish to delete node 20. After removing node 20 the tree of Figure 15.17 results.

A single right rotation pivoting on node 15 restores balance locally. But a consequence of this rotation is to bring node 12 up from level 3 to level 2, thus causing the root node to go out of balance. The tree after doing a right rotation on node 15 is shown in Figure 15.18.

The restored AVL tree resulting from a single right rotation on node 10 is shown in Figure 15.19.

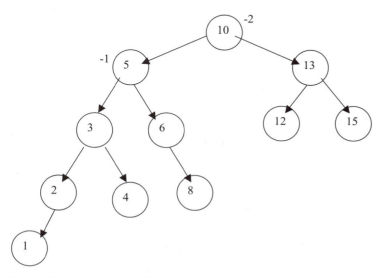

Figure 15.18. Result of right rotation on node 15.

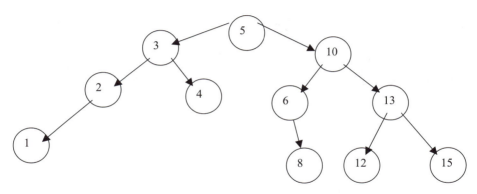

Figure 15.19. Restored AVL tree.

15.14 Splay Tree

Splay trees are ordinary binary search trees that employ a splaying operation in the search path from root to node (node being accessed or inserted) that causes the node to become the new root node of the tree. The resulting tree will generally not be well balanced and in fact may be poorly balanced. But it can be shown that the amortized cost of performing a large sequence of insert or access operations is $O(n \log_2 n)$, the same as an AVL tree.

Splaying

There are two distinct mechanisms for moving an accessed node to the root position. Suppose we are accessing some node with a parent and grandparent node.

1. If the path from grandparent to child involves a descent to the left and then to the right or a descent to the right and then to the left (opposite directions), a zig-zag rotation is required (to be illustrated later).
2. If the path from grandparent to child involves a descent to the left and again to the left or a descent to the right and again to the right (same direction), a zig-zig rotation is required (to be illustrated later).

Figure 15.20 illustrates the case where a zig-zag rotation is required with respect to X.

A left rotation on node P must be followed by a right rotation on node G. This produces the result shown in Figure 15.21.

Figure 15.22 shows a configuration of nodes that is suitable for zig-zig rotations on X.

A right rotation on node G must be followed by a right rotation on node P. This produces the result shown in Figure 15.23.

Since the splay operation always moves an accessed (or inserted) node to the root of the tree, this data structure is particularly efficient in applications in which repeated access to an element occurs frequently. The most frequently accessed nodes are always near the top of a splay tree.

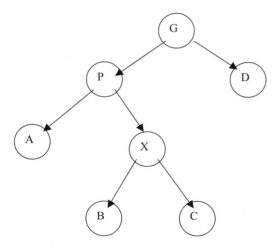

Figure 15.20. Zig-zag case for splaying.

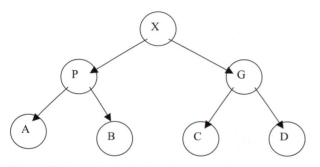

Figure 15.21. Splay tree after zig-zag rotations.

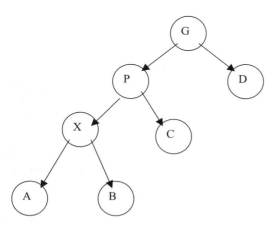

Figure 15.22. Splay tree configuration for zig-zig rotations.

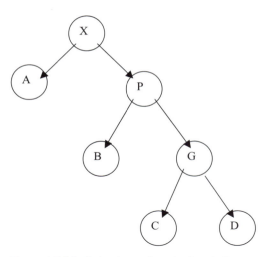

Figure 15.23. Splay tree after zig-zig rotations.

15.15   Implementation of Class *SplayTree*

Listing 15.7 presents the details of class *SplayTree*.

Listing 15.7   Class *SplayTree*

```
/** Implementation of splay tree
*/
package foundations;
import java.util.*;

public class SplayTree extends BinarySearchTree {

  // Commands

  /** Add obj to the table; must be Comparable */
  public void add (Comparable obj) {
    super.add(obj);
    touch(obj); // Defined below
  }

  // Queries

  /** Return true if the table contains obj */
  public boolean has (Comparable obj) {
    if (this.maxLevel() >= 2)
      touch(obj);
    return super.contains(obj);
  }

  // Internal methods and fields
  private SearchTreeNode [] info;
```

```java
private char [] direction;
private int infoIndex = 0;

private void touch (Comparable obj) {
  info = new SearchTreeNode [numberElements];
  direction = new char [numberElements];
  infoIndex = 0;
  SearchTreeNode current = root;
  info[0] = current;
  boolean found = false;
  while (current != null && !found) {
    if (obj.compareTo(current.contents) == 0) {
      found = true;
    }
    else {
      if (obj.compareTo(current.contents) < 0) {
        current = current.left;
        direction[infoIndex] = 'L';
        info[++infoIndex] = current;
      }
      else {
        current = current.right;
        direction[infoIndex] = 'R';
        info[++infoIndex] = current;
      }
    }
  }
  if (found)
    splay(root);
}

private void splay (SearchTreeNode node) {
  SearchTreeNode temp;
  while (infoIndex >= 2) {
    if (direction[infoIndex - 1] == direction[infoIndex - 2]) {
      // zig-zig
      if (direction[infoIndex - 1] == 'R') {
        temp = leftRotate(info[infoIndex - 2]);
        if (infoIndex > 2) {
          if (direction[infoIndex - 3] == 'R')
            info[infoIndex - 3].right = temp;
          else
            info[infoIndex - 3].left = temp;
        }
        else
          root = temp;
        temp = leftRotate(info[infoIndex - 1]);
        if (infoIndex > 2) {
```

```
        if (direction[infoIndex - 3] == 'R')
          info[infoIndex - 3].right = temp;
        else
          info[infoIndex - 3].left = temp;
      }
      else
        root = temp;


    }
    else {
      temp = rightRotate(info[infoIndex - 2]);
      if (infoIndex > 2) {
        if (direction[infoIndex - 3] == 'R')
          info[infoIndex - 3].right = temp;
        else
          info[infoIndex - 3].left = temp;
      }
      else
        root = temp;
      temp = rightRotate(info[infoIndex - 1]);
      if (infoIndex > 2) {
        if (direction[infoIndex - 3] == 'R')
          info[infoIndex - 3].right = temp;
        else
          info[infoIndex - 3].left = temp;
      }
      else
        root = temp;
    }
  }
  else { // zig-zag
    if (direction[infoIndex - 2] == 'R') {
      temp = rightRotate(info[infoIndex - 1]);
      info[infoIndex - 2].right = temp;
      temp = leftRotate(info[infoIndex - 2]);
      if (infoIndex > 2) {
        if (direction[infoIndex - 3] == 'R')
          info[infoIndex - 3].right = temp;
        else
          info[infoIndex - 3].left = temp;
      }
      else
        root = temp;


    }
    else {
      temp = leftRotate(info[infoIndex - 1]);
```

```
          info[infoIndex - 2].left = temp;
          temp = rightRotate(info[infoIndex - 2]);
          if (infoIndex > 2) {
            if (direction[infoIndex - 3] == 'R')
              info[infoIndex - 3].right = temp;
            else
              info[infoIndex - 3].left = temp;
          }
          else
            root = temp;
        }
      }
      infoIndex -= 2;
    }
    if (infoIndex == 1)
      if (direction[0] == 'R')
        root = leftRotate(info[0]);
      else
        root = rightRotate(info[0]);
  }

  protected SearchTreeNode rightRotate (SearchTreeNode t) {
    SearchTreeNode returnNode;
    SearchTreeNode temp;
    temp = t;
    returnNode = t.left;
    temp.left = returnNode.right;
    returnNode.right = temp;
    return returnNode;
  }

  protected SearchTreeNode leftRotate (SearchTreeNode t) {
    SearchTreeNode returnNode;
    SearchTreeNode temp;
    temp = t;
    returnNode = t.right;
    temp.right = returnNode.left;
    returnNode.left = temp;
    return returnNode;
  }
}
```

Explanation of Listing 15.7

1. Class *SplayTree*, like class *AVLTree*, extends class *BinarySearchTree*.

2. Two internal arrays, *info* and *direction*, are used to store the nodes and directions of descent in the search path from the root to the node being accessed.

3. Method *touch*, invoked by the query *has* and the command *add*, loads the arrays *info* and *direction* with search path information.

4. The query *has* replaces the parent query *contains*. This is essential because *contains* is used in *add* and *remove* (in class *BinarySearchTree*) and we do not wish splaying to be activated each time *contains* is invoked.

5. The private method *splay* uses the info and direction arrays to determine whether zig-zig or zig-zag rotations are needed. The *while* loop moves up the tree starting at the accessed node two levels with each iteration until the top of the tree is reached.

The reader should study the details of method *splay* and verify that it works.

15.16   Skip List

Skip lists are a relatively recent invention designed by W. Pugh.[1] They represent a creative way to utilize lists to implement the search table abstraction. Even though this chapter is titled "Search Trees," we examine the skip list structure because it is quite interesting and represents an alternative to AVL trees because of the high performance of a skip list.

A sequence of linked lists is maintained. The list at the bottom holds all the information. The list directly above the bottom list holds roughly half the data, the list above it roughly one-quarter of the data, and so on. The exact elements held at each level are determined probabilistically from the level directly below.

More formally, a skip list structure contains a series of lists $\{L_1, L_2, \ldots, L_t\}$. Each list L_i stores a subset of the items in list L_{i+1}. The items in L_i are nondecreasing and always contain a first item that is $-\infty$ and a last item that is ∞. Figure 15.24 shows a skip list.

L_t is the top list; L_1 is the bottom list.

We add an item to list L_1 first. By flipping a virtual coin (using a random number generator), we determine whether the item is added to list L_2. If it is (say when the coin comes up heads), we determine whether the item is also added to list L_3 (with another "heads"). We continue this process until we reach the top list, L_t. The probability of the item being added to all the lists would be $(1/2)^t$ where t represents the number of lists. This schema leads to the observation made earlier that as one moves up the lists from L_1, each higher list has roughly 1/2 the number of elements as the list directly below it.

Because of the skip list structure, the computational complexity associated with searching the list is high. The search process begins at the top list through a series of scan and drop operations. This is best illustrated with a diagram. See the skip list in Figure 15.24.

Suppose we wish to search for element 30. Since 30 is not in the top list (list 6), we drop to the list directly below it (list 5). We scan to the right until the element we are searching for exceeds an element in list 5. We drop to list 4. We again

---

[1] Pugh, W., "Skip lists: a probabilistic alternative to balanced trees," *Communications of the ACM*, Vol. 35, pp. 668–676, 1990.

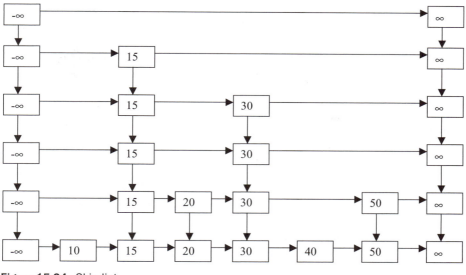

Figure 15.24. Skip list.

scan to the right, this time encountering item 30 in list 4. Our search process required two comparison operations compared to the four comparison operations that would have been required if we had used an ordered list structure.

Suppose we wish to search for element 40. From list 6 we drop down to list 5. Since 40 is greater than 15, we drop down to list 4 (through the node that contains 15). We scan list 4 discovering that 40 is greater than 30. We drop (through the node containing 30) down to list 3, then list 2, and finally list 1 where we find element 40. This time the search effort is the same as a linear search.

15.17 Implementation of Skip List

Listing 15.8 presents an implementation of class *SkipList*.

Listing 15.8 Class *SkipList*

```
/**
 * Implementation of Skip List without duplicates.
 * This is a dynamic implementation.
 * The size is specified upon construction to determine the number
 * of levels, which remains fixed.
 */
package foundations;
import java.util.*;

public class SkipList implements SearchTable {

    // Fields
    private int numberElements;
```

```java
private int levels;
private int capacity;
private Node start;
private Random rnd = new Random();
private int [] numValues;


// Constructor
public SkipList (int capacity) {
  // Build skeletal structure of list
  this.capacity = capacity;
  levels = (int) (1.75 * Math.log(capacity));
  numValues = new int[levels + 1];
  start = new Node(new SmallestComparable(), null, null);
  Node below1 = start;
  Node below2 = new Node(new LargestComparable(), null, null);
  below1.after = below2;
  Node above1, above2;
  // Build vertical towers down to level 1
  for (int index = levels - 1; index >= 1; index--) {
    above1 = below1;
    above2 = below2;
    below1 = new Node(new SmallestComparable(), null, null);
    below2 = new Node(new LargestComparable(), null, null);
    below1.after = below2;
    above1.down = below1;
    above2.down = below2;
  }
  numberElements = 0;
  for (int i = 1; i <= levels; i++)
    numValues[i] = 2;
  // Warm up random number generator
  for (int i = 0; i < 10000; i++)
    rnd.nextBoolean();
}


// Commands

/** Remove all objects from the table if found
*/
public void makeEmpty () {
  levels = (int) (1.75 * Math.log(capacity));
  numValues = new int[levels + 1];
  start = new Node(new SmallestComparable(), null, null);
  Node below1 = start;
  Node below2 = new Node(new LargestComparable(), below1, null);
  below1.after = below2;
  Node above1, above2;
```

```
    // Build vertical towers down to level 1
    for (int index = levels - 1; index >= 1; index--) {
      above1 = below1;
      above2 = below2;
      below1 = new Node(new SmallestComparable(), null, null);
      below2 = new Node(new LargestComparable(), null, null);
      below1.after = below2;
      above1.down = below1;
      above2.down = below2;
    }
    numberElements = 0;
    for (int i = 1; i <= levels; i++)
      numValues[i] = 2;
}

/** Add obj to the table; must be Comparable */
public void add (Comparable obj) {
  int index = levels;
  Node current = start;
  Node previous = current;
  Node newNode = null;
  Node aboveLevel = null;
  // Determine the level up to which the new insertion will rise
  int riseTo = 1;
  while (head())
    riseTo++;
  do {
    // Scan to the right as long as node's content < obj
    while (current.contents.compareTo(obj) < 0) {
      previous = current;
      current = current.after;
    }
    if (index <= riseTo) { // Perform insertion at this level
      newNode = new Node(obj, previous.after, null);
      numValues[index]++;
      previous.after = newNode;
      if (aboveLevel != null)
        aboveLevel.down = newNode;
      aboveLevel = newNode;
    }
    current = previous;
    index--;
    current = current.down;
    previous = current;
  }
  while (index >= 1 && current != null);
  numberElements++;
}
```

```java
/** Remove obj from table, if found
*/
public void remove (Comparable obj) {
  if (this.contains(obj)) {
    int index = levels;
    Node current = start;
    Node previous = current;
    // Scan down until the obj is found
    Node begin = start;
    do {
      current = begin;
      while (current != null &&
             current.contents.compareTo(obj) != 0) {
        previous = current;
        current = current.after;
      }
      if (current == null) {
        begin = begin.down;
        index--;
      }
    } while (current == null);
    // Drill down and remove nodes
    previous.after = current.after;
    begin = begin.down;
    while (begin != null) {
      current = begin;
      while (current.contents.compareTo(obj) != 0) {
        previous = current;
        current = current.after;
      }
      previous.after = current.after;
      begin = begin.down;
    }
    numberElements--;
  }

}


// Queries


/** Return true if the container is empty
*/
public boolean isEmpty () {
  return numberElements == 0;
}
```

```java
/** Return the number of objects in the container
*/
public int size () {
  return numberElements;
}

/** Return true if the table contains obj
*/
public boolean contains (Comparable obj) {
  int index = levels;
  Node current = start;
  Node previous = current;
  do {
    // Scan to the right as long as node's content < obj
    while (current.contents.compareTo(obj) < 0) {
      previous = current;
      current = current.after;
    }
    if (current.contents.compareTo(obj) == 0)
      return true;
    current = previous;
    index--;
    current = current.down;
    previous = current;
  }
  while (index >= 1);
  return current != null;
}

/** Return obj if in table
*    useful when obj is a key & returns an Association
*/
public Comparable get (Comparable obj) {
  int index = levels;
  Node current = start;
  Node previous = current;
  do {
    // Scan to the right as long as node's content < obj
    while (current.contents.compareTo(obj) < 0) {
      previous = current;
      current = current.after;
    }
    if (current.contents.compareTo(obj) == 0)
      return current.contents;
    current = previous;
    index--;
```

```
      current = current.down;
      previous = current;
    }
    while (index >= 1);
    return null;
  }

  public int numberLevels () {
    return levels;
  }

  public int [] numValues () {
    return numValues;
  }

  /** Return an iterator on all elements
  */
  public Iterator elements () {
    Vector v = new Vector();
    // Get node at left at level 1
    Node current = start;
    while (current.down != null)
      current = current.down;
    current = current.after;
    for (int i = 1; i <= numberElements; i++) {
      v.addElement(current.contents);
      current = current.after;
    }
    return v.iterator();
  }

  // Internal methods
  boolean head () { // Simulates fair coin
    return rnd.nextBoolean() == true;
  }

  private class Node {

    // Fields
    private Comparable contents;
    private Node after, down;

    // Constructor
    public Node (Comparable contents, Node after, Node down) {
      this.contents = contents;
      this.after = after;
      this.down = down;
    }
  }
}
```

```
private class SmallestComparable implements Comparable {
  public int compareTo( Object obj) {
    return -1;
  }
}

private class LargestComparable implements Comparable {
  public int compareTo (Object obj) {
    return 1;
  }
}
}
```

Explanation of Listing 15.8

Class *SkipList* implements *SearchTable*.

There are six fields that define the state of a skip list. These include *numberElements, levels, capacity, start* (the *Node* with value $-\infty$ at the top level), *rnd* (a random number generator), and *numValues* (an array that holds the number of elements at each level).

The constructor takes a capacity as input and uses it to determine the number of levels. This capacity input does not restrict the actual number of elements added to the skip list. It just provides a basis for setting the number of levels. The value $1.75 * log(capacity)$ provides a good approximation of how many levels are needed so that there will be approximately one element at the highest level. Using a *for* loop, the skeletal structure of the skip list is constructed. The contents of every node must be of type *Comparable*. This includes the elements that must represent $-\infty$ and ∞.

How can we provide surrogates for $-\infty$ and ∞ and make them *Comparable*? We create two small inner classes, *SmallestComparable* and *LargestComparable*, with the following:

```
private class SmallestComparable implements Comparable {
  public int compareTo(Object obj) {
    return -1;
  }
}

private class LargestComparable implements Comparable {
  public int compareTo(Object obj) {
    return 1;
  }
}
```

The first of these classes defines *compareTo* so that it always returns -1. The second of these classes defines *compareTo* so that it always returns 1.

In the constructor for *SkipList* we assign *new SmallestComparable()* to all the left column nodes and *new LargestComparable( )* to all the right column nodes.

A third inner class, *Node*, provides links *after* and *down* to enable scanning through a list and dropping to the next lower list.

Method *add* first determines the level to which the inserted new item will rise. A *do while* loop performs the ordered linked-list insertion.

Method *remove* scans each list, starting at the top list, until the element being removed is located. It then drills down removing all occurrences of the node that need to be removed.

Methods *contains* and *get* follow a similar logic starting at the top list and scanning until the element being sought is found or is greater than some list element. This is repeated until the element being sought is found.

The query *elements* defines a local *Vector* object and loads it with all the elements obtained from the bottom list. It then returns the *iterator* object associated with this *Vector*.

A probabilistic analysis of the skip list structure (beyond the scope of these notes) reveals that search time is of $O(\log_2 n)$.

15.18   Putting It All Together

This chapter has examined four implementations of a *search table*: binary search tree, AVL tree, splay tree, and skip list. The last three of these attempt to provide for fast search, add, and remove operations.

The relationship among these classes is shown in the UML diagram of Figure 15.25.

Another GUI tree laboratory application has been written. This application enables the user to visualize binary search tree, AVL tree, and splay tree add and remove operations (method *remove* is not implemented for *AVLTree*). As the user specifies integer-valued elements, a display panel shows the actual tree representation for small-sized trees (thirty nodes or fewer). The tree laboratory also allows the performance of AVL trees and skip lists to be compared. It allows the ACE and maximum level of binary search trees, AVL trees, and splay trees to be compared.

Several screen shots from the application in progress are shown in the next several figures. Figure 15.26 shows the results of two experiments. Random AVL trees, BSTs (binary search trees), and splay trees are constructed using the same random values and their average path length and max level are compared. The AVL tree clearly is the winner. The second experiment generates an AVL tree and skip list from the same values – 10,000 random values in this case. The times to construct and then access each of its nodes are compared for the two data structures. The skip list is the winner (almost a tie). Considering the relative simplicity of the skip list structure, it is quite amazing that it does so well.

The tree shown in Figure 15.27 results from the sequential insertion of 100, 50, 200, 150, 250, and 175. Figure 15.28 shows the tree after element 200 is removed.

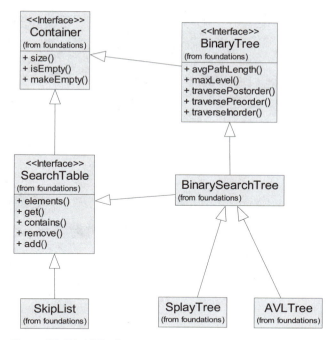

Figure 15.25. UML diagram.

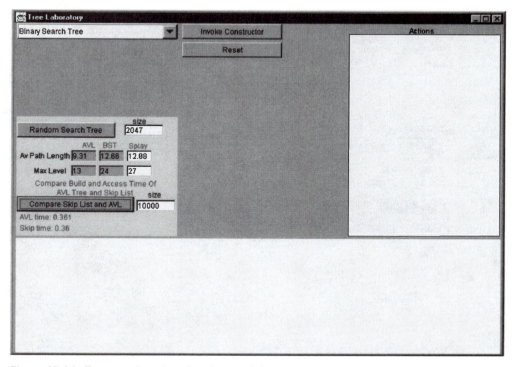

Figure 15.26. Two experiments using the tree laboratory.

Figure 15.27. Binary search tree.

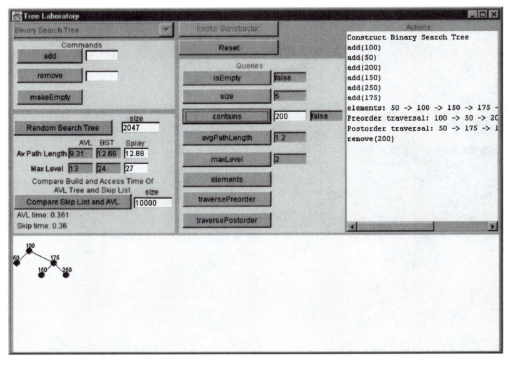

Figure 15.28. Binary search tree after removing 200.

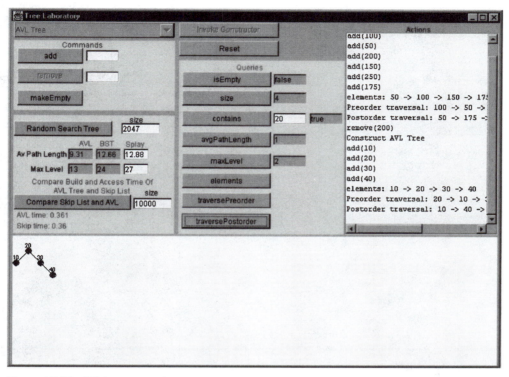

Figure 15.29. AVL tree.

After the "Reset" button is clicked, the AVL tree is chosen from the combo box and the constructor invoked.

Figure 15.29 shows the tree resulting from the sequential insertion of 10, 20, 30, and 40.

The addition of element 35 produces (after a type 2 rotation) the tree shown in Figure 15.30.

Finally, if the user clicks "Reset" and chooses "Splay Tree" and then adds elements 10, 20, 30, and 40 the tree shown in Figure 15.31 is obtained.

The reader is encouraged to experiment with the tree laboratory.

15.19   Reusable Class *DrawTree*

In the screen shots taken from the tree laboratory in the previous section there are several tree structures painted in a panel component and integrated into the user interface. This helps the user visualize the tree structures that are constructed.

A reusable component, *DrawTree*, was designed for this purpose. This component was also used to render the expression trees presented in the previous chapter and may be used to render any binary tree.

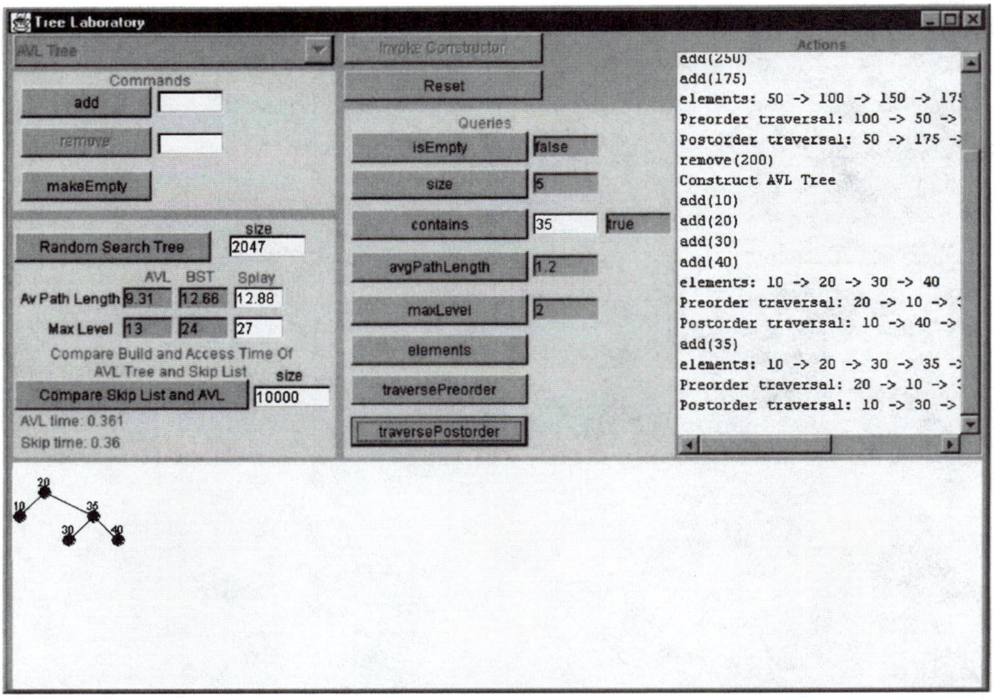

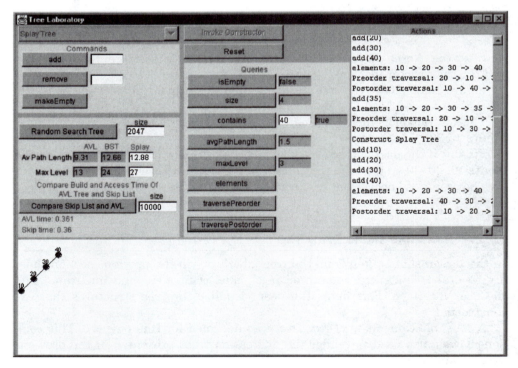

Figure 15.30. AVL tree after the insertion of 35.

Figure 15.31. Splay tree.

The constructor for class *DrawTree* is given as follows:

```
public DrawTree (SearchTreeNode root, int size, JPanel panel,
               Color color, int labelSize) {
  // Details not shown here
}
```

The user must send the root node of the tree to be rendered, the size of the tree, a *JPanel* component that captures the drawing, the color to be used for the nodes, and links between nodes and the font size for the node labels. All of the logic for drawing such a tree onto the panel is encapsulated in class *DrawTree*. This is in the spirit of object-oriented software construction in which a class performs a specialized activity – tree drawing in this case – letting the application programmer focus on other aspects of his or her application.

The details of class *DrawTree* are presented in Listing 15.9.

Listing 15.9 Class *DrawTree*

```
/** Produces a JPanel containing a binary tree
*/
package foundations;
import javax.swing.*;
import java.awt.*;

public class DrawTree {

  // Fields

  private int size;
  private SearchTreeNode [] nodes;
  private int [] levels;
  private int nodesIndex = -1;
  private final int diameter = 10;
  private JPanel panel;
  private Color color;
  private SearchTreeNode root;
  private int labelSize;

  // Constructor

  public DrawTree (SearchTreeNode root, int size, JPanel panel,
                 Color color, int labelSize) {
    this.color = color;
    this.root = root;
```

```
      this.panel = panel;
      this.size = size;
      this.labelSize = labelSize;
      color = Color.red;
      if (root != null)
        constructTree();
  }

  // Commands

  public void update (SearchTreeNode root, int size) {
      clearPanel();
      this.root = root;
      this.size = size;
      constructTree();
  }

  public void clearPanel () {
      Graphics g = panel.getGraphics();
      g.setColor(panel.getBackground());;
      g.drawRect(panel.getVisibleRect().getBounds().x,
                 panel.getVisibleRect().getBounds().y,
                 panel.getVisibleRect().getBounds().width,
                 panel.getVisibleRect().getBounds().height);
      g.fillRect(panel.getVisibleRect().getBounds().x,
                 panel.getVisibleRect().getBounds().y,
                 panel.getVisibleRect().getBounds().width,
                 panel.getVisibleRect().getBounds().height);
  }

  // Internal methods
  private void build (SearchTreeNode n, int level) {
      if (n != null) {
        build(n.left, level + 1);
        nodesIndex++;
        nodes[nodesIndex] = n;
        levels[nodesIndex] = level;
        build(n.right, level + 1);
      }
  }

  private void drawLineSegment (Point pt1, Point pt2) {
      Graphics g = panel.getGraphics();
      g.setColor(color);
      g.drawLine(pt1.x + diameter / 2, pt1.y + diameter / 2,
                 pt2.x + diameter / 2, pt2.y + diameter / 2);
  }
```

```
  private int index (SearchTreeNode n) {
    for (int i = 0; i < size; i++)
      if (nodes[i] == n)
        return i;
    return -1;
  }


  private void drawNode (Point pt, String str) {
    Graphics g = panel.getGraphics();
    g.setColor(color);
    g.drawOval(pt.x, pt.y, diameter, diameter);
    g.fillOval(pt.x, pt.y, diameter, diameter);
    g.setColor(Color.black);
    g.setFont(new Font("Times Roman" , Font.PLAIN, 9));
    String drawStr = (str.length() > labelSize) ?
                            str.substring(0, labelSize) : str;
    g.drawString(drawStr, pt.x, pt.y);
  }


  private void constructTree () {
    nodesIndex = -1;
    nodes = new SearchTreeNode[size];
    levels = new int[size];
    build(root, 1);
    for (int index = 0; index < size; index++) {
      drawNode(new Point(index * 20, levels[index] * 20),
               nodes[index].contents.toString());
      if (nodes[index].left != null) {
        SearchTreeNode left = nodes[index].left;
        int indexLeft = index (left);
        drawLineSegment(new Point(index * 20,
                     levels[index] * 20),
          new Point(indexLeft * 20, levels[indexLeft] * 20));
      }
      if (nodes[index].right != null) {
        SearchTreeNode right = nodes[index].right;
        int indexRight = index (right);
        drawLineSegment(new Point(index * 20,
                     levels[index] * 20),
          new Point(indexRight * 20,
                   levels[indexRight] * 20));
      }
    }
  }
}
```

Explanation of Listing 15.9

The private (internal) method *build* uses an in-order traversal to load up two array fields, *nodes* and *levels*. The private method *constructTree* uses the information in the arrays *nodes* and *levels* to draw the nodes and links. The horizontal position of each node is proportional to the index in which the node is stored in the *nodes* array and the vertical position of the node is held in the *levels* array.

The private methods *drawLine* and *drawNode* use the graphic context of the *panel* component that is input to place their pixels onto this graphics context.

Method *constructTree* iterates through all the nodes stored in the *nodes* field and draws links to their left and right children, if any.

15.20 Summary

❏ This chapter has presented the details of four *SearchTable* implementations: *BinarySearchTree, AVLTree, SplayTree,* and *SkipList.*

❏ The *BinarySearchTree* performs well only if the tree is relatively balanced.

❏ The *AVLTree, SplayTree,* and *SkipList* perform efficiently regardless of the data that are added to these structures.

❏ The performance of all binary tree types is dependent on the degree of balance in the tree.

❏ An AVL tree is always nearly optimally balanced.

❏ A splay tree has an amortized performance that is equal to $O(n \log_2 n)$.

❏ A skip list performs almost as well as an AVL tree.

15.21 Exercises

1 For the binary tree shown in Figure Exercise 1:

    a. Compute the average internal path length.
    b. What is the sequence of nodes visited using a preorder traversal?
    c. What is the sequence of nodes visited using a in-order traversal?
    d. What is the sequence of nodes visited using a postorder traversal?
    e. Sketch the tree that results if node 70 is deleted from the tree.
    f. Sketch the tree that results if node 90 is deleted from the original tree.

To answer questions 2, 3, 4, and 5 you will need to create a new class, *SpecialBinarySearchTree*, that extends *BinarySearchTree* and is in package *foundations*. Create your *SpecialBinarySearchTree* in a subdirectory *foundations*. You must run your new class from the directory just outside *foundations* using **java foundations.SpecialBinarySearchTree**. The answers to Exercises 2, 3, 4, and 5 will be contained in the single file *SpecialBinarySearchTree.java*.

Include a function *main( )* in your *SpecialBinarySearchTree* class that tests each of the functions designed in Exercises 2, 3, 4, and 5.

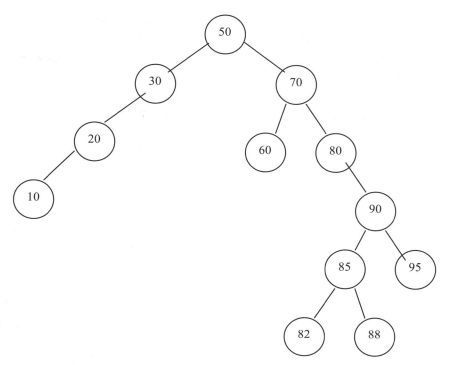

Figure Exercise 1.

2 Implement a query *int level (Comparable item)* in class *SpecialBinary-SearchTree* that returns the level of an item in the *SpecialBinarySearchTree*. The root node is defined as having level 0.

3 Implement a query *boolean isPerfectlyBalanced ()* in class *SpecialBinarySearchTree* that returns *true* if the search tree is perfectly balanced and otherwise returns *false*.

4 Implement a query *boolean isAVL ()* in class *SpecialBinarySearchTree* that returns *true* if the search tree is an AVL tree and otherwise returns *false*.

5 Implement a query *int minimumDepth ()* in class *SpecialBinarySearchTree* that returns the level of the leaf node whose level is closest to the root level.

6 Construct an experiment that confirms that the amortized cost of inserting nodes into a splay tree is logarithmically related to the number of nodes.

7 Revise the implementation of class *SkipList* so that each node points backwards and upwards in addition to pointing to the right and downwards. Test your new implementation.

8 Can you deduce any relationship between the postorder traversal of a binary tree and the preorder traversal of its mirror image?

9   Find all the binary trees such that the preorder and postorder traversals visit the nodes in exactly the same order.

10 Do the leaf nodes in a binary tree occur in the same order for preorder, inorder, and postorder traversals? If so, justify your contention.

11 Explain, prove, or justify that if we are given the preorder and postorder traversals of a binary tree, the binary tree structure may be constructed.

16

Hashing and Sets

Hash tables are containers that represent a collection of objects inserted at computed index locations. Each object inserted in the hash table is associated with a hash index. The process of hashing involves the computation of an integer index (the hash index) for a given object (such as a string). If designed properly, the hash computation (1) should be fast, and (2) when done repeatedly for a set of keys to be inserted in a hash table should produce hash indices uniformly distributed across the range of index values for the hash table. The term "hashing" is derived from the observation that there should be little if any obvious association between the object being inserted and its hash index. Two closely related objects such as the strings "time" and "lime" should generally produce unrelated hash indices. Thus hashing involves distributing objects into what appears to be random (but reproducible) locations in the table.

When two distinct objects produce the same hash index, we refer to this as a **collision**. Clearly the two objects cannot be placed at the same index location in the table. A collision resolution algorithm must be designed to place the second object at a location distinct from the first when their hash indices are identical.

The two fundamental problems associated with the construction of hash tables are:

1. the design of an efficient hash function that distributes the index values of inserted objects uniformly across the table

2. the design of an efficient collision resolution algorithm that computes an alternative index for an object whose hash index corresponds to an object previously inserted in the hash table

We shall consider each of these problems in this chapter.

The standard Java package *java.util* provides an efficiently designed and robust *Hashtable* class and an approximately equivalent *HashMap* class. We shall explore class *Hashtable* in this chapter. We also examine the *Set* abstraction and its implementation in this chapter.

16.1 Hashing and Collision Resolution

Although any kind of object may be put into hash tables we shall focus on objects of type *String*. Most standard Java classes provide a *hashCode()* query function that returns an *int* for a given instance of the class. The *hashCode()* value may be used to determine the index location for insertion of an object in a hash table. In the event of a collision, the final destination of the object (index location) must be determined using a collision resolution algorithm, as indicated earlier.

Can one build a perfect hash function in which a unique index value may be associated with an arbitrary string? The answer is yes in theory, but no in practice.

Suppose one maps each character of a string to an integer using the conversion:

A -> 1

B -> 2

...

Z -> 26

Other special characters such as apostrophes may be assigned additional numbers. As an example, suppose that there are twenty-seven possible values, one for each character (e.g., letters map to 1...26 and interior apostrophe maps to 27). Let us consider the hash value for a string of length 10. The perfect hash function would be:

```
hashIndex = word [0] + word [1] * 27 + word [2] * 27² + word [3] * 27³
          + word [4] * 27⁴ + word [5] * 27⁵ + word [6] * 27⁶
          + word [7] * 27⁷ + word [8] * 27⁸ + word [9] * 27⁹
```

In the worst case, when every character maps to the value 27, the index range would go up to:

$$(27 + 27^2 + 27^3 + \cdots + 27^{10}) \sim 3 \times 10^{14}.$$

For strings of length greater than 10 the index range would be even greater. It is therefore impractical to build a perfect hash function for strings of arbitrary length. It must also be recalled that the string itself must be stored in the table. The memory requirements for this are overwhelming!

In a practical hash table, only a limited number of strings can be stored. If English words are being stored, only a fraction of all possible words (over one million have been identified) can fit in memory and be available for fast access. A typical hash function will produce collisions when building such a table.

A hash table, like all containers, has a given size. This represents the actual number of objects stored in the table. The ratio of a hash table's size to its capacity is defined as the **load factor** of the hash table. That is, *load factor = size/capacity*.

If each object in a hash table is associated with a unique hash index (and this is unlikely in practice), it would take only one comparison operation to determine whether a specified object were present or not present in the hash table. The hash index would be computed for the object and the object would be compared to the contents of the table at the hash index location. The object would either be present or not present. Because of collisions it is often the case that two or more comparison operations must be performed before determining whether a specified object is present or not present in a hash table. We define the number of comparison operations required to determine the presence of a specified object as the **number of probes**. We can compute the **average number of probes** for a given hash table. This is a measure of the efficiency of the table – smaller values indicate a higher efficiency. The ACE statistic for a binary search tree (average comparison effort) discussed in Chapter 15 is a similar measure of search efficiency for a container. The smaller the value of ACE or average number of probes, the faster the average access time.

We shall compare the performance of hash tables with balanced binary trees later.

16.2 Bit Operations

Before continuing with our discussion of hashing and collision resolution, we review the Java language's support for low-level bit operations.

The *BitSet* class stores a sequence of bits. It is actually an array of bits. The key operations of class *BitSet* are:

```
// Constructor
BitSet (int nbits)

// Commands
void set (int bit)        // sets the bit to true (on = 1)
void clear (int bit)      // sets the bit to false (off = 0)
void and (BitSet other)   // logically AND receiver bit set with other
void or (BitSet other)    // logically OR receiver bit set with other
void xor (BitSet other)   // logically XOR receiver bit set with other

// Queries
boolean get (int bit)     // return true if the bit is on
                          // otherwise return false
```

We illustrate the use of bit sets in producing prime numbers. Suppose we wish to compute all the prime numbers between 2 and 1,000,000. One algorithm for computing prime numbers uses the Sieve of Eratosthenes. It efficiently eliminates all numbers in the desired range that are integer multiples of potential prime numbers. By starting at the lowest numbers, only the prime numbers remain.

We first define a bit set that can hold 1,000,000 bits. Next we turn off (set to *false*) all the bits that are multiples of numbers known to be prime using the Sieve of Eratosthenes. When completed, the indexed bits that remain on (have a *true* value) after this process are themselves the prime numbers.

Listing 16.1 presents the details of a class called *Primes* that implements this algorithm, computes primes up to 1,000,000, and displays on the console the prime numbers up to 5,000.

Listing 16.1 Sieve of Eratosthenes Using Class *BitSet*

```java
/** An application program that computes the prime numbers from 2 to
 *   one million using bit sets and the Sieve of Eratosthenes algorithm.
 *   Prime numbers are output to the console up to the value printTo.
 */
import java.util.*;

public class Primes {
  private final static int SIZE = 1000000;
  private final static int printTo = 5000;


  // Commands
  public void computePrimes () {
    BitSet b = new BitSet (SIZE);
    int count = 0;
    int i;

    // Set all the bits from 2 to 1,000,000
    for (i = 2; i < SIZE; i++)
      b.set (i);

    // eliminate (turn off) multiples of prime numbers
    i = 2;      // start with smallest prime number
    while (i * i < SIZE) {
      if (b.get(i)) {
        count++;
        int k = 2 * i;
        while (k <= SIZE) {
          b.clear (k);
          k += i;
        }
      }
      i++;
    }


    // Display results
    for (i = 2, count = 0; i < SIZE; i++)
      if (b.get (i)) {
        if (i <= printTo)
          System.out.print (i + " ");
        count++;
      }
    System.out.println ("\nNumber of primes between 2 and "
                            + SIZE + " = " + count);
  }
```

```
public static void main (String[] args) {
  Primes app = new Primes();
  app.computePrimes();
  }
}
```

Let us walk through this algorithm.

The initial bit set, indexed from 0 to SIZE − 1, looks like:

(0, 0, 1, ..., 1, 1, 1).

In the first *while* loop, since *b.get (2)* returns true, we assign *k* the value 4. We clear bits 4, 6, 8, 10 . . . from the bit set (integer multiples of 2). The bit set now looks like:

(0, 0, 1, 1, 0, 1, 0, 1, 0, 1, 0, ...).

Now the variable *i* is incremented to 3. Since this bit is on, we assign *k* the value 6. We clear 6, 9, 12, 15, . . . from the bit set (integer multiples of 3). The bit set looks like:

(0, 0, 1, 1, 0, 1, 0, 1, 0, 0, 0, 1, 0, 1, 0, 0, 0...).

Now the variable *i* is incremented to 4 and then to 5, since bit 4 is cleared. We assign *k* the value 10 and clear bits in positions 10, 15, 20, 25, ... This pattern continues until we have reached the square root of SIZE. Why can we safely stop at this point?

The output of Listing 16.1 is not shown because of its length.

16.3 Perfect Hash Function

Suppose that we wish to map any English word of five characters or less to a unique index value (in an array). We can accomplish this using the following hash function:

```
hashIndex = word [0] + word [1] * 27 + word [2] * 27² + word [3] * 27³
            + word [4] * 27⁴
```

The largest index possible would be $27 * (1 + 27 + 27^2 + 27^3 + 27^4) = 14,900,787$. Listing 16.2 presents the details of this hash function in a class called *PerfectHash*.

The hash indices of several words are given in the following table after applying the perfect hash function:

Word	Hash index
disk	230611
drive	3097282
car	13152
cars	387129

Listing 16.2   Class *PerfectHash*

```java
/** A perfect hash function for words of five characters or less.
*/
import java.util.*;

public class PerfectHash {

  private BitSet data = new BitSet (14900787);

  private int convert (char ch) {
    if (ch >= 'a' && ch <= 'z')
      return ch - 'a' + 1;
    else if (ch == '\'')
      return 27;
    else
      return 0;
  }

  // Commands

  public void insert (String word) {
    if (word.trim().length() <= 5)
      data.set (hashIndex (word));
  }

  // Queries

  public int hashIndex (String word) {
    if (word.trim().length() <= 5) {
      String str = word.toLowerCase().trim();
      int sum = convert (str.charAt (0));
      int multiplier = 27;
      for (int index = 1; index < str.length(); index++) {
        sum += convert (str.charAt (index)) * multiplier;
        multiplier *= 27;
      }
      return sum;
    }
    else
      return -1;
  }

  public boolean contains (String word) {
    return data.get(hashIndex (word));
  }
}
```

16.4 Collisions

In the previous section a perfect hash function was defined, one that associates a unique index with every word. The problem is that it works only for words with length equal to or less than five characters.

In this section we investigate the occurrence of collisions. To do this we hash 109,580 distinct English words and count the number of collisions using arrays of increasing size to hold the string values. We use the predefined query *hashCode( )* for class *String* in the Java 2 Platform to hash the words in file *distinct.txt*. Query *hashCode( )* is good but not perfect; therefore, we should expect some collisions.

This file of distinct words, *distinct.txt*, has the following properties:

Properties of File *distinct.txt*

```
Number of words of length 1 = 1
Number of words of length 2 = 140
Number of words of length 3 = 853
Number of words of length 4 = 3129
Number of words of length 5 = 6918
Number of words of length 6 = 11492
Number of words of length 7 = 16881
Number of words of length 8 = 19461
Number of words of length 9 = 16694
Number of words of length 10 = 11882
Number of words of length 11 = 8374
Number of words of length 12 = 5812
Number of words of length 13 = 3677
Number of words of length 14 = 2101
Number of words of length 15 = 1159
Number of words of length 16 = 583
Number of words of length 17 = 229
Number of words of length 18 = 107
Number of words of length 19 = 39
Number of words of length 20 = 29
Number of words of length 21 = 11
Number of words of length 22 = 4
Number of words of length 23 = 2
Number of words of length 24 = 0
Number of words of length 25 = 1
Number of words of length 26 = 0
Number of words of length 27 = 0
Number of words of length 28 = 1
Number of words of length 29 = 0
Number of words of length 30 = 0

Total number of words = 109580
```

Listing 16.3 shows the details of this experiment. Collisions are computed for the 109,580 words when hashed into tables of different sizes, ranging from

SIZE $= 10{,}980$ to $10 *$ SIZE. It is expected that the number of collisions goes down as hash table size increases (i.e., the load factor goes down). Of course, increased size (decreased load factor) wastes space in the table.

Listing 16.3 Collision Experiment

```
/** An application that determines the number of collisions among
 *    109,580 distinct words using the hashCode() function of class
 *    String and tables of increasing size.
 */
import java.io.*;


public class CollisionExperiment {


  // Fields
  private final int NUMBER_WORDS = 109580;
  String [] table;


  public void computeCollisions () {
    int hashIndex = 0;
    try {
      System.out.println ("Size\t\t\tCollisions");
      for (int size = NUMBER_WORDS; size <= 10*NUMBER_WORDS;
        size += NUMBER_WORDS) {
        table = new String[size];
        BufferedReader diskInput = new BufferedReader (
                          new InputStreamReader (
                          new FileInputStream (
                          new File("distinct.txt"))));
        // Insert each line of disk input file into hash table
        int collisions = 0;
        String line = diskInput.readLine();
        while (line != null && line.length() > 0) {
          hashIndex = Math.abs(line.hashCode()) % size;
          if (table[hashIndex] == null)
            table[hashIndex] = line;
          else
            collisions++;
          line = diskInput.readLine();
        }
        System.out.println (size + "\t\t\t" + collisions);
      }
    }
    catch (Exception ex) {}
  }
```

```
  static public void main (String[] args) {
    CollisionExperiment app = new CollisionExperiment();
    app.computeCollisions();
  }
}
```

The output from Listing 16.3 is the following:

```
Size          Collisions
109580          40309
219160          23422
328740          16538
438320          12627
547900          10264
657480          8740
767060          7500
876640          6568
986220          5964
1095800         5310
```

The number of collisions decreases as the size of the table increases.

16.5   Class *Hashtable*

In this section we examine the standard Java class *Hashtable* provided in package *java.util*. The skeletal structure of parts of class *Hashtable* is given in Listing 16.4.

Listing 16.4   Skeletal Structure of Portions of Class *Hashtable*

```
/** Skeletal structure of portions of class Hashtable
*/

public class Hashtable {

  // Constructors
  public Hashtable () {
    /* Constructs a new empty hashtable with a default capacity and
       load factor that is 0.75.
    */
    ...
  }

  public Hashtable (int initialCapacity) {
    /* Constructs a new empty hashtable with the specified initial
       capacity and default load factor.
    */
    ...
  }
```

```
public Hashtable (int initialCapacity, float loadFactor) {
  /* Constructs a new empty hashtable with the specified initial
     capacity and the specified load factor.
   */
  ...
}

// Commands

/** Empties hashtable
 */
public void clear () { ... }

/** Maps the specified key to the specified value in the table.
 */
public put (Object key, Object value) { ... }

/** Removes the key and its corresponding value from the table.
 */
public remove (Object key) { ... }

// Queries

/** Returns the number of keys in the table.
 */
public int size () { ... }

/** Returns true if the specified object is a key in the table.
 */
public boolean containsKey (Object key) { ... }

/** Returns true if the table maps one or more keys to this value.
 */
public boolean containsValue (Object value) { ... }

/** Returns the value to which the specified key is mapped in the
 *   table.
 */
public Object get (Object key) { ... }

/** Returns an enumeration of the values in the table.
 */
Enumeration elements () {...}

/** Returns an enumeration of the keys in this hashtable.
 */
public Enumeration keys () { ... }
}
```

If the number of objects stored in the table exceeds the capacity multiplied by the load factor, the table is dynamically increased in size. This ensures that the specified load factor is never exceeded.

We now perform another experiment whose goal is to determine the speed of information access using class *Hashtable*. We load the same set of 109,580 distinct English words into a *Hashtable*, which uses the *hashCode()* method from class *String* to determine the index in the table to store each word. We then output the time that it takes to search the constructed hash table for all the words that have been inserted into the table. Listing 16.5 shows the details of this experiment.

Class *Hashtable* stores associations and computes the table index by hashing the key. Thus the *hash.put(line, line)* statement in Listing 16.5 simply lets the word serve as both key and value.

Listing 16.5 **Experiment to Determine the Speed of Class *Hashtable***

```java
/** Application to determine the speed of Hashtable.
*/
import java.io.*;
import java.util.*;
import java.text.*;

public class HashTest {

  // Internal fields
  private final int SIZE = 109580;
  private int count = 0;
  private long elapsedTime = 0L;
  private Hashtable hash;

  public void performTest () throws Exception {
    long elapsedTime = 0L;
    long startTime, endTime;
    DecimalFormat df = new DecimalFormat("0.##");
    BufferedReader diskInput;
    String line;
    hash = new Hashtable(250000);
    diskInput = new BufferedReader (new InputStreamReader (
                            new FileInputStream (
                            new File ("distinct.txt"))));
    // Insert each line of disk input file into hash table
    line = diskInput.readLine();

    while (line != null) {
      hash.put(line, line);
      line = diskInput.readLine();
    }
    System.out.println ("hash.size() = " + hash.size());
```

```
    System.out.println ("Checking words against hash table");
    elapsedTime = 0;
    diskInput = new BufferedReader (new InputStreamReader (
                                new FileInputStream (
                                new File ("distinct.txt"))));
  line = diskInput.readLine();
  while (line != null) {
    startTime = System.currentTimeMillis();
    if (hash.containsKey(line))
      count++;
    endTime = System.currentTimeMillis();
    elapsedTime += endTime - startTime;
    line = diskInput.readLine();
  }
  System.out.println ("Words found in hash table = " + count);
  System.out.println ("Words checked per second = " +
                    (int) (count * 1000.0 / elapsedTime) +
                    " words per second.");
  }

public static void main (String[] args) throws Exception {
  HashTest app = new HashTest();
  app.performTest();
  }
}
```

Typical output from Listing 16.5 is the following:

```
hash.size() = 109580
Checking hash table words against hash table
Words found in hash table = 109580
Correctly spelled words checked per second = 608777 words
  per second.
```

These results were obtained using a Pentium-III PC with 256 MB RAM, running at 500 MHz, under Windows NT. The *hashCode()* algorithm is fast!

16.6 Collision Resolution

We shall examine two algorithms for collision resolution, **linear chaining** and **coalesced chaining**. Both provide collision resolution within the space allocated for the hash table. A third type of collision resolution called **separate chaining** builds linked lists of objects that hash to the same index. Separate chaining avoids the problem of overlapping chains (to be described in the next section) at the expense of requiring that extra memory be allocated for each collision. Separate chaining is used in standard class *Hashtable*. Coalesced chaining is more complex but significantly more efficient than linear chaining. In this section we explore the details of linear chaining and coalesced chaining.

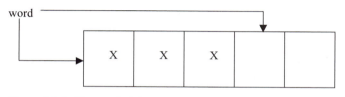

Figure 16.1. Linear chaining.

16.6.1 Linear Chaining

Linear chaining involves sequentially searching the hash table for an empty location if the initial location given by the hash index is occupied by another word. The sequential search starts at the hash index for the given word. When the highest index location in the table is reached, the search continues by wrapping to the lowest index location in the table. As long as there is at least one empty index location in the hash table, this process eventually terminates. For high load factors the collision resolution chains begin to overlap, adding even more time required to find an object in the table.

Figure 16.1 shows a word that ends up three index locations to the right of its initial destination because of linear chaining collision resolution.

Algorithm for Word Insertion Using Linear Chaining

1. *Obtain hash index for word.*
2. *If table at hash index is empty, insert the word at this location.*
3. *If the table at the hash index is occupied with a different word, sequentially increment the index until the word is encountered or an empty index location is found.*
4. *If the loop in step 3 terminates because of an empty index location, insert the word at this empty location.*

The number of probes associated with the insertion of a word using linear chaining is equal to the number of index locations touched before the word is inserted. For the insertion shown in Figure 16.1, the number of probes equals 4.

When a hash table is relatively empty, the likelihood of a collision is small. As the load factor increases (ratio of the number of words to the capacity of the table), the likelihood of a collision increases. Collisions force sequential chains of words to be formed. As collision chains get substantial in size, the likelihood of them getting even larger increases. This is based on the assumption that a good hash function produces hash indices that are uniformly distributed across the hash table. A large collision chain presents a bigger target than an isolated word. The big get bigger! Chains eventually overlap making the problem even worse.

At high load factors when many collision chains have formed, the average number of probes required to search for a word in the table using linear chaining increases significantly.

The algorithm for searching for a word in the hash table using linear chaining is the following:

Algorithm for Word Access Using Linear Chaining

1. *Obtain hash index for word.*
2. *If table at hash index is empty, word is not present.*
3. *If the table at the hash index is occupied with a different word, sequentially increment the index until the word is found or an empty index location is found.*
4. *If the loop in step 3 terminates because of an empty index location, the word is not in the table.*

We next examine the effect that load factor has on the performance of a hash table using linear chaining. We use the average number of probes as a measure of the table's efficiency. To accomplish this we design a simulation experiment that uses a uniformly distributed random index to simulate a good hash function. As virtual words are added at random index locations we keep track of the number of probes required for each insertion. At the end we output the average number of probes. Listing 16.6 provides the details of our simulation experiment.

Listing 16.6   **Efficiency of Linear Chaining versus Load Factor: A Simulation**

```java
/** An application that simulates the performance of linear chaining.
*/
import java.text.*;
import java.util.*;

public class LinearChainingApp {

  // Fields
  int probes;
  boolean [] words = new boolean [1000]; // Holds virtual words
  Random rnd = new Random();
  int count;

  public void generateTable (double loadFactor) {
    // Empty the table
    for (int i = 0; i < 1000; i++)
      words[i] = false;
    count = (int) (1000 * loadFactor);
    probes = 0;
    for (int i = 0; i < count; i++) {
      int hashIndex = rnd.nextInt(1000);
      while (words[hashIndex] == true) {
        hashIndex++;
        probes++;
```

```
      if (hashIndex == 1000)
         hashIndex = 0;
      }
      words[hashIndex] = true;
      probes++;
    }
  }

  static public void main (String[] args) {
    DecimalFormat df = new DecimalFormat("#.00");
    LinearChainingApp app = new LinearChainingApp();
    System.out.println (
            "Load Factor\t\t\tAverage Number of Probes");
    for (double lf = 0.1; lf <= 0.9; lf += 0.1) {
      app.generateTable(lf);
      System.out.println(df.format(lf) + "\t\t\t\t" +
                  df.format((double) app.probes / app.count));
    }

    for (double lf = 0.91; lf < 1.0; lf += 0.01) {
      app.generateTable(lf);
      System.out.println(df.format(lf) + "\t\t\t\t" +
                  df.format((double) app.probes / app.count));
    }
  }
}
```

The output of the simulation in Listing 16.6 for linear chaining is:

Load Factor	Average Number of Probes
.10	1.06
.20	1.16
.30	1.24
.40	1.36
.50	1.45
.60	1.84
.70	3.02
.80	2.67
.90	4.16
.91	5.35
.92	4.87
.93	6.98
.94	7.33
.95	9.88
.96	11.59
.97	9.66
.98	12.80
.99	20.12

For load factors up to 0.6, the performance of the table is relatively independent of the number of words in the table. Above this load factor the performance starts to degrade and above a load factor of 0.8 degrades rapidly.

A balanced binary search tree with 1,000 nodes has an ACE (average comparison effort) of about 9. That is, it would take an average of approximately 9 comparison operations to locate an arbitrary object in the search tree. This is approximately equivalent to a hash table using linear chaining at a load factor of 0.95. If the load factor is controlled and kept moderate, say under 0.6, the expected performance of a hash table is approximately four times faster than a balanced binary search tree. This improvement in performance applies to insertion and searching.

16.6.2 Coalesced Chaining

Coalesced chaining attempts to forestall the buildup of long collision chains (contiguous sequences of words) by maintaining a collision resolution index (CRI) that is not correlated to the current hash index. This CRI is initialized to "point" to the highest "available" index in the table. Each time a collision occurs, the word is placed at the CRI location if the location is unoccupied. If the location is occupied, the CRI is sequentially reduced by 1 until an empty location is found. An array is maintained to store link information for later searching. Each time a collision occurs, the chain of links (each link being an index location in the table) is followed to the end and the new location given by the CRI is added to the collision chain.

The algorithm for coalesced chaining is presented in more detail below.

Algorithm for Coalesced Chaining

1. *Initialize link array so that the value at each index location equals -1 (indicates no linking).*

2. *Initialize the collision resolution index (CRI) to the highest index in the hash table.*

3. *Obtain the hash index for the word being inserted.*

4. *If the hash table is empty at the given hash index, insert the word at this index.*

5. *If the table is occupied with a different word at the hash index, determine whether the link array contains a value other than -1 at the hash index. If it does, traverse the link array to find the index of the last location in the collision chain. If the word to be inserted is found in the collision chain, abort the insertion process (duplicate words are not allowed).*

6. *Determine the CRI by finding the first available location to resolve the collision, starting at the present CRI and decrementing the CRI value sequentially until an empty location is found. At least one empty location must be available in the hash table to assure that this loop terminates.*

7. *Update the link array with the CRI value and insert the word at the CRI.*

To further clarify the algorithm presented above, we consider a simple example. Suppose we have a small table with capacity 10 and index locations 0 to 9. Suppose further that we wish to insert the following 7 words represented by the letters A,

Hash table   **CRI**

				A			B		C
0	1	2	3	4	5	6	7	8	9

Link array

-1	-1	-1	-1	-1	-1	-1	-1	-1	-1

Figure 16.2. Hash table and link index after insertion of words A, B, and C.

B, C, D, E, F, and G. These words have hash values given in the following table:

Word	Hash Index
A	4
B	7
C	9
D	7
E	6
F	7
G	4

The situation after words A, B, and C have been inserted is shown in Figure 16.2.

Now consider the insertion of word D. Its hash index equals 7. Since this location is occupied, coalesced-chaining collision resolution must be brought into action. Since the link array at index 7 holds the value −1, there is no collision chain to traverse. The CRI is decremented until an empty location is found. This is location 8. The word D is inserted at index 8 and the value 8 is inserted in the link array at index 7 (indicating that from location 7 one must go to location 8 to find word D). The word E is inserted directly at index 6 (its hash index) since that location is empty.

Now we consider the insertion of word F whose hash index equals 7. This location is occupied. The link value at index 7 is 8 (from the insertion of word D). The CRI is decremented to 5, the first empty index. The link index is not changed. The situation after word F is inserted is shown in Figure 16.3.

Hash table   **CRI**

				A	F	E	B	D	C
0	1	2	3	4	5	6	7	8	9

Link array

-1	-1	-1	-1	-1	-1	-1	8	5	-1

Figure 16.3. Hash table and link index after insertion of words A, B, C, D, E, and F.

Hash table   **CRI**

			G	A	F	E	B	D	C
0	1	2	3	4	5	6	7	8	9

Link array

-1	-1	-1	-1	3	-1	-1	8	5	-1

Figure 16.4. Hash table and link index after all words have been inserted.

Finally, we consider the insertion of word G. Since index 4 is occupied we go to the collision chain, if any, at index 4 (from the link array). There is no collision chain yet formed. The CRI is decremented to index 3, the first empty location. The final hash table with all 7 words is shown in Figure 16.4.

It is interesting to determine the average number of probes for a hash table that uses coalesced chaining and compare the results to those of linear chaining. Because the collision resolution index is not correlated to the hash index, we would expect better average performance. The results are surprising and quite dramatic.

Listing 16.7 shows the details of this simulation experiment with the results shown below the listing.

Listing 16.7   Efficiency of Linear Chaining versus Load Factor: A Simulation

```
/** Simulating the performance of coalesced chaining.
*/
import java.text.*;
import java.util.*;

public class CoalescedChainingApp {

  // Fields
  final int SIZE = 1000;
  int probes;
  boolean [] words = new boolean [SIZE];
  int [] link = new int [SIZE];
  Random rnd = new Random();
  int count;
  int cri; // collision resolution index

  // Commands

  public void generateTable (double loadFactor) {
    // Empty the table
    for (int i = 0; i < SIZE; i++)
      words[i] = false;
```

```
   // Reset the link array
   for (int i = 0; i < SIZE; i++)
     link[i] = -1;
   cri = SIZE - 1;
   count = (int) (SIZE * loadFactor);
   probes = 0;

   for (int i = 0; i < count; i++) {
     int hashIndex = rnd.nextInt(SIZE);
     if (words[hashIndex] == false) {
       words[hashIndex] = true;
       probes++;
     }
     else { // collision resolution required
       // Scan to end of collision chain
       int index = hashIndex;
       while (link[index] != -1) {
         probes++;
         index = link[index];
       }
       // Find cri
       while (words[cri] == true)
         cri--;
       words[cri] = true;
       link[index] = cri;
       probes++;
     }
   }
 }


 static public void main (String[] args) {
   DecimalFormat df = new DecimalFormat("#.00");
   CoalescedChainingApp app = new CoalescedChainingApp();
   System.out.println (
             "Load Factor\t\t\tAverage Number of Probes");
   for (double lf = 0.1; lf <= 0.9; lf += 0.1) {
     app.generateTable(lf);
     System.out.println(df.format(lf) + "\t\t\t\t" +
             df.format((double) app.probes / app.count));
   }
   for (double lf = 0.91; lf <= 1.0; lf += 0.01) {
     app.generateTable(lf);
     System.out.println(df.format(lf) + "\t\t\t\t" +
             df.format((double) app.probes / app.count));
   }
 }
}
```

The results for coalesced chaining, shown below, are remarkable. Even when the load factor is 99 percent, the average number of probes is close to one. When comparing these results to those of linear chaining in Listing 16.6, it is clear that coalesced chaining is significantly better. Coalesced chaining is an "in-place" version of separate chaining.

Output of Listing 16.7 for Coalesced Chaining

```
Load Factor          Average Number of Probes
.10                  1.00
.20                  1.01
.30                  1.00
.40                  1.03
.50                  1.04
.60                  1.12
.70                  1.17
.80                  1.14
.90                  1.18
.91                  1.19
.92                  1.19
.93                  1.21
.94                  1.37
.95                  1.27
.96                  1.28
.97                  1.25
.98                  1.25
.99                  1.34
```

16.7 Set

The *Set* abstraction is specified by the interface *Set* repeated from Chapter 10 in Listing 16.8. Interface *Set* provides a minimal set of commands and queries for the *Set* abstract data type.

Listing 16.8 Interface *Set*

```
/** Interface Set
*/
package foundations;

public interface Set extends Container {

  // Commands

  /** Add obj to the set
  */
  public void add(Object obj);
```

```
    /** Remove obj from the set
    */
    public void remove(Object obj);

    // Queries

    /** Return the union of self with s
    */
    public Set union(Set s);

    /** Return intersection of receiver with s
    */
    public Set intersection(Set s);

    /** Return difference of receiver with s
    */
    public Set difference(Set s);

    /** Return true if receiver is a subset of s
    */
    public boolean subset(Set s);

    /** return true if obj is in the set
    */
    public boolean contains(Object obj);
}
```

A set is a container that does not allow duplicates and provides fast access to information. In addition to the usual container operations (*makeEmpty*, *isEmpty*, and *size* from *Container* plus new methods *add*, *remove*, and *contains*), a *Set* supports the binary operations of *union*, *intersection*, *difference*, and *subset*. These are formulated as queries since they return information and leave the state of the receiver object intact.

We shall employ the standard class *BitSet* described in Section 16.2, to implement *Set*. We call this class *BSet* because of the internal dependence on *BitSet*. Listing 16.9 presents the implementation of *BSet*.

Listing 16.9   Class *BSet*

```
/** A bit set implementation of Set.
*/
package foundations;
import java.util.*;

public class BSet implements Set {

    // Fields
```

```
private BitSet data;
private int capacity;

// Constructors

public Bset (int capacity) {
  data = new BitSet (capacity);
  this.capacity = capacity;
}

public Bset (BitSet b) {
  data = b;
  this.capacity = b.size();
}

// Commands

/** Remove all objects from the container if found
*/
public void makeEmpty () {
  for (int i = 0; i < capacity; i++)
    data.clear(i);
}

/** Add obj to the set
*/
public void add (Object obj) {
  data.set(Math.abs(obj.hashCode()) % capacity);
}

/** Remove obj from the set
*/
public void remove (Object obj) {
  data.clear(Math.abs(obj.hashCode()) % capacity);
}

// Queries

/** Return true if the container is empty
*/
public boolean isEmpty () {
  for (int i = 0; i < capacity; i++)
    if (data.get(i)) {
      return false
      break;
    }
  return true;
}
```

```
/** Return the number of objects in the container
*/
public int size () {
  int count = 0;
  for (int i = 0; i < capacity; i++)
    if (data.get(i))
      count++;
  return count;
}

/** Return the union of self with s */
public Set union (Set s) {
  BitSet local = new BitSet(capacity);
  for (int i = 0; i < capacity; i++)
    if (data.get(i) || ((BSet) s).data.get(i))
      local.set(i);
  return new BSet(local);
}

/** Return intersection of receiver with s
*/
public Set intersection (Set s) {
  BitSet local = new BitSet(capacity);
  for (int i = 0; i < capacity; i++)
    if (data.get(i) && ((BSet) s).data.get(i))
      local.set(i);
    return new BSet(local);
}

/** Return difference of receiver with s
*/  public Set difference (Set s) {
  BitSet local = new BitSet(capacity);
  for (int i = 0; i < capacity; i++)
    if (data.get(i) && !((BSet) s).data.get(i))
      local.set(i);
  return new BSet(local);
}

/** Return true if receiver is a subset of s
*/
public boolean subset (Set s) {
  BSet testSet = (BSet) this.intersection(s);
  // Compare testSet and this
  boolean returnValue = true;
  for (int i = 0; i < capacity; i++)
    if (data.get(i) != testSet.data.get(i)) {
      returnValue = false;
```

```
      break;
    }
  return returnValue;
}

/** Return true if obj is in the set
*/
public boolean contains (Object obj) {
  return data.get (Math.abs(obj.hashCode()) % capacity);
}

public static void main (String[] args) {
  Set s = new BSet(10000000);

  s.add (new Integer(5));
  s.add (new Integer(17));
  s.add (new Integer(2317));
  s.add (new Integer(9876543));
  if (s.contains (new Integer(5)))
    System.out.println ("5 is present");
  else
    System.out.println ("5 is not present");
  if (s.contains(new Integer(17)))
    System.out.println ("17 is present");
  else
    System.out.println ("17 is not present");
  if (s.contains (new Integer(2317)))
    System.out.println ("2317 is present");
  else
    System.out.println ("2317 is not present");
  if (s.contains (new Integer(2318)))
    System.out.println ("2318 is present");
  else
    System.out.println ("2318 is not present");
  if (s.contains (new Integer(9876543)))
    System.out.println ("9876543 is present");
  else
    System.out.println ("9876543 is not present");
  if (s.contains (new Integer(9876544)))
    System.out.println ("9876544 is present");
  else
    System.out.println ("9876544 is not present");
  s.remove(new Integer(2317));
  if (s.contains (new Integer(2317)))
    System.out.println ("2317 is present");
  else
    System.out.println ("2317 is not present");
```

```
    Set t = new BSet(10000000);
    t.add(new Integer(5));
    t.add(new Integer(17));
    t.add(new Integer(18));
    t.add("Hello");
    t.add("World");
    Set u = t.union(s);
    Set i = t.intersection(s);
    System.out.println("s.size() = " + s.size());
    System.out.println("t.size() = " + t.size());
    System.out.println("u.size() = " + u.size());
    System.out.println("i.size() = " + i.size());

    if (s.subset(u))
      System.out.println("s is a subset of u");
    else
      System.out.println("s is not a subset of u");

    if (s.subset(i))
      System.out.println("s is a subset of i");
    else
      System.out.println("s is not a subset of i");

    Set d = u.difference(s);
    if (d.contains("Hello"))
      System.out.println("d contains Hello");
    else
      System.out.println("d does not contain Hello");
    System.out.println("The size of set d = " + d.size());
  }
}
```

The Output for Listing 16.8 Is:

```
5 is present
17 is present
2317 is present
2318 is not present
9876543 is present
9876544 is not present
2317 is not present
s.size() = 3
t.size() = 5
u.size() = 6
i.size() = 2
s is a subset of u
s is not a subset of i
```

```
d contains Hello
The size of set d = 3
```

Explanation of Listing 16.8

Two private fields are provided: *data* of type *BitSet* and *capacity* (type *int*). The two constructors that are provided initialize the *data* and *capacity* fields.

The command *makeEmpty* sends the *clear()* message to each bit in *data*. The command *add* enables the bit (sets its value to true) at the location given by the absolute value of the *hashCode()* applied to the object being put in the *BSet*. Command *remove* works the same way using *clear()* instead of *set()* to remove the bit.

Query *isEmpty* scans *data* returning true if all bit locations have value *false*. Query *size* scans data returning the number of bit locations that have value *true*. Query *union* takes the logical "or" operator "||" of each bit location of the receiver's data and the data of the input and returns a new *BSet* built from the "or'ed" data. Query *intersection* works the same way using the "and" operator "&&". The analysis of the remaining queries is left as an exercise for the reader.

It is important to construct a *SetLab* GUI application that allows each of the commands and queries to be fully exercised and tested. This is left as an exercise for the reader.

16.8   Summary

Hash tables and sets are containers and share the common property that duplicates are not allowed. Hashing may be used in the implementation of a set. Major points made about hashing and sets are:

❏ Hashing is the process of calculating an integer index to represent an object. This object may then be stored in a hash table at the hashed index. The ratio of objects in a hash table to its capacity is called its "load factor."

❏ A perfect hashing operation produces a unique index for all objects it hashes: The index is uniformly distributed over the range of indices in the hash table. A hash table with a perfect hashing function can theoretically have a load factor of one.

❏ The craft of designing hash functions falls far short of the ideal hashing function desired. As a result, practical hashing functions sometimes cause collisions.

❏ A collision occurs when two different objects hash to the same index. Reducing the load factor of a hash table may reduce the relative frequency of collisions.

❏ There are several algorithms for resolving collisions. These include linear chaining, coalesced chaining, and separate chaining among others.

❏ The ideal performance of a hash table is O(1). This performance is degraded because of collisions and the need to resolve those collisions.

❏ Coalesced chaining provides better performance than linear chaining.

❏ Sets are containers that do not allow duplicates. Set-specific operations include union, intersection, and difference (plus potentially others).

❑ A *BitSet* is a representation of a set wherein elements are represented by a unique index into an array of bits (possibly through hashing). The value of the bit indicates absence (value = 0) or presence (value = 1) of the element.

16.9 Exercises

1 For the words (total of 109,580) in file *distinct.txt* (found in the Chapter 16 folder in the downloadable notes), you are to build a test class that examines the relative uniformity of the *hashCode()* method of class *String*.

   a. Calculate the range, mean, and standard deviation for the distribution of raw hash codes.
   b. Repeat for rescaling the raw hash codes to fit within a hash table of sizes from 0.1x to 1.0x in steps of 0.1x, where x = 109,580.
   c. Repeat for rescaling the raw hash codes to fit within a hash table of sizes from 1.0x to 10.0x in steps of 1.0x, where x = 109,580.
   d. For parts a., b., and c. plot histograms of the resulting hash codes. Use a bin size of 1 percent (resulting in 100 bins) for each scale used.

2 Another collision resolution scheme called *double hashing* computes two hash indices for each object. One index is the primary hash index. If a collision occurs, the second hash index is added as an increment to the first until an empty location is found. Implement and test an algorithm for double hashing using the words in *distinct.txt*. Use various load factors as was done for linear chaining in Listing 16.6. Compare your results with those obtained for linear chaining and coalesced chaining.

3 The collision resolution scheme called *separate chaining* uses a hash table of linear lists. Collisions are resolved by adding each object to the list in its appropriate hashed index location in the hash table. Implement and test, using the words in *distinct.txt*, a separate chaining resolution scheme. Describe in detail the design you use for the hash table. Compare your results with those obtained from other collision resolution schemes. Use various initial load factors as was done for linear chaining in Listing 16.6. Calculate and compare the actual load factor after the tables are built with the initial load factor.

4 Develop logic for the number of probes for "unsuccessful" searches in a hash table using the model introduced in Listing 16.6 for "successful" search. Unsuccessful search is defined as the process of deciding, based on searching the table, that an element is not in the table. It is a given condition that the element being sought is not in the table. The key is determining when a search of the table confirms that fact. Perform this experiment for two or more of the collision resolution schemes with various load factors. A really interesting project computes the average number of probes for successful and unsuccessful search, for all collision resolution schemes, and for a wide range of load factors. For extra credit, the projects should be UI-based and plot the "average number of probes versus load factor" curves for all variations on success versus nonsuccess and collision resolution schemes. Think of this as a hashing laboratory. Additional details are given below.

Project Details:

a. Write a class called *CollisionResolution* that does the following:

- For load factors of 0.25, 0.50, 0.75, 0.85, 0.90, and 0.95, build hash tables by simulating the actual hashing of data values to indices in the table. Store a boolean "true" in each hashed index. If a new datum hashes to an index containing "true" then we have a collision. This collision is to be resolved using a collision resolution scheme. The hashing simulation should approximate an ideal hash function, that is, provide a uniformly distributed set of indices over the table (there is still a possibility of collisions).
- Calculate the average number of probes for the following three collision resolution schemes: linear chaining, double hashing as described in Exercise 2, and coalesced chaining.
- Display the results of all experiments in tabular form.
- Plot (using whatever means) the average number of probes versus the load factor for all experiments on the same graph (3 resolution schemes – successful versus unsuccessful = 6 curves). Choose an appropriate scale to make the graph easily readable.

b. Guidelines and hints/suggestions

- Use three hash tables, one for each collision resolution scheme.
- The hash tables may be reinitialized and reused for each load factor.
- Compute the average number of probes for successful search while building the hash tables (see Listing 16.6 for hints).
- Compute the average number of probes for unsuccessful search after the tables are built.

5   Provide an analysis of all methods in class *BSet* in Listing 16.8.

6   Design, develop, and implement a set laboratory that provides interactive testing of all commands and queries in implementing classes for interface *Set*. The laboratory should include hooks for implementing class *BSet* and one other class called *SetE*. Test the laboratory using the provided implementation of class *BSet* in package *foundations*.

17

Association and Dictionary

We are all familiar with the concept of a dictionary as a fairly large book containing words and definitions. The words are always in alphabetical order to help us look up a particular word. Having the words in alphabetical order is a convenient feature but is not required. There may be other ways to find words in the dictionary, especially if our dictionary is in electronic form. Most words in a dictionary have several definitions. We associate each word with its definitions. Thus, we may characterize a dictionary as a container (possibly ordered) of associations between words and their meanings.

To take our reasoning a step further in our attempt to understand the required behavior of a dictionary, we never add definitions to a dictionary unless they are associated with a word. On the other hand, as we are building the dictionary we may add words without definitions on the promise that the definitions will be added later for those words. And finally, as we fine tune our understanding, we may change definitions for words that are already in the dictionary. We may wish to remove entries in the dictionary or access them in various ways. For example, we may wish to access a list of the words only, the meanings only, or the entire list of entries.

In Chapter 10 we defined interface *Dictionary* as an extension of the *Container* interface, interface *OrderedDictionary* as an extension of *SearchTable*, and supporting class *Association*. The relationships among *Dictionary*, *OrderedDictionary*, *Association*, and other classes are illustrated in Figure 17.1. Implementing classes for *Dictionary* and *OrderedDictionary* will use instances of *Association*. Queries for accessing keys, values, and elements of a dictionary or ordered dictionary return iterators on the contained objects.

In this chapter we begin with a brief discussion of class *Association* and then focus on interface *Dictionary* and its implementation, and on *OrderedDictionary* and its implementation. We present selected details for two implementations of *Dictionary* plus a dictionary laboratory for testing the features of *Dictionary*. We also present selected details for two implementations of *OrderedDictionary* and an ordered dictionary laboratory for testing the features of *OrderedDictionary*.

17.1 The *Association* Abstract Data Type

Associations represent pairs of objects called *keys* and *values*. There is a one-to-one correspondence between a *key* and its *value*. Associations have internal state

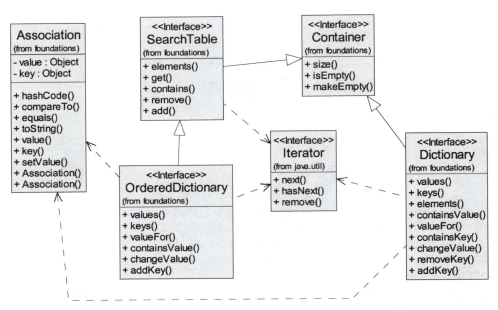

Figure 17.1. Interfaces *Dictionary* and *OrderedDictionary* and class *Associations*.

and behavior as specified by class *Association*. The instance variable *key* is essential for creation of an instance of *Association*. The instance variable *value* may initially be null. The class definition for *Association* is repeated in Listing 17.1 from Chapter 10.

The requirement that a *key* be assigned on creation of an instance of *Association* is enforced by not providing a null parameter constructor. The one-parameter constructor creates an instance with a specified *key* and assigns null to *value*. The two-parameter constructor creates an instance of *Association* and initializes both *key* and *value*. Once an instance is created, its *key* cannot be changed (it is immutable).

The single command, *setValue(Object value)*, allows one to set or change the *value* after an instance has been created. The two constructors and the single command are consistent with the above described behavior and rules for creating instances of *Association*.

Listing 17.1 Class *Association*

```
/** Class Association
*    An instance must initialize a key on creation.
*    If used as a comparable Association, keys must be comparable and
*      comparison is based on keys only.
*    Note that equals() does not enforce the comparable feature and
*      requires equality of both key and value.
*/
package foundations;
import java.io.Serializable;
```

```
public class Association extends Object
                             implements Comparable, Serializable {
  // Fields

  private Object key;
  private Object value;

  // Constructors

  /** Create an instance with specified key and null value
   */
  public Association (Object key) {
    this(key, null);
  }

  /** Create an instance with specified key and value
   */
  public Association (Object key, Object value) {
    this.key = key;
    this.value = value;
  }

  // Commands

  /** Set the value
   */
  public void setValue (Object value) {
    this.value = value;
  }

  // Queries

  /** return key
   */
  public Object key () {
    return key;
  }

  /** Return value
   */
  public Object value () {
    return value;
  }

  /** Return a String representation.
   *    Return a String of the form <key:value>
   */
```

```
public String toString () {
  return "<" + key + ":" + value + ">";
}


/** Implement Comparable method compareTo
 *  Compare based only on key; key must be Comparable
 */
public int compareTo (Object obj) {
  return ((Comparable)key).compareTo(((Association)obj).key());
}


/** Override inherited Object method equals()
 */
public boolean equals (Object obj) {
  if (obj instanceof Association)
    return (key.equals(((Association)obj).key)
            && value.equals(((Association)obj).value));
  else
    return false;
}


/** Override inherited Object method hashCode().
 *   Return a unique int representing this object
 */
public int hashCode () {
  int bits1 = key.hashCode();
  int bits2 = value.hashCode();
  return (bits1 << 8)^(bits2 >> 8);
}
}
```

Further Discussion of Listing 17.1

Fields *key* and *value* represent the internal state of an association. These two fields have *private* visibility to enforce the intended behavior of instances of the class, even for potential subclasses of *Association* and other classes in the *foundations* package.

The class has six queries, two for accessing the fields, three that are inherited from *Object* and overridden, and one promised by implementing interface *Comparable*. The default implementations for *toString, equals*, and *hashCode* in class *Object* are redefined to apply specifically to instances of *Association*. We want a special string representation for showing association instances. For example, if *key = CS2* and *value = A second course in computer science*, then *toString* returns the following string:

```
<CS2:A second course in computer science>
```

The *equals(Object obj)* method returns *true* if the *key* and *value* of the receiver are equal to the *key* and *value* of the parameter *obj*. The algorithm for *hashCode* is designed to include features of both the *key* and the *value*. The *compareTo* query returns the result of applying *compareTo* to the keys of the receiver and parameter associations. The class for *key* must implement *Comparable*. By implementing *compareTo* using only the key, we enable the ability to find an instance when only its key is known. This feature is important for implementations of interface *SearchTable* covered in earlier chapters and in this chapter for implementers of interface *OrderedDictionary*.

The one-to-one relationship between *key* and *value* may appear to imply that this class does not represent our familiar dictionary, with multiple definitions for any word. However, *value* may be any object, including an array, thus allowing multiple definitions for each key.

17.2 The *Dictionary* Interface

In Listing 17.2 we again present interface *Dictionary*. It adds three commands *(addKey(Object key, Object value)*, *removeKey(Object key)*, and *changeValue(Object key, Object value))* and six queries *(containsKey(Object key)*, *valueFor(Object key)*, *containsValue(Object value)*, *elements()*, *keys()*, and *values())* to enhance those inherited from *Container*. Notice that the parameters are instances of *Object*.

Listing 17.2 Interface *Dictionary*

```
/** Interface Dictionary
 *    A dictionary contains instances of Association: key-value pairs
 *    A class for a key must implement equals() from class Object
 */
package foundations;
import java.util.*;

public interface Dictionary extends Container {

  // Commands

  /** Add an association <key-value>
   *    If the key already exists, set its value
   */
  public void addKey (Object key, Object value);

  /** Remove association with key if found
   */
  public void removeKey (Object key);

  /** Change value for specified key
   *    Throw NoSuchElementException if key not found.
   */
  public void changeValue (Object key, Object value);
```

```
// Queries

/** Return true if key is in dictionary
 */
public boolean containsKey (Object key);

/** Return value for specified key
 *    Throw NoSuchElementException if key not found
 */
public Object valueFor (Object key);

/** Return true if the dictionary contains obj as a value
 */
public boolean containsValue (Object value);

/** Return iterator over the entries - Associations
 */
public Iterator elements ();

/** Return iterator over all keys
 */
public Iterator keys ();

/** Return iterator over all values
 */
public Iterator values ();
}
```

The complete behavior of a dictionary includes commands and queries from interface *Dictionary* plus those inherited from interface *Container* and optionally selected methods from *Object*. Implementing classes must implement all these commands and queries. An example design is illustrated in Table 17.1 for a class named *ImplementsDictionary*. The inherited *Container* methods include command *makeEmpty* plus queries *size* and *isEmpty*. Interface *Dictionary* adds three new commands and six new queries. The queries *containsKey(Object key)* and *containsValue(Object value)* return a *boolean* based on whether parameters *key* or *value*, respectively, are contained anywhere in the dictionary. Query *valueFor(Object key)* returns the *value* for the specified *key*. Three new queries return iterators on the entries (associations), keys, or values. It is usually desirable to override the *toString* query from class *Object*.

The three queries that return iterators may optionally use an inner class to implement the *Iterator* interface. Two potential constructors are shown that initialize a dictionary to some default capacity or specified capacity. Depending on the actual class chosen for internal data representation, additional constructors or modifications to the two shown in Table 17.1 may be required.

Table 17.1   Public Interface Design for Implementing Classes of *Dictionary*

Constructors

public ImplementsDictionary( )	Create an empty dictionary with default capacity.
public ImplementsDictionary(int capacity)	Create an empty dictionary with specified capacity.

Commands

public void addKey(Object key, Object value)	Add <key:value> as a new association in the dictionary; if key already present change its value.
public void removeKey(Object key)	If found, remove contained association with specified key.
public void changeValue(Object key, Object value)	Change value for specified key; throw exception if key not found.
public void makeEmpty( )	Make the dictionary empty (from Container).

Queries

public boolean containsKey(Object key)	Return true if key is in the dictionary.
public boolean isEmpty( )	Return true if dictionary is empty (from Container).
public int size( )	Return the number of associations (from Container).
public Object valueFor(Object key)	Return the value for specified key; throw exception if key not found.
public boolean containsValue(Object value)	Return true if value is in the dictionary.
public Iterator elements( )	Return an iterator on the associations in the dictionary.
public Iterator keys( )	Return an iterator on the keys in the dictionary.
public Iterator values( )	Return an iterator on the values in the dictionary.
public String toString( )	Override from Object to return a string giving all associations with form: { <key1:val1>, <key2:val2>,... }

17.3   Implementing the *Dictionary* Interface

The first step in designing a class that implements the *Dictionary* interface is to choose a data structure representing the contained associations. There are several options including a linear dynamic list such as represented by the Java class *java.util.Vector* or a hash table such as represented by the Java class *java.util. Hashtable*. Additionally, we may use an implementation of the *List* interface defined in the *Container* hierarchy, or our own implementation of a hash table. A static array may also be used but is not recommended since we would have to manage the dynamic sizing of the dictionary.

We discussed concepts and implementations for the *List* interfaces in Chapter 13. Concepts and details for hashing are discussed in Chapter 10. For now we choose to use existing classes in package *java.util, Vector*, and *Hashtable*, as two options to represent the contained data in a dictionary.

The *Vector* class represents a dynamic list of objects whose order is dependent on the history of additions and removals. It has methods including those specified for *List, IndexableList*, and *PositionableList*. We might characterize it as an "industrial strength" list. For a vector of size n, the search performance is O(n) and on average requires $n/2$ steps to find an object in the vector. It always requires n steps to determine that an object is not in the vector. The only way we can search a vector is to start at the front and iterate over indices from 0 to size -1.

As discussed in Chapter 16, a *Hashtable* stores an object in a particular index of an array that is uniquely determined from the hash code of the object. The time to find an object in a hash table is constant, given by the time to compute a hash code (index) and check the object in that hashed index. Its performance is O(1), that is, one step independent of size n. In a well-designed hash table this performance is approximately achievable for both successful and unsuccessful searches.

The implementation for *java.util.Hashtable* requires that contained objects be instances of *java.util.Map.Entry*, a conceptual equivalent of our *Association* class. It hashes only the key to get an index for storing the map entries. In essence, *Hashtable* is an industrial strength implementation for a variation on *Dictionary*. Our *Dictionary* interface is a somewhat simpler version of a dictionary. In using *Hashtable* to implement *Dictionary* we will be using only part of the feature set in *Hashtable*.

In choosing either *Vector* or *Hashtable* as our container of associations for the *Dictionary* implementation, we must read and follow any constraints imposed by these classes. Specifically of interest are the following constraints.

Constraints for Using Class *Vector*

1. Contains a dynamic array of instances of *Object*.
2. Contained objects are accessible by index or position.
3. No special constraints on the contained objects.
4. Methods specific to key or value are not handled by *Vector* and must be handled internally in our implementing class.

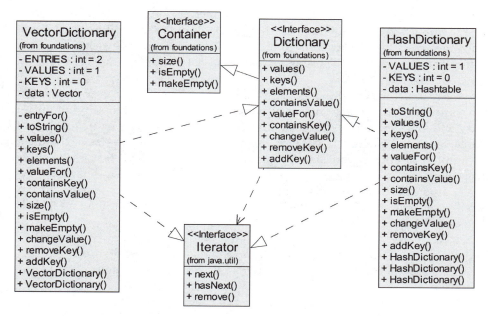

Figure 17.2. Class diagram for two implementations of interface *Dictionary*.

Constraints for Using Class *Hashtable*

1. Contains a dynamic array of instances of *Map.Entry*.

2. *Map.Entry* instances are similar to *Association* instances.

3. New objects are added using method *put(Object key, Object value)*.

4. Neither *key* nor *value* may be null in method *put()*. This is a variation from our earlier discussion that *Dictionary* should be able to accept commands to add an association with value = null, that is, <keyObject:null>.

5. Contained objects are accessible by a hash index on the *key*.

6. The class representing *key* must implement *equals()* and *hashCode()* from *Object*

We wish to develop implementations for *Dictionary* using both *Vector* and *Hashtable* as the containers of our associations. These two choices will illustrate the details required in implementing *Dictionary* and serve as actualized implementations for use in demonstrating the dictionary laboratory.

Figure 17.2 shows the major classes required for implementing *Dictionary* using *HashTable* and *Vector*.

17.3.1 Implementation of *Dictionary* Using a *Hashtable*

Complete details are given in Listing 17.3 for the source file *HashDictionary.java* that uses class *Hashtable* to implement *data*. Class *HashDictionary* is a *Hashtable* implementation of interface *Dictionary*. In addition to the methods required by interfaces *Container* and *Dictionary*, method *toString* inherited from *Object* is also overridden.

HashDictionary has three fields: (1) *data*, which is the contained *Hashtable*; (2) *KEYS*; and (3) *VALUES*, which are *int* parameters for controlling the type of iteration returned by queries *keys* and *values*. The last two are *static* since we need only one copy of each. There is no direct support by *Hashtable* for iteration over the entries.

Three constructors are provided that take advantage of three ways to initialize the contained *Hashtable*. They represent flexible options for specifying initial capacity and maximum load factor (default is 0.75). The capacity is the number of available "buckets" (default is 101) for storing entries. When the size of the hash table (number of entries contained) equals capacity times load factor, the table capacity is increased (to capacity * 2 + 1) and the table is rehashed (based on new capacity). It is wise to set an initial capacity large enough so that rehashing is not required, while not wasting storage space. A load factor between 0.5 and 0.75 is recommended to reduce time spent in collision resolution.

The inner class *HashIterator* encapsulates field *entries* as an *Enumeration* (Java 1.1 version of an *Iterator*) since *Hashtable* does not provide direct support for *Iterator*. The methods in *HashIterator* send corresponding messages to the enumeration.

Details of method *toString* are shown in the listing. Since *Hashtable* does not support an iteration over the entries, we must use an inefficient implementation that iterates over the keys and uses *valueFor(key)* to get the value. Method *valueFor(key)* must iterate to find the key and then send message *get(key)* to the encapsulated hash table to get the value. We could use a similar approach to implement *elements*.

Listing 17.3   Class *HashDictionary*

```
/** class HashDictionary - an implementation of interface Dictionary
 *                        - uses java.util.Hashtable for data
 */
package foundations;
import java.util.*;

public class HashDictionary implements Dictionary {

  // Fields
  private Hashtable data;
  private static int KEYS = 0;        // iterator control
  private static int VALUES = 1;      // iterator control

  // Constructors

  /** Construct dictionary with default capacity and load factor 0.75
   */
  public HashDictionary () {
    data = new Hashtable();
  }
```

```java
/** Construct dictionary with initialCapacity and load factor 0.75
*/
public HashDictionary (int initialCapacity) {
  data = new Hashtable(initialCapacity);
}


/** Construct a dictionary with initialCapacity and loadFactor
 *    Hashtable constraint: required range 0.0 < loadFactor < 1.0
 *    Hashtable constraint: recommended loadFactor is 0.5 --> 0.75
*/
public HashDictionary (int initialCapacity, float loadFactor) {
  data = new Hashtable(initialCapacity, loadFactor);
}


// Commands

/** Add an association <key-value>
 *    If the key already exists, set its value
 *    Hashtable constraint: neither key nor value can be null
 *    Hashtable constraint: if key not there add it with value
*/
public void addKey (Object key, Object value) {
  data.put(key, value);
}


/** Remove association with key if found
*/
public void removeKey (Object key) {
  data.remove(key);
}


/** Change value for specified key
 *    Throw NoSuchElementException if key not found.
 *    Hashtable constraint: no direct support
*/
public void changeValue (Object key, Object value) {
  if (data.containsKey(key))
    data.put(key, value);
  else
    throw new NoSuchElementException("Key not found");
}


/** Remove all objects from the container if found
*/
public void makeEmpty () {
  data.clear();
}
```

```
// Queries

/** Return true if the container is empty
*/
public boolean isEmpty () {
  return data.isEmpty();
}

/** Return the number of keys in the dictionary
*/
public int size () {
  return data.size();
}

/** Answer true if obj is in the container as a value
*/
public boolean containsValue (Object value) {
  return data.contains(value);
}

/** Return true if key is in dictionary
*/
public boolean containsKey (Object key) {
  return data.containsKey(key);
}

/** Return value for specified key
*    Throw NoSuchElementException if key not found
*/
public Object valueFor (Object key) {
  if (containsKey(key))
    return data.get(key);
  else
    throw new NoSuchElementException("Key not found" );
}

/** Return iterator over the entries - Associations
*/
public Iterator elements () {
  return null; // not supported by Hashtable
}

/** Return iterator over all keys
*/
public Iterator keys () {
  return new HashIterator(KEYS);
}
```

```java
/** Return iterator over all values
*/
public Iterator values () {
  return new HashIterator(VALUES);
}


/** Override method toString() from class Object
*    Return in set notation all entries in the dictionary
*    Notation is: {<key1:value1>, <key2:value2>,...}
*/
public String toString () {
  String str = "{" ;
  Object key = null;
  if (isEmpty())
    return str + " }" ;
  else {
    try {
      for (Iterator i = new HashIterator(KEYS);
                                      i.hasNext();){
        key = i.next();
        str = str + " <" + key + ":" + this.valueFor(key)
                  + ">," ;

      }
    } catch (Exception ex) { }
    return str.substring(0, str.length() - 1) + " }" ;
  }
}

/** private class HashIterator implements Iterator
*/

private class HashIterator implements Iterator {

  // Fields

  /** java.util.Hashtable does not return an Iterator
  *    It returns an Enumeration on the keys or values
  */
  private Enumeration entries;
  private int type; // enumeration over keys or elements

  // Constructor

  /** Field entries iterates over keys or values
  */
  private HashIterator (int type) {
    entries = (type == KEYS) ? data.keys() : data.elements();
    this.type = type;
  }
```

```
// Commands

public void remove () {  // not used - null implementation
}

// Queries

public boolean hasNext () {
  return entries.hasMoreElements();
}

public Object next () {
  return entries.nextElement();
}
  }
}
```

Tip

> Notice that the class header for *HashDictionary* promises to *implement* interface *Dictionary*. Since *java.util* also has a *Dictionary* class, why do we not get a name conflict? In fact, *java.util.Dictionary* is an abstract class whose use is no longer recommended; it is retained for backward compatibility with previous versions of Java. The compiler knows that we are referring to the *foundations* version of *Dictionary* because it is the only interface named *Dictionary*. WARNING: When using the label *Dictionary* to represent a type (as is done in the dictionary laboratory where we import both *foundations.** and *java.util.**) we must use a fully qualified name label (e.g., *foundations.Dictionary*) so the compiler knows which *Dictionary* we are using.

Discussion of Listing 17.3

The choice of *Hashtable* as the contained data in *HashDictionary* presents some choices. The good news is that all commands and most queries in *HashDictionary* are easily implemented by invoking an appropriate method in *Hashtable*. However, some of these methods are slightly different than our original specification for *Dictionary*. Entries in *Hashtable* require that both the key and value be non-null. This is a small concession in the behavior of our command *addKey(key, value)* and is acceptable. The method for changing the value of a specified key in *Hashtable* has the same behavior as *addKey()*. We must take control to ensure that our specification for *changeValue()* is satisfied. We do not allow *changeValue()* to work unless the *key* parameter is already in the dictionary. New comments are added to the source code where constraints are imposed.

Method *toString()* from *Object* is overridden to provide a custom string representation for the dictionary. It lists the key-value pairs as elements in a set; for example,

```
{ <key1:value1>, <key2:value2>, ... }
```

Inner class *HashIterator* implements the *Iterator* interface in a way to provide iteration over the keys or values by specifying *int type* as *KEYS* or *VALUES*. This inner class and its fields and constructors are *private* to strictly enforce its supporting role for class *HashDictionary*. No client class may create an instance of *HashIterator*. Client classes do require access to the iterator commands and queries; thus, command *remove( )* and queries *hasNext( )* and *next( )* are *public*. This visibility for methods is also consistent with the *java.util.Iterator* interface.

17.3.2   Implementation of *Dictionary* Using a *Vector*

Selected details are given in Listing 17.4 for the source file *VectorDictionary.java* that uses class *java.util.Vector* to implement *data*. Class *VectorDictionary* is a *Vector* implementation of interface *Dictionary*. Most of the details are left as an exercise for the reader.

Listing 17.4   Class *VectorDictionary*

```java
/** VectorDictionary implements interface Dictionary using
 *    java.util.Vector
 */
package foundations;
import java.util.*;

public class VectorDictionary implements Dictionary {

  // Fields
  private Vector data;
  private static int KEYS = 0;      // iterator control
  private static int VALUES = 1;    // iterator control
  private static int ENTRIES = 2;   // iterator control
  // Constructors

  /** Construct dictionary with default capacity
   */
  public VectorDictionary () {
    // Left as an exercise
  }

  /** Construct dictionary with initialCapacity
   */
  public VectorDictionary (int initialCapacity) {
    // Left as an exercise
  }
```

```
// Commands

/** Add an association <key-value>
*    If the key already exists, set its value
*/
public void addKey (Object key, Object value) {
  // Left as an exercise
}


/** Remove association with key if found
*/
public void removeKey (Object key) {
  // Left as an exercise
}


/** Change value for specified key
*    Throw NoSuchElementException if key not found.
*/
public void changeValue (Object key, Object value) {
  // Left as an exercise
}


/** Remove all objects from the container if found
*/
public void makeEmpty () {
  // Left as an exercise
}


// Queries

/** Return true if the container is empty
*/
public boolean isEmpty () {
  // Left as an exercise
  return true;
}


/** Return the number of keys in the dictionary
*/
public int size () {
  // Left as an exercise
  return 0;
}
```

```java
/** Answer true if obj is in the container as a value
*/
public boolean containsValue (Object value) {
  // Left as an exercise
  return false;
}


/** Return true if key is in dictionary
*/
public boolean containsKey (Object key) {
  // Left as an exercise
  return false;
}


/** Return value for specified key
*    Throw NoSuchElementException if key not found
*/
public Object valueFor (Object key) {
  // Left as an exercise
  return null;
}


/** Return iterator over entries - Associations
*/
public Iterator elements () {
  return new VectorIterator(ENTRIES);
}


/** Return iterator over all keys
*/
public Iterator keys () {
  return new VectorIterator(KEYS);
}


/** Return iterator over all values
*/
public Iterator values () {
  return new VectorIterator(VALUES);
}


/** Override method toString() from class Object
*    Return in set notation all entries in the dictionary
*    Notation is: {<key1:value1>, <key2:value2>,...}
*/
```

```java
public String toString () {
  // Left as an exercise
  return null;
}


/** Query - private - return entry for specified key,
*                    return null if key not found
*/
private Association entryFor (Object key) {
  // Left as an exercise
  return null;
}


/** private class VectorIterator implements Iterator
*   returns ENTRIES, KEYS, or VALUES based on type
*/

private class VectorIterator implements Iterator {

  private Iterator elements;
  private int type;

  /** Field entries iterates over keys or values
  */
  private VectorIterator (int type) {
    elements = data.iterator();
    this.type = type; // iterate over keys, values, or elements
  }

  public boolean hasNext () {
    return elements.hasNext();
  }

  public Object next () {
    return (type == ENTRIES)
           ? (Association)elements.next()
           : (type == KEYS)
             ? ((Association)elements.next()).key()
             : ((Association)elements.next()).value();
  }

  public void remove () {
    // not used - null implementation
  }
}
}
```

Discussion of Listing 17.4

Since we may iterate over the objects contained in *Vector*, class *VectorDictionary* and its inner class *VectorIterator* provide iterator access to entries as well as keys and values. A fourth field, *private static int ENTRIES*, provides support for iteration over entries. A private method *entryFor(Object key)* returns the association entry for the specified *key*, if found. It is intended for use by query *valueFor()* and also by commands *addKey*, *removeKey*, and *changeValue*. An instance of *VectorIterator* is created with a specified value for *type*. This value is then used by query *next* to return the next entry, key, or value.

17.4 The Dictionary Laboratory

A dictionary laboratory is presented that tests all constructors, commands, and queries for the *Dictionary* implementations. It can test both the *Hashtable* and *Vector* implementations (*HashDictionary* and *VectorDictionary*, respectively) and accept three different pluggable implementations (class names ending in E) left as exercises. Figure 17.3 shows a class diagram for the dictionary laboratory and its major supporting classes.

Full implementations are provided in the *foundations* package for *HashDictionary* and *VectorDictionary*. Partial implementations are provided for the three classes *HashDictionaryE*, *DictionaryE*, and *VectorDictionaryE*; the remaining details may be assigned as exercises. All five classes may be exercised from the dictionary laboratory.

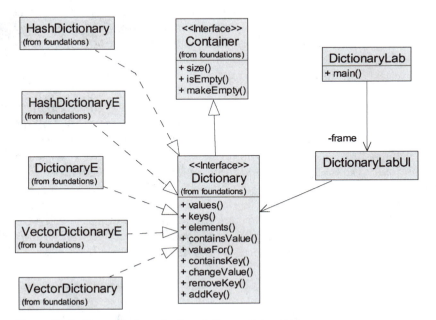

Figure 17.3. Class diagram for the dictionary laboratory.

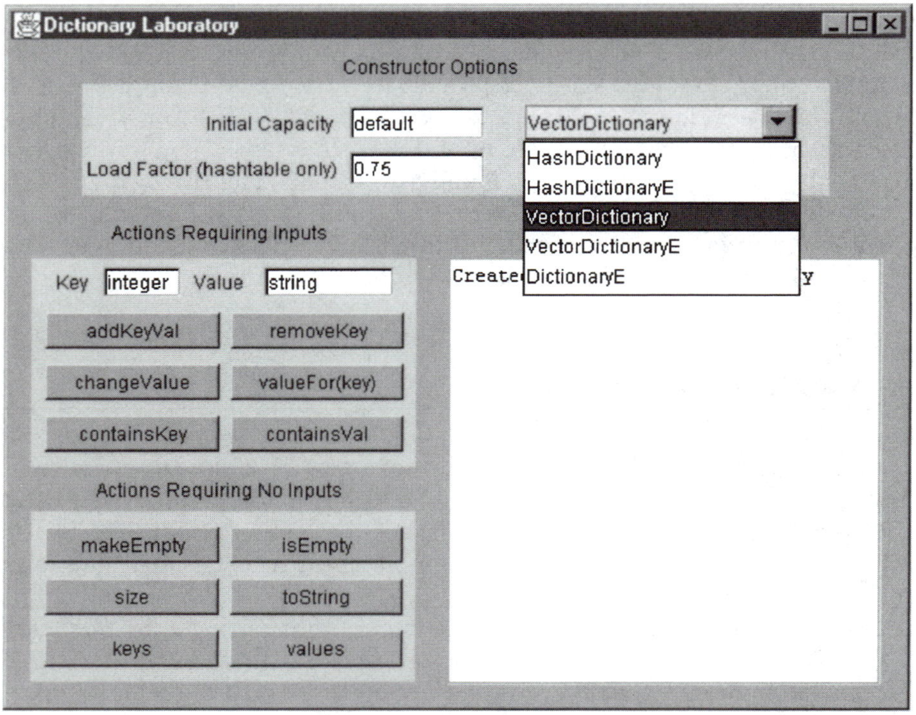

Figure 17.4. Preliminary screen shot of the dictionary laboratory.

Figure 17.4 shows a screen shot of the dictionary laboratory, illustrating the options for implementing classes as selected from the *combo box*. *VectorDictionary* has been selected, which enables the buttons. Entries into the dictionary are arbitrarily constrained to have integer keys and string values. This allows us to show different issues for reading integers and strings from a text field in the source file for *DictionaryLab*.

Another screen shot of the dictionary laboratory is shown in Figure 17.5 after creation of an instance of *HashDictionary* and exercising a number of operations.

One might ask why we would want a dictionary that is not ordered. To answer this question we must first look at how the dictionary is implemented. We have presented two options: (1) a hash table (*Hashtable*) or (2) an indexable list (*Vector*). Both of these do have order. The order is just based on something other than the relative magnitudes of the contained objects. Both use an array to store the objects. The index in the array for a given object is computed from a hashing function for *Hashtable* and is a victim of the history of insertions and removals for *Vector*. An "ordered" dictionary would have objects stored from smallest to largest. In terms of efficiency of lookup operations, the unordered hash table implementation is the best. It requires a fixed time to find any object, regardless of the size of the dictionary. Its time complexity is $O(1)$ versus $O(n)$ or $O(\log_2 n)$ for typical implementations of ordered dictionaries. The *Vector* implementation of *Dictionary* has time complexity $O(n)$.

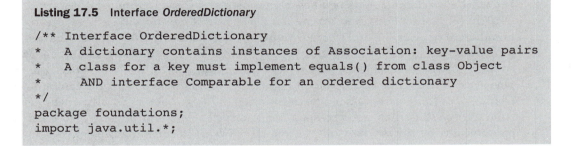

Figure 17.5. Screen shot of the dictionary laboratory after exercising options.

17.5   The *OrderedDictionary* Interface

An ordered dictionary is a dictionary whose entries are ordered in terms of its keys. Interestingly enough, interface *OrderedDictionary* extends not *Dictionary*, but *SearchTable*. This allows us to enforce the comparable property of keys in an ordered dictionary. Recall that a search table contains comparable objects. Although an ordered dictionary is a kind of dictionary, it is more precisely a kind of search table whose contained elements are associations. The relationships among interfaces *OrderedDictionary*, *SearchTable*, and *Dictionary* were shown in Figure 17.1. Listing 17.5 shows the source for interface *OrderedDictionary*, repeated from Chapter 10.

Listing 17.5 Interface *OrderedDictionary*

```
/** Interface OrderedDictionary
 *    A dictionary contains instances of Association: key-value pairs
 *    A class for a key must implement equals() from class Object
 *      AND interface Comparable for an ordered dictionary
 */
package foundations;
import java.util.*;
```

```
public interface OrderedDictionary extends SearchTable {

  // Commands

  /** Add an association <key-value› ; value may be null
  */
  public void addKey (Comparable key, Object value);

  /** Changes value for specified key
  *    Throw NoSuchElementException if key not found.
  */
  public void changeValue (Comparable key, Object value);

  // Queries

  /** Return true if key is in dictionary
  */
  public boolean containsValue (Object value);

  /** Return value for specified key
  *    Throw NoSuchElementException if key not found
  */
  public Object valueFor (Comparable key);

  /** Return an iterator on the keys
  */
  public Iterator keys ();

  /** Return an iterator on the values
  */
  public Iterator values ();
}
```

The complete behavior of an ordered dictionary includes commands and queries from interface *OrderedDictionary*, plus those inherited from interfaces *Search-Table* and *Container*, plus optionally selected methods from *Object*. Implementing classes must implement all these commands and queries. An example design is illustrated in Table 17.2 for a class named *ImpOrderedDictionary*. The inherited *Container* methods include command *makeEmpty* plus queries *size* and *isEmpty*. Interface *SearchTable* adds two new commands and three new queries. Interface *OrderedDictionary* adds two new commands and three new queries. The set of commands and queries for an *OrderedDictionary* is essentially the same as that for a *Dictionary*. The major difference is the requirement that an ordered dictionary contain *Comparable* objects. The *remove* command from interface *SearchTable* performs the equivalent function of *removeKey* in dictionary. The *add* command from *SearchTable* accepts a single association as a parameter. Finally, query *get* from *SearchTable* has no corresponding query for *Dictionary*. It is also desirable to override the *toString* query from class *Object* in implementing classes for *OrderedDictionary*.

Table 17.2   Public Interface Design for Implementing Classes of *OrderedDictionary*

Constructors

public ImpOrderedDictionary( )	Create an empty ordered dictionary with default capacity.
public ImpOrderedDictionary(int capacity)	Create an empty ordered dictionary with specified capacity.

Commands

public void add(Comparable obj)	Add a new association, obj, to the ordered dictionary (from SearchTable).
public void addKey(Comparable key, Object value)	Add <key:value> as a new association in the ordered dictionary; if key already present change its value. Value may be null.
public void remove(Comparable key)	If found remove contained association with specified key.
public void changeValue(Comparable key, Object value)	Change value for specified key; throw exception if key not found.
public void makeEmpty( )	Make the ordered dictionary empty (from Container).

Queries

public boolean contains(Comparable key)	Return true if key is in the ordered dictionary (from SearchTable).
public boolean isEmpty( )	Return true if dictionary is empty (from Container).
public int size( )	Return the number of associations (from Container).
public Object valueFor(Comparable key)	Return the value for specified key; throw exception if key not found.
public boolean containsValue(Object value)	Return true if value is in the ordered dictionary.
public Comparable get(Comparable key)	Return the association with given key, throw exception if key not found (from SearchTable).
public Iterator elements( )	Return an iterator on the associations in the ordered dictionary (from SearchTable).
public Iterator keys( )	Return an iterator on the keys in the ordered dictionary.
public Iterator values( )	Return an iterator on the values in the ordered dictionary.
public String toString( )	Override from Object to return { <key1:val1>, <key2:val2>,... }

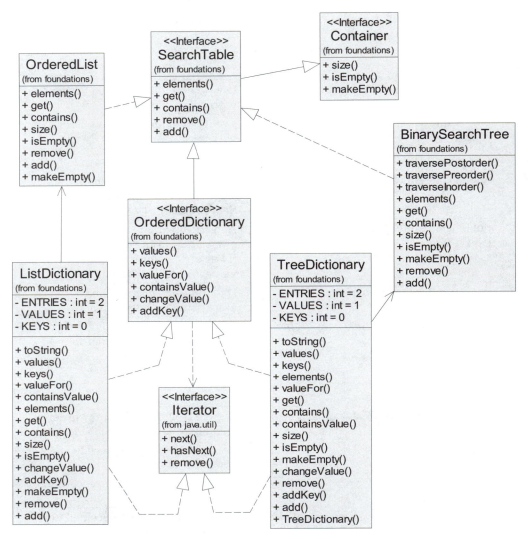

Figure 17.6. Class diagram for implementing classes of *OrderedDictionary*.

The three queries that return iterators may optionally use an inner class to implement the *Iterator* interface. Two potential constructors are shown that initialize an ordered dictionary to some default capacity or specified capacity. Depending on the actual class chosen for internal data representation, additional constructors or modifications to the two shown in Table 17.2 may be required.

17.6   Implementing the *OrderedDictionary* Interface

We previously presented two data structures that implement interface *Search-Table*: class *OrderedList* in Chapter 13 and class *BinarySearchTree* in Chapter 15. Either of these data structures may be used as the actual container for an ordered dictionary. The advantage of using an encapsulated binary search tree or ordered list for our ordered dictionary class is that most of the commands and queries are already implemented. We need only send the appropriate message to the encapsulated data object. Figure 17.6 shows a class diagram for two implementing classes of interface *OrderedDictionary*. Both implementing classes of *OrderedDictionary* encapsulate an instance called *data* that is the selected data structure.

Only the public commands and queries are shown for classes *OrderedList* and *BinarySearchTree*, although each has a number of private or protected supporting methods. It is interesting to note that classes *TreeDictionary* and *ListDictionary* have only public methods. This is a direct consequence of their reuse of existing classes, for *data*, that implement interface *SearchTable*.

TreeDictionary and *ListDictionary* must also implement interface *Iterator* in support of the *keys*, *values*, and *elements* queries. This may be done directly or by using an inner class for the iterators.

Listing 17.6 shows limited details for a class called *TreeDictionary* that implements interface *OrderedDictionary*. It is left as an exercise to complete the implementation details.

Listing 17.6 A *BinarySearchTree* Implementation of Interface *OrderedDictionary*

```
/** class TreeDictionary - implementation of OrderedDictionary
 *                        - uses a BinarySearchTree for data
 */
package foundations;
import java.util.*;

public class TreeDictionary implements OrderedDictionary {

  // Fields
  private BinarySearchTree data;
  private static int KEYS = 0;          // iterator control
  private static int VALUES = 1;        // iterator control
  private static int ENTRIES = 2;       // iterator control


  // Constructors

  /** Construct an empty dictionary
   */
  public TreeDictionary () {
    // left as an exercise
  }


  // Commands

  /** Add an association to the dictionary
   */
  public void add (Comparable obj) {
    // left as an exercise }
```

```
/** Add an association <key-value>
 *    If the key already exists, set its value
 *    BinarySearchTree requirement: add() overwrites existing element
 */
public void addKey (Comparable key, Object value) {
  // left as an exercise
}

/** Remove association with key if found
 *    Association.compareTo() uses only keys, value not needed
 */
public void remove (Comparable key) {
  // left as an exercise }

/** Change value for specified key
 *    Throw NoSuchElementException if key not found.
 */
public void changeValue (Comparable key, Object value) {
  // left as an exercise
}

/** Remove all objects from the container if found
 */
public void makeEmpty () {
  // left as an exercise
}

// Queries

/** Return true if the container is empty
 */
public boolean isEmpty () {
  // left as an exercise
  return true;
}

/** Return the number of keys in the dictionary
 */
public int size () {
  // left as an exercise
  return 0;
}

/** Answer true if obj is in the container as a value
 */
public boolean containsValue (Object value) {
  // left as an exercise
  return false;
}
```

```java
/** Return true if key in the dictionary
 */
public boolean contains (Comparable key) {
  // left as an exercise
  return false;
}


/** Return entry for key
 *    Throw NoSuchElementException if key not found
 */
public Comparable get (Comparable key) {
  // left as an exercise
  return null;
}


/** Return value for specified key
 *    Throw NoSuchElementException if key not found
 */
public Object valueFor (Comparable key) {
  // left as an exercise
  return null;
}


/** Return iterator over all entries
 */
public Iterator elements () {
  // left as an exercise
  return null;
}


/** Return iterator over all keys
 */
public Iterator keys () {
  // left as an exercise
  return null;
}


/** Return iterator over all values
 */
public Iterator values () {
  // left as an exercise
  return null;
}
/** Override method toString() from class Object
 *    Return in set notation all entries in the dictionary
 *    Notation is: {<key1:value1>, <key2:value2>,...}
 */
```

```
public String toString () {
  // left as an exercise
  return "" ;
 }
}
```

An implementation for *OrderedDictionary* using an *OrderedList* has essentially the same form as the *BinarySearchTree* implementation in Listing 17.6, except that *data* is an *OrderedList*. It is left as an exercise to provide the complete implementation of class *ListDictionary* with the partial template shown in Listing 17.7.

Listing 17.7 *ListDictionary* Implementation of *OrderedDictionary*

```
/** Class ListDictionary - implements OrderedDictionary
 *   Uses an instance of OrderedList for data;
 */
package foundations;
import java.util.*;

public class ListDictionary implements OrderedDictionary {

  // Fields
  OrderedList data;

  // All remaining details left as an exercise
}
```

Next we look at details of an ordered dictionary laboratory for testing implementations of *OrderedDictionary*. The *foundations* package provides complete implementations for *TreeDictionary* and *ListDictionary*.

17.7 The Ordered Dictionary Laboratory

The ordered dictionary laboratory is designed to illustrate and test features of implementing classes for interface *OrderedDictionary*. It allows the user to optionally select from the two fully implemented classes, *TreeDictionary* and *ListDictionary*, or from three implementations left as exercises. Figure 17.7 shows a class diagram representing the design features of the ordered dictionary laboratory.

Classes *TreeDictionaryE* and *ListDictionaryE* are partial implementations of *TreeDictionary* and *ListDictionary*. Details of these classes are left as an exercise. Additionally, class *OrderedDictionaryE* may be used for a custom implementation of *OrderedDictionary*.

A screen shot of the ordered dictionary laboratory is shown in Figure 17.8 after selection of the *TreeDictionary* implementing class and performing a number of operations on the ordered dictionary. The ordered dictionary laboratory is designed to accept strings for *key* and *value*. Notice that the keys are ordered independently of their insertion order.

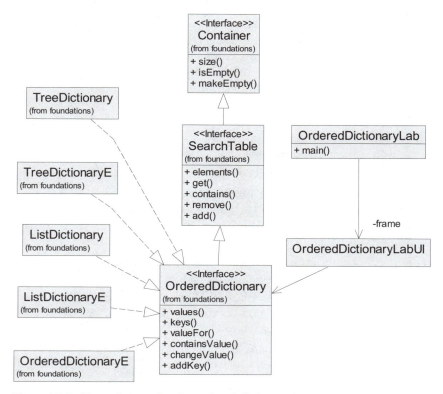

Figure 17.7. Class diagram for the ordered dictionary laboratory.

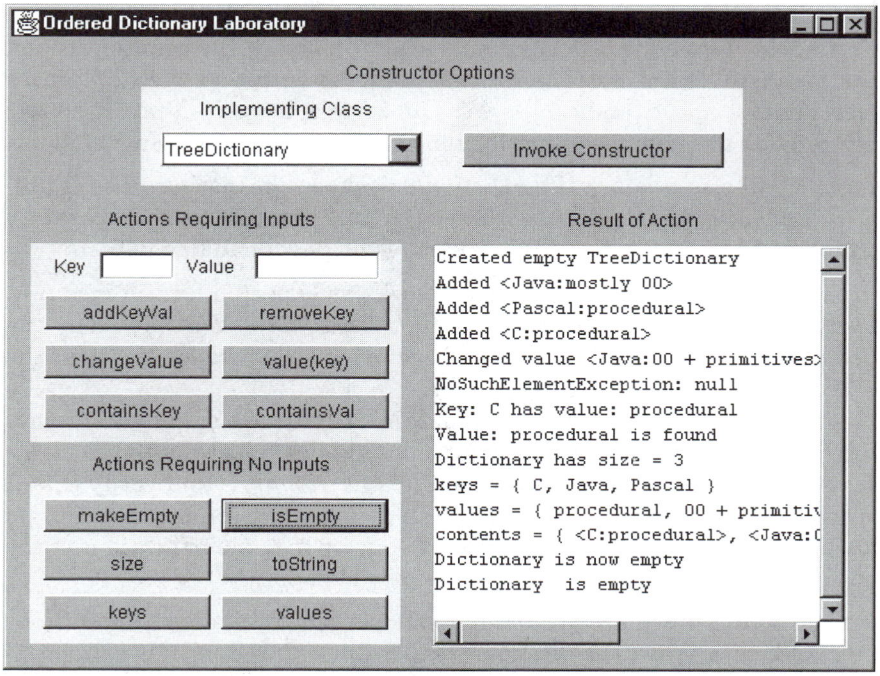

Figure 17.8. Screen shot of the ordered dictionary laboratory.

17.8 Summary

This chapter adds additional detail to class *Association* and introduces details for the dictionary as a container. It defines two kinds of dictionaries: *Dictionary* and *OrderedDictionary*. Laboratories are presented that allow testing of implementing classes for interfaces *Dictionary* and *OrderedDictionary*. Properties for associations and dictionaries are:

❏ An *association* represents a *key:value* pair.

❏ Dictionaries contain associations. The elements in the dictionary may be ordered on the keys of its contained associations or may be nonordered.

❏ A *dictionary* contains elements whose internal order depends on the details of its implementing classes. It is said to be "nonordered." It contains instances of *Object*. Interface *Dictionary* extends *Container*. A *dictionary* does not use the comparable property of its contained associations.

❏ An *ordered dictionary* contains elements whose internal order is based on the values of the elements. Its contained objects must be *Comparable*. For this reason, interface *OrderedDictionary* extends *SearchTable*.

❏ A *dictionary* may be implemented as a hash table or a linear list. Lookup performance of the hash table is O(1) compared to O(n) for the list.

❏ An *ordered dictionary* may be implemented as a binary search tree or an ordered list. Lookup performance for the binary search tree is O(n $\log_2$ n) compared to O(n) for the ordered list.

17.9 Exercises

1   Develop a test class called *AssociationTest* that tests all the commands and queries for instances of *Association*. Pay close attention to the differences between queries *equals* and *compareTo*. Be certain to verify that these two queries provide the behavior described in the discussion of Listing 17.1.

2   A complete solution to class *HashDictionary* (shown in Listing 17.3) is provided in the *foundations* package and works with the dictionary laboratory (found in the *DictionaryLab* folder as part of the downloadable notes).

    a. Verify that the dictionary laboratory works as expected for the *java.util. Hashtable* implementation in class *HashDictionary*. You may copy the entire *DictionaryLab* folder into a directory of your choice and run the batch file named *Goui.bat*.

    b. Folder *DictionaryLab\foundations* contains a skeletal implementation for *Dictionary* called *HashDictionaryE* that compiles and runs but does little else. Complete all details for class *HashDictionaryE* and verify that it works using the dictionary laboratory. In your implementation of *HashDictionaryE*, use a hash table of your own implementation as the data structure that contains the dictionary elements.

3   A complete solution to class *VectorDictionary* is provided in the *foundations* package and works with the dictionary laboratory (found in the *DictionaryLab* folder as part of the downloadable notes).

a. Verify that the dictionary laboratory works as expected for the *java.util.-Vector* implementation in class *VectorDictionary*. You may copy the entire *DictionaryLab* folder into a directory of your choice and run the batch file named *Goui.bat*.

b. Folder *DictionaryLab\foundations* contains a skeletal implementation for *Dictionary* called *VectorDictionaryE* (similar to Listing 17.4) that compiles and runs but does little else. Complete all details for class *VectorDictionaryE* and verify that it works using the dictionary laboratory. In your implementation of *VectorDictionaryE*, use *java.util.Vector* as the data structure that contains the dictionary elements.

4   Folder *DictionaryLab\foundations* contains a skeletal implementation for *Dictionary* called *DictionaryE* that compiles and runs but does little else. Complete all details for class *DictionaryE* and verify that it works using the dictionary laboratory. In your implementation of *DictionaryE*, use any data structure of your choice that contains the dictionary elements. Write a detailed description of the chosen data structure and describe its performance features. Compare your data structure with the hash table and list implementations.

5   A complete solution to class *TreeDictionary* is provided in the *foundations* package and works with the ordered dictionary laboratory (found in the *OrderedDictionaryLab* folder as part of the downloadable notes).

a. Verify that the ordered dictionary laboratory works as expected for the *foundations.BinarySearchTree* implementation in class *TreeDictionary*. You may copy the entire *OrderedDictionaryLab* folder into a directory of your choice and run the batch file named *Goui.bat*.

b. Folder *OrderedDictionaryLab\foundations* contains a skeletal implementation for *OrderedDictionary* called *TreeDictionaryE* (similar to Listing 17.6) that compiles and runs but does little else. Complete all details for class *TreeDictionaryE* and verify that it works using the ordered dictionary laboratory. In your implementation of *TreeDictionaryE*, use a binary search tree of your own implementation as the data structure that contains the dictionary elements.

6   A complete solution to class *ListDictionary* is provided in the *foundations* package and works with the ordered dictionary laboratory (found in the *OrderedDictionaryLab* folder as part of the downloadable notes).

a. Verify that the ordered dictionary laboratory works as expected for the *foundations.OrderedList* implementation in class *ListDictionary*. You may copy the entire *OrderedDictionaryLab* folder into a directory of your choice and run the batch file named *Goui.bat*.

b. Folder *OrderedDictionaryLab\foundations* contains a skeletal implementation for *OrderedDictionary* called *ListDictionaryE* that compiles and runs but does little else. Complete all details for class *ListDictionaryE* and verify that it works using the ordered dictionary laboratory. In your implementation of *ListDictionaryE*, use your own implementation of an ordered list as the data structure that contains the dictionary elements.

7   Folder *OrderedDictionaryLab\foundations* contains a skeletal implementation for *OrderedDictionary* called *OrderedDictionaryE* that compiles and runs but does little else. Complete all details for class *OrderedDictionaryE* and verify that it works using the ordered dictionary laboratory. In your implementation of *OrderedDictionaryE*, use any data structure of your choice. It may be a class that implements *SearchTable* or a totally new class that implements *OrderedDictionary* directly. Write a detailed description of the chosen data structure and describe its performance features. Compare your data structure with the binary search tree and ordered list implementations.

18

Sorting

Sorting involves rearranging information in some container, usually an array, so that the information is stored from smallest to largest (ascending order) or from largest to smallest (descending order). The need to sort is fundamental. We are interested in finding efficient algorithms to accomplish the task.

We shall assume throughout this chapter that the entities to be sorted are *Comparable*. That is, they may be compared using the query *compareTo*.

All the sorting methods are presented as static functions with an array of *Comparable* as the first parameter and the number of elements to be sorted as the second parameter. Although this represents a departure from the normal pattern of object-oriented class construction, we believe it is justified. As long as the array of elements to be sorted are *Comparable* the user should not be burdened with having to create an instance of a sorting class in order to rearrange the elements in the array that requires sorting.

18.1 Simple and Inefficient Sorting Algorithms

We consider two relatively simple sorting algorithms in this section before turning our attention to more efficient sorting.

18.1.1 Selection Sort

The array is scanned from index 1 to index n and the location of the largest value is obtained. This value is interchanged with the nth value. This assures that the largest value is placed in the rightmost position (index n).

The array is again scanned, this time from index 1 to index $n - 1$. The location of the largest value is obtained. This value is interchanged with the $(n - 1)$st value.

This pattern is continued, each time finding the location of the largest value and then interchanging it with the rightmost position in a range of values that shrinks by one each time.

Listing 18.1 shows Java code that accomplishes selection sort. It is assumed that the numbers in the array are stored in index locations 1 to n (i.e., we allocate one extra index in the array to allow "natural" indexing to be used).

Listing 18.1 Selection Sort

```
public static void selectionSort (double [] data, int size) {
  int maxIndex, index1, index2;
  double max, temp;

  for (index1 = size; index1 >= 2; index1--) {
    max = data [1];
    maxIndex = 1;
    for (index2 = 2; index2 <= index1; index2++)
      if (data [index2] > max) {
        maxIndex = index2;
        max = data [index2];
      }
    temp = data [index1];
    data [index1] = data [maxIndex];
    data [maxIndex] = temp;
    if (lab.display && index1 % 500 == 0)
      lab.displayData(size);
  }
}
```

Complexity of Selection Sort

We seek to determine how the computational effort increases as a function of problem size for large problem size n.

Each iteration in the selection sort algorithm requires many comparisons followed by a single exchange. On the first iteration, it takes computation time proportional to n ($n - 1$ comparisons plus an exchange) to compute the maximum value. On the second iteration, it takes computation time proportional to $n - 1$. On the third iteration, it takes computation time proportional to $n - 2$. The overall computation time is therefore proportional to $n + (n - 1) + (n - 2) + \cdots + 1$. This well-known arithmetic series has a sum equal to $n * (n + 1)/2$. For large n, this is proportional to n^2 since we can disregard the linear term in the polynomial.

We therefore can say that selection sort is $O(n^2)$. For large n, if we double the size of the array that we are sorting, we quadruple the computational effort. This can cause serious problems if n is large.

18.1.2 Bubble Sort

During the first iteration, each element in the array is compared to its next element (element one index higher). If the second element is smaller than the first element, the two elements are interchanged; otherwise they are left alone. Upon the conclusion of this first iteration, the largest element in the array is guaranteed to be in the rightmost position, n.

During the second iteration, the elements are again compared two at a time and interchanged if they are out of order (second element being smaller than the first) and left alone if they are in order. These comparisons stop after the $(n-2)$nd element is compared to the $(n-1)$st element.

On subsequent iterations, element comparisons and possible interchanges are performed on a shrinking range of elements. Boolean parameter *exchanged* is set to *false* prior to each iteration of the inner *for* loop. If no exchanges are made, the array is sorted and Bubble Sort halts.

Listing 18.2 shows the details of the Bubble Sort method.

Listing 18.2   Bubble Sort

```java
public static void bubbleSort (Comparable [] data, int size) {
   int index1, index2;
   Comparable temp;
   boolean exchanged;

   for (index1 = size; index1 >= 2; index1--) {
     exchanged = false;
     for (index2 = 1; index2 <= index1 - 1; index2++) {
       if (data [index2].compareTo(data [index2 + 1]) > 0) {
         temp = data [index2];
         data [index2] = data [index2 + 1];
         data [index2 + 1] = temp;
         exchanged = true;
       }
     }
     if (!exchanged)
       break;
   }
}
```

Complexity of Bubble Sort

We again seek to determine how the computational effort increases as a function of problem size for large problem size n.

The same reasoning process as given above leads to the conclusion that the complexity is $O(n^2)$. On the first iteration there are $n-1$ comparison operations. On the next iteration there are $n-2$ and so forth.

Bubble Sort generally performs worse than Selection Sort, although both have time complexity $O(n^2)$. This can be attributed to the fact that Bubble Sort does more swapping of elements in the array. Both do an equivalent number of comparisons. For example, on the first iteration, there are $(n-1)$ comparisons and a maximum of $(n-1)$ exchanges (Selection Sort had only one exchange). For an array of elements that are almost sorted, Bubble Sort does exceptionally well. This is because it breaks out of the algorithm as soon as no swaps are made (when *exchanged* remains *false*).

18.2 Efficient Sorting Algorithms

18.2.1 Quick Sort

This algorithm, developed by Tony Hoare, is considered by many to be the fastest sorting algorithm in existence. It employs a "divide and conquer" strategy in which the sorting of a large array is replaced by the sorting of two smaller arrays. Each of these in turn is replaced by two still smaller arrays. This process of replacing a large problem by two smaller problems continues recursively until the array is of size 2.

The outer structure of method *quickSort* is given in Listing 18.3.

Listing 18.3 Outer Structure of Quick Sort

```
public static void quickSort (Comparable [] data, int low, int high) {
  int partitionIndex;

  if (high - low > 0) {
    partitionIndex = partition (data, low, high);
    quickSort (data, low, partitionIndex - 1);
    quickSort (data, partitionIndex + 1, high);
  }
}
```

The genius of this algorithm is the concept and implementation of method *partition*. This method returns an index location, *partitionIndex*, which contains a value that splits the array into two disjoint subsets. In the left subset, consisting of all array elements whose indices are less than the partition index, the values are less than the partition value. In the right subset, consisting of all array elements whose indices are greater than the partition index, the values are equal to or greater than the partition value. If all the left subset values are sorted and all the right subset values are sorted, then since all the left subset values are less than all the right subset values, the entire array is sorted. This forms the basis for the recursion in Listing 18.3. It gives the best performance if method *partition* divides the array in half at each level.

Figure 18.1 shows the array before and after *partition* does its work. The *partition* algorithm arbitrarily chooses the element at index *low* as the partition element (**5** in the figure). It then proceeds to find the required index location (*partitionIndex*) in the array to which the partition element must be moved.

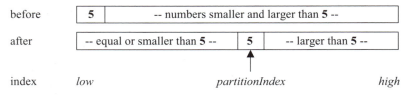

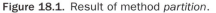

Figure 18.1. Result of method *partition*.

Listing 18.4 shows the code that implements the *partition* algorithm.

Listing 18.4 Partition Method

```
private static int partition (Comparable [] data, int low, int high) {
  int k, j;
  Comparable temp, p;

  p = data [low]; // Partition element
  // Find partition index (j).
  k = low;
  j = high + 1;
  do {
    k++;
  } while (data [k].compareTo(p) <= 0 && k < high);
  do {
    j--;
  } while (data [j].compareTo(p) > 0);
  while (k < j) {
    temp = data [k];
    data [k] = data [j];
    data [j] = temp;
    do {
      k++;
    } while (data [k].compareTo(p) <= 0);
    do {
      j--;
    } while (data [j].compareTo(p) > 0);
  }
  // Move partition element (p) to partition index (j).
  if (low != j) {
    temp = data [low];
    data [low] = data [j];
    data [j] = temp;
  }
  return j;  // Partition index
}
```

Complexity of Quick Sort (Informal Argument)

If, on the average, the partition function bisects the array into two relatively equal subsets, then the number of times this may happen is $\log_2 n$. This implies that the partition function will be invoked approximately $\log_2 n$ times. Each time it is invoked it requires linear time to perform its work. Although this time is in general less than n (because only a portion of the array is being partitioned), an upper bound for *partition* would be O(n). Therefore, the complexity of Quick Sort is bounded by O($n \log_2 n$).

This is significantly more efficient than O(n^2). If, for example, the problem size were $n = 1,000,000$, the ratio of n^2 to $n \log_2 n$ would be approximately equal to

$10^{12}/20 * 10^6$. That is, the inefficient algorithm would take about 50,000 times longer to execute than the efficient Quick Sort algorithm.

We walk through a simple example to illustrate the operation of the partition function.

Consider an array with the following values. The partition element, p, equals 5 (always the first element in the array).

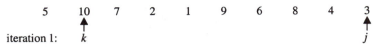

Steps in iteration 1 are the following. The index k is incremented from the leftmost position until the first element is found that is larger than p. In this case, k is 2 corresponding to element 10. The index j is decremented from the rightmost position until the first element is found that is equal to or less than p. In this case, j is 10 corresponding to element 3.

Since k is less than j, we interchange the values at these indices (swap 10 and 3). The new array is:

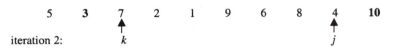

In iteration 2 we again increment index k until we find the first element that is larger than p. We decrement the index j until we find the first element that is equal to or less than p. The value of k is 3 and the value of j is 9. After interchanging the values (swap 7 and 4) at these indices the new array is:

5	3	4	2	1	9	6	8	7	10

iteration 3:
           $\uparrow$ $\uparrow$
           j k

We continue this pattern as long as the index k is less than the index j. In iteration 3, k reaches index 6 (containing element 9) and j reaches index 5 (containing element 1). Since k is no longer less than j the *while* loop terminates.

The final step is to interchange the value at index *low* (equal to 1) with the value at index j (equal to 5). We swap elements 5 and 1. This leads to the array:

1	3	4	2	5	9	6	8	7	10

      $\uparrow$
    partitionIndex = 5

The *partition* algorithm has produced elements in index locations smaller than *partitionIndex* (the partition element) whose values are smaller than 5 and values in index locations greater than *partitionIndex* whose values are greater than 5. That is exactly the purpose of method *partition*.

Consider the situation where the array starts out as sorted. You will be asked to show as an exercise that the Quick Sort algorithm turns in its worst performance, $O(n^2)$, when the input data are already sorted. How ironic!

18.2.2 Gap Sort

Recently a new sorting algorithm that is a small variant of Bubble Sort has been invented. This algorithm is called Gap Sort. Gap Sort starts off by comparing elements that are separated by a given *gap*. If the elements being compared are out of order (the second element is smaller than the first), they are interchanged. An iteration is completed after all the elements that can be compared (not all of them) are compared (the 1st element is compared to the element in index $1 + gap$, the 2nd element is compared to the element in index $2 + gap, \dots$, the $n - gap$ element is compared to the nth element).

On the next iteration, the value of *gap* is reduced by a constant factor called the "shrink factor," a number greater than 1. Again all the elements that can be compared are compared. During each subsequent iteration, the *gap* is reduced by the shrink factor until it reaches a value equal to or less than 1. At this time the *gap* is frozen at 1.

The code for this algorithm is given in Listing 18.5. The constant *SF* (shrink factor) is assigned a value greater than 1.0 outside of this procedure, initially equal to size.

Listing 18.5 Gap Sort

```
public static void gapSort (Comparable [] data, int size) {
  int index;
  int gap, top;
  Comparable temp;
  boolean exchanged;
  double SF = 1.3;

  gap = size;
  do {
    exchanged = false;
    gap = (int) (gap / SF);
    if (gap == 0)
      gap = 1;
      for (index = 1; index <= size - gap; index++) {
        if (data [index].compareTo(data [index + gap]) > 0) {
          temp = data [index];
          data [index] = data [index + gap];
          data [index + gap] = temp;
          exchanged = true;
        }
      }
  } while (exchanged || gap > 1);
}
```

The algorithm is almost identical to Bubble Sort. If the gap were set to 1, then pure Bubble Sort would result.

By comparing *data [index]* with *data [index + gap]*, the smaller elements are brought more quickly from right to left, whereas in ordinary Bubble Sort, these smaller elements migrate very slowly from right to left.

What makes this algorithm nothing short of amazing is that it works very efficiently only when the shrink factor is very close to the value 1.3. For any shrink factors that deviate even slightly from this magic value, the algorithm dramatically slows down to the speed of ordinary Bubble Sort. Nobody really understands what is so special about the magic shrink-factor value 1.3. This is an open question.

18.3   Binary Search

An additional static function to add to class *Sorting* is *binarySearch*. This method allows one to efficiently search an array after the array has been sorted.

Listing 18.6   Binary Search

```
public static boolean binarySearch (Comparable [] data, int first,
                                     int last, Comparable value) {
  int middle = (first + last) / 2;
  if (data [middle].compareTo(value) == 0)
    return true;
  else if (value.compareTo(data [middle]) < 0) {
    if (first <= middle - 1)
      return binarySearch (data, first, middle - 1, value);
    else
      return false;
  }
  else if (value.compareTo(data [middle]) > 0) {
    if (middle + 1 <= last)
      return binarySearch (data, middle + 1, last, value);
    else
      return false;
  }
  return false; // This line is never reached
}
```

The algorithm for *binarySearch* uses a "divide and conquer" approach to search and provides time performance of $O(\log_2 n)$.

18.4   Sort Laboratory

An application program, Sort Lab, is available for your use. In this program each of the sorting algorithms (Selection Sort, Bubble Sort, Gap Sort, and Quick Sort) are implemented. A provision for visualizing the data as sorting progresses is available as well as a provision for timing the various algorithms using the algorithm of your choice. Figure 18.2 shows a graphical display indicating the progress of a Bubble Sort.

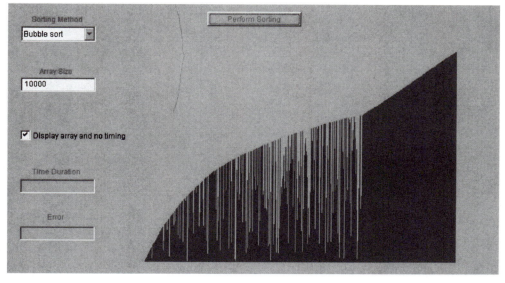

Figure 18.2. The sort laboratory.

18.5 Summary

❑ The need to sort is fundamental. We are interested in finding efficient algorithms to accomplish the task.

❑ All the sorting methods are presented as static functions with an array of *Comparable* as the first parameter and the number of elements to be sorted as the second parameter.

❑ Quick Sort, developed by Tony Hoare, is considered by many to be the fastest sorting algorithm in existence. It employs a "divide and conquer" strategy in which the sorting of a large array is replaced by the sorting of two smaller arrays. Each of these in turn is replaced by two still smaller arrays. This process of replacing a large problem by two smaller problems continues recursively until the array is of size 2.

18.6 Exercises

1 Discuss the advantages, if any, and disadvantages, if any, of making each sorting method a static method.

Consider the following data set in an array:

5, 11, 15, 14, 13, 12, 17, 10, 8, 4, 2, 6, 9, 3, 1.

Walk through the following sorting methods (Exercises 2 through 5) and count the number of interchange operations that are required for each sorting method.

2 Walk through and count the number of interchange operations required using Selection Sort.

3 Walk through and count the number of interchange operations required using Bubble Sort.

4 Walk through and count the number of interchange operations required using Gap Sort.

5 Walk through and count the number of interchange operations required using Quick Sort.

6 Implement Selection Sort if the data are held in a vector.

7 Implement Bubble Sort if the data are held in a vector.

8 Implement Quick Sort if the data are held in a vector.

9 Implement a Selection Sort on a two-dimensional array declared as follows:

Comparable [][] data;

if the sorting is to be done on the data in column 0.

10 Show that the worst-case performance of Quick Sort occurs when the input data are already sorted.

11 How might you modify the Quick Sort algorithm to guarantee $O(n \log_2 n)$ performance for all input data?

Unified Modeling Language Notation

This appendix presents a brief introduction to UML notation as used in the book. For more detailed discussion of UML, its history, notation, documentation, and uses, the reader is referred to the UML Web page for Rational Software Corporation:

http://www.rational.com/uml/

A.1 Representing Classes in UML

UML notation provides a rich variety of options for graphically representing the details of a class. The basic icon for a class is a rectangular box with one, two, or three compartments as shown in Figure A.1. The compartments contain strings and special symbols. The *Name* compartment is required. The two *List* compartments typically contain attributes and operations and may be suppressed as desired. Within each compartment, UML offers many options for amount of detail to be shown.

Among the options for detail to be shown in the three compartments are the following:

- *String* – an identifier representing a class name, field name, or method name.
- *<<stereotype-string>>* – A string in guillemets is a stereotype. Stereotypes may be thought of as categories that further qualify a class, field, or method. For example, we may use the stereotype *<<interface>>* to identify a class that is a Java interface. We may apply the stereotype *<<final>>* to a constant field and the stereotypes *<<command>>* or *<<query>>* to methods.
- +, −, # − Visibility is indicated using a "+" symbol for *public*, a "−" symbol for *private*, a "#" symbol for *protected*, or no symbol for *package* (Java default).
- *{property-string}* – A string in curly braces is used to identify additional properties for a class, field, or method.

The template for a class name is

ClassName

The default visibility for a class is *public*. Nonpublic classes may be identified using a property string. Property strings may also be used to identify the package to which a class belongs. Class names are typically boldface for emphasis.

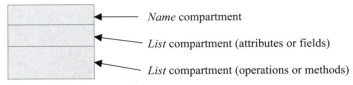

Figure A.1. UML icon for representing a class.

An abstract class or interface class name is usually displayed in italics with the addition of stereotypes *<>* or *<<interface>>*.
The template for fields is given by:

> *visibility name* : *type-expression = initial-value* {*property-string*}

where:
> *visibility* is a +, −, #, or no symbol,
> *name* is the name of the field,
> *type-expression* is the type of the field, separated from *name* by a colon,
> *initial-value* is the default initialization value for the field, after equals,
> *property-string* is as defined above in curly braces.

All parts of the field template are optional except the *name*. A stereotype, if used, is displayed first.
The template for methods is given by:

> *visibility name* (*parameter-list*) : *return-type-expression* { *property-string*}

where:
> *visibility* is a +, −, #, or no symbol,
> *name* is the name of the method,
> *parameter-list* is a comma-separated list of *parameter:type* elements
>   enclosed in parentheses,
> *return-type-expression* is the type returned by the method, separated from
>   *parameter-list* by a colon,
> *property-string* is as defined above in curly braces.

Figure A.2 shows several options for displaying abstract class *Vehicle* from Chapter 1 using UML. A particular display of a class may selectively include any combination of features of the class. The minimal display is one compartment with the class name.

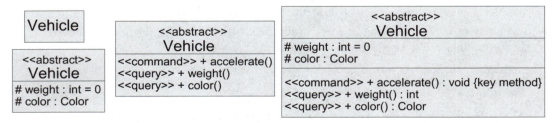

Figure A.2. Options for displaying class *Vehicle*.

The left column in Figure A.2 shows the minimal display for class *Vehicle* and an enhanced display including the field *List* compartment. Class *Vehicle* is identified as abstract in two ways: (1) by italicizing the class name and (2) by using the stereotype *<>*. Fields *weight* of type *int* and *color* of type *Color* have *protected* visibility and *weight* is initialized to 0.

The middle column shows class *Vehicle* with the field *List* compartment suppressed and the method *List* compartment visible. Method *accelerate* is abstract (italicized) and is a *<<command>>*. Methods *weight* and *color* both are stereotype *<<query>>*. All three methods have *public* visibility.

The right column shows all details included in the specification for class *Vehicle*. Return types (parameters too, if there are any) are shown for all methods. A property string identifies *accelerate* as a *key method* (one that must be implemented by subclasses).

A few additional options for displaying a class are shown in subsequent examples.

A.2 Representing Relationships among Classes in UML

There are a number of possible relationships among classes, five of which are significant for Java. These five relationships are:

1. Extension – a subclass *extends* its parent class.
2. Implementation – a class *implements* an interface class.
3. Association – two classes have an association to each other. Higher order and more complex associations are also possible but are not used in this book.
4. Using – a class uses another class, such as a utility class.
5. Inner – a class may contain an inner class (defined within the containing class).

Notation for extension and implementation is shown in UML in Figure A.3. The directed arrows may optionally be further qualified by attaching stereotypes or property strings to them. The property string *venue* is the discriminant for distinguishing subclasses of *Vehicle*. The *Vehicle* class *implements* interface *Serializable*. An alternative way to distinguish an *extends* relationship and an *implements* relationship is to make the arrow dashed for the *implements* relationship.

An association between two classes implies a strong dependence. There are many varieties of associations and a rich set of symbols and adornments to characterize them in UML. A single solid line connecting the two classes denotes an association. The association may have a name and each class may have a role name. Communication between the two classes may be bidirectional (the default) or unidirectional as indicated by a simple arrowhead. A using relationship between two classes is typically utilitarian and a somewhat weaker relationship than an association. A single dashed line connecting the two classes denotes a using relationship. A using relationship may be characterized by the same set of adornments available for an association. Figure A.4 shows examples of associations and using relationships.

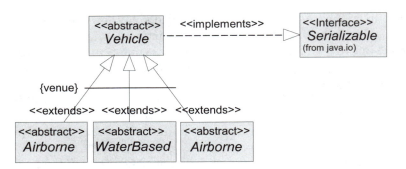

Figure A.3. Extension and implementation in UML.

Class *BinaryTreeHeap* uses class *Vector* (for intermediate storage to enable iteration). It has (an association) two instances of *HeapNode* (the *root* and *last* nodes). *BinaryTreeHeap* initiates communication in all as indicated by the arrows. *HeapNode* has a bidirectional association with itself (a reference to its *parent*, also an instance of *HeapNode*). Communication may be initiated in either direction.

Another association of interest is that of an aggregation. An aggregation is a whole–part relationship. The whole is an aggregate of its parts. Figure A.5 shows a simple example of an aggregation plus additional adornments for associations.

Aggregation is shown as a diamond at the class representing the "whole," class *JetPlane* in Figure A.5. Class *JetPlane* is an aggregate of one (1) *Fuselage*, *Avionics*, one-to-eight (1...8) instances of *Engine*, and zero-or-one (0...1) *TailHook*. It has one-or-more (1...*) *FlightCrew* members and zero-or-more (0...*) instances of *Passenger*. *ControlTower* is an *observer* of *JetPlane* and has a bidirectional *comm* (communication) association with *FlightCrew*. And *JetPlane* uses a *Runway*. The dashed line connecting associations from *JetPlane* to *Avionics* and *Fuselage* indicates that additional aggregate parts exist. Figures A.4 and A.5 show only part of the rich set of relationships among classes and qualifying details. The reader is referred to the UML documentation for additional details on associations and other UML notation.

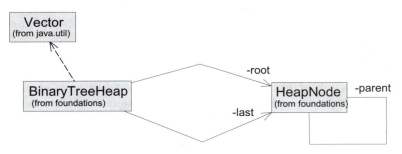

Figure A.4. Associations and using relationships among classes.

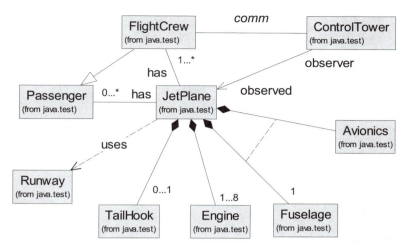

Figure A.5. Aggregation shows a whole–part relationship.

An inner class may be shown as a class within a class. In addition to the inner class relationship, there may be another dependency between the two classes. This dependency cannot be extension or implementation, but it can be an association or using relationship. A simple example is shown in Figure A.6 for class *LinkedStack*, which implements the *Stack* interface and has an inner class *Node*. Class *LinkedStack* has an association with its inner class through its field *top*. Notes may be added to diagrams using a rectangle with a bent upper right corner. A dashed line connects the note to its target UML component.

A.3 Representing Packages in UML

A package is represented as a tabbed folder. Subpackages may be shown as folders within folders and classes within a package may also be shown. Some simple examples using packages and classes in the Java platform are shown in Figure A.7. Package *java* contains (among others) subpackages *util* and *awt*. One interface in *java.util* is *Observer*. The *awt* package contains many classes and subpackages including class *Component* and package *event*. Subpackage *event* contains class *ActionEvent* and others.

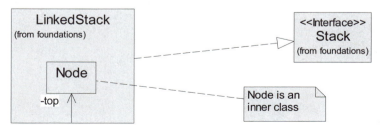

Figure A.6. Inner classes.

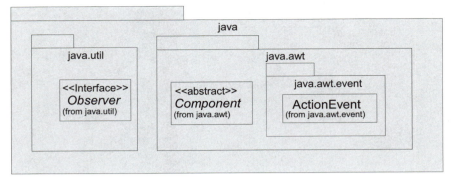

Figure A.7. Packages in UML.

A.4 Representing Objects in UML

A rectangular box with two compartments, appropriate strings, and symbols inside represents an object in UML. The top compartment contains the object name and its class in the form shown.

> *objectName : ClassName*

Presentation options include (1) the object name only and (2) the class name only (preceded by the colon). The bottom compartment is optional and shows details of the fields and their values for this particular object in the form below.

> *fieldName : type = value*

Examples are shown in Figure A.8.

Object *aPoint* is implied as an instance of class *Point* by its name. It is the simplest representation for an object in UML. Object *bPoint* in the second icon is clearly identified as an instance of *Point*. The third icon is an instance of *Point* with no name; that is, it is anonymous. The fourth icon shows *bPoint* again and identifies its fields, their types, and current values.

A.5 Representing Interactions among Objects in UML

UML provides two kinds of diagrams for illustrating interactions among objects. These interaction diagrams are (1) collaboration diagrams and (2) sequence diagrams. They show essentially the same information in two separate forms. Both are part of the dynamic model for an object-oriented design. That is, they show

Figure A.8. Objects in UML.

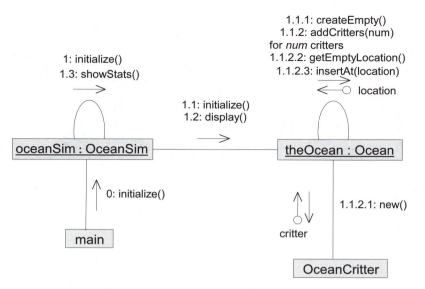

Figure A.9. Collaboration (object interaction) diagram in UML.

features of the software that are valid while the software is running. Most tools for generating UML diagrams provide an automatic conversion from one to the other.

A sequence diagram shows a time-sequential display of messages passing among objects, usually in a linear time display from top to bottom. A collaboration diagram shows objects displayed arbitrarily on a page with links (lines) connecting those objects that interact. A directional arrow close to the link and a string identifying the message being sent indicates message passing. An arrow with a circle at one end and a string identifies objects returned as a result of a message sent. Messages may be numbered to indicate their sequence in both the sequence and collaboration diagrams.

We illustrate only a collaboration diagram. The book uses only one collaboration diagram in Chapter 6 to illustrate details of event handling in Java and no sequence diagrams.

Figure A.9 shows some of the features of a collaboration diagram in UML. It shows two objects, *oceanSim* and *theOcean*, plus one class, *OceanCritter*. Details are shown for initializing the ocean simulation. Numbered messages are shown hierarchically. For example, message *1: initialize()* sent by object *oceanSim* to itself consists of three parts: *1.1: initialize(), 1.2: display()* both sent to object *theOcean*, and *1.3: showStats()* sent to itself.

As a more detailed explanation of Figure A.9, we may use a sequential list of messages showing hierarchical level by indentation.

```
// initialize an instance of OceanSim
0: initialize() - main sends initialize() to object oceanSim
```

```
1: initialize() - oceanSim sends message initialize() to itself
  1.1: initialize() - oceanSim sends initialize() to theOcean
    1.1.1: createEmpty() - sent by theOcean to itself
    1.1.2: addCritters(num) - sent by theOcean to itself
      for num critters - loop
      1.1.2.1: new() - theOcean sends to class OceanCritter
              - object critter is returned
      1.1.2.2: getEmptyLocation() - theOcean to theOcean
                            - returns location object
      1.1.2.3: insertAt(location) - theOcean to theOcean
  1.2: display() - oceanSim sends to theOcean
  1.3: showStats() - oceanSim sends to itself.
// initialize routine is complete
```

Complexity of Algorithms

Two resources coveted by software developers are memory space and execution time. Among the factors that determine the memory footprint of an application or its execution time is the algorithm chosen in the application (there may of course be many algorithms used within an application).

The space taken by an algorithm is related to the information structure used to hold the data and any other information structures required to support the computational process. These are usually defined as fields in the data structure class.

The time required to execute an algorithm is dependent on the structure of the algorithm. We are usually concerned with the worst-case time, the best-case time, and the average time, to be defined in the following paragraphs. Sometimes these are the same. These execution times are usually related to one or more parameters that determine the size of the problem being solved. To be conservative we normally rely on worst-case time when comparing two algorithms.

The worst-case time is the longest time that any problem of specified size takes to execute. The best-case time is the shortest time that any problem of specified size takes to execute. The average-case time is an estimate of the time required for an average problem of specified size.

For worst-case, best-case, and average-case times, we are normally concerned with asymptotic time complexity – in plain English, the time required to complete an algorithm as a function of problem size when the problem size is assumed to be large.

Let us consider an example. Suppose we wish to characterize the time for searching a linear linked list for a particular element as in the list implemented by class *SinglyLinkedList* of Chapter 13. The best-case time occurs when the element being sought is the first element in the list. The time is a constant, independent of the size of the list. The worst-case time occurs when the element being sought is the last element. In this case the time required is directly proportional to the size of the list, say n. The average-case time implies that it takes $n/2$ to complete the search (equivalent to finding an element halfway into the list).

We use "big O" notation to characterize the asymptotic complexity of an algorithm. Formally, an algorithm whose computation time is given by a function $f(n)$ is considered to be $O(g(n))$ if and only if $|f(n)| <= a * g(n)$ for all $n >= n_0$, where a and n_0 are constants. If this relationship holds, we say "function f is big O of g."

For the list example, the worst-case time would be $O(n)$ since for any n the time required to find the last element (worst case) is less than or equal to some constant times n. This is also the average-case time complexity since we do not take constants into account in big O representation. The best-case time for a linear linked list would be constant complexity or $O(1)$.

Algorithm complexity can sometimes be determined by carefully observing the structure of the program that implements the algorithm. If a simple loop is required to compute the desired result with some size parameter, say n, as the upper limit, the complexity of this portion of the algorithm is $O(n)$. This is based on the simple idea that each iteration of the loop contributes an equal share of overhead to the overall computational complexity. So, for example, the following segment of code contributes $O(n)$ complexity:

```
for (int index = 0; index < n; index++) {
  /* Some sequence of steps */
}
```

Let us consider an algorithm structure based on two nested loops as follows:

```
for (int index1 = 0; index1 < n; index1++) {
  for (index2 = 0; index2 < n; index2++) {
    /* Some sequence of steps */
  }
}
```

Here each loop is bounded by the size parameter n. If we again assume that each time the sequence of steps is executed it contributes an equal share to the overall overhead of the algorithm, we merely have to estimate the total number of steps as a function of n. For each value of the outer *index1*, the inner loop is executed n times. Since the outer loop is executed n times, the overall number of steps is proportional to n^2. Therefore the nested loops given above contribute $O(n^2)$ complexity to the overall algorithm.

It is easy to show that triply nested loops would contribute $O(n^3)$ and so on. Sometimes the structure of a loop is subtle. Consider the following loop structure:

```
index = 1;
while (index < n) {
  index *= 2;
  /* Some sequence of steps */
}
```

In the above loop, the number of iterations is given by $\log_2(n)$. This is because *index* is multiplied by two after each iteration.

In comparing algorithms we usually compare their asymptotic complexity (big O function). In Chapter 15 it is shown that a balanced binary search tree is able to locate an arbitrary element with average time complexity of $\log_2(n)$. We have already seen that a linked list requires $O(n)$. How different are these algorithms in terms of their computational efficiency?

As an example, suppose that we have n equals 1,000,000 in each structure. The ratio of performance between a binary search tree and linked list of size one million is approximately:

$$\log_2(1{,}000{,}000)/1{,}000{,}000 = 20/1{,}000{,}000 = 1/50{,}000.$$

That is, the balanced search tree requires a computational effort that is 1/50,000 of that of the linked list.

To further illustrate the profound effect that the structure of an algorithm has on its performance, let us consider a relatively simple but challenging problem.

Suppose we are given an array of size n of real numbers, with the stipulation that the array must contain at least one positive and one negative number. Within such an array we define a subarray as contiguous values from some lower index to some higher index, where the lower and higher indices may be the same. For example, the array of size 3 shown below has the following subarrays:

value1	value2	value3
1	2	3

```
Subarrays
1
2
3
1, 2
2, 3
1, 2, 3
```

Suppose we consider the sum of values within each subarray. These are given as follows:

```
Subarray    Sum of values

1           value1
2           value2
3           value3
1, 2        value1 + value2
2, 3        value2 + value3
1, 2, 3     value1 + value2 + value3
```

Our problem is to compute the sum of values that is largest among all possible subarrays of a given array. Let us work the solution to such a problem by hand for the new array given below with values shown.

1	-2	3	1	-1	2

After some careful inspection and trial and error, it appears that the subarray defined by the contiguous elements in index values 3, 4, 5, and 6 provides the largest possible sum of subarray values.

How can we implement an algorithm as a Java function that returns this largest sum? The signature of this function would be:

```
int largestSumBruteForce (int [] data, int size);
```

Here *data* holds the array of values and *size* represents the number of elements in the array to be considered.

We consider and compare two algorithms for solving this problem. The first algorithm that employs a brute-force approach enumerates every possible subarray, computes its sum, and keeps track of the largest sum to date. We consider this algorithm first in Listing B.1.

Listing B.1   Brute-Force Algorithm for Computing Largest Sum of Values in Subarray

```
/** Precondition:
    Data contains at least one positive and one negative value.
    This function returns the largest sum among all subarrays.
*/
int largestSumBruteForce (int [] data, int size) {
  int largest = Integer.MIN_VALUE;
  for (int index1 = 0; index1 < size; index1++)
      for (int index2 = index1; index2 < size; index2++) {
          int sum = 0;
          for (int index3 = index1; index3 <= index2; index3++)
              sum += data[index3];
          if (sum > largest)
              largest = sum;
      }
  return largest;
}
```

From our previous discussion, since the structure of this code is characterized by three nested loops, the asymptotic complexity is given by $O(n^3)$. This implies that for large n, if one doubles the size of the array, the computational effort increases by a factor of 8.

A much more clever approach to solving this problem is given in Listing B.2. Since the structure of the clever algorithm in Listing B.2 is a single loop, its asymptotic complexity is $O(n)$. It should be dramatically clear that a cleverly constructed algorithm can be significantly more efficient than one that works correctly by brute force.

Listing B.2 A Clever Algorithm for Computing Largest Sum of Values in Subarray

```
int largestSumClever (int [] data, int size) {
  int maxSoFar = Integer.MIN_VALUE;
  int maxEndingHere = 0;
  for (int index = 0; index < size; index++) {
    if (maxEndingHere + data[index] > 0)
        maxEndingHere += data[index];
    else
      maxEndingHere = 0;
    if (maxEndingHere > maxSoFar)
        maxSoFar = maxEndingHere;
  }
  return maxSoFar;
}
```

As an exercise, the reader should construct a benchmark program that loads an array of increasing size with random values from $-5,000$ to 5,000. For each size array the same values should be used for both algorithms. The time it takes to return the largest value should be computed and output in a table for each of the two algorithms.

Installing and Using Foundations Classes

C.1   Installing the Foundations Classes

All the foundations classes and the supporting source files for the book are contained in a single compressed file named *foundations.zip*. This file may be downloaded from the Cambridge University Press Web site at *http://www.cup.org*.

Extract the entire contents of the *foundations.zip* file into the directory of your choice. We will refer to this directory as *user-dir* in our discussion. A typical choice for *user-dir* might be *C:\CS2notes*. The structure of directories and files created in *user-dir* by the extraction is shown in Figure C.1.

Chapters 2 and 10, plus the appendices, have no supporting Java files. Each folder has supporting source files for laboratories and test programs discussed in its corresponding chapter. The entire structure is only 1.8 MB (1.13 MB of that is in a single file called *distinct.txt* containing words for use by examples in Chapter 16). File *foundations.jar* contains all the compiled class files for the *foundations* package.

A typical directory structure for the chapter folders is shown in Figure C.2 for Chapters 9 and 14. The *docs* folder in Chapter 9 provides *javadoc* generated documentation for class *foundations.Fraction*. Each GUI laboratory has application and user-interface source files plus a batch file that compiles and runs the application. These laboratories were developed using JBuilder3. The *foundations* folders contain compilable (do-nothing) source file stubs that are to be used in specific exercises. The *support* folders typically contain short test programs that are console-based or source file stubs to be used in exercises. In some cases batch files are included for compiling and executing the test programs.

C.2   Using *foundations.jar* with the Java 2 Platform

In the Java 2 Platform there are several options for setting up and using classes in third-party archives such as *foundations.jar*. We describe below the setup method that is simplest and least dependent on other setup/installation options used in an existing Java installation (including various IDEs). We use the *classpath* environment variable to locate and use the *foundations* classes.

If the *classpath* enviroment variable does not exist, create it. If it does exist, modify it. You must include the following as part of a semicolon-separated list of

Name	Size	Type
ch11–Stack-Queue		File Folder
ch12-StackApp		File Folder
ch13-Lists		File Folder
ch14-Tree-Heap-PQ		File Folder
ch15-SearchTree		File Folder
ch16-Hashing-Sets		File Folder
ch17-Dictionary		File Folder
ch18-Sorting		File Folder
ch1-OOfund		File Folder
ch3-Classes		File Folder
ch4-Inheritance		File Folder
ch5-GUI		File Folder
ch6-JavaGUI		File Folder
ch7-Throwable		File Folder
ch8-Recursion		File Folder
ch9-ADT		File Folder
foundations.jar	73KB	Executable Jar File

Figure C.1. Top-level folders and *jar* file extracted from *foundations.zip*.

directories for the *classpath* variable:

    .;*user-dir*\ *foundations.jar*

The dot (".") represents the current directory. The second term is the fully qualified path to the Java archive *foundations.jar*. Replace *user-dir* with the actual path. When you invoke the compiler and interpreter for Java, the *foundations* classes should now be found.

The above changes to the *classpath* environment variable require that you have administrator access to the platform on which Java is installed. If you do not have such access, there is an alternative that will still allow you to use the foundations classes. This alternative is to use the *-classpath* switch when invoking the

```
| -- ch9-ADT
|           | -- Counter       // A GUI application for the Counter ADT
|           | -- docs          // javadoc documentation for class Fraction
|           | -- FractionLab   // The Fraction Laboratory
|                   | -- support // Information and support files
|
|     . . .
|
| -- ch14-Tree-Heap-PQ
|           | -- ExpressionTree    // The ExpressionTree Laboratory
|           |       | -- support // Supporting test and exercise files
|           | -- Heap              // The Heap Laboratory
|           |       | -- foundations  // source stubs for exercises
|           |       | -- support      // console-based test files
|           | -- PriorityQueue     // The PriorityQueue Laboratory
|           |       | -- foundations  // source stubs for exercises
|           |       | -- support      // console-based test files
|
|     . . .
|
```

Figure C.2. Typical directory structure for laboratories and support files.

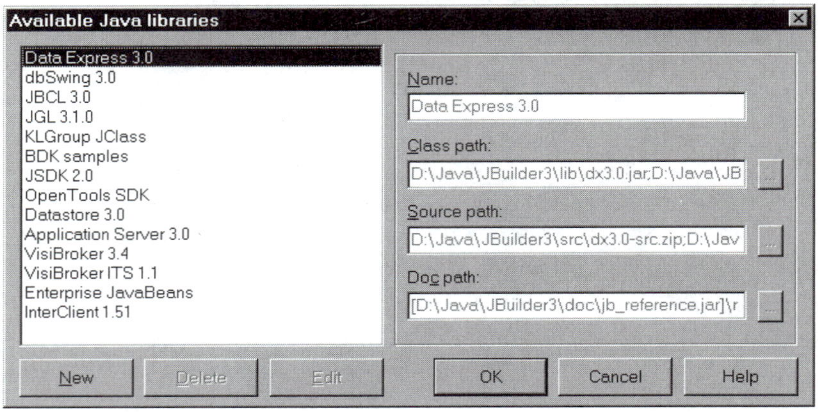

Figure C.3. Default Project Properties window in JBuilder.

Java compiler *javac.exe* and interpreter *java.exe*. In this case, use the following template for invoking the compiler and interpreter on *SourceFile.java*:

> *javac -classpath ".;user-dir\foundations.jar" SourceFile.java*
>
> *java -classpath ".;user-dir\foundations.jar" SourceFile*

C.3   Using *foundations.jar* with JBuilder

We describe below the details for using the *foundations.jar* archive with JBuilder3. Most other IDEs also provide a way to do the same thing. All the labs were designed using JBuilder. You may create a project, include the source files for a given laboratory, and compile and run the lab from within JBuilder. The advantage to the reader is that the UI component of each laboratory appears in the *Design* view of JBuilder exactly as it was constructed. This makes it easy to modify the design visually.

To include *foundations.jar* in JBuilder requires that the *Project Properties* be modified. While it is preferable to modify the default properties, the following steps may be applied to each project independently as well.

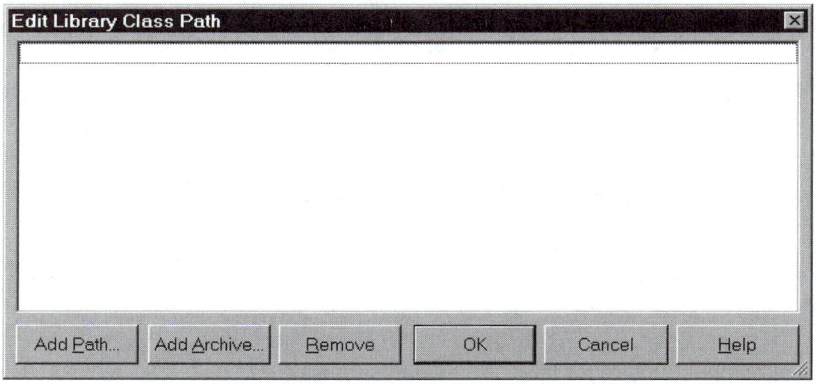

Figure C.4. Setting the path to archive *foundations.jar*.

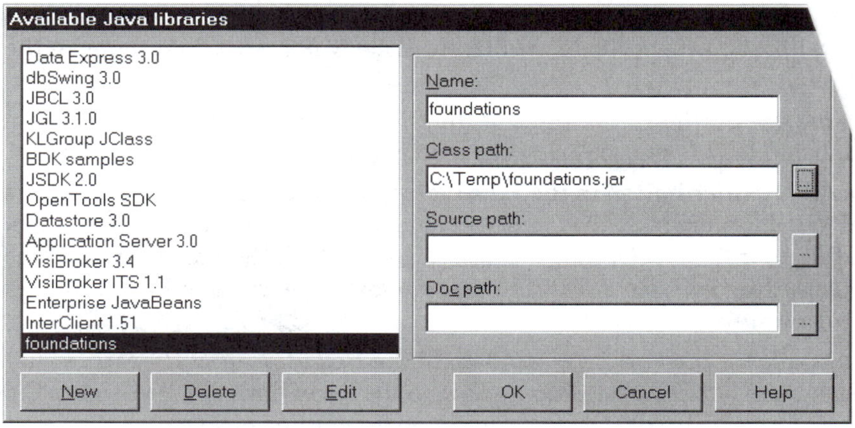

Figure C.5. Library *foundations* is now available.

1. From the *Project* menu of JBuilder, open the *Default Project Properties* window. Select the *Paths* tab and click the *Libraries* button near the bottom. This opens a window titled *Available Java Libraries*. Typically there are a number of libraries already in the list. See Figure C.3.

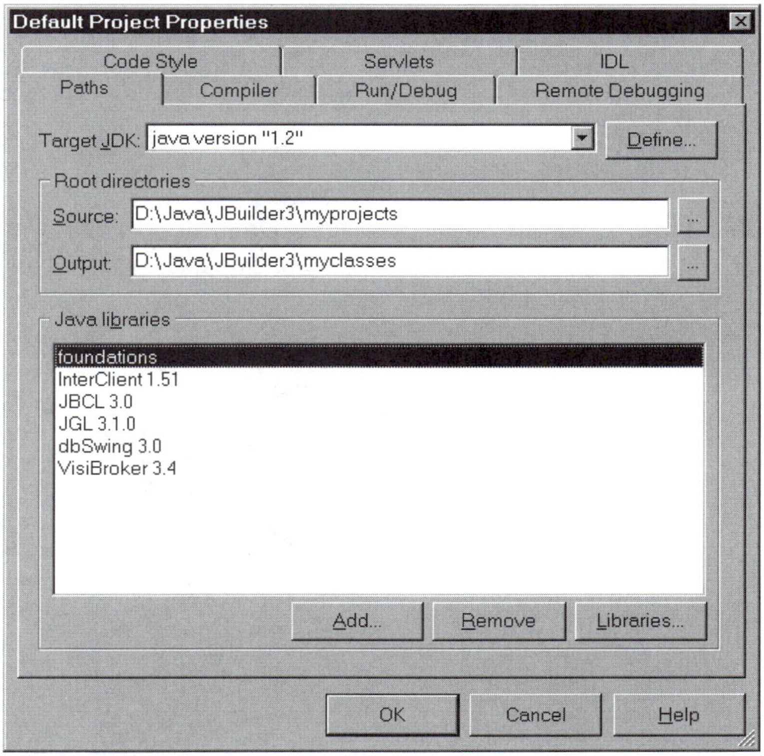

Figure C.6. Library *foundations* is now part of the Default Project Properties.

2. Click the *...y* button at bottom left in the *Available Java libraries* window. This adds a *...* ibrary entry called *untitled*. Edit the *Name:* text field to make the name *...* library equal to *foundations*.

3. Click *...rowse* button to the right of the *Class path:* text field. This opens a *...*eled *Edit Library Class Path*. See Figure C.4.

4. C*...* win*...dd Archive* button in the *Edit Library Class Path* window. This opens *...* Windows browser that lets you navigate to your *foundations.jar* file. *...*ding your *foundations.jar* file and clicking *OK* on the *Edit Library Class* *...*dow, the *Available Java libraries* window appears as in Figure C.5. In *...*re, *user-dir* is *C:\Temp*.

*...*e *Available Java libraries* window. In the *Default Project Properties* win- *...*ck the *Add* button to add *foundations* to the list of libraries. See Figure C.6 *...* final result. JBuilder now has access to *foundations* classes.

Index

Citations followed by t and f refer to tables and figures respectively.